W9-CJN-823

ANECDOTES
FROM
HISTORY

ANECDOTES
FROM
HISTORY

being a collection of
1000 anecdotes, epigrams and episodes
illustrative of
English and World History

COMPILED BY
GRANT UDEN

BASIL BLACKWELL

631 10810 6

Printed in Great Britain by Alden & Mowbray Ltd
at the Alden Press, Oxford
and bound by the Kemp Hall Bindery

Fashnable fax and polite annygoats ...

W. M. Thackeray, *The Yellowplush Papers*

'I may be famous, but I've never heard of it. What did Sir Robert say?'

Dr. Bottwink hesitated.

'Perhaps it would be improper for me to quote it,' he said. 'It is probably not included in young ladies' history books.'

Cyril Hare, *An English Murder*

TO
RICHARD COOPER

FOREWORD

I have been asked by the publishers to prepare a book of anecdotes and episodes which might be of some assistance, not only to the general reader, but to students and teachers of history; and I could do no better than to try to assemble the sort of book I myself would have been glad to have at my elbow in the years when I was teaching, and lecturing in, that most difficult of all subjects.

It seems to me that, do as we will and labour as conscientiously as we may, it is the little, even trivial, incidents and remarks that abide when all else is in danger of being discarded and forgotten; so that things in themselves unimportant gain in stature and significance because, by reason of them, great events and wider issues are more easily held in mind.

Mere erudition can command our respect, but rarely our memory. The ordinary reader and listener—which means most of us—cheerfully ignores the well-founded pronouncements of the scholar and seizes resolutely on the time-honoured tales of Alfred and the Cakes, Drake playing bowls, and all the rest. And who shall say that he is wrong to do so? More, who, on solid grounds and quotable evidence, will totally deny their truth? Whether or no the trumpets of Joshua rang round the city of palm trees, the fact is that the walls of Jericho *did* fall down flat, strangely and suddenly. In our own day, the long discredited story of the king who retrieved a lady's garter and made it the badge of the most illustrious order of chivalry in Christendom, has now convincing evidence to support it.* As I write, eminently respectable archaeologists are digging to establish the historicity of Arthur's Camelot.

Rarely can anyone satisfactorily and finally separate fact from legend and rumour, especially when the subject of them lived centuries ago. It is not even possible with our contem-

---

* See Margaret Galway, *Joan of Kent and the Order of the Garter*, Birmingham University Historical Journal, Vol. I.

poraries. Pope John and Sir Winston Churchill already have such a wealth of anecdote surrounding them that no one will ever separate hard truth from mere gossip and invention. It was ever so.

And does it matter? If the story does not distort and destroy what we are fairly sure is truth, but serves to emphasize and sharpen it, should its origins worry us unduly? It is a difficult question; and at least I have demanded a fairly respectable pedigree for what I have included. But, respectable or not, perhaps we should all recall the words of a great student and teacher of history:*

> ... from these familiar tales we can learn most clearly what our forefathers thought of the great men and women who came before them. These stories survived because they brought out most emphatically the particular traits in the characters of the heroes which the popular imagination considered to be most significant. ... And the stories should be left at that. The touch of the rationaliser ruins them. ...
>
> Should we tell these stories to-day? At least, I feel, we should realise how we cut ourselves off from the past if we do not. More and more the historian has to concern himself with what is regarded as the essential substructure of society. ... And yet life, the actual life of individuals, goes on in the despised superstructure. Its twists and turns produce dramatic episodes, tragic or comic, pathetic or just plain exciting, and moments which test men and women so that their true character is displayed. These make good stories, which men feel instinctively to be significant, and much of the significance of History will be lost if they are ignored.

G. U.

* Robert Birley, Head Master of Eton, address to the Historical Association, 1955.

ARRANGEMENT

Entries are in alphabetical order, usually under a main personality or event. It is possible for anecdotes about a character to occur under more than one heading; e.g. while there are several entries for EDWARD III, the story of the Black Prince winning his spurs is placed under CRECY, BATTLE OF. In other cases, while specific major events occur as separate entries, more general material about the period may be found under a supplementary heading; e.g. while there are anecdotes, etc., under TRAFALGAR and WATERLOO, other stories about the wars in general are included under NAPOLEONIC WARS.

Probably the quickest way to see what material is available for a particular period is to scan the chronological index, arranged in centuries, at the end of the book.

ACKNOWLEDGEMENTS

The author and publisher wish to thank the following for permission to reproduce copyright material from the sources shown

ALLEN & UNWIN LTD for the extract from *A Social History of the Navy*, 1960 by Michael Lewis
AMERICAN HERITAGE PUBLISHING Co INC for the extract from 'The Hanging of John Brown', *American Heritage*, No. 2, 1955
JOHN BAKER PUBLISHERS LTD for the extract from *A House of Kings* edited by Edward Carpenter
ARTHUR BARKER LTD for the extract from *Black Mastiff* by M. Coryn
B. T. BATSFORD LTD for the extract from *Trafalgar* by Oliver Warner
G. BELL & SONS LTD for the extract from *Little Madam* by Janet Mackay
ERNEST BENN LTD for the extracts from *Charles James Fox* by John Drinkwater and *Spain's Uncertain Crown* by R. Sencourt
A. & C. BLACK LTD for the extracts from *A History of England for Schools* by M. W. Keatinge and N. L. Frazer and *Lives of the Fathers* Vol. I by F. W. Farrar; and DOUBLEDAY & CO INC for the extract from *The Civil War* in America by Alan Barker
WILLIAM BLACKWOOD & SONS LTD for the extract from *Ships and Men* by David Hannay
BLANDFORD PRESS LTD for the extract from *John Wesley, Anglican* by Garth Lean
THE BODLEY HEAD for the extracts from *The Whispering Gallery-Leaves from a Diplomat's Diary* and *Cole of Norfolk* by A. M. Stirling; and HOLT, RINEHART AND WINSTON INC for the extract from *The Romanovs* by E. L. Almedingen
BURNS & OATES LTD for the extract from *A Short History of Medieval England* by A. Gordon Smith
CAMBRIDGE UNIVERSITY PRESS for the extracts from *Cambridge History of English Literature*, Vol. 4, *A History of the Crusades* by Sir Steven Runciman and *Change in the Farm* by T. Hennell
JONATHAN CAPE LTD for the extract from *Queen Elizabeth I* by J. E. Neale
CHATTO & WINDUS LTD for the extract from *The Naval Side of British*

History by Geoffrey Callender; and MISS D. E. COLLINS for the extract
from *A Short History of England* by G. K. Chesterton
THE CLARENDON PRESS for the extract from *Historical Portraits*, Part I
by C. R. L. Fletcher
COLLINS PUBLISHERS for the extracts from *The Trial of Charles I*
by C. V. Wedgewood and *Diaries and Letters 1930–39* by Harold
Nicolson
CONSTABLE PUBLISHERS for the extracts from *Shepherds of Britain* by
A. Gosset and *An Autobiography* by Sir Edmund Hornby; and
McGRAW-HILL BOOK Co for the extract from *Florence Nightingale* by
Cecil Woodham Smith
CONSTABLE YOUNG BOOKS LTD for the extract from *Collector's Casebook*
by Grant Uden
CURTIS BROWN LTD and the authors for the extracts from *A Laugh a
Day* by Irvin S. Cobb, *A Short History of Europe* by H. A. L. Fisher and
The Spanish Royal House by Sir Charles Petrie
THE DAILY TELEGRAPH for the extracts from 'Albany', 22 January
1967 and 'When the Tsar's House Struck' by William Gerhardie,
12 March 1967
GERALD DUCKWORTH & Co LTD for the extract from *Royal Dukes*
by Roger Fulford
ELEK BOOKS LTD for the extract from *Diplomatic Courier* by Michael
O'Brien Twohig; and ABELARD-SCHUMAN LTD for the extract from
The Borgias by Anny Latour
THE SUNDAY EXPRESS for the extract from the article by Quintin
Hogg, 2 April 1967
EVANS BROTHERS LTD for the extract from *The Ascendancy for France*
by H. O. Wakeman
FABER & FABER LTD for the extract from *Ask the Fellows Who Cut the
Hay* by George Ewart Evans
VICTOR GOLLANCZ LTD for the extract from *Peace in their Time* by
Emery Kelen
HAMISH HAMILTON LTD and HARPER & ROW INC for the extracts
from *American Aspects* by D. W. Brogan
GEORGE G. HARRAP & Co LTD for the extract from *The Englishman
and His Books* by Amy Cruse
WILLIAM HEINEMANN LTD for the extracts from *South* by Sir Ernest
Shackleton and *The Richmond Papers* by A. M. W. Stirling
JULIAN HERBAGE for the extract from his article 'Handel in England'
THE HISTORICAL ASSOCIATION for the extract from *Common Errors in
History*

DAVID HIGHAM ASSOCIATES LTD for the extracts from *The Age of Scandal* by T. H. White

HODDER & STOUGHTON LTD for the extracts from *The Great Arab Conquests* by Sir John Bagot Glubb and *The Enemy at Trafalgar* by Edward Fraser; and A. P. WATT & SON LTD for the extract from *Twenty Five Years* by Edward, Viscount Grey of Falloden

HOUGHTON MIFFLIN Co for the extract from *Branch Ricky* by Arthur Mann

HUTCHINSON PUBLISHING GROUP LTD for the extracts from Beau Brummell by Lewis Melville and *Let Me Tell You* by A. C. R. Carter

WILLIAM KIMBER & CO LTD and ANTHONY SHEIL ASSOCIATES LTD for the extract from *The Green Baize Door* by Ernest King

VISCOUNT LAMBTON for the extracts from 'Political Reminiscences', *History Today* August 1961 and 'Recollections of Lord Palmerston', *History Today* March 1961 by C. G. Barrington

MAJOR GENERAL J. D. LUNT for the extract from his article 'Jeb Stuart: Cavalier of the Confederacy', *History Today*, August 1961

MACDONALD & CO LTD for the extract from *Intelligible Heraldry* by Sir Christopher and Adrian Lynch

THE MACMILLAN CO, NEW YORK and WILLIAM KIMBER & CO LTD for the extract from *Panama, The Canal, The Country and the People* by Albert Edwards

MACMILLAN & CO LTD and ALFRED A. KNOPF INC for the extract from *Of Whales and Men* by R. B. Robertson

MACMILLAN & CO LTD for the extracts from *Wessex Tales* by Thomas Hardy and *History of the British Army*, Vol. II by Sir John Fortescue; and CURTIS BROWN LTD for the extract from *Variety of Man* by C. P. Snow

DAVID MACKAY CO INC for the extract from *Lincoln's Secretary, A Biography of John G. Nicolay* by Helen Nicolay

THE MARYLAND HISTORICAL SOCIETY for the extract from *A Quarter Century of Growth of the Maryland Historical Society*, March 1965

METHUEN & CO LTD for the extracts from *More Medieval Byways* by L. F. Salzman and *The Sailors Whom Nelson Led* by Edward Fraser

JOHN MURRAY for the extract from *Parliamentary Reminiscences and Reflections 1808–1885* by Lord George Hamilton

THOMAS NELSON & SONS LTD for the extracts from *Chaucer in His Time* by Derek Brewer and *Sea Wolves and the Mediterranean* by E. Hamilton Currey

THE OXFORD HISTORICAL SOCIETY for the extract from *Collecteana*, 2nd Series

OXFORD UNIVERSITY PRESS for the extract from *Edwardian England* by P. K. Kemp

MRS. JOYCE PEARSON for the extract from *Lives of the Wits* by Hesketh Pearson

A. D. PETERS & CO for the extract from *The Great Lucifer* by Margaret Irwin

THE DUKE OF PORTLAND for the extract from *Men, Women and Things* by the late Duke of Portland

ROUTLEDGE & KEGAN PAUL LTD for the extract from *Bertrand of Brittany* by Roger Varcel

HUGH ROSS WILLIAMSON for the extract from his book *John Hampden*

C. W. SCOTT-GILES for the extract from his book *The Romance of Heraldry*

CHARLES SCRIBNER'S SONS LTD for the extract from *F. D. R. My Boss* by Grace Tully

THE SOCIETY OF AUTHORS for the extract from *Sea Life in Nelson's Time* by John Masefield

A. WATKINS INC for the extract from *My Forty Years with Ford* by Charles E. Sorenson

WEIDENFELD & NICOLSON and SIMON AND SCHUSTER INC for the extract from *Monarchy* by Harold Nicolson

ARNOLD WHITRIDGE for the extract from his article 'Cuba's Role in American History,' *History Today* June 1961

SIR MARTIN WILSON for the extract from *Impressions and Memoirs* by Lord Ribblesdale

The author and publisher have made every effort to clear all copyright material, but in spite of their efforts, it has been impossible to trace the holders of some of the extracts. In the event of any unforeseen infringements, they express their regrets, and would welcome any information which would remedy such oversight in future editions.

ANECDOTES FROM HISTORY

ADOLPHUS FREDERICK, DUKE OF CAMBRIDGE (1774–1850), seventh son of George III.

Conversation in Church

But perhaps his finest and most eccentric efforts were reserved for church. He became very deaf and always sat right in front of the church, where he was seen by the whole congregation. This might not have been so serious if he had not made a practice of being heard all over the church as well, in a running commentary on the service. No doubt many of his funnier remarks are apocryphal as, for example, the story that when the clergyman came to the commandment 'Thou shalt do no murder,' a loud voice replied: 'I don't: I leave that to my brother Ernest.' But it was a common occurrence to hear in reply to the clergyman's 'Let us pray,' an agreeable 'By all means' from the Duke, or, in answer to a prayer for rain, 'Amen, but you won't get it till the wind changes,' or, in answer to the sentence, 'For we brought nothing into the world, neither may we carry anything out,' the reply, 'True, true—too many calls upon us for that.'

SOURCE: Roger Fulford, *Royal Dukes*, Gerald Duckworth & Co., 1933, pp. 304–305.

ALBERT (FRANCIS CHARLES AUGUSTUS EMMANUEL) PRINCE (1819–1861), husband of Queen Victoria and Prince Consort.

i. '*Let's hear no more of it, ma'am*'

Of Lord Melbourne and his strong common sense Lord Shaftesbury, in 1882, told me the following characteristic story.

When the Queen became engaged to Prince Albert, she wished him to be made King Consort by Act of Parliament, and urged her wish upon the Prime Minister, Lord Melbourne. At first that sagacious man simply evaded the point, but when her Majesty insisted on a categorical answer—'I thought it my duty to be very plain with her. I said: "For God's sake, let's hear no more of it, ma'am; for if you once get the English people into the way of making kings, you will get them into the way of unmaking them." '

SOURCE: George W. E. Russell, *Collections and Recollections*, Smith, Elder & Co., 1903, Ch. XXII.

ii. *Albert and Court etiquette*

A pleasing instance of the ultra-German etiquette fomented by Prince Albert was told me by an eyewitness of the scene. The Prime Minister and his wife were dining at Buckingham Palace very shortly after they had received an addition to their family. When the ladies retired to the drawing-room after dinner, the Queen said most kindly to the Premier's wife:

'I know you are not very strong yet, Lady ——; so I beg you will sit down. And, when the Prince comes in, Lady D—— shall stand in front of you.'

This device of screening a breach of etiquette behind the portly figure of a British Matron always struck me as extremely droll.

SOURCE: ibid, Ch. III.

iii. *'You are exposing my flank'*

That the above sort of device continued to be used at a later period is clear from the recently published memoirs of Mildred, Lady Buxton. Speaking of a banquet in honour of the German Emperor at the beginning of this century, she says:

The Emperor was in the uniform of an English Field-Marshal— red. The King was in the clothes of a German Field-Marshal —green. (He looked as if he must burst.) The Prince of Wales (a sailor) looked furious and uncomfortable in the uniform of the *Garde de Corps*—white, piped with grass-green with a bright orange sash. . . .

We all stood about till we were ready to drop. Lord Ripon at last came up to me and asked if I would stand in front of him while he sat down as he thought he should die, so I did for quite a long time, and if I moved at all a plaintive voice was heard to say:

'Oh don't you move, you are exposing my flank.'

See also GREAT EXHIBITION.

ALDHELM (or EADHELM) ST. (640?–709). Abbot of Malmesbury and Bishop of Sherborne. He was an accomplished teacher, with many ideas about education which are reckoned as 'modern' today, a poet, and a great builder of churches.

Aldhelm the Minstrel

Aldhelm had observed with pain that the peasantry were become negligent in their religious duties, and that no sooner was the church service ended than they all hastened to their homes and labours, and could with difficulty be persuaded to attend to the exhortations of the preacher.

He watched the occasion, and stationed himself in the character of a minstrel on the bridge over which the people had to pass, and soon collected a crowd of hearers by the beauty of his verse. When he found that he had gained possession of their attention, he gradually introduced among the popular poetry which he was reciting to them, words of more serious nature, till at length he succeeded in impressing upon their minds a truer feeling of religious devotion.

SOURCE: William of Malmesbury, *Gesta Pontificum Anglorum*; quoted *Old England*, Vol. i, p. 59.

B

ALEXANDER THE GREAT (356–323 B.C.), King of Macedon; conqueror of the Persian empire; penetrated as far as the Punjab.

i. *The taming of Bucephalus*

When Philonicus, the Thessalian, offered the horse named Bucephalus in sale to Philip,* at the price of thirteen talents, the king, with the prince and many others, went into the field to see some trial made of him. The horse appeared extremely vicious and unmanageable, and was so far from suffering himself to be mounted, that he would not bear to be spoken to, but turned fiercely upon all the grooms. Philip was displeased at their bringing him so wild and ungovernable a horse and bade them take him away. But Alexander, who had observed him well, said:

'What a horse are they losing, for want of skill and spirit to manage him!'

Philip at first took no notice of this; but, upon the prince's often repeating the same expression . . . he said:

'Young man, you find fault with your elders, as if you knew more than they, or could manage the horse better.'

'And I certainly could,' answered the prince.

'If you should not be able to ride him, what forfeiture will you submit to for your rashness?'

'I will pay the price of the horse.'

Upon this all the company laughed, but the king and prince agreeing as to the forfeiture, Alexander ran to the horse, and laying hold of the bridle, turned him to the sun; for he had observed, it seems, that the shadow which fell before the horse, and continually moved as he moved, greatly disturbed him. While his fierceness and fury lasted, he kept speaking to him softly and stroking him; after which he gently let fall his mantle, leaped lightly upon his back, and got his seat very safe. Then, without pulling the reins too hard, or using either whip or spur, he set him a-going. As soon as he perceived his uneasiness abated, and that he wanted only to run, he put him in a full gallop, and pushed him on both with the voice and the spur.

* Philip of Macedon, father of Alexander.

Philip and all his court were in great distress for him at first, and a profound silence took place. But when the prince had turned him and brought him straight back, they all received him with loud acclamations, except his father, who wept for joy, and, kissing him, said:

'Seek another kingdom, my son, that may be worthy of thy abilities; for Macedonia is too small for thee.'

SOURCE: Plutarch's *Lives*; trans. J. and W. Langhorne, 1831.

ii. *'I will not steal a victory'*

On the eve of the battle of Arbela, 331 B.C., Alexander's counsellors advised him to fall on the army of Darius at night, before it was drawn up in order.

The oldest of his friends, and Parmenio in particular, when he beheld the plain . . . all illumined with the torches of the barbarians, and heard all the . . . noise from their camp, like the bellowings of an immense sea, were astonished at their numbers, and observed among themselves how arduous an enterprise it would be to meet such a torrent of war in open day. They waited upon the king, therefore . . . and advised him to attack the enemy in the night. . . . Upon which he gave them that celebrated answer:

'I will not steal a victory.'

SOURCE: ibid.

iii. *Darius tries to buy off Alexander*

It was about this time that he received a letter from Darius, in which that prince proposed, on condition of a pacification and future friendship, to pay him ten thousand talents in ransom of the prisoners, to cede to him all the countries on this side the Euphrates, and to give him his daughter in marriage. Upon his communicating these proposals to his friends, Parmenio said:

'If I were Alexander, I would accept them.'

'So would I,' said Alexander, 'if I were Parmenio.'

SOURCE: ibid.

See also DIOGENES.

ALEXANDER III (1845–1894), Emperor of Russia. Nicknamed 'little bull' by his family.

Duty dance

... he had two qualities which streaked even his earliest years with light; a big heart and a vehement honesty, its expressions all too often disconcerting to many members of his father's household and his own. . . . Once at a ball at Wiesbaden, when a German cousin, strictly adhering to conventions, thanked him 'for the great pleasure of the dance,' Alexander cut her short:

'Why can't you be honest? It was just a duty neither of us could have relished. I have ruined your slippers and you have made me nearly sick with the scent you use.'

SOURCE: E. L. Almedingen, *The Romanovs*, The Bodley Head, 1966, p. 272.

ALFONSO XIII (1886–1941), King of Spain; driven into exile, through the pusillanimity of his ministers, 1931.

i. *The King speaks out*

I am not an absolute monarch. I am only absolute inasmuch as I can offer my life for my country, and this I have done and do with pleasure, but I am without responsibility. . . .

Responsibility has been conferred upon Parliament, and it is a severe thing to say, but it is the bald truth, that Parliament is not living up to its duties, and the many schemes presented to it which would be of great benefit to the country do not make headway. There is profuse debate, in which the desire to improve the project does not appear, but rather a wish that it shall not prosper for the better service of political ends. Time passes and the Government falls; other men take office and again the King signs the same scheme for presentation to the Cortes, and those who formerly supported it, but failed to secure its passage, by law of political logic, being in opposition, now oppose it. . . . I know my ground and I know what I can say. And because I know this, and in view of the state of things I have described, I feel the necessity for the Provinces to start a movement in support of the King, and then, in Parliament, the welfare of the nation, and not political interests, will triumph. Then the politicians will behave as they ought. . . .

SOURCE: speech at Cordova, reported in *The Times*, February 2, 1924; only made public in Spain four years later.

ii. 'Which speech?'

Nearly three years after he had made this speech the King was again in Cordova, and the Alcade told him that his great speech would never be forgotten, it had been illuminated on parchment by the finest artists in the city, and hung in the room in which it was delivered.

'Which speech?' asked the King. 'The one I made or the one they said I made?'

'The one you made, Your Majesty,' said the Alcade.

SOURCE: Sir Charles Petrie, *The Spanish Royal House*, Geoffrey Bles, 1958, p. 229.

iii. *An unusual revolution*, 1923

Hardly had he [King Alfonso] got to sleep again, when he was rung up once more, this time by General Primo de Rivera.

'Your Majesty,' he said, 'I have revolted with the garrison of Barcelona to the cry of *Viva el Rey* and *Viva España*. I place myself and the troops at Your Majesty's disposal. The Ministry must go out of the window, but we are loyal to Your Majesty.'

At this Don Alfonso rubbed his eyes, as if to assure himself that he was awake, and said to his *aide-de-camp*:

'Am I awake? Am I dreaming? Am I mad? I don't understand a revolution which places itself at the disposal of the King. What does it mean?'

SOURCE: described by King Alfonso personally to Sir Charles Petrie and included ibid., p. 232. The government did, in fact, 'go out of the window' and General Primo de Rivera took over power by royal decree.

ALFRED (849–901), King of the West Saxons; called 'the Great'.

i. *Alfred learns to read*

He was loved by his father and mother, and even by all the people, above all his brothers, and was educated altogether at the court of the king. . . . His noble nature implanted in him from his cradle a love of wisdom above all things; but, with shame let it be spoken, by the unworthy neglect of his parents and nurses, he remained illiterate even till he was twelve years old or more; but he listened with serious attention to the Saxon poems which he often heard recited, and easily retained them in his docile memory. . . .

On a certain day, therefore, his mother was showing him and his brother a Saxon book of poetry, which she held in her hand, and said:

'Whichever of you shall the soonest learn this volume shall have it for his own.'

Stimulated by these words, or rather by the Divine inspiration, and allured by the beautifully illuminated letter at the beginning of the volume, he spoke before all his brothers, who, though his seniors in age, were not so in grace, and answered:

'Will you really give that book to one of us, that is to say, to him who can first understand and repeat it to you?'

At this his mother smiled with satisfaction, and confirmed what she had before said. Upon which, the boy took the book out of her hand, and went to his master to read it, and in due time brought it to his mother and recited it.

After this he learned the daily course, that is, the celebration of the hours, and afterwards certain psalms, and several prayers, contained in a certain book which he kept day and night in his bosom, as we ourselves have seen, and carried about with him to assist his prayers, amid all the bustle and business of his present life.

SOURCE: Asser, Bishop of Sherborne, *Life of Aelfred*; in *Six Old English Chronicles*, trans. J. A. Giles.

ii. *Alfred in the camp of the Danes*

For nine successive years, battling with his enemies, sometimes deceived by false treaties and sometimes wreaking his vengeance on the deceivers, he was at last reduced to such extreme distress ... that he was compelled to retreat to a certain island named Adelingia, which from its marshy situation was hardly accessible. He was accustomed afterwards, when in happier circumstances, to relate to his companions in a lively and agreeable manner his perils there, and how he escaped them. . . . Not long after [receiving encouragement from St. Cuthbert in a dream], venturing from his concealment, he hazarded an experiment of consummate art. Accompanied only by one of his faithful adherents, he entered the tent of the Danish king under the disguise of a mimic, and being admitted, in his assumed capacity of jester, to every corner of the banqueting-room, there was no object of secrecy that he did not minutely attend to both with eyes and ears. Remaining there several days, until he had satisfied his mind on every matter which he wished to know, he returned to Adelingia, and, assembling his companions, pointed out the indolence of the enemy and the easiness of their defeat.

SOURCE: William of Malmesbury, *Gesta Regum Anglorum*, iii, Part I; inc. in Keatinge and Frazer, *A History of England for Schools*, 1919.

iii. *Alfred and the cakes*

At this time King Alfred, of whom we have already had much to say, was leading a hazardous life in great difficulties with a few of his nobles and also some soldiers and vassals among the woods and swamps of the county of Somerset. For he was destitute, except for what he could get openly or by stealth by raiding the heathen or even the Christians who had submitted to heathen rule. And, as we read in the life of St. Neot, he lay in hiding with a certain cowherd. Now it happened that one day a countrywoman, the wife of that cowherd, decided to bake some loaves, as the king was sitting by the hearth, seeing to his bow and arrows and other gear. When the unfortunate woman saw the loaves burning at the fire, she ran up quickly and took them away, upbraiding the invincible king and saying:

'Hi! man, when you see the cakes are burning, why can't you turn them round?'

SOURCE: Asser, *De Rebus Gestis Ælfredi*, Matthew Parker's edition, 1574; trans. Robert Birley in *The Undergrowth of History*, Historical Association, 1955. Birley adds that, though Asser was a contemporary of Alfred's and his Life was written before the King died, 'Parker included in his edition extensive extracts from a work usually known as The Annals of St. Neots. . . . One of his longest interpolations begins in the passage . . . "And, as we read in the Life of St. Neot." The story of Alfred and the Cakes, therefore, has nothing to do with Asser's life and it is to the Annals that we must first turn.' *The Annals of St. Neots* was written in the early 12th Century. But Birley gives evidence that there was probably an earlier life of St. Neot, and that the original story of Alfred and the cakes, though it is not given by Asser, can possibly be dated to not long after A.D. 1000.

iv. *The New Historians prove too much*

In 1872, when University College, Oxford, celebrated the thousandth anniversary of its foundation, Lord Sherbrooke, as an old Member of the College, made the speech of the evening. His theme was a complaint of the iconoclastic tendency of the New Historians. Nothing was safe from their sacrilegious research. Every tradition, however venerable, however precious, was resolved into a myth or a fable.

'For example,' he said, 'we have always believed that certain lands which this college owns in Berkshire were given to us by King Alfred. Now the New Historians come and tell us that this could not have been the case, because they can prove that the lands in question never belonged to the King. It seems to me that the New Historians prove too much—indeed, they prove the very point which they contest. If the lands had belonged to the King, he would probably have kept them to himself; but as they belonged to some-one else, he made a handsome present of them to the College.'

SOURCE: G. W. E. Russell, *Collections and Recollections*.

ALGIERS, BOMBARDMENT OF (August 27, 1816). The British government sent a fleet under Lord Exmouth (formerly Sir Edward Pellew) to Algiers to stamp out the corsairs and pirates of the north African coast, headed by the slave-trafficking Dey. Exmouth blasted the harbour and its batteries, destroyed the Dey's fleet and freed thousands of slaves.

The chaplain in the hen-coop

He [Doctor John Frowd, chaplain on the *Queen Charlotte* at Algiers] was a very little man, an irrepressible, unwearied chatterbox, with a droll interrogative face, a bald shining head, and a fleshy under-lip which he could push nearly up to his nose. . . .

As the action thickened, he was seized with a comical religious frenzy, dashing round the decks and diffusing spiritual exhortation amongst the half-stripped busy sailors, till the First Lieutenant ordered a hen-coop to be clapped over him, whence his little head, emerging, continued its devout cackle, quite regardless of the balls which flew past him.

SOURCE: Rev. W. Tuckwell, *Reminiscences of Oxford*, 1901.

AMERICAN CIVIL WAR, THE (1861–1865).

i. *The meaning of civil war*

The War was a civil war because it set brother against brother, father against son. Thousands of Northerners . . . served in the ranks of the Confederate Army. Thousands of Southerners served in the ranks of the Union Army . . . . Mrs. Lincoln's brothers fought for the South and two Crittenden brothers became generals in opposing armies. The son of the commander of the Confederate Navy served in the Union Navy.

SOURCE: D. W. Brogan, *American Aspects*, Hamish Hamilton, 1964, p. 29; first pub. in *Harper's Magazine* (*A Fresh Appraisal of the Civil War*).

ii. *Jeb gives a lesson and loses his hat*

James Ewell Brown Stuart, better known as 'Beauty' or just 'Jeb', was the best-known cavalry leader in the South. With his vast cinnamon-coloured beard and moustaches, a flamboyant style of dress and his inseparable personal banjo-player Sweeney, he became a legend in his life-time before being killed in action, with the rank of major-general, at the age of 30.

On one occasion he led his men right up to the Federal skirmish line, made them dismount, and then waited till the enemy infantry were within two hundred yards before he gave the order to fall back towards the horses. Once mounted, he led them away at a slow trot, and as soon as they were clear he halted them and delivered the following address:

'Attention! Now I want to talk to you men. You are brave fellows and patriotic, too, but you're ignorant of this kind of work, and I'm teaching you. I want you to observe that a good man on a good horse can never be caught. Another thing: Cavalry can *trot* away from anything, and a gallop is a gait unbecoming to a soldier unless he is going toward the enemy. Remember that. We gallop toward the enemy, and trot away, always. . . .'

In August [1862] he . . . succeeded in capturing General Pope's personal baggage, with all his papers and letters. . . . Stuart, who had lost his famous plumed hat when he was nearly captured by Federal cavalry at Verdiersville on August 17th, sent a letter to Pope which was later reprinted with glee by the Richmond papers:

'Major Genl. John Pope
Commanding, U.S. Army.
General: You have my hat and plume. I have your best coat. I have the honor to propose a cartel for a fair exchange of the prisoners.'

SOURCE: James Lunt, *Jeb Stuart: Cavalier of the Confederacy*, in *History Today*, August 1961, pp. 539–541.

iii. *Early attempts at secession*

There have been two overt attempts at secession already: one the secession of the southern students from the Medical School at Philadelphia; the second upon the election of Speaker Pennington when the South seceded from Congress, went out, took a drink, and came back. The third attempt will be when Old Abe is elected; they would again secede and this time would take two drinks and come back again.

SOURCE: a young Republican, Carl Schurz, in a speech; quoted Alan Barker, *The Civil War in America*, 1961, pp. 91–92.

iv. *An honest politician*

Simon Cameron of Pennsylvania was one of the Republican 'bosses'.

Thaddeus Stevens, when asked by Lincoln if Cameron was an honest man, replied:

'He would not steal a red-hot stove.'

On being challenged over this later, he replied:

'Oh, well, I apologise. I said Cameron would not steal a red-hot stove. I withdraw that statement.'

SOURCE: Alan Barker, *The Civil War in America*, 1961, p. 102.

When asked to describe an honest politician he [Simon Cameron] replied:

'One who when bought, stays bought.'

SOURCE: ibid.

v. *Dismissal of a General*

General George McClellan was dismissed by Lincoln in November 1862, for timidity in taking action against the Southern armies.

'He's got the slows, Mr. Blair. He is an admirable engineer, but he seems to have a special talent for a stationary engine.'

SOURCE: quoted Alan Barker, *The Civil War in America*, 1961, p. 122.

The following exchange with McClellan is also recorded:

Irritated by the inaction of General George B. McClellan . . . the President sent him this note:

'My dear McClellan:

If you don't want to use the army I should like to borrow it for a while.

Yours respectfully,
A. LINCOLN.'

SOURCE: Frances Cavanah and Lloyd E. Smith, *I am an American*, Whitman Publishing Co., Racine, Wisconsin, 1940, pp. 122–123.

vi. *Confederate bank-notes*

The Confederate states were always severely handicapped for lack of proper financial resources. The issue of large quantities of paper money by the Confederate government and by individual member states led to serious inflation.

One journalist described the portraits appearing on Confederate banknotes by commenting on 'that unchanging expression of ineffable melancholy which the engraver has given to all of them; for on the best specimens of Confederate currency Davis is doleful and Stephens saturnine, Hunter is heavy, Clay clouded with care, and Memminger is mournful.'

SOURCE: quoted Alan Barker, *The Civil War in America*, 1961, p. 143.

vii. *Gladstone on the South*

There is no doubt that Jefferson Davis and other leaders of the South have made an army; they are making, it appears, a navy; and they have made what is more than either, they have made a nation.

SOURCE: William Ewart Gladstone, in a speech at Newcastle-upon-Tyne, October 7, 1862.

viii. *The President meets the Commander-in-Cheif*

Lincoln looked for a long time for a general to command the Union forces and eventually decided on General Ulyssees Grant after he had won a series of battles. Grant was called to Washington and met Lincoln there, March 8, 1864.

At about 9½ P.M. the General came in—alone again excepting his staff—and he and the President met for the first time. The President, expecting him, knew from the buzz and movement in the crowd that it must be the General; and when a man of modest mien and unimposing exterior presented himself, the President said:

'This is General Grant, is it not?'

The General replied, 'Yes,' and the two greeted each other more cordially, but still with that modest deference, felt rather than expressed in word or action, so appropriate to both—the one the honored ruler, the other the honored victor of the nation and the time.

SOURCE: Helen Nicolay, *Lincoln's Secretary, A Biography of John G. Nicolay*, New York, Longmans, Green & Co., 1949.

ix. *Robert E. Lee makes history*

Lee is probably the only soldier who has ever been offered the command of both armies in a war.

SOURCE: D. W. Brogan, *American Aspects*, Hamish Hamilton, 1964, p. 30.

x. *Lee surrenders*

General Robert E. Lee, finding himself hopelessly hemmed in by overwhelming numbers, surrendered the Confederate Army to General Grant in April 1865.

Grant had not yet come up, and while waiting for his arrival General Lee seated himself upon some rails which Colonel Talcott of the Engineers had fixed at the foot of an apple tree for his convenience. This tree was half a mile distant from the point where the meeting of Lee and Grant took place, yet widespread currency has been given to the story that the surrender took place under its shade, and 'apple-tree' jewelry has been profusely distributed from the orchard in which it grew. . . .

The meeting between the two renowned generals took place at the house of a Mr. McLean . . . to which mansion, after exchanging courteous salutations, they repaired to settle the terms on which the surrender of the Army of Northern Virginia should be concluded.

A conversation here took place which General Grant, as he himself tells us, led to various subjects divergent from the immediate purpose of the meeting, talking of old army matters and comparing recollections with General Lee. As he says, the conversation grew so pleasant that he almost forgot the object of the meeting.

SOURCE: Armistead L. Long, *Memoirs of Robert E. Lee*, 1887.

xi. *The farmers keep their horses*

The arms, artillery, and public property were to be turned over to an officer appointed to receive them, the officers retaining their side-arms and private horses and baggage. In addition to this, General Grant permitted every man of the Confederate army who claimed to own a horse or mule to retain it for farming purposes, General Lee remarking that this would have a happy effect. . . .

When, after his interview with Grant, General Lee appeared again, a shout of welcome instinctively ran through the army. . . . As he rode slowly along the lines hundreds of his devoted veterans pressed around the noble chief, trying to take his hand, touch his person, or even lay a hand upon his horse, thus exhibiting for him their great affection. The general then, with head bare and tears flowing freely down his manly cheeks, bade adieu to the army. In a few words he told the brave men who had been so true in arms to return to their homes and become worthy citizens.

Thus closed the career of the noble Army of Northern Virginia.

SOURCE: ibid.

xii. *Lincoln decides to issue the proclamation of slave emancipation*

I think the time has come now. I wish it were a better time. I wish that we were in a better condition. . . . When the rebel army was at Frederick, I determined, as soon as it should be driven out of Maryland, to issue a Proclamation of Emancipation such as I thought most likely to be useful. I said nothing to anyone; but I made the promise to myself, and (hesitating a little)—to my Maker. The rebel army is now driven out, and I am going to fulfil that promise.

SOURCE: Lincoln to his Cabinet, Sept. 22, 1862; *Inside Lincoln's Cabinet: The Civil War Diaries of Salmon P. Chase* (edit. David Donald), New York, Longmans, Green & Co., 1954.

xiii. *Sunday morning choice*

'It is now Sunday morning. I'll go to church and you may go to hell.'

SOURCE: Stephen A. Douglas, U.S. Senator from Illinois, to his hecklers in an anti-slavery audience, 1854.

xiv. *The preparation of the Gettysburg Address*

Lincoln was very silent all the previous evening after dinner. No one else being present he walked to and fro in his room apparently thinking deeply. He went to bed early, and when he came down to breakfast he looked unwell, and said he had slept little. On the train he was silent for a considerable while, and then he asked me for some writing paper. On his knee he then wrote out his speech in full, exactly as it has come down to us. The impression left on me was that Lincoln was merely transcribing from memory the words he had composed during the night.

When we reached the battlefield Lincoln was nervous and apparently not well. Everett spoke eloquently but very long.

Then Lincoln rose, holding in his hand the papers he had written in the train. He did not read, but spoke every word in a clear, ringing, resonant, vibrating voice, which obviously passed over the crowd. His speech occupied only a few minutes in delivery. It was listened to with breathless attention and when it came to an end there was at first no cheering, but an audible indrawing of deep breath as from an audience that had been profoundly moved. In the silence of the next moment

Everett leapt to his feet again and said, as nearly as I can remember, this:

'We have just listened to a speech that will live through the ages.'

SOURCE: related to Hall Caine by John Hay, Lincoln's close friend, who accompanied him to Gettysburg; quoted A. R. C. Carter, *Let Me Tell You*, Hutchinson & Co., 1940, pp. 231–232.

xv. *The Address*

Fourscore and seven years ago our fathers brought forth upon this continent a new nation, conceived in liberty, and dedicated to the proposition that all men are created equal. Now we are engaged in a great civil war, testing whether that nation, or any nation so conceived and so dedicated, can long endure. We are met on a great battlefield of that war. We have come to dedicate a portion of that field as a final resting-place of those who here gave their lives that a nation might live. It is altogether fitting and proper that we should do this. But in a larger sense we cannot dedicate, we cannot consecrate, we cannot hallow this ground. The brave men, living and dead, who struggled here, have consecrated it far above our power to add or detract. The world will little note, nor long remember, what we say here, but it can never forget what they did here. It is for us, the living, rather to be dedicated here to the unfinished work they have thus far so nobly advanced. It is rather for us to be here dedicated to the great task remaining before us, that from these honoured dead we take increased devotion to that cause for which they here gave the last full measure of devotion; that we here highly resolve that the dead shall not have died in vain, that this nation, under God, shall have a new birth of freedom; and that government of the people, by the people, and for the people, shall not perish from the earth.

SOURCE: *Speeches and Letters*, 1907.

See also LINCOLN, ABRAHAM.

AMERICAN INDEPENDENCE, WAR OF (1775–1783).

i. '*In the name of Jehovah and the Continental Congress*'

Colonel Ethan Allen (1737–1789), American officer, captures Ticonderoga, May 10, 1775.

... directions were privately sent me from the then colony (now state) of Connecticut, to raise the Green Mountain Boys, and, if possible, with them to surprise and take the fortress, Ticonderoga. This enterprise I cheerfully undertook; and, after first guarding all the several passes that led thither, to cut off all intelligence between the garrison and the country, made a forced march from Bennington, and arrived at the lake opposite to Ticonderoga, on the evening of the ninth day of May, 1775, with two hundred and thirty valiant Green Mountain Boys; and it was with the utmost difficulty that I procured boats to cross the lake. However, I landed eighty-three men near the garrison, commanded by Col. Seth Warner; but the day began to dawn, and I found myself under a necessity to attack the fort, before the rear could cross the lake. . . .

The men being, at this time, drawn up in three ranks, each poised his firelock. I ordered them to face to the right; and, at the head of the centre file, marched them immediately to the wicket-gate . . . where I found a sentry posted, who instantly snapped his fusee at me: I ran immediately towards him, and he retreated through the covered way into the parade within the garrison, gave a haloo, and ran under a bomb-proof. My party, who followed me into the fort, I formed on parade in such a manner as to face the two barracks which faced each other. The garrison being asleep, except the sentries, we gave three huzzas which greatly surprised them. One of the sentries made a pass at one of my officers with a charged bayonet, and slightly wounded him: My first thought was to kill him with my sword; but, in an instant, I altered the design and fury of the blow to a slight cut on the side of the head; upon which he dropped his gun, and asked quarter, which I readily granted him, and demanded of him the place where the commanding officer kept; he shewed me a pair of stairs in the front of a barrack, on the west side of the garrison, which led to a second

C

story in said barrack, to which I instantly repaired, and ordered the commander, Capt. Deleplace, to come forth instantly, or I would sacrifice the whole garrison; at which the Capt. came immediately to the door, with his breeches in his hand; when I ordered him to deliver to me the fort instantly; he asked me by what authority I demanded it; I answered him:

'In the name of the great Jehovah, and the Continental Congress.'

. . . This surprise was carried into execution in the gray of the morning of the tenth day of May, 1775. The sun seemed to rise that morning with superior lustre; and Ticonderoga and its dependencies smiled on its conquerors, who tossed about the flowing bowl, and wished success to Congress, and the liberty and freedom of America.

SOURCE: *A Narrative of Col. Ethan Allen's Captivity . . . containing his Voyages and Travels With the most remarkable occurrences respecting himself . . .*, 1807.

An American writer, Ben C. Clough, comments: 'Right for him if he really said: "In the name of the Great Jehovah and of the Continental Congress." He says he did. Oral tradition has it, however, that his language was less polite.'

ii. *Bunker Hill, June 17, 1775*

'Men, you are all marksmen—don't one of you fire until you see the whites of their eyes.'

SOURCE: Israel Putnam, American Revolutionary General (1718–1790); Frothingham, *History of the Siege of Boston*, 1873. The order has also been attributed to Colonel William Prescott.

iii. *Sequel to a sermon*

Last Thursday, after hearing a very good sermon, I went with the multitude into King Street to hear the Proclamation for Independence read and proclaimed. Some field-pieces with the train were brought there. The troops appeared under arms, and all the inhabitants assembled there (the small-pox prevented many thousands from the country), when Colonel Crafts read from the balcony of the State House the proclamation. Great attention was given to every word. As soon as he ended, the cry from the balcony was, 'God save our American States,' and then three cheers which rent the air. The bells rang, the privateers fired, the forts and batteries, the cannon were discharged, the platoons followed, and every face appeared joyful. . . . After dinner the King's Arms were taken down from the State House, and every vestige of him from every place in which it appeared, and burnt in King Street. Thus ends royal authority in this State. And all the people shall say Amen.

SOURCE: Mrs. John Adams to her husband, July 21, 1776, from Boston; Charles Francis Adams (edit.), *Familiar Letters to John Adams and His Wife, Abigail Adams, During the Revolution*, 1876.

iv. *Surrender at Saratoga*, October 17, 1777

About 10 o'clock, we marched out, according to treaty, with drums beating & the honours of war, but the drums seemed to have lost their former inspiriting sounds, and though we beat the Grenadier's march, which not long before was so animating, yet then it seemed by its last feeble effort, as if almost ashamed to be heard on such an occasion. . . .

The meeting between Burgoyne and Gates was well worth seeing. He paid Burgoyne about as much respect as if he was the conqueror, indeed, his noble air, tho prisoner, seemed to command attention and respect from every person.

SOURCE: *The Journal of Lieutenant William Digby*; in *The British Invasion from the North* (edit. James Phinney Baxter), 1887.

v. *Mrs. Ackland seeks her husband*

In the engagements leading up to the great American victory of Saratoga, October 17, 1777, an English officer in General Burgoyne's army, Major Ackland, was shot through both legs, captured and removed to the headquarters of the American General Poor. Ackland's wife, who had accompanied him throughout the campaign, immediately sought permission from Burgoyne to go to her husband. The American historian Lossing wrote:

'Though I was ready to believe,' says Burgoyne 'that patience and fortitude, in a supreme degree, were to be found, as well as every other virtue, under the most tender forms, I was astonished at this proposal. After so long an agitation of spirits, exhausted not only for want of rest, but absolutely want of food, drenched in rain for twelve hours together, that a woman should be capable of such an undertaking as delivering herself to an enemy, probably in the night, and uncertain of what hands she might fall into, appeared an effort above human nature.

The assistance I was able to give was small indeed. I had not even a cup of wine to offer her. All I could furnish her with was an open boat, and a few lines, written upon a dirty wet paper, to General Gates [the commanding American General] recommending her to his protection. . . .'

She set out in an open boat upon the Hudson, accompanied by Mr. Brudenell, the chaplain, Sarah Pollard, her waiting maid, and her husband's valet, who had been severely wounded while searching for his master upon the battle-field. It was about sunset when they started, and a violent storm of rain and wind, which had been increasing since the morning, rendered the voyage tedious and perilous in the extreme.

It was long after dark when they reached the American outposts; the sentinel heard their oars, and hailed them. Lady Harriet returned the answer herself. The clear, silvery tones of a woman's voice amid the darkness filled the soldier on duty with superstitious fear, and he called a comrade to accompany him to the river bank.

The errand of the voyagers was made known, but the faithful guard, apprehensive of treachery, would not allow them to land until they sent for Major Dearborn. They were invited by that officer to his quarters, where every attention was paid to them, and Lady Harriet was comforted by the joyful tidings that her husband was safe. In the morning she experienced parental tenderness from General Gates, who sent her to her husband, at Poor's quarters, under a suitable escort.

SOURCE: Benson John Lossing (1813–1891); quoted Sir Edward Creasy, *The Fifteen Decisive Battles of the World* (32nd edition, 1886), pp. 488–490.

vi. *Lord Cornwallis fails to lead his army*

The British surrender at Yorktown, October 19, 1781.

Every eye was prepared to gaze on Lord Cornwallis, the object of peculiar interest and solicitude; but he disappointed our anxious expectations; pretending indisposition, he made General O'Harra his substitute as the leader of his army. This officer was followed by the conquered troops in a slow and solemn step, with shouldered arms, colors cased and drums beating a British march. . . . The royal troops, while marching through the line formed by the allied army, exhibited a decent and neat appearance, as respects arms and clothing, for their commander opened his store and directed every soldier to be furnished with a new suit complete, prior to the capitulation. But in their line of march we remarked a disorderly and un-soldierly conduct, their step was irregular, and their ranks frequently broken.

SOURCE: Surgeon James Thacher, *A Military Journal.*

vii. *Lord North's resignation,* 1782

A more interesting scene had not been acted within the walls of the House of Commons, since February, 1743, when Sir Robert Walpole retired from power. Nor did that First Minister by any means display in the last moments of his political life, the equanimity, suavity, and dignity manifested by his successor.

Lord North ordered his Coach to remain at the House of Commons in waiting, on that evening. In consequence of so unexpected an event as his resignation, and the House breaking up at such an early hour, the housekeeper's room became crowded to the greatest degree; few persons having directed their carriages to be ready before midnight.

In the midst of this confusion, Lord North's Coach drove up to the door; and as he prepared to get into it, he said, turning to those persons near him, with that unalterable equanimity and good temper which never forsook him:

'Good-night, Gentleman. You see what it is to be in the secret.'

SOURCE: Sir N. William Wraxall, *Historical Memoirs of My Own Time*, 1815, Vol. 2, pp. 151–152.

ANDREWS, JOHN (1720–1817), dragoon.

The last parade of John Andrews

John Andrews, who was at Dettingen, Fontenoy and Culloden, among other battles, 'served his country . . . with fidelity' for 81 years and turned up for his last parade when over 90 on Lexden Heath, near Colchester, in 1811. The troops were being reviewed by the Prince Regent and the Duke of York, and the former asked who the old soldier in his faded uniform was.

The Earl [of Chatham] replied:

'Why, 'tis old Andrews, the oldest soldier in the service . . . now on half-pay.'

An *aide-de-camp* was directly sent to request the old veteran's attendance, who of course soon attended, and a long and interesting conversation ensued, of which the following forms a part:

Duke of York. 'How old are you Andrews, and how long have you been in the service?'

Andrews. 'Why, your Royal Highness, I am now ninety years old and have been in the service about 70 years.'

His Royal Highness, seeing that he was drest in an old suit of Regimentals, enquired how long he had worn them?

'Why, your Royal Highness, about 40 years,' replied Andrews, at which the Prince took up the skirt of his coat, for the purpose of feeling the texture, and remarked that 'such cloth was not made nowadays.'

'No,' replied the old veteran, 'nor such men neither.'

SOURCE: Edward Paulett Strutt, *Note-books*; quoted Hector Bolitho, *The Galloping Third*, John Murray, 1963.

ANNE BOLEYN (1507–1536), second queen of Henry VIII; crowned on Whit Sunday, 1533, after a secret marriage in January; executed May 19, 1536.

i. *Beginning of a courtship*

There came to me in the night the most afflicting news possible. I have to grieve for three causes: first, to hear of my mistress' sickness, whose health I desire as my own, and would willingly bear the half of yours to cure you. Secondly, because I fear to suffer yet longer that absence which has already caused me so much pain. . . . Thirdly, because the physician I trust most is at present absent, when he could do me the greatest pleasure. However, in his absence I send you the second: I beseech you to be governed by his advice, and then I shall hope soon to see you again.

SOURCE: Henry VIII to Anne Boleyn, when she was critically ill during an epidemic of the sweating sickness; *State Papers.*

ii. *End of a courtship*

I heard say the executioner was very good, and I have a little neck.

SOURCE: Anne Boleyn to Sir W. Kingston, on the morning of her execution; recorded by him in a letter to Thomas Cromwell. By one of the ironies of history, Anne spent the night before her coronation and the night before her execution in the same room in the Tower of London.

ANNE (1665–1714), Queen of Great Britain. Anne was a stickler for correctness in dress at Court.

The wrong wig

Once Lord Bolingbroke came to her in a tie-wig instead of a full-bottomed one, and although she had sent for him in the greatest haste she was thoroughly disconcerted.

'I suppose,' she said crossly, 'that the next time his lordship appears at Court he will come in his nightcap.'

SOURCE: J. H. Jesse, *Continuation of Memoirs of the Court of England from the Revolution in 1688 . . .* ; Christopher Hibbert, *The Court at Windsor*, Longmans, 1964, p. 94.

ARKWRIGHT, SIR RICHARD (1732–1792), engineer and inventor.

The subterranean barber

When Sir Richard Arkwright went first to Manchester, he hired himself to a petty barber; but being remarkably frugal, he saved money out of a very scanty income. With these savings he took a cellar, and commenced business; at the cellar head he displayed this inscription:

'Subterranean shaving with keen razors, for one penny.'

The novelty had a very successful effect, for he soon had plenty of customers; so much so, that several brother tonsors, who before had demanded twopence a piece for shaving, were obliged to reduce their terms. They also styled themselves subterranean shavers, although they all lived and worked above ground. Upon this Arkwright determined on a still further reduction, and shaved for a halfpenny.

A neighbouring cobbler one day descended the original subterranean tonsor's steps in order to be shaved. The fellow had a remarkably strong, rough beard. Arkwright, beginning to lather him, said he hoped he would give him another half-penny, for his beard was so strong it might spoil his razor. The cobbler declared he would not. Arkwright then shaved him for the half-penny, and immediately gave him two pairs of shoes to mend. This was the basis of Arkwright's extraordinary fortune; for the cobbler, struck with this unexpected favour, introduced him to the inspection of a cotton machine. . . . The plan of this Arkwright got possession of: and it gradually led him to the dignity of a knighthood, and the accumulation of half a million of money.

SOURCE: Thomas Byerley and Joseph Clinton Robertson, *The Percy Anecdotes*, 1820–1823.

ARMADA, THE SPANISH or **'INVINCIBLE'**(July–August, 1588).

i. *Drake at bowls*

The Queen had received such assurance they [the Armada] were so disabled from coming this year by storm, that she made

Secretary Walsingham send for four of her first-rate Ships to be brought home to Chatham. But their return was prevented by the Intelligence which Captain Thomas Fleming brought into the harbour on the 19th of July, that he had discovered the Enemy approaching from the Lizard-Point in Cornwall. The Captains and Commanders were then it seems at Bowls upon the Hoe at Plymouth; and the Tradition goes, that Drake would needs see the Game up, but was soon prevailed to go and play at Rubbers with the Spaniards. All Hands were now at Work to warp out the Ships, which, with the admirable Industry of the Seamen, was very speedily perform'd, the Wind blowing stiffly into the Haven from the South-west.

SOURCE: William Oldys, *The Life of Sir Walter Raleigh* . . . , 1736; quoted in Robert Birley, *The Undergrowth of History*, Historical Association, 1955, which contains an admirable examination of the bowls story. The first printed mention of it occurs 36 years after the Armada in Thomas Scott, *The Second Part of Vox Pupuli or Gondemar appearing in the likeness of Matchiavell in a Spanish Parliament*, 1624.

ii. *Two against a galleon*

Much speech is of two gentlemen of the court that went to the navy at the same time, whose names are Thomas Gerard, and William Hervy, to me not known, but now here about London spoken of with great fame. These two adventured out of a ship-boat, to scale the great galliass, wherein Moncada was, and entered the same only with their rapiers; a matter commonly spoken, that never the like was hazarded before, considering the height of the galliass compared to a ship-boat.

SOURCE: *The Copie of a Letter sent out of England to Don Bernadin Mendoza, Ambassadour in France for the King of Spaine, declaring the State of England . . . found in the Chamber of Richard Leigh, a Seminarie Priest* . . . (Harleian Miscellany).

iii. *Drake has a mind to wrestle a fall*

We have the army of Spain before us and mind, with the grace of God, to wrestle a fall with them. There was never anything pleased me better than seeing the enemy flying with a southerly wind to the northward ... if we live, I doubt not so to handle the matter with the Duke of Sidonia as he shall wish himself at Saint Marie Port among his orange trees.

SOURCE: Drake to Sir Francis Walsingham, when the remnants of the Armada were standing northward; quoted Julian Corbett, *Sir Francis Drake*, Macmillan, 1901, p. 170.

iv. *Drake summarizes the achievements of the Invincible Armada*

With all their great and terrible ostentation, they did not in all their sailing round about England so much as sink or take one ship, bark, pinnance, or cock-boat of ours, or even burn so much as one sheep-cote on this land.

SOURCE: John Strype (1643–1737); quoted Sir Edward Creasey, *The Fifteen Decisive Battles of the World*.

ASKEW, ANNE (1521–1546), Protestant martyr; examined for heresy, tortured on the rack, and burnt at Smithfield.

'*To the very end*'

Then the lieutenant caused me to be loosed from the rack. Incontinently I swooned, and then they recovered me again. After that I sat two long hours reasoning with my lord chancellor upon the bare floor, whereas he with many flattering words persuaded me to leave my opinion. But my Lord God (I thank His everlasting goodness) gave me grace to persevere, and will do (I hope) to the very end.

SOURCE: John Bale, ... *Examinacyon of Anne Askewe*, 1547–1548; quoted William Haller, *Foxe's Book of Martyrs and the Elect Nation*, Jonathan Cape, 1963, p. 60.

ASTOR, LADY NANCY (1879–1964), the first woman member of the House of Commons.

A newspaper magnate's widest circulation

Viscount Waldorf Astor owned Britain's two most influential newspapers, the *Times* and the *Observer*, but his American wife,

Nancy, had a wider circulation than both papers put together.

SOURCE: Emery Kelen, *Peace in Their Time*, Victor Gollancz, p. 330.

ATHANASIUS, ST. (296?–373), Bishop of Alexandria.

Unorthodox baptisms by the future saint

. . . one day Alexander [bishop of Alexandria] had been keeping the 'birthday' of his martyred predecessor Peter, and was expecting some of his clergy to a banquet at his house. His windows looked towards the sea, and as he stood gazing out of them towards the present harbour he saw a group of boys upon the shore. They were playing at Church ceremonies, and, thinking that they were going a little too far, he called some of the clergy to witness the scene, and then sent them to bring the boys into his presence.

After a little pressure, the boys admitted that in play they had made Athanasius bishop, and that he had baptised some of them . . . by immersion in the sea, with all legitimate forms. Finding that the questions had been duly put and the answers correctly given, the Archbishop . . . determined to recognise the baptism as valid, but to follow it up by confirmation.

SOURCE: based on Rufinus, who visited Alexandria in 372; F. W. Farrar, *Lives of the Fathers*, Adam & Charles Black, 1907, Vol. I, p. 453.

ATTERBURY, FRANCIS (1662–1732), Bishop of Rochester and Dean of Westminster. Deprived of his offices and banished for his Jacobite sympathies.

'Atterbury's Pad'

A specimen of the dexterous wit of Atterbury in debate is related in connection with the history of the Occasional Conformity and Schism Bills, December 1718. On that occasion, Lord Coningsby rebuked the Bishop for having, the day before, assumed the character of a prophet.

'In Scripture,' said this simple peer, 'I find a prophet very like him, namely Balaam, who, like the right reverend lord, drove so very furiously that the ass he rode upon was constrained to open his mouth and reprove him.'

The luckless lord having sat down, the bishop rose with a demure and humble look, and having thanked his lordship for taking so much notice of him, went on to say that 'the application of Balaam to him, though severe, was certainly very happy. . . . There wanted, however, the application of the ass; and it seemed as if his lordship, being the only person who had reproved him, must needs take that character upon himself.'

From that day, Lord Coningsby was commonly recognised by the appellation of 'Atterbury's Pad'*.

SOURCE: *The Book of Days* (edit. R. Chambers), W. & R. Chambers, 1864, Vol. I, p. 335.

AUGUSTUS FREDERICK, DUKE OF SUSSEX (1773–1843), sixth son of George III. He formed a library of 50,000 books; followed a very progressive line in politics, supporting the Reform Bill of 1832, and often being critical of the royal family; refused to be buried with the rest of them.

i. *Early to bed*

As he used to tell his young aide-de-camp, Mr. Keppel, the present Earl of Albemarle, he was an early sufferer in a good cause. When only seven years old he was, by order of the king, locked up in his nursery, and sent supperless to bed, for wearing Admiral Keppel's election colours.

SOURCE: Percy Fitzgerald, *The Royal Dukes and Princesses . . .*, 1882, Vol. II, p. 77. George III's exasperation is understandable, since Keppel was opposed by a candidate of the King's own choosing.

See GEORGE III for an account of the King's personal canvassing.

ii. *A wonderful voice*

His vanity is so undisguised that it wears the form of frankness, and therefore gives no disgust. I mentioned to him that I had

* Pad = an easy-paced horse.

heard of his excellence in singing, and he agreed that he possessed it without the least hesitation, adding:

'I *had* the most wonderful voice that ever was heard—three octaves—and I do understand music. I practised eight hours a day in Italy. One may boast of a voice, as it is a gift of nature.'

SOURCE: Mrs. Trench; quoted ibid., Vol. II, p. 62.

iii. *Lord Eldon's letter*

In contravention of the Royal Marriage Act, the Duke married Lady Augusta Murray in Rome, in 1793. In an effort to get the marriage validated, the Duke, on his return to England, decided to have the ceremony repeated in this country, and the banns were given out at St. George's, Hanover Square, apparently without anyone realizing that one of the royal Dukes was involved. The marriage was later declared void. Lord Eldon gave this account of the situation:

It seemed singular that banns should be published where one of the parties was of the royal family, and that the clergyman publishing the banns should not be struck upon reading of the name; it appeared, however, that in the parish there were many of the name (I think Augustus Frederick) by which he was called in the publication. Then, great blame was imputed to the rector for publishing the banns without inquiry as to the residence of the parties in the parish; so it was proposed to call upon the clergy of the church, St. George's, Hanover Square, to account for the marriage having taken place by banns, without the proper residence of the party in the parish, and without their knowing the parties. The rector first appeared: he said he had two most respectable curates, and he had always solemnly enjoined them not to marry parties without having first inquired about their residence. The curates were then examined, and they said theirs was a most respectable parish clerk, who wore a gown, and they had always most solemnly given a like injunction to him. The clerk was then called, and he declared that no man in the parish had a more excellent careful wife than he had, and that he daily gave her most solemnly a like injunction. She then made her appearance, and said that she must sometimes be about her own, and not about parish business;

but that she had two female servants, as discreet as any in the parish, and she had always given them a like solemn injunction, when anybody brought a paper about publication of banns in her and her husband's absence, to make proper inquiries about the parties' residence.

All this put Lord Thurlow [Lord Chancellor] out of humour, and he then said to me angrily, 'Sir, why have you not prosecuted, under the Act of Parliament, all the parties concerned in this abominable marriage?' To which I answered that it was a very difficult business to prosecute; that the Act it was understood, had been drawn by Lord Mansfield, and *Mr. Attorney General* Thurlow and Mr. Solicitor-General Wedderburne, and unluckily they had made all parties present at the marriage guilty of a felony; and as nobody could prove the marriage except a person who had been present at it, there could be no prosecution, because nobody present could be compelled to be a witness. This put an end to the matter.

SOURCE: Percy Fitzgerald, *The Royal Dukes and Princesses . . .*, 1882, Vol. II. pp. 54–55.

iv. *Marginal comment*

'I don't believe a word of it.'

SOURCE: handwritten comment on the Athanasian Creed in the margin of his prayer book.

AUSTERLITZ, BATTLE OF (December 2, 1805): won by Napoleon on the anniversary of his coronation against the combined armies of Austria and Russia.

'*Roll up that map*'

'Roll up that map; it will not be wanted these ten years.'

SOURCE: said of the map of Europe by William Pitt, Prime Minister, on receiving news of the battle, which destroyed the European coalition he had built up. Philip Henry, fifth Earl Stanhope, *Life of the Right Hon. William Pitt*, 1862, Vol. iv, p. 369.

BACON, FRANCIS, BARON VERULAM and VISCOUNT ST. ALBANS (1561–1626), Lord Chancellor and essayist.

i. *Bacon-versus-Sir Edward Coke*

Coke was Attorney-General at the time. The exchange took place in the Exchequer court when Bacon was recommending the re-seizure of the lands of George Moore, 'a relapsed recusant and fugitive'.

Mr. Attorney kindled at it, and said, 'Mr. Bacon, if you have any tooth against me, pluck it out, for it will do you more hurt than all the teeth in your head will do you good.'

I answered coolly in these words: 'Mr. Attorney, I respect you; I fear you not; and the less you speak of your own greatness, the more I shall think of it.'

He replied, 'I think scorn to stand upon terms of greatness towards you, who are less than little, less than the least. . . .'

Herewith stirred, I said no more than this: 'Mr. Attorney, do not depress me so far, for I have been your better, and may be again when it pleases the queen.'

SOURCE: *A true remembrance of the abuse I received from Mr. Attorney-General, publicly in the Exchequer, the first day of term*, in a letter to Robert Cecil; quoted *The Percy Anecdotes*, 1820–1823.

ii. *Bacon's province*

I have taken all knowledge to be my province.

SOURCE: a letter to Lord Burleigh, 1592.

iii. *The broken reed*

'It is my act, my hand, my heart: I beseech your lordships to be merciful to a broken reed.'

SOURCE: Bacon's answer, when, having confessed to charges of bribery and corruption, he was asked by a committee of the House of Lords whether he subscribed the confession.

iv. *The justest judge*

Bacon did not attempt to defend himself, although he declared, and apparently with truth, that he was 'the justest judge in

England these fifty years', but he also declared that his disgrace was 'the justest censure in Parliament that was these two hundred years'.

SOURCE: M. W. Keatinge and N. L. Frazer, *A History of England for Schools*, A. & C. Black, 1911.

v. *The last experiment*

His devotion to science appears to have been the immediate cause of his death. Travelling in his carriage when there was snow on the ground, he began to consider whether flesh might not be preserved by snow as well as by salt. In order to make the experiment he alighted at a cottage near Highgate, bought a hen, and stuffed it with snow. This so chilled him that he was unable to return home, but went to the Earl of Arundel's house in the neighbourhood, where his illness was so much increased by the dampness of the bed into which he was put that he died in a few days. . . . In a letter to the earl, the last which he wrote, after comparing himself to the elder Pliny, 'who lost his life by trying an experiment about the burning of Mount Vesuvius', he does not forget to mention his own experiment, which, says he, 'succeeded excellently'.

SOURCE: *Chambers's Cyclopaedia of English Literature*, W. & R. Chambers, new edition, 1901, Vol. I.

BACON, SIR NICHOLAS (1509–1579), Lord Keeper of England; father of Francis Bacon.

i. *The Lord Keeper's signal*

. . . he was loaden with a corpulent body, especially in his old age, so that he would be not only out of breath, but almost out of life, with going from Westminster Hall to the Star Chamber; insomuch, when sitting down in his place, it was some time before he could recover himself; and therefore it was usual in that court that no lawyer should begin to speak, till the lord keeper held up his staff as a signal for him to begin.

SOURCE: Thomas Fuller, *The English Worthies*, 1662, 1952 edition, George Allen & Unwin, pp. 531–532.

ii. *The great man in the little house*

He gave for his motto, *Mediocria Firma* [A middle course is safe];
... never attaining, because never affecting, any great estate ....
And therefore when Queen Elizabeth, coming thither [to his
house at Gorhambury, Hertfordshire] in progress, told him:

'My lord, your house is too little for you.'

'No, madam,' returned he, no less wittily than gratefully, 'but
it is your highness that hath made me too great for mine house.'

SOURCE: ibid., p. 532.

BALACLAVA, BATTLE OF (October 25, 1854).

The Charge of the Light Brigade

C'est magnifique, mais ce n'est pas la guerre.
(It is magnificent, but it is not war.)

SOURCE: Maréchal Bosquet.

BALFOUR, ARTHUR JAMES, first **EARL OF BALFOUR**
(1848–1930), statesman; Prime Minister, 1902–1905, Foreign
Secretary, 1916–1919, etc.

The young Balfour is not infallible

Comment on Balfour, when he was a junior Fellow of Trinity,
Cambridge:

'We are none of us infallible—not even the youngest of us.'

SOURCE: Dr. W. H. Thompson, Master of Trinity; in George W.
E. Russell, *Collections and Recollections*, Smith, Elder & Co., 1903,
Ch. XIX.

BANNOCKBURN, BATTLE OF (June 24, 1314). The battle in
Stirlingshire in which Edward II's forces were completely routed,
with disastrous losses, by Robert Bruce of Scotland.

The 30,000 that remained

A splenetic Englishman said to a Scotchman ... that no man
of taste would think of remaining any time in such a country as
Scotland. To which the canny Scot replied:

D

'Tastes differ; I'se tak' ye to a place, no far frae Stirling, whaur thretty tousand of your countryman ha' been for five hundred years, an' they've nae thotcht o' leaving' yet.'

SOURCE: John Timbs, *A Century of Anecdote, 1760–1860.*

BEAUFORT, MARGARET, Countess of Richmond and Derby (1443–1509), Mother of Henry VII. An early patron of Caxton. The Oxford women's college, Lady Margaret Hall, is named after her.

i. *What more could be expected?*

She was a gentlewoman, a scholar and a saint, and after having been three times married she took a vow of celibacy. What more could be expected of any woman?

SOURCE: said by Miss Elizabeth Wordsworth, first Principal of the college. It was by Margaret Beaufort's first marriage, to Edmund Tudor, Earl of Richmond, that she became the mother of the first Tudor king.

ii. *The Countess offers to become a laundress*

The Lady Margaret, Countess of Richmond, mother to King Henry the seventh, a most worthy Patroness of good Letters, would often say, On the condition that Princes of Christendom would combine themselves, and march against the common enemy the Turk, she would most willingly attend them, and be their Laundress in the camp.

SOURCE: William Camden, *Remains Concerning Britain*, 7th impression, 1674, p. 296.

BECKET, THOMAS (1118?–1170), Archbishop of Canterbury. Canonized in 1173 by Pope Alexander III.

i. *The rage of Henry II*

When the news of this [the excommunications and suspensions by Becket] reached King Henry at Bur-le-Roi, near Bayeux, following so swiftly on Thomas's refusal to absolve the ex-communicated bishops, he lost his temper. The Angevin demon burst through his reserve and he shouted the words which he was for ever after to regret.

'What sluggards and knaves,' he cried, 'have I fed in my house that they are faithless to their lord and let him be tricked so infamously by one upstart clerk!'

SOURCE: Philip Lindsay, *Kings of Merry England*, Ivor Nicholson & Watson, 1935, p. 183.

ii. *No traitor, but a priest*

Inspired by fury the knights called out:

'Where is Thomas Becket, traitor to the king and realm?'

As he answered not, they cried out the more furiously:

'Where is the archbishop?'

At this, intrepid and fearless . . . he descended from the stair where he had been dragged by the monks in fear of the knights, and in a clear voice answered:

'I am here, no traitor to the king, but a priest. Why do you seek me?'

SOURCE: Edward Grim's eyewitness account, in *Materials for the History of Becket*, Rolls Series, 1875–1885.

BEDE or **BÆDA** (673–735): monk of Jarrow; teacher, historian, scholar, and author of some fifty works, including *The Ecclesiastical History of the English Nation*, 'the first fruits of the Christian scholarship of England'. His translation of the Gospel of St. John, completed on his death-bed, is unfortunately lost. The story was told by Cuthbert in a letter to Cuthwin.

The last task completed

Having said much more, he passed the day joyfully till the evening; and the boy, above mentioned, said:

'Dear master, there is yet one sentence not written.'

He answered,

'Write quickly.'

Soon after, the boy said:

'The sentence now is written.'
He replied:
'It is well. You have said the truth. It is ended.'

SOURCE: letter from Cuthbert to Cuthwin, trans. Henry Morley in *Illustrations of English Religion*; inc. in *The Cambridge Book of Prose and Verse in Illustration of English Literature* . . . (edit. George Sampson), C.U.P., 1924, pp. 65–66.

BEDS.

i. *The Great Bed of Ware*

Few objects of antiquarian curiosity acquired more notoriety than a bedstead or bed, of unusually large dimensions, preserved at Ware, twenty miles from London, on the road to Cambridge. Shakespeare employs it as an object of comparison in his play of *Twelfth Night*, bearing date 1614, where Sir Toby Belch says:

'As many lies as will lie in this sheet of paper, though the sheet were big enough for the bed of Ware in England.'

Nares, in his *Glossary**** says:

'This curious piece of furniture is said to be still in being, and visible at the Crown or at the Bull in Ware. It is reported to be twelve feet square, and to be capable of holding twenty or twenty-four persons.' And he refers to Chauncey's Hertfordshire† for an account of the bed receiving at once twelve men and their wives, who lay at the top and bottom in this mode of arrangement—first two men, then two women, and so on alternately—so that no man was near to any woman but his wife.‡

SOURCE: John Timbs, *Nooks and Corners of English Life*, 1867, p. 179.

* Nares, Robert, *A Glossary; or a Collection of Words . . . which have been thought to require Illustration in the Works of English Authors*, 1822.

† Sir Henry Chauncy, *The Historical Antiquities of Hertfordshire*, 1700.

‡ In fact, it doesn't work out! It can be done, but the sleeping arrangements need a little modification.

ii. *The last traveller with a bed?*

Formerly, wealthy persons travelled with their bed in their carriage. Mr. Beckford, of Fonthill,* was, probably, the last person who so travelled in England, some forty years since, when the writer's informant saw the unpacking of the bed, at the inn-door at Salt Hill.

SOURCE: ibid., p. 180. Considerable care was taken in the transport and erection of royal beds, and it was ordered that 'a yoman with a daggar is to searche the strawe of the kynges bedde that there be none untreuthe therin'.

BENBOW, JOHN (1653–1702), Admiral. An officer much celebrated in song and story, who came up the hard way to flag rank, and was a tough customer not popular with some of his more gently born colleagues. In the War of the Spanish Succession (1702–1713), Benbow was sent to prevent the French occupying some of the Spanish West Indian possessions. Despite heroic efforts by Benbow, during which he was seriously wounded, he failed in his action with the French Admiral Ducasse through the shameful failure of a number of the English captains, who refused to bring their ships into action.

The cowardly captains

Admiral Ducasse knew very well that his squadron had been saved through the disgraceful conduct of Benbow's captains, and he was too true a sailor to regard it in any but the proper light. He sent the following letter to Benbow:

> Sir,
>   I had little hope on Monday last but to have supped in your cabin [i.e., to have been taken prisoner]; but it pleased God to order it otherwise, and I am thankful for it. As for

---

* William Beckford (1759–1844), a wealthy collector who spent large sums on his mansion at Fonthill Giffard, which his extravagances compelled him to sell in 1822.

those cowardly captains who deserted you, hang them up;
for, by God, they deserve it.

Ducasse.

SOURCE: *The Book of Days* (edit. R. Chambers), 1865, Vol. II,
p. 543. Two of the captains were, in fact, convicted by a court
martial and shot; and one was imprisoned and cashiered. Benbow
died soon after as the result of his wounds.

BERLIN, TREATY OF (1878). Concluded after the war between
Russia and Turkey, the parties being those two countries plus Great
Britain, Germany, Austria, France and Italy. The congress was
under the presidency of Bismarck, and the British plenipotentiaries
were Disraeli and the Marquis of Salisbury. They obtained the
right for Great Britain to administer Cyprus.

Lord Odo's diplomacy

When the Congress of the Powers assembled at Berlin in the
summer of 1878, our Ambassador in that city of stucco palaces
was the loved and lamented Lord Odo Russell, afterwards Lord
Ampthill, a born diplomat if ever there was one. . . . On the
evening before the formal opening of the Congress, Lord
Beaconsfield arrived in all his plenipotentiary glory, and was
received with high honours at the British Embassy. In the
course of the evening one of his private secretaries came to
Lord Odo Russell and said:

'Lord Odo, we are in a frightful mess, and we can only turn
to you to help us out of it. The old chief has determined to open
the proceedings of the Congress in French. He has written out
the devil's own long speech in French and learnt it by heart, and
is going to fire it off at the Congress tomorrow. We shall be the
laughing stock of Europe. He pronounces *épicier* as if it rhymed
with *overseer*, and all his pronunciation is to match. It is as much
as our places are worth to tell him so. Can you help us?'

Lord Odo listened with amused good humour to this tale of
woe, and then replied:

'It is a very delicate mission that you ask me to undertake,
but then I am fond of delicate missions. I will see what I can do.'

And so he repaired to the state bedroom, where our venerable Plenipotentiary was beginning those elaborate processes of the toilet with which he prepared for the couch.

'My dear Lord,' began Lord Odo, 'a dreadful rumour has reached us.'

'Indeed! Pray, what is it?'

'We have heard that you intend to open the proceedings tomorrow in French.'

'Well, Lord Odo, what of that?'

'Why, of course, we all know that there is no one in Europe more competent to do so than yourself. But then, after all, to make a speech in French is a commonplace accomplishment. There will be at least half a dozen men at the Congress who could do it almost, if not quite, as well as yourself. But, on the other hand, who but you can make an English speech? All these Plenipotentiaries have come from the various Courts of Europe expecting the greatest intellectual treat of their lives in hearing English spoken by its greatest living master. The question for you, my dear Lord, is—will you disappoint them?'

Lord Beaconsfield put his glass in his eye, fixed his gaze on Lord Odo, and then said:

'There is much force in what you say. I will consider the point.'

And the next day he opened the proceedings in English.

Now, the psychological conundrum is this—Did he swallow the flattery. . .? Or did he see through the manœuvre, and recognise a polite intimation that a French speech from him would throw an air of comedy over all the proceedings of the Congress, and perhaps kill it with ridicule?

SOURCE: George W. E. Russell, *Collections and Recollections*, Smith, Elder & Co., 1903, Ch. XXIV.

BISMARCK, OTTO VON (1815–1898), German statesman.

i. *The origin of 'Blood and Iron'*

Place in the hands of the King of Prussia the strongest possible military power, then he will be able to carry out the policy you wish; this policy cannot succeed through speeches, and shooting-matches, and songs; it can only be carried out through blood and iron.

SOURCE: Speech to the Prussian House of Deputies, Jan. 28, 1886.

ii. *Bismarck's wife has a theory*

I must tell you that my wife has a theory that only thin people can talk English well. According to this, neither you nor I will make our mark in that language.

SOURCE: Bismarck to journalist Henri de Blowitz, 1878; de Blowitz, *My Memoirs*, Edwin Arnold, 1903, p. 157.

iii. *'You had better send for an interpreter'*

I remember an incident that I shall never forget. We [Bismarck, Thiers and Favre, French statesmen] were discussing a question about which we could not come to an understanding. M. Thiers held his own in the most spirited manner possible. M. Jules Favre was pathetic, gesticulating in the most tragic way, but, nevertheless, no progress was made with our business. All at once I began to talk German. M. Thiers looked at me in amazement.

'You know we do not understand German,' he said.

'Certainly,' I replied in French. 'When I am discussing matters with people with whom I believe I can finally come to an understanding, I speak their language, but when I see that it is useless to argue with them I talk my own language. You had better send for an interpreter.'

SOURCE: ibid., p. 162.

BLACK HOLE OF CALCUTTA, THE (June 21, 1756). One of the blackest crimes of history, perpetrated by Suray-ud-Daulah, ruler of Bengal, after his capture of the British fort at Calcutta.

No more than three and twenty

Figure to yourself, my friend, if possible, the situation of a hundred and forty-six wretches, exhausted by continual fatigue and action, crammed together in a cube of eighteen feet, in a close sultry night, in Bengal, shut up to the eastward and southward (the only quarters from whence air could reach us) by dead walls, and by a wall and door to the north, open only to the westward by two windows, strongly barred with iron, from which we could receive scarce any the least circulation of fresh air. . . .

About a quarter after six in the morning, the poor remains of 146 souls, being no more than three and twenty, came out of the Black-hole alive, but in a condition which made it very doubtful whether they would see the morning of the next day. . . .

SOURCE: John Zephaniah Holwell, letter in *Annual Register*, 1758. Holwell succeeded Clive as temporary governor of Bengal. For a much fuller extract from Holwell's narrative, see *They Saw it Happen*, 1689–1897, Basil Blackwell, 1958.

BLENHEIM, BATTLE OF (August 13, 1704): fought during the third campaign of the War of the Spanish Succession.

i. *Marlborough before the battle*

Marlborough's words at the council of war, when a battle was resolved on . . . deserve recording. We know them on the authority of his chaplain, Mr. (afterwards Bishop) Hare, who accompanied him throughout the campaign. . . . Marlborough's words to the officers who remonstrated with him on the seeming temerity of attacking the enemy in their position, were:

'I know the danger, yet a battle is absolutely necessary; and I rely on the bravery and discipline of the troops, which will make amends for our disadvantages.'

SOURCE: Sir Edward Creasey, *The Fifteen Decisive Battles of the World*, 1851.

ii. *Compliment from a prisoner of war*

The most distinguished prisoner taken at Blenheim was Marshal Tallard, who was opposed to Marlborough commanding the left of the Allied forces. Part of Tallard's captivity was spent in the congenial surroundings of Chatsworth, the great Derbyshire mansion of the Dukes of Devonshire.

It was on this fine house that Marshal Tallard . . . is reported to have passed a singularly elegant enconium, after being invited thither by the noble owner. On taking leave of his Grace, he observed:

'My lord, when I come hereafter to compute the time of my captivity in England, I shall leave out the days of my enjoyment at Chatsworth.'

SOURCE: Thomas Byerley and Joseph Clinton Robertson, *The Percy Anecdotes*, 1820–1823.

BOADICEA or **BOUDICCA** (?–62), Queen of the Iceni of Norfolk and Suffolk; led revolt against the Roman Ninth Legion.

The Queen starts a hare

. . . Boadicia, Princess then of the parts of Norfolk and Suffolk, exceedingly injured by them [i.e. the Romans], animated the Britains to shake off the Roman bondage, and concluded:

'Let the Romans, which are no better than Hares and Foxes, understand that they make a wrong match with Wolfs and Greyhounds.'

And with that word, let an Hare out of her lap, as a foretoken of the Romans' fearfulness.

SOURCE: William Camden, *Remains Concerning Britain*, 7th impression, 1674. Camden adds, tersely, 'but the success of the battel proved otherwise'. Boadicea, described by the Greek historian Dio Cassius as very tall, fierce-eyed and tawny-haired, took poison when defeated by Suetonius Paullinus.

BOLINGBROKE, HENRY ST. JOHN, VISCOUNT (1678–1751), statesman. See also WALPOLE, SIR ROBERT, for some mention of his career. He was created Viscount Bolingbroke and Baron St. John of Lydiard Tregoze in 1712.

i. *Penalty of the peerage*

Lord Bolingbroke's father said to him on his being made a lord:
'Ah, Harry, I ever said you would be hanged, but now I find
that you will be beheaded.'

SOURCE: Joseph Spence, *Anecdotes*.

ii. *The difficulty about good laws*

'It is a very easy thing to devise good laws: the difficulty is to
make them effective.'

SOURCE: Lord Bolingbroke, quoted Spence's *Anecdotes*.

BONNER, EDMUND (1500?–1569), Bishop of London; several
times imprisoned. In 1549 accused of not being sufficiently
zealous in enforcing the use of the new Prayer Book, and was
ordered to preach at St. Paul's, bringing out some points laid
down for him in advance; but he still failed to acknowledge the
Supremacy of the King, was deprived of his office and sent to
prison in the Marshalsea.

Retort rumbustious

Then it was that one jeeringly saluted him, 'Good morrow,
bishop quondam [one-time bishop].'

To whom Bonner as tartly returned, 'Good morrow, *knave
semper* [knave always].'

SOURCE: Thomas Fuller, *The English Worthies*, 1662, 1952 edition,
George Allen & Unwin, p. 627.

BORGIAS, THE. It has been said that no family in history has
achieved such notoriety as that of the Borgias in the 15th Century.
Its most famous, or infamous, members were Pope Alexander
VI, and his children Cesare and Lucretia. Their chief weapon,
about which many rumours and exaggerations have been
circulated, was poison.

The meaning of 'to have drunk'

And the famous Borgia poison? It is a fact that from 1500, 'to
have drunk' meant 'to have been poisoned by the Borgias'.

Cattanei, who kept Isabella d'Este regularly informed, wrote to her from Rome:

'Every night the magistrates kill one another; they give a fine example to the Italians by teaching them what they will have to do at the Pope's death, when there will be a dearth of friends or places to offer refuge. The Spanish ambassador who was in Venice at the time of the League is very gravely ill, and it is suspected that he drank. From the very beginning he was warned not to have food outside his house.'

SOURCE: Anny Latour, *The Borgias* (trans. Neil Mann), Elek Books, 1963, pp. 124–125.

It is one of the ironies, or perhaps comforts, of history that Alexander VI's great grandson, Francisco Borgia, who renounced his wordly rank and entered the Society of Jesus, was canonized as Saint Francis Borgia in the 17th Century.

BOSWELL, BATTLE OF (August 22, 1485). The battle, fought in Leicestershire, which, with the death of Richard III, brought to an end the male line of Plantagenet and established the House of Tudor in the person of Henry VII.

i. *The sleeping sentry*

Richard lost nothing of his vigilance or unrelenting sternness in his last hours. Going the rounds at Bosworth, he found a sentinel asleep, and stabbed him, with the remark:

'I found him asleep, and have left him as I found him.'

SOURCE: John Timbs. *Ancestral Stories and Traditions of Great Families*, 1869, p. 315.

ii. *The Jockey of Norfolk ignores a warning*

The 'Jockey of Norfolk' was Sir John Howard, 1st Duke of Norfolk (1430?–1485), 'jockey' at that time having nothing to do with horses, but being a diminutive form of 'John'. 'Dickon' in the following verse stood for 'Richard'.

Sir John was a faithful follower of Richard III. Before the Battle of Bosworth he found a warning note, apparently written by some of his friends, in his tent:

Jockey of Norfolk, be not too bold,
For Dickon thy master is bought and sold.

Howard disregarded the warning and fell leading the van of Richard's forces.

SOURCE: Burke's *Peerage and Baronetage*, etc.

When Charles, thirteenth Duke of Norfolk, had completed his restoration of Arundel Castle, he proposed to entertain all the descendants of his ancestor, Jock of Norfolk, who fell at Bosworth field; but gave up his intention on finding that he should have to invite upwards of six thousand persons.

SOURCE: Samuel Pepys, *Diary*, Everyman's Library edition, Vol. i, p. 634, footnote.

iii. *The last of the mediæval kings*

But whatever else may have been bad or good about Richard of Gloucester, there was a touch about him which makes him truly the last of the mediæval kings. It is expressed in the one word which he cried aloud as he struck down foe after foe in the last charge at Bosworth—'Treason!' For him, as for the first Norman kings, treason was the same as treachery; and in this case at least it was the same as treachery. When his nobles deserted him before the battle, he did not regard it as a new political combination, but as the sin of false friends and faithless servants. Using his own voice like the trumpet of a herald, he challenged his rival to a fight as personal as that of the two paladins of Charlemagne. His rival did not reply, and was not likely to reply. The modern world had begun. The call echoed unanswered down the ages; for since that day no English king has fought after that fashion. Having slain many, he was himself slain and his diminished force destroyed.

So ended the war of the usurpers; and the last and most doubtful of all the usurpers, a wanderer from the Welsh marches, a knight from nowhere, found the crown of England under a bush of thorn.

SOURCE: G. K. Chesterton, *A Short History of England*, Chatto & Windus, 1917.

It was Sir William Stanley's last-minute treachery that turned the day, so that the warning to the Jockey of Norfolk (above) was well-founded. It was Stanley who was handed the gold crown of England from beneath the thorn bush where it had rolled from Richard's battered helmet, and set it on the head of Henry Tudor.

He was the only English king to be crowned on the field of battle. If confirmation be needed of the story of the crown beneath the bush, it may be found in the fact that Henry VII caused the device of the crown hidden in a bush to be incorporated in the design for his tomb in Westminster Abbey, and also in the glass for the windows of the Chapel.

iv. *Henry gives away his sword after the battle*

One of the Welsh knights who followed Henry Tudor to Bosworth Field was Richard-ap-Howel of Tremostyn.

When the battle was over, Henry invited him to court, but the honest Welshman nobly replied:

'I will dwell among mine own people.'

Henry then presented him with the sword and belt he had worn that day, with which, attended by his followers, he retreated into Wales, the little king of half a county.

SOURCE: W. Hutton, *The Battle of Bosworth Field . . .* , 1813.
See also RICHARD III.

BOYNE, BATTLE OF THE (July 1, 1690). Fought between the troops of William III and those of James II, who had fled the country eighteen months before but had landed in Ireland with a French force in an effort to regain his kingdom.

The King hides the hole in his coat

By three or four in the afternoon the whole of our army [King William's] was encamped. As soon as it had settled down the king began to reconnoitre the hostile camp and the fords of the river. During the whole time the artillery was directing its fire against us, with little loss to us, it is true, but to the great danger of the king. Posterity may have difficulty in believing how this great prince escaped with his life.

It may be mentioned that the enemy, having perceived through their field glasses that the king was reconnoitring their camp . . . pointed their artillery at the group. The second shot which they fired—it was from a 6 pounder—almost overthrew the king. The ball passed so near his back, that his doublet, his waistcoat and his coat were burnt about a hand's breadth, and the skin grazed so closely that it bled.

Those about his Majesty thought he was dangerously wounded, but he said with great coolness, 'It is nothing; but the ball came very near.' The King then asked for his cloak, in order to hide the hole burnt in his coat, and went on further . . . he remained two or three hours longer on horseback, lest the report that he was wounded should spread through the camp and alarm the troops.

SOURCE: account by the Danish emissary, L. Barbé, who was in Ireland to report on the war to Christian V of Denmark; *Notes and Queries*, July 14, 1877; quoted Hector Bolitho, *The Galloping Third*, John Murray, 1963.

BRADFORD, JOHN (1510?–1555), Protestant martyr; chaplain to Bishop Ridley (q.v.); burnt at Smithfield.

'There, but for the grace of God . . .'

But for the grace of God, there goes John Bradford.

SOURCE: remark on seeing criminals on their way to execution. His exclamation is more familiarly rendered as 'There, but for the grace of God. . .'.

BRAHE, TYCHO (1546–1601), famous Danish astronomer. During a duel, fought in complete darkness, following an argument about some mathematical problem, Brahe lost a portion of his nose.

The man with the gold and silver nose

As Tycho was not used to going around without a nose, and did not like to, he went to the expense of purchasing a new one. He was not satisfied, as some others might have been, to put on a wax one, but, being a nobleman of wealth, ordered a nose made of gold and silver so soberly painted and adjusted that it seemed of a natural appearance.

SOURCE: Peter Gassendi's life of Brahe, pub. in Latin, 1654. Willem Jansson Blaer, who spent two years with Brahe, told Gassendi that Tycho commonly carried a small box, filled with salve or glue, in his pocket, which he could apply whenever the nose became wobbly.

BRAY, THE VICAR OF.

i. *'I'll still be the Vicar of Bray, sir'*

The vicar of Bray, in Berkshire, was a papist under the reign of Henry the Eighth, and a Protestant under Edward the Sixth; he was a papist again under Mary, and once more became a Protestant in the reign of Elizabeth. When this scandal to the gown was reproached for his versatility of religious creeds, and taxed for being a turncoat and an inconstant changeling . . . he replied:

'Not so neither; for, if I changed my religion, I am sure I kept true to my principle; which is, to live and die the vicar of Bray!'

SOURCE: Isaac D'Israeli, *The Curiosities of Literature*, 1881 edition, Vol. 1, p. 196. Opinion differs as to who was the original turncoat vicar. One guess is Simon Aleyn (1540–1588) who, according to Thomas Fuller, was a Protestant in the reigns of Henry VIII, Edward VI and Elizabeth, and a Catholic under Mary. Another candidate is Simon Symonds who is stated to have been an Independent in the Protectorate, a High Churchman under Charles II, a Catholic under James II, and a Moderate in the reign of William III.

ii. *The Bishop who loved the Kitchen better than the Church*

D'Israeli says:

'How has it happened that this vicar should be so notorious and one in much higher rank, acting the same part, should have escaped notice. Dr. Kitchen [Anthony Kitchin (1477–1563)] bishop of Llandaff, from an idle abbot under Henry VIII was made a busy bishop; Protestant under Edward, he returned to his old master under Mary; and at last took the oath of supremacy under Elizabeth, and finished as a parliament Protestant. A pun spread the odium of his name; for they said he had always loved the Kitchen better than the Church.'

BRIAND, ARISTIDE (1862–1932), French socialist statesman. One of the authors of the Locarno Pact.

i. *Rebuke to a diplomat*

He was simple, sentimental, ironical, ponderous, and lazy. Once he rebuked a Latin American diplomat who brought him a heap of documents to study.

'You don't suppose I've lost my incapacity for work, do you?'

ii. *The man who bleated about peace*

In an after-lunch speech, Briand picked up the drawing of a cartoon and poked fun at himself:

'I see a stooped little man standing on the shoulders of a formidable God of War, trying to convince him. . . .'

He continued for a while in his velvety way, the very model of an easy-witted Frenchman. Then his tone changed and he dropped the picture on the table.

'They say,' he thundered, 'that all I do here is to bleat about peace.'

His eyes took on the steel blue of Breton waters, his cheeks flushed, his voice dropped. Almost in a whisper he said:

'Yes, with my last breath I will bleat about peace,' and sat down.

SOURCE: Emery Kelen, *Peace in Their Time*, Victor Gollancz, 1964, p. 175.

iii. *'One must dream a little'*

Briand said: 'It is not enough to act, one must dream a little.'

SOURCE: ibid., p. 176.

E

BRINDLEY, JAMES (1716–1772), engineer; constructed over 365 miles of canals, including the Bridgewater Canal (Manchester and Liverpool) and Grand Trunk Canal (Rivers Trent and Mersey).

i. *The genius who went to bed*

Brindley could hardly read, and his spelling to the day of his death remained almost the most wonderful thing about him. . . . Mr. Smiles mentions one extraordinary habit of this self-taught genius; when he had to come to a decision, or to make a calculation, requiring long thought, he used to go to bed for a day, or even two or three days, and then rise with his plan matured in his head; to drawings or models he hardly ever resorted.

SOURCE: C. R. L. Fletcher, *Historical Portraits, 1700–1850*, Oxford, 1919, Part I, pp. 253 and 255.

ii. *Why God created rivers*

Such was the enthusiasm with which this extraordinary man engaged in all schemes of inland navigation, that he seemed to regard all rivers with contempt, when compared with canals. It is said, that in an examination before the House of Commons, when he was asked for what purpose he apprehended rivers were created, he replied, after some deliberation:

'To feed navigable canals.'

SOURCE: William Hone, *The Everyday Book*, 1830, Vol. II, entry for Sept. 27.

BROUGHAM, HENRY, BARON BROUGHAM AND VAUX (1778–1868). Lord Chancellor; formed Society for the Diffusion of Useful Knowledge; founded London University; active in the abolition of slavery movement.

i. *Conceit* . . .

. . . I think I have . . . indicated what a rascal Brougham was. Still, something more should be stated, showing his conceit and rascality.

As to the first, here is an anecdote to the point. There is near Alnmouth [on the coast of Northumberland] a ford on the Aln which you may ride when the tide is not too high; one day my Grandfather, who had Brougham staying with him at Howick, proceeded to cross by this ford, when the marks by the river side indicated that it was rather doubtful if the crossing was safe. Halfway over, Lord Grey, who led the way, turned in his saddle and said:

'Brougham, can you swim?'

Brougham replied:

'I never have swam, but have no doubt I could if I tried.'

One is reminded of the man who, when he was asked whether he could play the fiddle, answered that he did not know because he had never made the attempt.

ii. ... and uncleanness

Brougham, in one of his speeches, held up his hands and said:

'At least these two hands are clean.'

This was known to those in whose company he lived to be physically at least, untrue, as he was personally of dirty habits; that it was a lie in any other sense was not known.

SOURCE: Charles George Barrington, *Political Recollections; History To-day*, August 1961, pp. 572 and 574. The charge of lack of physical cleanliness is substantiated by the *Creevey Papers*, where a lady says of Brougham at the theatre: 'you never saw such an object, or anything half so dirty'.

iii. *Final Word*

'I never want to see his ugly face again.'

SOURCE: King William IV on the fall of Melbourne's government in 1834 and Brougham's consequent loss of office.

BROWN, JOHN (1810–1859), abolitionist, raided plantations, killed pro-slavery settlers, and transported the slaves to Canada; captured the U.S. armoury and arsenal at Harpers Ferry, Virginia.

John Brown's body

At eleven o'clock, escorted by a strong column of soldiers, the prisoner entered the field. . . . He wore the same seedy and dilapidated dress that he had at Harpers Ferry and during his trial, but his rough boots had given place to a pair of particoloured slippers and he wore a low crowned broad brimmed hat (the first time I had ever seen him with a hat). . . . He stepped from the waggon with surprising agility and walked hastily toward the scaffold pausing a moment as he passed our group to wave his pinioned arm & bid us good morning. I thought I could observe in this a trace of bravado—but perhaps I was mistaken, as his natural manner was short, ungainly and hurried. He mounted the steps of the scaffold with the same alacrity and there, as if by previous arrangement, he immediately took off his hat and offered his neck for the halter which was as promptly adjusted by Mr. Avis the jailer. A white muslin cap or hood was then drawn over his face and the Sheriff not remembering that his eyes were covered requested him to advance to the platform. The prisoner replied in his usual tone:

'You will have to guide me there.'

The breeze disturbing the arrangement of the hood the Sheriff asked his assistant for a pin. Brown raised his hand and directed him to the collar of his coat where several old pins were quilted in. The Sheriff took the pin and completed his work.

He was accordingly led forward to the drop, the halter hooked to the beam, and the officers supposing that the execution was to follow immediately took leave of him. In doing so, the Sheriff enquired if he did not want a handkerchief to throw as a signal to cut the drop. Brown replied, 'No, I don't care; I don't want you to keep me waiting unnecessarily.'

These were his last words, spoken with that sharp nasal twang peculiar to him, but spoken quietly and civilly, without impatience or the slightest apparent emotion. In this position he stood for five minutes or more, while the troops that composed the escort were wheeling into the positions assigned them. I stood within a few paces of him and watched narrowly during these trying moments to see if there was any indication of his giving way. I detected nothing of the sort. . . .

Col. Smith said to the Sheriff in a low voice, 'We are ready.'

The civil officers descended from the scaffold. One who stood near me whispered earnestly, 'He trembles, his knees are shaking.'

'You are mistaken,' I replied, 'it is the scaffold that shakes under the footsteps of the officers.'

SOURCE: David Hunter Strother, reporting for *Harper's Weekly*; Boyd B. Stutler, *The Hanging of John Brown*, American Heritage, The Magazine of History, No. 2, February 1955.

BRUCE, ROBERT DE (1274–1329), King of Scotland.

Bruce and the spider

There seems to be no contemporary authority for the famous story of how the despairing Bruce, outlawed and harried, recovered heart through watching in a cave the dauntless efforts of a spider to make its web, despite its many falls. But the widely circulated and cherished story has had its effect.

Spiders are treated with peculiar respect in Scotland, and, especially ... no one who claims consanguinity with Bruce will kill, or suffer one to be killed in his presence.

SOURCE: Sir Herbert Maxwell, *Robert the Bruce*, 1897, p. 15.

The popular tradition is that in the spring of 1305, Robert Bruce was crowned at Scone ... but, being attacked by the English, he retreated first to the wilds of Athole, and then to the little island of Rathlin, off the north coast of Ireland, and all supposed him to be dead. While lying ... in Rathlin, he one day noticed a spider near his bed try six times to fix its web on a beam in the ceiling.

'Now shall this spider,' said Bruce, 'teach me what I am to do, for I also have failed six times.'

The spider made a seventh effort, and succeeded; where-upon Bruce left the island ... and, collecting together 300 fol-lowers, landed at Carrick, and at midnight surprised the English garrison in Turnberry Castle; he next overthrew the earl of Gloucester, and in two years made himself master of well-nigh all Scotland. . . .

SOURCE: Rev. Cobham Brewer, *Reader's Handbook* . . . new edition, 1911.

See also BANNOCKBURN and DOUGLAS, SIR JAMES.

BRUMMELL, GEORGE BRYAN (1778–1840), called **BEAU BRUMMELL,** leader of fashion and intimate of the Prince Regent.

i. *A breach of etiquette*

We have it on the authority of Brummell that when he and Moira were closeted with the Prince at Carlton House, the Regent asked the Beau to ring the bell, whereupon Brummell, forgetful of etiquette said:

'Your Royal Highness is close to it.'

The host was furious, and, but for Lord Moira's tactful intervention, would have ordered Brummell to leave the Palace. The Beau then and afterwards confessed himself at fault:

'I was on such intimate terms with the Prince that if we had been alone I could without offence have asked him to ring the bell, but with a third person in the room I should never have done so—I knew him so well.'

SOURCE: Lewis Melville, *Beau Brummell*, Hutchinson & Co., 1924, p. 99.

ii. '*Who's your fat friend?*'

The estrangement took place apparently in 1812 [i.e. between the Prince of Wales and Brummell]. In April of the following year, the Dandy Club, as Byron called Watier's, or rather its four leaders, Brummell, Lord Alvaney, Sir Henry Mildmay, and Henry Pierrepoint, having had a wonderful run of luck at Hazard, decided to give a ball at the Argyle Rooms. The first question to be settled was, should or should not the Prince Regent be invited? His Royal Highness had already quarrelled with Brummell and was no longer on good terms with Sir Henry Mildmay. It was thought that this was an opportunity which might bring old friends together. Henry Pierrepoint, who was popular at Carlton House, was deputed to ask the Prince if he would come to the ball. To the general pleasure, he accepted the invitation. On the evening, His Royal Highness duly appeared, and there stood the four hosts to receive him.

He shook hands with Lord Alvaney; he shook hands with Pierrepoint; he looked the others full in the face—and passed on. The insult was deliberate—it was probably premeditated. Everyone present was horrified. A silence fell over the assembly. But Brummell was equal to the occasion.

'Alvaney,' he said quietly, but in a voice that penetrated the room, 'who's your fat friend?'

After this there could be no question of reconciliation.

SOURCE: ibid., pp. 101–102.

iii. 'Our failures'

Brummell's greatest triumph was his neck-cloth. The neck-cloth was then a huge clinging wrap, worn without stiffening of any kind, and so bagging out at the front: Brummell, in a moment of inspiration such as rarely comes to a man in a life-time, decided to have his starched. The conception was, indeed, a stroke of genius. What labour Brummell and his valet, Robinson—himself a character—must have expended on experiments to discover the exact amount of stiffening that would produce the best result, and how many hours for how many days must they have worked together in private, before disclosing the invention to the world of fashion.

Even later, most mornings could Robinson be seen coming out of the Beau's dressing-room with masses of crumpled linen on his arms.

'Our failures,' he would say to the assembled company in the outer rooms.

SOURCE: ibid., pp. 50–51.

BRUNEL, SIR MARC ISAMBARD (1769–1849), civil engineer; engineer of the Thames Tunnel, 1825–1843.

Absence and presence of mind

Brunel was a little man, with a head so large that an Irishman once said, 'Why, that man's face is all head!'

Many amusing anecdotes are told of his blunders during his moods of inventive abstraction; as, for instance, caressing a lady's hand, who sat next to him at table, thinking it was his wife's; forgetting his own name . . . and getting into wrong coaches, and travelling long distances ere he discovered his mistake.

At other times he shewed rare presence of mind. Once, when [he was] inspecting the Birmingham railway, trains, to the horror of the bystanders, were observed to approach from opposite directions. Brunel, seeing retreat to be impossible, buttoned his coat, brought the skirts close round him, and, placing himself firmly between the two lines of rail, the trains swept past, and left him unscathed.

SOURCE: *The Book of Days* (edit. R. Chambers), 1864, p. 685.

BUCKINGHAM, GEORGE VILLIERS, first **DUKE OF** (1592–1628), Court favourite.

i. *The libel in Coleman Street*

> Who rules the Kingdom? The King!
> Who rules the King? The Duke!
> Who rules the Duke? The Devil!

SOURCE: Contemporary saying; quoted John Timbs, *Ancestral Stories and Traditions of Great Families*, 1869, p. 143.

The original, according to D'Israeli, was taken down from a post in Coleman Street, and carried to the Lord Mayor, who had it conveyed to the King. The King suggested a double watch be set to prevent the display of similar libels.

ii. *The Letter in the Assassin's Hat*

On August 23, 1628, Buckingham was assassinated at Portsmouth by an army officer named John Felton. In Felton's hat was found a paper which said:

'That man is cowardly base, and deserveth not the name of a gentleman or soldier, that is not willing to sacrifice his life for the honour of his God, his king, and his country. Let no man commend me for the doing of it, but rather discommend themselves as the cause of it; for if God had not taken away our hearts for our sins, he would not have gone so long unpunished.'

SOURCE: quoted ibid., p. 148. The original note has disappeared. It was in John Evelyn's possession for some time.

BULWER, SIR HENRY (1801–1872) **(BARON DALLING AND BULWER).** Victorian diplomatist. Among other appointments, secretary of embassy at Constantinople, ambassador at Madrid, Washington and Constantinople. Wroth, mentioned in the following anecdote, was a lawyer and a member of the staff of Sir Edmund Hornby, Judge of the Supreme Consular Court.

Umbrella, not apology

On one occasion, just as I was going south on circuit, I had to give Wroth instructions to go up in the *Stationaire* gun-boat to the Danube, there having been a row between the Helots and the Ionians. . . . Of course, I notified the Ambassador what I had done, but no sooner was my back turned than Bulwer sent for Wroth and insisted on his following his instructions and ignoring mine. Wroth offered to be guided by them when they were not contrary to those given him by me. On which Bulwer abused him like a pickpocket before the whole Embassy, and told him that he was only an underling and that he could dismiss him at his pleasure.

Wroth declined to discuss the question of the Ambassador's authority over him, leaving that for me to do, adding that he would beg to remind His Excellency that he was a gentleman and would insist on being treated as such, and left the room.

The first Secretary of Embassy and the Oriental Secretary, who had been at Cambridge with Wroth, remonstrated with Bulwer but without effect, and on the servant saying that Mr. Wroth desired to return, Bulwer triumphantly turned round to them saying:

'I knew better than you how to treat those Court fellows. He has come to apologise'; and when Wroth re-entered the room began to say: 'If you have come to apologise, I shall . . .'

But here Wroth cut him short by saying that he had only come back for his umbrella, which he had forgotten, and stalked out.

SOURCE: Sir Edmund Hornby, *An Autobiography*, Constable & Co., 1929, pp. 119–120.

BUNYAN, JOHN (1628–1688), Trial of: in 1661, Bunyan was brought before Sir John Kelyng(e) at the Bedford Assizes, and sentenced to imprisonment for absenting himself from church and preaching 'to the great disturbance and distraction of the good subjects of this kingdom, contrary to the laws of our sovereign lord the King'.

'I would preach again tomorrow'

Then said Kelynge:

'Hear your judgment. You must be had back to prison and there lie for three months following, and if then you do not submit to go to church and leave off preaching, you must be banished the realm.'

If, after such banishment, he was again found in the country without special licence from the King, he was told he should stretch by the neck for it. The gaoler was then ordered to remove his prisoner, who, as he went down, gave a parting look at his judge, and left these farewell words behind him:

'I am at a point with you; for if I were out of prison to-day, I would preach the gospel again to-morrow, by the help of God!'

SOURCE: John Brown, *John Bunyan*, 1885, 3rd edition, p. 153.

BURKE, EDMUND (1729–1797), statesman.

i. *The dagger scene in the House of Commons*

The great Whig, as is well known, was carried by the French Revolution out of all power of sober judgment.... When at the height of the rabies, having to speak on the second reading of the Alien Bill, December 28, 1792, he called in, in passing, at the office of Sir Charles M. Lamb, under-secretary of state. It was only three months from the massacre of Paris. England was in high excitement about the supposed existence of a party amongst ourselves, who were supposed to fraternise with the ... reformers of France and imitate their acts. Some agent for that party had sent a dagger to a Birmingham manufacturer, with an order for a large quantity after the same pattern. It was a coarsely-made weapon, a foot long in the blade, and fitted to serve equally as a stiletto and as a pike-head.

The Birmingham manufacturer, disliking the commission, had come to the under-secretary's office to exhibit the pattern dagger, and ask advice. He had left the weapon, which Burke was thus enabled to see. The illustrious orator, with the under-secretary's permission, took it along with him to the House, and, in the course of a flaming tirade about French atrocities, and probable imitations of them in England, he drew the dagger from his bosom, and threw it down on the floor, as an illustration of what every man might shortly expect to see levelled at his own throat. There were of course sentiments of alarm raised by the scene; but probably the more general feeling was one of derision.

SOURCE: *The Book of Days* (edit. R. Chambers), 1865, Vol. I, p. 36.
See also FRENCH REVOLUTION.

ii. *Mrs. Burke clears up*

In his House Burke is quiet if not contradicted in anything; but walks about heedless of every concern—knowing nothing of Servants, expenses, etc. He is very careless of his papers—would drop on the floor a paper though it contained treason as he would do a newspaper cover. Mrs. Burke watches over every-thing, collects his scraps, arranges and dockets every paper.

'My dear Jane,' will Burke say, 'I want such a paper.' It is produced. As conversation proceeds he calls for others. She produces them. He sometimes asks for one which she cannot remember.

'Yes, yes, yes, my dear Jane!' . . .

She examines.

SOURCE: Joseph Farington, *The Farington Diary* (edit. James Greig), Hutchinson & Co., 1922, Vol. I, p. 192.

BYNG, JOHN (1704–1757) **EXECUTION OF.** Admiral of the Blue John Byng, an honest and courageous officer, was sent in 1756 with a poorly manned and equipped fleet to relieve the island of Minorca. After some indecision and a half-hearted engagement, Byng sailed to Gibraltar. Brought home under arrest and court-martialled, he was acquitted of treachery and cowardice but found guilty of a lack of resolution in doing his utmost to relieve Minorca and defeat the French. He was shot on the quarter-deck of his own ship, despite a good deal of protest and the efforts of Pitt to secure his pardon.

i. *'Pour encourager les autres'*

Dans ce-pays-ci il est bon de tuer de temps en temps un amiral pour encourager les autres.

(In this country [England] it is thought well to kill an admiral from time to time to encourage the others.)

SOURCE: Voltaire, *Candide*, 1759, Ch. 23.

ii. *The Admiral takes an easy leave*

While he felt like a victim, he acted like a hero. . . . He took an easy leave of his friends, detained the officers not a moment, went directly to the deck, and placed himself in a chair with neither ceremony nor tightness. Some of the more humane officers represented to him, that his face being uncovered might throw reluctance into the executioners, and besought him to suffer a handkerchief. He replied with the same unconcern:

'If it will frighten *them*, let it be done; they would not frighten me.'

His eyes were bound; they shot, and he fell at once.

SOURCE: Horace Walpole, *Memoirs*, pub. 1822–1845.

iii. *Boswell transcribes an epitaph*

> To the perpetual Disgrace
> of publick Justice,
> The Honourable John Byng, Esq.
> Admiral of the Blue,
> Fell a Martyr to political
> Persecution,
> March 14th, in the Year 1757;
> when Bravery and Loyalty
> were insufficient Securities
> for the Life and Honour of
> A Naval Officer.

SOURCE: transcribed by James Boswell in Southill Church, Bedfordshire, en route for Scotland, 1781, with Doctor Johnson.

CAEDMON (fl. about 670).

'What shall I sing?'

There was in this abbess's [i.e. Hilda's] monastery a certain brother, particularly remarkable for the grace of God, who was wont to make pious and religious verses, so that whatever was interpreted to him out of Scripture, he soon after put the same into poetical expressions of much sweetness and humility, in English, which was his native language. . . . Others after him attempted, in the English nation, to compose religious poems, but none could ever compare with him, for he did not learn the art of poetry from men, but from God . . . for, having lived in a secular habit till he was well advanced in years, he never learned anything of versifying; for which reason, being some-times at entertainments when it was agreed, for the sake of mirth, that all present should sing in their turns, when he saw the instrument come towards him he rose up from the table and returned home.

Having done so at a certain time, and gone out of the house where the entertainment was, to the stable, where he had to take care of the horses that night, he there composed himself to rest at the proper time. A person appeared to him in his sleep and, saluting him by his name, said:

'Caedmon, sing some song to me.'

He answered:

'I cannot sing; for that was the reason why I left the entertainment and retired to this place, because I could not sing.'

The other, who talked to him, replied:

'However, you shall sing.'

'What shall I sing?' rejoined he.

'Sing the beginning of created things,' said the other.

Hereupon he presently began to sing verses to the praise of God, which he had never heard. . . .

In the morning he came to the steward, his superior, and, having acquainted him with the gift he had received, was conducted to the abbess, by whom he was ordered, in the presence of many learned men, to tell his dream, and repeat the verses, that they might all give their judgment what it was, and whence his verse proceeded. They all concluded that heavenly grace had been conferred on him by our Lord.

They expounded to him a passage in holy writ, either historical or doctrinal, ordering him, if he could, to put the same into verse. Having undertaken it, he went away and, returning the next morning, gave it to them composed in most excellent verse.

Whereupon, the abbess, embracing the grace of God in the man, instructed him to quit the secular habit, and take upon him the monastic life; which, being accordingly done, she associated him to the rest of the brethren in her monastery, and ordered that he should be taught the whole series of sacred history. Thus Caedmon, keeping in mind all he heard, . . . converted the same into most harmonious verse; and, sweetly repeating the same, made his masters in their turn his hearers.

SOURCE: The Venerable Bede, *The Ecclesiastical History of the English Nation*, Book IV, Ch. XXIV.

CALENDAR, REFORMATION OF THE (1751). The centuries have seen a number of efforts to formulate an accurate calendar, one of the problems being to make the true equinox coincide with the calendar equinox, and the real new moons with the calendar new moons. The modern, or Gregorian calendar, was introduced by Gregory XIII in 1582. It was not adopted by Great Britain till 1752, when, to rectify the error in the old-style calendar the 11 days between September 2 and 14 were omitted, and the beginning of the year moved from March 25 to January 1.

'Who stole the eleven days?'

The Protestant populace of England . . . were . . . violently inflamed against the statesmen who had carried through the bill for the change of style; generally believing that they had been defrauded of eleven days (as if eleven days of their destined lives) by the transaction. Accordingly, it is told that for some time afterwards, a favourite opprobrious cry to unpopular statesmen, in the streets and on the hustings was:

'Who stole the eleven days? Give us back the eleven days!'

SOURCE: *A Book of Days* (edit. R. Chambers), 1864, Vol. I, p. 105.

CANUTE or **CNUT** (994?–1035), King of the English, of Denmark and Norway.

i. *Canute commands the waves*

King Canutus, commonly called Knute, walking on the sea-sands near to Southampton, was extolled by some of his flattering followers, and told that he was a King of Kings, the mightiest that reigned far and near; that both sea and land were at his command. But this speech did put the godly King in mind of the infinite power of God, by whom Kings have and enjoy their power, and thereupon he made this demonstration to repel their flattery. He took off his cloak and, wrapping it round together, sate down upon it near to the sea, that then began to flow, saying:

'Sea, I command thee that thou touch not my feet!'

But he had not so soon spoken the word but the surging wave dashed him. He then, rising up and going back, said:

'Ye see now, my lords, what good cause you have to call me a King, that am not able by my commandment to stay one wave. No mortal man doubtless is worthy of such an high name, no man hath such command, but one King which ruleth all.'

SOURCE: William Camden, *Remains Concerning Britain*, 7th impression, 1674. This is a late version of the story told earlier by Ranulf Higden (d. 1364) in *Polychronicon* and other early chronicles such as that to which the name of Matthew of Westminster has become attached. There is no contemporary or near-contemporary authority for it.

ii. *Memories of Canute*

During the Second World War the Danish Foreign Minister paid a visit to the famous Swannery at Abbotsbury.

The distinguished visitor said to the chief keeper:

'I don't suppose you see many Danes hereabouts.'

'Oh, I don't know. We had Canute here a thousand years ago,' replied the countryman.

SOURCE: Newspaper report.

CARACTACUS or **CARADOC** (fl. 50), King of the Britons; resisted the Romans for nine years before being captured.

Caractacus in Rome

Caractacus fled for protection to Cartismandua, queen of the Brigantes. But adversity has no friends. By that princess he was loaded with irons and delivered up to the conqueror. He had waged war with the Romans during the last nine years. His fame was not confined to his native island; it passed into the provinces, and spread all over Italy. Curiosity was eager to behold the heroic chieftain, who, for such a length of time, made head against a great and powerful empire. Even at Rome the name of Caractacus was in high celebrity.

The emperor, willing to magnify the glory of the conquest,

bestowed the highest praise on the valour of the vanquished king. He assembled the people to behold a spectacle worthy of their view. . . . The followers of the British chief walked in procession. The military accoutrements, the harness and rich collars, which he had gained in various battles, were displayed with pomp. The wife of Caractacus, his daughter, and his brother, followed next: he himself closed the melancholy train. The rest of the prisoners, struck with terror, descended to mean and abject supplications. Caractacus alone was superior to misfortune. With a countenance still unaltered, not a symptom of fear appearing, no sorrow, no condescension, he behaved with dignity even in ruin. Being placed before the tribunal, he delivered himself in the following manner:

'. . . A reverse of fortune is now the lot of Caractacus. The event to you is glorious, and to me humiliating. I had arms, men, and horses; I had wealth in abundance: can you wonder that I was unwilling to lose them? The ambition of Rome aspires to universal dominion: and must mankind, by consequence, stretch their necks to the yoke? I stood at bay for years: had I acted otherwise, where, on your part, had been the glory of conquest, and where, on mine, the honour of a brave resistance? I am now in your power: if you are bent on vengeance, execute your purpose; the bloody scene will soon be over, and the name of Caractacus will sink into oblivion. Preserve my life, and I shall be, to late posterity, a monument of Roman clemency.'

Claudius granted him a free pardon, and the same to his wife, his daughter, and his brother.

SOURCE: Tacitus, *Annals* (trans. Arthur Murphy), J. M. Dent & Sons (Everyman's Library), 1908, Books XXXVI–XXXVII.

CAREY, ROBERT, first **EARL OF MONMOUTH** (1560?– 1639). One of the most colourful characters of his period, with some literary gifts and a dashing quality about a number of his actions. His best-known exploit was to ride from London to Edinburgh, a distance of some 400 miles, in about sixty hours, conveying the news of Queen Elizabeth's death to King James of

Scotland. This was despite a bad tumble at Norham. It was also in defiance of the wishes of the Government, who arranged for a much more dignified and less break-neck commission to journey with the momentous tidings. It duly arrived—two days after Carey.

Carey was no stranger to the London–Scotland route. Fourteen years earlier, for a wager of £2000, he had walked from London to Berwick—a distance of 342 miles—in twelve days, and won his money.

Among his writings is a vivid and moving account of the last days of Queen Elizabeth.

i. *The sighs of Queen Elizabeth*

I took my journey about the end of the year 1602. When I came to court, I found the Queen ill disposed, and she kept her inner lodging; yet she, hearing of my arrival, sent for me. I found her in one of her withdrawing chambers, sitting low upon her cushions. She called me to her; I kissed her hand, and told her it was my chiefest happiness to see her in safety, and in health, which I wished might long continue. She took me by the hand, and wrung it hard, and said:

'No, Robin, I am not well,' and then discoursed with me of her indisposition, and that her heart had been sad and heavy for ten or twelve days; and in her discourse, she fetched not so few as forty or fifty great sighs. I was grieved at the first to see her in this plight; for in all my lifetime before, I never knew her fetch a sigh, but when the Queen of Scots was beheaded.

SOURCE: *Memoirs*, first printed 1759.

ii. *Salute to the new King*

Very early on Saturday, I took horse for Edinburgh, and came to Norham about twelve at noon, so that I might well have been with the King at supper time. But I got a great fall by the way; and my horse, with one of his heels, gave me a great blow on the head, that made me shed much blood. It made me so weak, that I was forced to ride a soft pace after: so that the King was newly gone to bed by the time I knocked at the gate. I was quickly let in; and carried up to the King's Chamber. I kneeled by him, and saluted him by his title of 'England, Scotland, France, and Ireland'.

SOURCE: ibid.

CAROLINE AMELIA ELIZABETH (1768–1821), Queen of George IV.

> *Most Gracious Queen, we thee implore*
> *To go away and sin no more,*
> *But if that effort be too great,*
> *To go away at any rate.*

SOURCE: quoted in Lord Colchester's Diary, November 15, 1820.

CAT-O'-NINE TAILS. The Navy's chief weapon for punishment in former times.

i. *The shower of molten lead*

I would not use it on a bull, unless in self-defence; the shaft is about a foot and a half long, and covered with green or red baize, according to taste; the thongs are nine, about twenty-eight inches in length, of the thickness of a goose-quill, and with two knots in each. Men describe the first blow as like a shower of molten lead.

SOURCE: Dr. Gordon Stables, surgeon in the Royal Navy, 1863–1871.

ii. *The degradation of the cat*

My firm conviction is the bad man was very little the better; the good man very much the worse. The good man felt the disgrace, and was branded for life. His self-esteem was permanently maimed, and he rarely held up his head or did his best again.

SOURCE: quoted John Masefield, *Sea Life in Nelson's Time*, Methuen & Co., 1905, pp. 159–160.

CATHERINE II (1683–1727), Empress of Russia, wife of Peter III.

The sentry who guarded the snowdrops

At the time of my first stay at St. Petersburg, in 1859, I had an example of another Russian peculiarity. During the first spring days it was then the custom for everyone connected with the Court to promenade in the Summer Garden between Paul's Palace and the Neva. There the Emperor had noticed a sentry standing in the middle of a grass plot; in reply to the question why he was standing there, the soldier could only answer:

'Those are my orders.'

The Emperor therefore sent one of his adjutants to the guard-room to make inquiries; but no explanation was forthcoming except that a sentry had to stand there winter and summer. The source of the original order could no longer be discovered.

The matter was talked of at Court, and reached the ears of the servants. One of these, an old pensioner, came forward and stated that his father had once said to him as they passed the sentry in the Summer Garden:

'There he is, still standing to guard the flower; on that spot the Empress Catherine once noticed a snowdrop in bloom unusually early, and gave orders that it was not to be plucked.'

This command had been carried out by placing a sentry on the spot, and ever since then one had stood there all the year round.

SOURCE: Otto, Prince von Bismarck, *Reflections and Reminiscences,* 1898; Tauchnitz edition (trans. A. J. Butler), 1899, Vol. I, p. 277.

CAVOUR, CAMILLO BENSO, COUNT OF (1810–1861), Italian statesman; formerly banker, manufacturer and farmer. He had a favourite trick of rubbing his hands together.

'Things are going well'

'Cavour is rubbing his hands,' used to be said at Turin, 'things are going well.'

SOURCE: William de la Rive, *Reminiscences of the Life and Character of Count Cavour,* 1862, p. 108.

CAXTON, WILLIAM (1422?–1491), first English printer; 'Governor of the English Nation' in the Low Countries.

i. *Caxton on English womanhood*

The women of this country be right good, wise, pleasant, humble, discreet, sober, chaste, obedient to their husbands, true, secret, steadfast, ever busy and never idle, temperate in speaking and virtuous in all their works. Or at least should be so.

SOURCE: Willam Caxton, *The Dictes and Sayings of the Philosophers*, 1477 (spelling modernized).

ii. *Caxton's nine most worthy men*

For it is notoriously known through the universal world that there be nine worthy and the best that ever were. That is to wit, three Paynims [pagans], three Jews, and three Christian men.

SOURCE: Caxton's prologue to Malory's, *The Noble Histories of King Arthur and of Certain of his Knights*, 1485. The nine nominated are:

Hector of Troy
Alexander the Great
Julius Caesar

Joshua
David
Judas Maccabeus

King Arthur
Charlemagne
Godfrey of Bouillon

iii. *Flemish spoken in Kent*

It was a territory [the Weald of Kent, where Caxton was born] with almost a language of its own, a broad dialect which visitors found it difficult to understand and complicated by the fact that a good deal of Flemish was mixed up with it. Edward III had encouraged a large number of cloth-makers from Flanders to settle in the Weald, and they had established themselves so strongly that even some of their foreign ways of speech filtered into the Kentish dialect.

In after years, Caxton often told with much amusement of a traveller named Sheffield, a mercer, who called at a farmhouse and asked for eggs. The housewife shook her head, saying she did not understand French. This made the traveller angry, because he spoke no French either and thought the woman must be either stupid or impertinent. But one of his friends, better versed in the speech of the countryside, said that what they really wanted was some 'eyren'. This was the Flemish word, and the good-wife immediately understood and supplied the mercer with eggs.

SOURCE: Caxton's Prologue to Virgil's *Eneydos*, 1490; Grant Uden, *The Knight and the Merchant*, Faber, 1965, pp. 87–88.

CECIL, WILLIAM, BARON BURGHLEY (1520–1598). The greatest of Elizabeth's ministers and one of the greatest in English history, guiding the destinies of this country for forty years and skilfully managing its capricious queen. His industry and devotion to duty were remarkable. In his younger days, he had his less responsible moments, but seems to have shown his gift for managing affairs at the same time.

i. *Young Cecil recovers his losses*

A mad companion having enticed him to play, in a short time he lost all his money, bedding and books to his companion, having never used play before. And being afterwards among his other company, he told them how such a one had misled him, saying he would presently have a device to be even with him. And with a long trouke he made a hole in the wall, near his playfellow's bed-head, and, in a fearful voice, spake through the trouke:

'O mortal man, repent! Repent of thy horrible time consumed in play, cozenage and lewdness, or else thou art damned and canst not be saved.'

Which, being spoken at midnight, when he was all alone, so amazed him as drove him into a sweat for fear. Most penitent and heavy, the next day, in presence of the youths, he told with trembling that a fearful voice spake to him at midnight, vowing never to play again; and, calling for Mr. Cecil, asked him forgiveness on his knees, and restored to him all his money, bedding and books. So the two gamesters were both reclaimed with this merry device, and never played more.

SOURCE: quoted Charles Knight, *Old England*, Book V, Ch. III.

ii. *Burghley's good head*

When the treasurer, in the latter part of his life, was much afflicted with gout, the queen always made him sit down in her presence with some obliging expression.

'My Lord,' she would say, 'we make use of you, not for your bad legs, but for your good head.'

SOURCE: quoted John Macdiarmid, *Lives of British Statesmen*, 1820, Vol. i, p. 291.

iii. *Queen Elizabeth stoops to Burghley*

Incredible was the kindness which Queen Elizabeth had for him, or rather for herself in him, being sensible that he was so able a minister of state. Coming once to visit him, being sick of the gout at Burghley House in the Strand, and being much heightened with her head attire (then in fashion) the lord's servant who conducted her through the door, 'May your highness,' said he, 'be pleased to stoop.'

The queen returned, 'For your master's sake I will stoop, but not for the king of Spain's.'

SOURCE: Thomas Fuller, *The English Worthies*, 1662, 1952 edition, George Allen & Unwin, p. 336.

CHAMBERLAIN, JOSEPH (1836–1914), statesman.

i. *'A human mole'*

I was in his company a good many times, both socially and officially, but I never knew him when his mind was not busy evolving some 'scheme' to the exclusion of every other thought in the universe.

'I was made to burrow,' I once heard him say.

'Yes,' sighed Balfour, who was standing near, 'a sort of human mole.'

'Better than being a sort of languid giraffe,' came Joey's fierce retort—after the philosopher had moved out of earshot.

SOURCE: (anon.) *The Whispering Gallery*, John Lane, 1926, pp. 37–38.

ii. *An original view of the case*

Mr. Chamberlain, as is well known, does not devote any particular attention to taking exercise; indeed, he never troubles about it at all. The story goes that once, whilst on a visit to the United States, he was taken somewhat unwell, and, in consequence, consulted a doctor, who, questioning him as to his habits and mode of life, became somewhat horrified on being told of his patient's exploits in the way of cigars.

'Mr. Chamberlain,' said he, 'I think, if I may say so, that you smoke a great deal too much.'

'Perhaps I do,' was the imperturbable reply, 'but, then, you must remember I don't take any exercise'—an original view of the case which completely dumbfounded the physician.

SOURCE: *Reminiscences of Lady Dorothy Nevill* (edit. Ralph Nevill), Thomas Nelson & Sons, 1906.

iii. *Twilight of a statesman*

One pleasant memory of Prince's Gardens: almost opposite lived the great Joseph Chamberlain. I often saw him. He would come into the gardens opposite, always in a frock coat and tall silk hat, with an orchid in his button-hole. He had been a partial invalid for some five years and was a little uncertain in his walk. His valet and first footman, Ernest Pink, in livery, tall hat, with leather cockade, would follow slowly behind him carrying a chair. When Joey . . . stopped, Pink would at once place the chair gently against his knees and Joe would sit down. After two or three minutes Joe would beckon him and Pink would take him by the arm, assist him to his feet and, bolt upright, but very slowly, he would set off and Pink would follow with the chair. Round and round the gardens they would go for an hour, stopping, resting, and starting again—and then Joe would go in.

SOURCE: Ernest King, *The Green Baize Door*, William Kimber, 1963, p. 25.

CHARLEMAGNE or CHARLES THE GREAT (742?–814), King of the Franks and Lombards, and Western Emperor.

i. *The Might of Charlemagne*

This story gives a vivid impression of the spectacular reputation Charlemagne had acquired towards the end of his career and in the next generation. Charlemagne had crossed the Alps to crush the King of the Lombards. The Lombard leader was watching from the walls of Pavia, accompanied by Count Ogger, who was in exile from Charlemagne's court.

First of all, he saw only a thick cloud of dust; it was caused by the engines of war by which the walls of the capital were to be battered.

'Here is Charles' cried Didier, 'with this great army.'

'No,' answered Ogger.

Then there appeared a huge crowd of common soldiers.

'Surely Charles advances triumphant in the midst of this host.'

'Not yet,' replied Ogger.

Next there appeared the body of guards, veteran warriors who never knew rest.

'Now Charles is coming!' said Didier, full of terror.

'No,' answered Ogger, 'not yet.'

After these came the bishops, abbots, clerks of the royal chapel, and counts. Then Didier cried, choking with fear,

'Let us go down and hide ourselves in the bowels of the earth, far from this terrible foe.'

'When you see the harvest fields shaking with terror,' said Ogger, 'then you may believe that Charles is approaching.'

As he said this, a dark cloud appeared, driven by the east wind, which converted the day into night. But the emperor advanced a little nearer, and the gleam of his arms lightened over Pavia. .... Then Charles himself appeared, clothed from head to foot in steel armour, a lance on his left hand, his right resting upon his invincible sword. Ogger recognised him and, struck with terror, trembled and fell, crying:

'It is he!'

SOURCE: a monk of St. Gall, writing in 884; quoted Victor Duruy, *A Short History of France*, 1873, Everyman's Library edition, J. M. Dent & Son, 1917, pp. 150–151.

ii. *The Emperor tries to write*

Charlemagne applied himself closely to study, of which, in the eyes of his father and grandfather, a warrior had no need. .... He even tried to write, and was accustomed always to keep under his pillow tablets and copies in order that he might practise forming letters whenever he found a moment of leisure.

SOURCE: ibid., p. 147.

iii. *The Emperor's stature*

Charles was large and strong, and of lofty stature, though not disproportionately tall (his height is well known to have been seven times the length of his foot).

SOURCE: Einhard, *The Life of Charlemagne*, written between 817 and 836.

CHARLES I (1600–1649), King of England.

i. *A Clergyman prays for limited blessings on Prince Charles*

In 1623, Prince Charles, accompanied by the Duke of Buckingham, went to Madrid with the object of bringing back the Infanta of Spain as Charles's bride. King James, apparently not wishing the issue to be prejudged, issued an order to the clergy, through the Bishop of London, that they were to limit their prayers to those for his safe return home. One clergyman seems to have misunderstood.

I'll tell you a jest. The Bishop of London, you know, gave order from his Majesty to the Clergy not to prejudicate the Prince's journey in their Prayers, but only to pray to God to return him home in safety again unto us, and no more. An honest plain preacher, being loath to transgress the Order given, desired in his Prayer 'that God would return our noble Prince home in safety again to us, and no more': supposing the words 'no more' to be a piece of the Prayer. . . .

SOURCE: letter from Joseph Mead to Sir Martin Stuteville, March 29, 1623. British Museum, Harleian MSS. Inc. in Henry Ellis, *Original Letters, Illustrative of English History*, 1st series, 1825, Vol. iii, pp. 137–138.

ii. *An unfortunate silence greets Charles I at his coronation*

My expectation was soon answered with his Majesty's approach: who, presenting himself bare-headed to the people (all the doors being then opened for their entrance), the Archbishop on his right hand and Earl Marshal on his left, the Bishop said in my articulate hearing:

'My masters and friends, I am here come to present unto you your King, King Charles, to whom the crown of his ancestors and predecessors is now devolved by lineal right, and he himself come hither to be settled in that Throne which God and his birth have appointed for him: and therefore I desire you by your general acclamation to testify your consent and willingness thereunto.'

Upon which, whether some expected he should have spoken more, others, not hearing well what he said, hindered those by questioning which might have heard . . . or the presence of so dear a King drew admiring silence, so that those which were nearest doubted what to do; but not one word followed, till my Lord of Arundel told them they should cry out:

'God save King Charles!'

Upon which, as ashamed of their first oversight, a little shouting followed.

SOURCE: letter from Symonds D'Ewes to Sir Martin Stuteville, February 4, 1626. British Museum, Harleian MSS. Inc. in *Original Letters, Illustrative of English History*, 1st series, 1825, Vol. iii, p. 217.

iii. *'The birds are flown'*

The King, finding his instruments thus discouraged, and being resolved to remove all obstructions in his way, went in person to the House of Commons, attended not only with his ordinary Guard of Pensioners, but also with those desperadoes that for some time he had entertained at Whitehall, to the number of three or four hundred, armed with partizans, sword and pistol. At the door of the House he left his Guard commanded by Lord Roxberry, entering accompanied only by the Prince Palatine; where, taking possession of the Speaker's Chair, and not seeing those that he looked for, he said:

'The birds are flown.'

For, upon being given notice by a lady of the Court of the King's intention, they were retired into the City. The King then demanded of the Speaker where such and such were, naming the five Members: to which he answered in these words:

'I have neither eyes to see, ears to hear, nor tongue to speak, save what this House gives me.'

The King replied:

'I think you are in the right.'

SOURCE: *Memoirs of Edmund Ludlow, Esq., Lieutenant General of the Horse* . . . printed in Switzerland, 1698, Vol. I, pp. 24–25.

iv. *The King's communion plate*

A proposal for providing the royal household with appropriate plate, during his imprisonment at Holdenby House, Northamptonshire.

At their next sitting [February 5, 1647] the Committee of the Lords and Commons proposed that the communion plate, which was formerly set on the altar in his Majesty's Chapel at White-Hall, consisting of 'one gilte shyppe, two gilt vases, two gilte euyres [ewers] should be melted down to make plate for the King's use at Holdenby, there being none remaining in the jewel office fit for service'.

SOURCE: George Baker, *History of Northamptonshire*; inc. in W. D. Fellowes, *Historical Sketches of Charles I . . . and the Principal Personages of that Period*, 1828, p. 27.

v. *The King is stuck in a window*

During his imprisonment at Carisbrooke Castle, Isle of Wight, Charles made an ineffectual and somewhat undignified attempt at escape in 1648.

The plan agreed upon was as follows: at the time appointed, Firebrace [the royalist, Henry Firebrace, page of the bed-chamber and clerk of the kitchen] was to throw something up against the window of the King's chamber, as a signal that all was clear, on which his majesty was to come out and let himself down by a cord provided for that purpose; being descended, Firebrace, under favour of darkness, was to conduct him across the court to the main wall of the castle, from which he was again to descend into the ditch, by means of another cord with a stick fastened across it, serving as a seat; beyond this wall was the counterscarp, which, being low, might be easily ascended; near this place Mr. Worsley and Mr. Osborne were to be ready mounted, having a spare horse, with pistols and boots for the King, while Mr. Newland remained at the sea-side with a large boat, ready to have conveyed his majesty wherever he should have thought fit to direct. At the appointed time, when all things were in readiness, and everyone instructed in his part, Firebrace gave the expected signal, on which the King attempted to get out of the window, but discovered, when it was too late, that he had been fatally mistaken; for, although he found an easy passage for his head [the king had previously tried the window, and was under the impression that where his head could go his body could easily follow] he stuck fast between the breasts and shoulders, without the power of advancing or returning; but, having the instant before mistrusted something of this nature, he had tied a piece of cord to the bar of the window, by the means of which he might force himself back again. Firebrace heard him groan, without being able to afford him the least assistance; however, the King at length, with much difficulty, having released himself from the window, placed a candle in it, as an intimation that his attempt was frustrated.

SOURCE: Horsley's *History of the Isle of Wight*; inc. in W. D. Fellowes, *Historical Sketches of Charles I . . . and the Principal Personages of that Period*, 1828, pp. 36–37.

vi. *Towards an incorruptible crown*

The execution of Charles I took place on January 30, 1649. He was attended on the scaffold by William Juxon, Bishop of London (1582–1663), later Archbishop of Canterbury.

The Bishop said:

'There is but one stage more; which, though turbulent and troublesome, yet it is a very short one; you may consider it will soon carry you a very great way; it will carry you from earth to heaven; and there you shall find, to your great joy, the prize you hasten to, a crown of glory.'

The King rejoined:

'I go from a corruptible to an incorruptible crown, where no disturbance can be, no disturbance in the world.'

'You are exchanged from a temporal to an eternal crown. A good exchange!'

Then the King asked the executioner:

'Is my hair well?' and, taking off his cloak and George [i.e., the Order of the Garter, whose jewel shows St. George killing the Dragon], he delivered his George to the Bishop, saying:

'Remember.'

SOURCE: Contemporary pamphlet, *King Charles, his Speech made upon the Scaffold*; recorded in many other places, including John Rushworth, *Historical Collections*, 1659–1710; and W. D. Fellowes, *Historical Sketches of Charles I . . . including the King's Trial and Execution*, 1828, p. 165.

vii. *The groan of the spectators*

Matthew Henry, son of Philip Henry, a non-conformist divine, told how:

'At the latter end of the year 1648, he had leave given him to make a visit to his Father at White-hall, with whom he stayed some time; there he was Jan. 30th when the King was beheaded, and with a very sad heart saw the tragical blow given. Two things he used to speak of, that he took notice of himself that day, which I know not whether any of the Historians mention. One was, that at the instant when the blow was given, there was such a dismal universal groan among the thousands of people that were within sight of it (as it were with one consent) as he never heard before; and desired he might never hear the like again, nor see such a cause for it.'

(*Note*: the other thing commented on by Henry was that, at the instant the blow was given, two troops of soldiers appeared, one marching from Charing Cross towards King Street, and the other from King Street towards Charing Cross, especially to disperse the people.)

SOURCE: Matthew Henry, *Life of Philip Henry*, 1698.

viii. *The Protector's last visit to the King*

If we are to accept a traditional story which has much to recommend it, we have something of a key to his [Cromwell's] state of mind. 'The night after King Charles was beheaded,' we are told, 'my Lord Southampton and a friend of his got leave to sit up by the body in the Banqueting House at White-hall. As they were sitting very melancholy there, about two o'clock in the morning, they heard the tread of somebody coming very slowly upstairs. By-and-by the door opened, and a man entered very much muffled up in his cloak, and his face quite hid it. He approached the body, considered it very attentively for some time, and then shook his head—sighed out the words, "Cruel necessity!"

'He then departed in the same slow and concealed manner as he had come. Lord Southampton used to say that he could not distinguish anything of his face, but that by his voice and gait he took him to be Oliver Cromwell.'

SOURCE: Samuel Rawson Gardiner, *Oliver Cromwell*, Goupil & Co., 1899, pp. 104–105.

ix. *Addison reads one of the King's whiskers*

I do not remember any other kind of work among the moderns which more resembles the performances I have mentioned [i.e., various examples of 'false wit'] than that famous picture of King Charles the First, which has the whole book of Psalms written in the lines of the face and the hair of the head. When I was last at Oxford I perused one of the whiskers; and was reading the other, but could not go so far in it as I would have done, by reason of the impatience of my friends and fellow-travellers, who all of them pressed to see such a piece of curiosity.

SOURCE: Joseph Addison, *The Spectator*, No. 58, May 7, 1711.

x. *The resurrected statue*

The bronze statue [of Charles I] by Le Sueur in the gardens at Whitehall was sold to a contractor to melt down. He had the forethought to bury it, though he offered to a gullible public a large number of pocket knives said to be hafted in metal from it. When Charles II returned he was able triumphantly to produce the statue intact. It stands today at the top of Whitehall.

SOURCE: C. V. Wedgwood, *The Trial of Charles I*, Collins, 1964.

See also CIVIL WAR; CROMWELL, OLIVER; HENRIETTA MARIA; WENTWORTH, THOMAS, etc.

CHARLES II (1630–1685), King of England.

i. *The escape of Charles II after the Battle of Worcester*, September 3, 1651

It is a great pity that there was never a journal made of that miraculous deliverance, in which there might be seen so many visible impressions of the immediate hand of God. When the darkness of the night was over, after the King had cast himself into that wood, he discerned another man, who had gotten upon an oak tree in the same wood, near the place where the King had rested himself, and had slept soundly.

The man upon the tree had first seen the King, and knew him, and came down, and was known to the King, being a gentleman of the neighbouring county of Staffordshire, who had served his late Majesty during the War, and had now been one of the few who had resorted to the King after his coming to

Worcester. His name was Careless, who had a command of Foot. .... He persuaded the King, since it could not be safe for him to go out of the wood, and that, as soon as it should be fully light, the wood itself would probably be visited by those of the country, who would be searching to find those whom they might make prisoners, that he would get up into that tree where he had been; where the boughs were so thick with leaves that a man would not be discovered there without a narrower enquiry than people usually make in places which they do not suspect.

The King thought it good counsel; and, with the other's help, climbed into the tree, and then helped his companion to ascend after him; where they sat all that day, and securely saw many who came purposely into the wood to look after them, and heard all their discourse. . . .

The day being spent in the tree, it was not in the king's power to forget that he had lived two days with eating very little, and two nights with as little sleep; so that, when the night came, he was willing to make some provision for both; and he resolved, with the advice and assistance of his companion, to leave his blessed tree; and, when the night was dark, they walked through the wood into those inclosures which were farthest from the highway, and, making a shift to get over hedges and ditches, after walking at least eight or nine miles, which were the more grievous to the King by the weight of his boots . . . before morning they came to a poor cottage, the owner whereof, being a Roman Catholic, was known to Careless. He was called up, and as soon as he knew one of them, he easily concluded in what condition they both were; and presently carried them into a little barn full of hay.

SOURCE: Edward, Earl of Clarendon, *The History of the Rebellion and Civil Wars in England*, 1707, Vol. iii, Part 2, pp. 413–414. The author had these particulars of the escape from the King himself. The King rested in the barn for two nights and three days, living on a diet of butter, bread and milk, till an envoy from Careless came to conduct him to another house. Careless (or Carlos), on the King's restoration, was granted a third of the tax on hay and straw in London and Westminster.

G

ii. *The Turkish Emperor contemplates a possible change of religion*

He was certainly a prince . . . of whom the divine providence had taken especial care; witness his miraculous escape at Worcester battle; his treatment in the royal oak, when thousands were rummaging the fields in quest of him; his restoration being without one drop of blood: so that the Turkish emperor said, if he were to change his religion, he would only do it for that of the king of Great Britain's God, who has done such wonderful things for him.

SOURCE: *Diary of Sir John Lauder, Lord Fountainhill (1646–1722)* in the Advocates' Library, Edinburgh, part of which was published by Sir Walter Scott in 1822. It appeared in full in 1840.

iii. *The Headmaster who kept his hat on*

Every one has heard of the famous Dr. Busby, head-master of Westminster, who, while shewing Charles II over the school, apologised to that merry monarch for keeping his hat on in the presence of royalty; 'for,' said he, 'it would not do for my boys to suppose that there existed in the world a greater man than Dr. Busby.'

SOURCE: *Reminiscences and Recollections of Captain Gronow*, 1892, first pub. 1862–1866.

iv. *Charles II nearly chooses a new Bishop*

Robert South (1634–1716), prebend of Westminster, was nearly made a bishop as a result of a rousing sermon he preached before Charles II in the Abbey. In the course of it he referred to Oliver Cromwell as:

'. . . a bankrupt beggarly fellow . . . entering the Parliament House with a threadbare torn cloak and greasy hat and perhaps neither of them paid for.'

Charles is said to have burst out laughing and said that South must be made a bishop at the next vacancy. But the King died before this occurred and South remained in his minor position. He was offered the position of Dean of Westminster when he was nearly eighty, but declined, saying:

'Such a chair would be too uneasy for an old, infirm man to sit in.'

SOURCE: Edward Carpenter (edit.), *A House of Kings*, John Baker, 1966, p. 192.

v. *Why Charles II read his speeches*

Charles the Second once demanded of Dr. Stillingfleet'* who was a preacher to the court, why he read his sermons before him, when on every other occasion his sermons were delivered extempore. The doctor answered that, overawed by so many and noble personages, and in the presence of his sovereign, he dared not to trust his powers.

'And now,' said the divine, 'will your majesty permit me to ask a question? . . . Why . . . does your majesty read your speeches, when it may be presumed that *you* can have no such reason?'

'Why, truly,' said the king, 'I have asked my subjects so often for money that I am ashamed to look them in the face.'

SOURCE: Thomas Byerley and Joseph Clinton Robertson, *The Percy Anecdotes*, 1820–1823.

vi. *The King counts the stones at Stonehenge*

There is a common notion that the stones cannot be counted twice alike; but when Charles II visited Stonehenge in 1651, he counted and recounted the stones, and proved to his satisfaction the fallacy of this notion.

SOURCE: John Timbs, *Nooks and Corners of English Life*, 1867, pp. 13–14.

vii. *Lord Rochester offers to govern*

John Wilmot, second Earl of Rochester (1647–1680), poet and courtier, was one of the most dissolute and obscene of the men about Charles II. The following is an extract from a conversation between the King and Rochester reported by the poet Waller.

The King: I believe the English are the most untractable people upon earth.

* Edward Stillingfleet (1635–1699), Bishop of Worcester.

Rochester: I most humbly beg your majesty's pardon, if I presume in that respect.

The King: You would find them so were you in my place, and obliged to govern.

Rochester: Were I in your majesty's place, I would not govern at all.

The King: How then?

Rochester: I would send for my good lord Rochester, and command him to govern.

The King: But the singular modesty of that nobleman—

Rochester: He would certainly conform himself to your majesty's bright example. How gloriously would the two grand social virtues flourish under his auspices!

The King: What can these be?

Rochester: The love of wine and women!

The King: God bless your majesty!

SOURCE: quoted Stephen Collet, *Relics of Literature*, 1823, pp. 51–52.

viii. *Epitaph for a King*

Rochester also produced the famous epitaph on Charles II:

> *Here lies a great and mighty king**
> *Whose promise none relies on;*
> *He never said a foolish thing,*
> *And never did a wise one.*

Charles replied:

'This is very true: for my words are my own, and my actions are my ministers'.'

ix. *The end of the Merry Monarch*

King Charles II died peaceably, on Friday, 6th of February, 1685, having taken the sacrament before from Dr. Kenn, Bishop of Bath and Wells. . . . The queen being unwell, was unable to attend him; but sent to ask his pardon wherein she had ever offended him; he said:

* An alternative first line is: *Here lies our sovereign lord, the king.*

'Ah, poor Kate, many a time have I wronged her, but she never did me any wrong.'

SOURCE: *Diary of Sir John Lauder, Lord Fountainhall (1646–1722)*, in the Advocates' Library, Edinburgh; partially published by Sir Walter Scott, 1822, and in full by the Bannantyne Club, 1840.

See also PLAGUE.

CHARLES V (1337–1380), King of France; called 'the Wise'.

A French Solomon

Two ladies contended for precedence in the court of Charles V. They appealed to the monarch, who, like Solomon, awarded:
'Let the elder go first.'
Such a dispute was never known afterwards.

SOURCE: John Timbs, *A Century of Anecdote, 1760–1860*.

CHARLES V (1550–1558), King of Spain and Holy Roman Emperor. Abdicated 1555.

The Emperor lights his guest

Whilst the Emperor Charles the Fifth, after the resignation of his estates, stayed ... for wind, to carry him his last journey into Spain, he conferred on a time with Seldius, his brother Ferdinand's Ambassador, till the deep of the night. And when Seldius should depart, the Emperor calling for some of his servants and no-one answering him (for those that attended upon him were some gone to their lodgings, and all the rest asleep) the Emperor took up the candle himself, and went before Seldius to light him down the stairs; and so did, not-withstanding all the resistance that Seldius could make. And when he was come to the stairs' foot, he said thus unto him:
'Seldius, remember this of Charles the Emperor, when he shall be dead and gone; that him whom thou hast known in thy time environed with so many mighty armies and guards of

soldiers, thou hast also seen alone, abandoned and forsaken, yea, even of his own domestical servants.'

SOURCE: Sir Walter Ralegh, *The Historie of the World*, 1614, Preface.

CHARLES VIII (reigned 1483–1498), King of France.

The conquest of Italy with a piece of chalk

Charles VIII invaded Italy in 1494 and had such an easy conquest that Pope Alexander VI said the French came with chalk in their hands, rather than swords to fight.

Thus it was that Charles, King of France, was allowed to seize Italy with chalk in hand.

SOURCE: Nicolo Machiavelli, *The Prince*. W. K. Marriott, in his translation of *The Prince*, Everyman edition, J. M. Dent & Son, 1908, comments: 'This is one of the *bon mots* of Alexander VI, and refers to the ease with which Charles VIII seized Italy, implying that it was only necessary for him to send his quartermasters to chalk up the billets for his soldiers to conquer the country. Cf. *The History of Henry VII*, by Lord Bacon:—"King Charles had conquered the realm of Naples, and lost it again, in a kind of a felicity of a dream. He passed the whole length of Italy without resistance: so that it was true what Pope Alexander was wont to say, that the Frenchman came into Italy with chalk in their hands, to mark up their lodgings, rather than swords to fight with." '

CHARLOTTE AUGUSTA MATILDA (1766–1828), Princess Royal of England.

The Princess and Miss Burney's stays

Afterwards I happened to be alone with this charming Princess and her sister Elizabeth, in the Queen's dressing-room. She then came up to me, and said:

'Now will you excuse me, Miss Burney, if I ask you the truth of something I have heard about you?'

'Certainly, ma'am.'

'It's such an odd thing, I don't know how to mention it; but I have wished to ask you about it this great while. Pray is it really true that, in your illness last year, you coughed so violently that you broke the whalebone of your stays in two?'

'As nearly true as possible, ma'am; it actually split with the force of the almost convulsive motion of a cough that seemed loud and powerful enough for a giant. I could hardly myself believe it was little I that made so formidable a noise.'

SOURCE: Fanny Burney's *Journal*, Sept. 29, 1786. Fanny Burney later Madame D'Arblay, was Second Keeper of the Robes to Queen Charlotte for five years.

CHARLOTTE SOPHIA (1744–1818), Queen of George III.

The bloom that wore off

Queen Charlotte had always been, if not ugly, at least ordinary, but in her later years her want of personal charms became, of course, less observable, and it used to be said that she was grown better looking. Mr. Croker one day said something to this effect to Colonel Disbrowe, her chamberlain.

'Yes,' replied he, 'I do think that the bloom of her ugliness is going off.'

SOURCE: John Timbs, *A Century of Anecdote, 1760–1860*. The Croker referred to is John Wilson Croker, politician and writer.

CHIANG KAI-SHEK (b. 1886), Marshal and President of the Chinese Republic; resigned January 1949 in the face of Communist successes.

'Why doesn't he generalize?'

... a great many Americans, when China gets out of hand, or into the wrong hands, think this can only be because of some gross error or even crime on the part of the official rulers of America. Even so simple an explanation as that Chiang made the mistake denounced in all the military text-books ... of commanding at long range and through favourites, is ignored.

People feel that Chiang's defeat (a disaster for America, I freely admit) *must* have been due to American folly or American treason. People refuse to believe that it might have had other, more important causes, above all the one admirably described by Senator Tom Connally:

'If he's a generalissimo, why doesn't he generalize?'

SOURCE: D. W. Brogan, *American Aspects*, Hamish Hamilton, 1964, pp. 12–13, first pub. in *Harper's Magazine* (*The Illusion of American Omnipotence*).

CHURCHILL, RANDOLPH HENRY SPENCER, commonly known as **LORD RANDOLPH CHURCHILL** (1849–1894), statesman; Chancellor of the Exchequer, leader of the House of Commons, etc.

On decimal points

'I never could make out what those damned dots meant.'

SOURCE: W. S. Churchill, *Lord Randolph Churchill*, Vol. II, p. 184.

CHURCHILL, SIR WINSTON (1620?–1688), royalist and politician; ancestor of Sir Winston Churchill, Prime Minister (1874–1965).

Sir Winston's lucky day

I have made great experience of the truth of it, and have set down Fryday as my own lucky day; the day on which I was born, christened, married, and I believe will be the day of my death. The day whereon I have had sundry deliverances from perils by sea and land, perils by false brethren, perils of lawsuits, &c. I was knighted (by chance unexpected of myself) on the same day, and have several good accidents happened to me on that day; and am so superstitious in the belief of its good omen, that I choose to begin any considerable action that concerns me on the same day.

SOURCE: Tract *Remarques on the 14th of October, being the auspicious birth-day of his present Majesty James II*, 1687; quoted Isaac D'Israeli, *Curiosities of Literature*.

CINCINNATUS, LUCIUS QUINTUS (519?–439? B.C.), Roman Consul.

'My field will not be sown this year!'

When Herodotus, taking advantage of the domestic troubles at Rome, possessed himself of the capitol, the Consul Valerius Publiola repulsed him, but fell dead at the head of his troops. Another consul was now to be elected, and after much deliberation the choice fell on Cincinnatus, in consequence of which the senate sent deputies to him to invite him to come and take possession of the magistracy. He was then at work in his field, and, being his own ploughman, he was dressed in a manner suitable to that profession. When he saw the deputies coming towards him, he stopped his oxen, very much surprised at seeing such a number of persons, and not knowing what they could want with him.

One of the company approached him, and requested him to put on a more suitable dress. He went into his hut, and having put on other clothes, he presented himself to those who were waiting for him outdoors. They immediately saluted him *Consul*, and invested him with the purple robe; the lictors ranged themselves before him ready to obey his orders, and begged him to follow them to Rome. Troubled at this sight, he for some time shed tears in silence. At last, recovering himself, he said only these words:

'My field will not be sown this year!'

SOURCE: Thomas Byerley and Joseph Clinton Robertson, *The Percy Anecdotes*, 1820–1823.

CIVIL WAR, GREAT or **GREAT REBELLION** (1642–1649).

i. *A Royalist prayer*

Prayer of Sir Jacob Astley (1579–1652), royalist, before the Battle of Edgehill, October 23, 1642; the first important battle of the Civil War, with the King present in person. The result was indecisive, with some advantage to the royalists.

'O Lord! thou knowest how busy I must be this day: if I forget thee, do not thou forget me.'

SOURCE: Sir Philip Warwick, *Memoires*, 1701, p. 229.

ii. *John Southcote joins the King*

Your grandfather at last with much importunity gained his father's and grandfather's consent. They equipped him very handsomely with arms and horses for himself and two or three men, and so he set forward with letters of recommendation to some of their acquaintance in the army, to present their son to the King. . . .

The first adventure he went upon, he was placed in a *corps de reserve* whilst the two armies were engaged . . . and I heard my father say that it was very irksome to him to stand still there in cold blood to be shot at, in sight of the two armies that were very warmly engaged. But after they had kept their post for about an hour, the right wing of the King's army forced their way through the enemy, and nailed up the cannon that had galled them for an hour very severely, and Oliver's army beginning to give way, they were called upon to pursue them in the flight; and this was the first occasion he had to make use of his little battle-axe, a weapon all the King's troops made use of, hanging in a ribbon that was tied about their wrists, which did not hinder their arm from making use of their pistol or sword as need required, and was a dead-doing thing whenever the horse broke in amongst the foot. It was very like the mason's lathing hammer, had a sharp little axe of one side and a hammer on the other, but most commonly made use of the hammer, which was sure to fell them to the ground with one rap upon their round heads.

SOURCE: a letter from Sir Edward Southcote to his son Philip; transcribed from the manuscript in the Priory of the Annunciation, Woodchester, by Father John Morris in *The Troubles of Our Catholic Forefathers*, 1872, Vol. i, p. 388.

iii. *A Cavalier calls on his brother and sister*

The army being now at no great distance from his brother and sister Stanford's, at Perry Hall, he [John Southcote] went thither for one day to divert himself; and the doors being open, he rode on horseback into the hall, and seeing lights up the stairs, which were broad and of easy ascent, he rode up the stairs, too, and never alighted from his horse till he came to the table where they were sitting at supper, who were much pleased with his frolic and glad to see him.

SOURCE: ibid, p. 389.

iv. *The knife-marks on the window-ledge*

During the siege of Gloucester by Charles I in 1643, his sons, the future Charles II and James II, stayed at Matson, near the city.

James the Second, after he came to the Crown, used frequently to mention the circumstances to his [George Selwyn's] grandfather when he went to Court; observing:

'My brother and I were generally shut up in a Chamber on the second Floor at Matson, during the day; where you will find that we have left the marks of our confinement, inscribed with our knives, on the ledges of all the windows.'

SOURCE: Sir N. William Wraxall, *Historical Memoirs of My Own Time*, 1810, Vol. II, p. 181. Matson was the Selwyns' family seat. George Augustus Selwyn (1719–1791) was M.P. for over 30 years and held a number of minor Government offices.

v. *Roundhead and Cavalier*

In the general, they were very honest men and well-meaning: some particular fools, or others, perhaps, now and then got in amongst them, greatly to the disadvantage of the more sober. They were modest in the apparel, but not in their language; they had the hair of their heads very few of them longer than their ears; whereupon, it came to pass that those who usually with their cries attended at Westminster . . . were by a nickname called *Round-heads*. The Courtiers again, having long hair and locks, and always swordes, at last were called by these men *Cavaliers*. . . .

SOURCE: William Lilly, *Monarchy or no Monarchy in England*, 1651; quoted John Timbs, *Nooks and Corners of English Life*, 1867, pp. 327–328. It seems that, at the outbreak of the Civil War, Cavalier was just as much a term of contempt as Roundhead. At one point, Charles I accused his opponents of attempting to 'render all persons of honour, courage, and reputation, odious to the common people under the style of *Cavaliers*'.

Of the word *Roundhead* . . . and the mixed fear and hatred it represented and provoked, decidedly the most characteristic example is furnished by the ever quaint and entertaining Bishop Hacket [John Hacket (1592–1670) bishop of Coventry and Lichfield], who tells a story of a certain worthy and honest Vicar of Hampshire who always . . . changed one word in the last verse of the Te Deum:

'O Lord, in thee have I trusted, let me never be a Roundhead!'

SOURCE: John Timbs, *Nooks and Corners of English Life*, 1867, p. 327.

vi. *A Cavalier toast*

(The name 'Cromwell' was usually pronounced 'Crumwell'.)

Among various kinds of 'ranting cavalierism' the Cavaliers during Cromwell's usurpation usually put a crumb of bread into their glass and, before they drank it off, with cautious ambiguity exclaimed:

'God send this crum well down!'

SOURCE: Isaac D'Israeli, *Curiosities of Literature*, 1881 edition, Vol. 2, p. 300.

vii. *Cromwell's definition of a good captain*

God hath given it to our handful; let us endeavour to keep it. I had rather have a plain russet-coated Captain that knows what he fights for, and loves what he knows, than that which you call 'a Gentleman' and is nothing else.

SOURCE: Letter to Sir William Spring and Maurice Barrow, from Cambridge, Sept. 1643.

In another letter in the same month, Cromwell expressed much the same idea. 'Gentlemen, it may be it provokes some spirits to see such plain men made Captains of Horse. It had been well that men of honour and birth had entered into these employments—but why do they not appear? Who would have hindered them? But, seeing it was necessary the work must go on, better plain men than none' (Sept. 28, 1643, to the same correspondents, from Holland, Lincolnshire).

viii. *The boy saboteur*

Incident during the siege of Warder Castle, when it was held by the Parliamentarian Edmund Ludlow.

The enemy was now beginning to draw about us, yet would not actually besiege us before they had endeavoured to reduce us by treachery. To this end, one Captain White, a Papist, of Dorsetshire, having found a boy at Shrewsbury fit for the purpose, gave him such instructions as he thought fit. He was not above twelve years of age. . . . This boy he sent to the Castle to desire of me to be admitted to turn the spit, or perform any other servile employment; to which I consented, his youth freeing him, as I thought, from any suspicion.

About three or four days after . . . a great wall-gun called a *Harquebuz de Croq*, being fired from the top of the Castle, burst in the middle. At night, as this boy was sitting with the Guard by the fire, some of them conceived a jealousy of him; and, strictly examining him about the cause of his coming, he affirmed it to be because the master whom he served had used him cruelly for speaking some words in favour of the Parliament. With which answer they, not being satisfied, threatened that unless he would confess the truth they would hang him immediately; and, to affright him, tied a piece of match [i.e. hempem rope used for firing cannon, etc.] about his neck and began to pull him up on a halbert. Upon this, he promised to confess all if they would spare his life; and, thereupon, acknowledged that Capt. White had hired him to number the men and arms in the Castle, to poison the arms, the well, and the beer, to blow up the ammunition, to steal away one of my best horses to carry him back to them; for which service he was to receive half-a-crown; confessing that he had accordingly poisoned two cannon and the harquebus that was broken, but pretended that his conscience would not give him leave to poison the water and the beer.

SOURCE: *Memoirs of Edmund Ludlow, Esq., Lieutenant General of the Horse* . . . , printed in Switzerland, 1698, Vol. 1, pp. 71–72.

CLEMENCEAU, GEORGES (1841–1929), Prime Minister of France; called 'The Tiger'. Sir Winston Churchill said of him that 'the old Tiger, with his quaint, stylish cap, his white moustache and burning eye, would have made a truer mascot for France than any barnyard fowl'.

i. *The incorruptible politician*

His refreshing cynicism darted out in every direction during a lunch to which he had invited me. It was quite an informal affair, and Georges was at the top of his form, playful and indiscreet.

Someone asked him why he had always been so disliked by the populace.

'Because I tell them the truth,' he replied.

'But why are you disliked by politicians?' he was asked.

'Because I am incorruptible,' he flashed back.

'Are you, then, the only honest politician in France?'

'But no! They are all honest'—a slight pause—'until temptation comes their way.'

SOURCE: (anon.) *The Whispering Gallery, being Leaves from a Diplomat's Diary*, John Lane, 1926, p. 194.

ii. *Clemenceau's onion soup*

In 1922, two years after he gave up the French premiership, Clemenceau was in America, and gave an address to the members and guests of the Maryland Historical Society.

The family of the late H. Crawford Black made his well-staffed home available for housing the distinguished guest. To the consternation of those making arrangements, it was learned that the great man demanded hot onion soup served to him in his room at exactly 'two hours past midnight'. The problem to be faced was not only that of finding a chef who could produce flawless French onion soup, but also that of finding one willing to prepare it at such an hour—not on one morning alone, but on the several mornings of the 'Tiger's' visit. The Society came through with flying colours and Franco-American relations did not suffer.

SOURCE: (article) Harold R. Manakee, *A Quarter-Century of Growth of the Maryland Historical Society*, Maryland Historical Magazine, March 1965, p. 60.

CLIVE, ROBERT, BARON CLIVE (1725–1774), soldier and Governor of Bengal.

i. *Clive runs a protection racket*

Dissatisfied with his pocket money as well as with what he was given to eat, dissatisfied with his whole position, the twelve-year-old boy decided to improve his lot by force. Since he was not provided with sufficient apples or sufficient pennies he obtained some for himself. He gathered all the dissatisfied children of his own age about him. Since there were sinister, dark deeds to be performed they trusted in sinister, dark Clive whose society they otherwise avoided, formed themselves into a gang and accepted his leadership. Soon some of the most expensive shop-windows belonging to the shopkeepers of Market Drayton were broken without them being able to convict a single one of the rascals who perpetrated it. And it was not long before the Market Drayton shopkeepers were filled with alarm. This was what young Bob had wanted to bring about. He set himself at the head of his gang, went from shop to shop in broad daylight and struck bargains.

'Your ... or your neighbour's ... window has been broken, Mr. So-and-so. ... No-one is in such a good position as I to protect you from the repetition of such an attack upon your property. It is true that I must receive a little compensation, shall we say twopence and a pound of apples a week. . . .'

'Two pence and a pound of apples a week,' the shopkeeper

would repeat thoughtfully, working out how great his chances were and how small the risks, and finally he would assent.

SOURCE: Wolf H. Harness, *Lord Clive, the Conqueror of India* (trans. Dorothy Harrison), Massie Publishing Co., 1939, pp. 85–86.

A good deal of the story of Clive's youthful indiscipline and insubordination is founded on local tradition, sometimes unsupported by satisfactory evidence; but, on the other hand, some of his relatives wrote of his 'wildness and a desire to dominate' and the 'fighting to which he is out of all measure addicted'. A contemporary account of Clive appeared in *Biographia Britannica*, 2nd edition, a good deal of material being supplied by Robert's cousin, Archdeacon Clive.

ii. *Clive climbs the church tower*

Perhaps to escape the consequences of some misdemeanour, Clive is said to have climbed the tower of Market Drayton church.

Here, just under the spire, some old stone gargoyles stretched far out beyond the edge of the tower, as water spouts.

Already the horrified men and women were gathering in the market place and with their heads thrown back were looking up at the old church tower in terror. A woman fainted, little girls screamed, the citizens shook their heads, the schoolboys yelled warnings heavenwards. They were all staring up at the water-spout on which, hardly recognisable at that dizzy height, young Bob stood with his hands in his trouser pockets. . . .

When the heads of some brave men appeared behind him, Bob Clive calmly turned round and announced that he would only abandon his dangerous position if he was granted absolute freedom from punishment. In order to bring the terrifying play to an end, they were prepared to yield.

SOURCE: ibid., p. 87.

iii. *A perceptive schoolmaster*

'If the lad should live to be a man and be given an opportunity for the exercise of his talents, few names will be greater than his.'

SOURCE: Doctor Eaton; *Biographia Britannica*, 2nd edition, p. 645.

iv. *Apology with reservations*

There is . . . the story of the time when he was ordered [while he was a clerk at Madras in the employment of the Honourable East India Company] to apologise for some piece of impertinence to the official in whose charge he was, and complied, but when the official invited him to dinner, he returned the answer:

'No, sir, the Governor ordered me to apologise, but he did not command me to dine with you.'

SOURCE: A. Mervyn Davies, *Clive of Plassey*, Nicholson & Watson, 1939; the story first appeared in *Biographia Britannica*, 2nd edition.

v. *Robert Clive chooses his wife*

Before the middle of the last century, Mr. Maskelyne, brother of Dr. Nevil Maskelyne, the Astronomer-Royal, went as a cadet to India, where he became acquainted with Mr. Clive, afterwards Lord Clive. The acquaintance ripened into friendship, and led to constant association.

There hung up in Mr. Maskelyne's room several portraits, among others a miniature which attracted Clive's frequent attention. One day, after the English mail had arrived, Clive asked Maskelyne if he had received any English letters . . . Maskelyne replied that he had, and read to his friend a letter he then held in his hand. A day or two after, Clive came back to ask to have the letter read to him again.

'Who is the writer?' enquired Clive.

'My sister,' was the reply. 'My sister, whose miniature hangs there.'

'Is it a faithful representation?' further asked Clive.

'It is,' rejoined Maskelyne, 'of her face and form; but it is unequal to represent the excellence of her mind and character.'

'Well, Maskelyne,' said Clive, taking him by the hand, 'you know me well, and can speak of me as I really am. Do you think that girl would be induced to come to India and marry me?'

. . . Maskelyne wrote home, and so recommended Clive's

H

suit that the lady acquiesced, went to India and, in 1753, was married at Madras to Clive.

SOURCE: Sir Bernard Burke, *The Rise of Great Families*, 1873, pp. 358–359.

vi. *One of Clive's ancestors*

Clive's great-great-grandfather was Colonel Robert Clive, member of Parliament for Bridgnorth and an officer in the Parliamentary army during the Civil War. It is said that the Shropshire royalists 'amended their litany' to read:

> *From Wem and from Wyche,*
> *And from Clive of the Styche,*
> *Good Lord, deliver us.*

SOURCE: Thomas Auden, *Memorials of Old Shropshire*, 1906. Styche was the Clive family estate in Shropshire, which they had held since the 15th Century.

COCKNEY, THE LONDON.

The antiquity of the term

London Cockneys. Let us observe the antiquity of this proverb, then the meaning; lastly the application thereof to Londoners. It is more than four hundred years old; for when Hugh Bigod added artificial fortifications to the natural strength of his castle at Bungay in Suffolk, he gave out this rhyme, therein vaunting it for impregnable:

> *Were I in my castle of Bungay,*
> *Upon the river of Waveney,*
> *I would not care for the king of Cockeney.*

Meaning thereby King Henry the Second, then peaceably possessed of London, whilst some other places did resist him. . . .

The name is generally fixed on such who are born within the sound of Bow Bell. . . . It is called Bow Bell because hanging in the steeple of Bow Church, and Bow Church because built upon *bows* or arches.

SOURCE: Thomas Fuller, *The English Worthies*, 1662, 1952 edition, George Allen & Unwin, p. 349.

COLBERT, JEAN BAPTISTE (1619–1683), French statesman; reorganized finances and 'directed five ministries'.

i. *Cardinal Mazarin's legacy*

'Sire, I owe you everything, but I think that I have in a measure paid my debt by giving you Colbert.'

SOURCE: Mazarin's words before his death to Louis XIV. Colbert had been one of the Cardinal's most effective officers.

ii. *Colbert on economy*

It is essential to save five shillings on unnecessary matters, and to pour out millions when your glory is concerned. A useless feast, costing 3000 livres, causes me incredible pain, but when it is a question of millions of gold for the Polish affair, I would sell all that I possess, I would hire out my wife and children, I would go on foot to the end of my days to supply them.

SOURCE: Colbert in a letter to Louis XIV; quoted Victor Duruy, *A Short History of France*, 1873, Everyman's Library edition, 1917, J. M. Dent & Sons, 1917, p. 137.

iii. *The disillusionment of Colbert*

The ambitions and extravagancies of the 'Sun King' prevented the economy being maintained on a sound basis. Colbert's efforts at limiting expenditure cost him the King's favour, and he died worn out and disappointed, refusing to read Louis XIV's last letter to him.

Had I done for God what I have done for that man, I should have won salvation ten times over. Now I know not what fate has in store for me.

SOURCE: Victor Duruy, *History of France*. The words will inevitably recall those ascribed to Cardinal Wolsey: 'Had I but served God as diligently as I have served the King, he would not have given me over in my gray hairs.'

COLERIDGE, SAMUEL TAYLOR (1772–1834), poet and philosopher.

i. *Coleridge's public lectures*

Coleridge's lectures were, unfortunately, extemporaneous. He
now and then took up scraps of paper on which he had noted
the leading points of his subject, and he had books about him
for quotation. On turning to one of these (a work of his own),
he said:

'As this is a secret which I confided to the public a year or two
ago, and which, to do the public justice, has been very faith-
fully kept, I may be permitted to read you a passage from it.'

SOURCE: Charles Robert Leslie, R.A., *Autobiographical Recollections*,
1860, Vol. I, p. 47.

ii. *Coleridge the conversationalist*

He drew me within the door of an unoccupied garden by the
road-side, and there, sheltered from observation by a hedge of
evergreen, he took me by the button of my coat, and, closing
his eyes, commenced an eloquent discourse, waving his right
hand gently, as the musical words flowed in an unbroken
stream from his lips. . . . I saw that it was of no use to attempt
to break away, so taking advantage of his absorption in his
subject, I, with my penknife, quietly severed the button from
my coat, and decamped. Five hours afterwards, in passing the
same garden, on my way home, I heard Coleridge's voice and,
looking in, there he was, with closed eyes—the button in his
fingers—and his right hand gracefully waving, just as when I
left him.

SOURCE: Charles Lamb; a story told by Lamb to J. R. Dix.

iii. *Wordsworth fails to understand*

Samuel Rogers used to tell a story of how he and Wordsworth
once listened while Coleridge spoke uninterruptedly for two

hours. Wordsworth showed profound attention, and every now and then nodded his head, as if to signify agreement. When they came away Rogers said:

'Well, for my part I could not make head or tail of Coleridge's oration; pray did you understand it?'

'Not one syllable of it,' was Wordsworth's reply.

SOURCE: Amy Cruse, *The Englishman and his Books*, Harrap, 1930, p. 247.

COLLECTIVE NOUNS.

A 15th Century collection

One of the amusements of the centuries has been the devising of words meaning a gathering of individuals belonging to the same kind or species. They gave many opportunities for sly humour and often shed light on the outlook of the times. The following examples are from a manuscript given to Walter Pollard of Plymouth by Thomas Imay, Clerk, in *c.* 1445.

A gaggle of women
A nonpatience of wives
A discreetness of priests
A converting of preachers
A threat of courtiers
A lying of pardoners
An eloquence of lawyers
A damning of jurors
A malpertness of pedlars
A rascal of boys
A drunkship of cobblers
A neverthriving of jugglers
A nontruth of sumners*
A waywardness of haywards†

* Or summoners, officers who charged delinquents before an ecclesiastical court.
† Parish officer in charge of fences, enclosures, etc.

COLLINGWOOD, CUTHBERT, first **BARON** (1750–1810), vice-admiral; second-in-command at Trafalgar, and took over command after Nelson's death.

i. *The Admiral who planted acorns*

It was said of Collingwood that whenever he walked about his estate he planted a number of acorns from a store he kept in his pocket, so that in future years there would still be oak for England's ships.

ii. *Collingwood and his 'Old Dreadnoughts'*

Collingwood owed something that day [Trafalgar] to the shooting of his 'Old Dreadnoughts'. They were the men he himself had trained so assiduously during the two years that Collingwood flew his flag in the *Dreadnought* previous to October, 1805. Week in, week out, throughout all that time, whenever the weather allowed, Collingwood used to practise his men every day, we are told, 'in firing at a mark, a cask with a flag on it, which had been hove overboard and allowed to drift until it was at a suitable distance to allow aiming to begin'.

Gunnery was Collingwood's hobby on board ship, and his 'Dreadnoughts' were taught their business under his eye, the Admiral often taking charge personally of the firing, and going down between decks to 'coach' the guns' crews himself. He made the *Dreadnought*, indeed, the best firing ship in the world of that time; unsurpassed alike in aiming straight and shooting quick. Under Collingwood's tuition they were trained to fire three broadsides in ninety seconds—a wonderful gunnery feat as it was considered in those days and for long afterwards.

SOURCE: Edward Fraser, *The Sailors Whom Nelson Led*, Methuen & Co., 1913, p. 245.

iii. *'Don't let there be a reflection against a cabin boy'*

However severe his outward aspect (and Collingwood never received from his captains half the affection which Nelson could summon at once, and keep throughout their lives), Collingwood was like Nelson in the generosity of his praise to dead and living alike. Captain Durham of the *Defiance* had an excellent example of the trait when he went to call on Collingwood in the *Euryalus* after the action [of Trafalgar].

As so often, Collingwood was writing in his cabin ... Durham mentioned several ships of which he had knowledge, and praised the noble conduct of some of the frigates. But 'the captain of the *Euryalus* hinted that there had been a want of exertion on the part of some particular ship'.

'Collingwood started up and said: "Sir, this has been a glorious victory for England and for Europe—don't let there be a reflection against a cabin boy." ' 'This', added Codrington, 'quite silenced the captain.'

SOURCE: Oliver Warner, *Trafalgar*, Batsford, 1959, p. 143.

iv. *'Send them to Collingwood'*

After all, the cat was not essential to discipline. This was proved time and time again while it was most in use. There were, of course, stubborn, brutal, and mutinous sailors. A fleet so manned could not lack such men. When such men were brought before Lord Nelson, he would say:

'Send them to Collingwood. He will tame them, if no one else can.'

Lord Collingwood was the man who swore, by the god of war, that his men should salute a reefer's coat, even when it were merely hung to dry. Yet he didn't tame his men by cutting their backs into strips. He would have his whole ship's company in perfect order, working like machines, with absolute, unquestioning fidelity. But he seldom flogged more than one man a month, and punished really serious offences, such as drunkenness, inciting to mutiny, and theft, with six, nine, or at most a dozen, lashes. His system tamed the hardest cases in the fleet—good men, whom Lord St. Vincent would have flogged to death, or sent to the yard-arm.

SOURCE: John Masefield, *Sea Life in Nelson's Time*, Methuen & Co., 1905, p. 159. One of Collingwood's sayings was: 'When a mutiny takes place on board a ship, it must be the fault of the Captain or officers.'

COLOUR BAR IN AMERICA, THE

The signing of Jackie Robinson

On May 17, 1954, the U.S. Supreme Court gave its decision that segregated schools were unconstitutional. A battle had been won seven years before when, in August 1945, in courageous defiance of the colour bar, Jackie Robinson, a negro baseball player, was signed on for the Brooklyn Dodgers, one of the most famous teams in the country. The man who signed him was Branch Rickey.

Rickey produced Papini's *Life of Christ* from the drawer of his desk. He often read the book himself as a guide to humility. It seemed appropriate to read aloud from it to a Negro baseball player who might become the first of his race to enter organized baseball.

'Can you do it? Can you do it?' Rickey asked over and over.

Shifting nervously, Robinson looked from Rickey to Sukeforth as they talked....

Did he have the guts to play the game no matter what happened? Rickey pointed out the enormity of the responsibility for all concerned: owners of the club, Rickey, Robinson, and all baseball. The opposition would shout insults, come in spikes first, throw at his head.

'Mr. Rickey,' Robinson said, 'they've been throwing at my head for a long time.'

Rickey's voice rose. 'Suppose I'm a player ... in the heat of an important ball game.' He drew back as if to charge at Robinson. 'Suppose I collide with you at second base. When I get up, I yell, "You dirty, black son of a ——".' He finished the castigation and added calmly, 'What do you do?'

Robinson blinked. He licked his lips and swallowed.

'Mr. Rickey,' he murmuered, 'do you want a ballplayer who's afraid to fight back?'

'I want a ballplayer with guts enough *not* to fight back!' Rickey exclaimed almost savagely. . . . ' 'Now I'm playing against you in a World Series!' Rickey stormed and removed his jacket for greater freedom. Robinson's hands clenched, trembled from the rising tension. 'I'm a hotheaded player. I want to win that game, so I go into you spikes first, but you don't give ground. . . . So I haul off and punch you right in the cheek!'

An oversized fist swung through the air and barely missed Robinson's face. He blinked, but his head didn't move.

'What do you do?' Rickey roared.

'Mr. Rickey,' he whispered, 'I've got two cheeks. That it?'

SOURCE: Arthur Mann, *Branch Rickey, American in Action*, Boston, Houghton Mifflin Company, 1957.

COLUMBUS, CHRISTOPHER (*c.* 1446 or 1451–1506), Genoese sailor; Admiral, Viceroy and Governor-General, under Ferdinand and Isabella of Spain, of all islands and continents discovered in the Western Ocean.

i. *Columbus is hailed as a god*

I had taken some Indians by force from the first island that I came to, in order that they might learn our language, and communicate to us what they knew respecting the country; which plan succeeded excellently, and was a great advantage to us, for in a short time, either by gestures and signs, or by words, we were enabled to understand each other. These men are still travelling with me, and although they have been with us now a long time, they continue to entertain the idea that I have descended from heaven; and on our arrival at any new place they published this, crying out immediately:

'Come, come and look upon beings of a celestial race.'

SOURCE: Columbus on his first voyage (1492–1493) in a letter to 'the noble Lord Raphael Sanchez, Treasurer to their most invincible Majesties'; Major, *Select Letters of Columbus*, Hakluyt Society, 1847.

ii. *Queen Isabella promises to find the money for the expedition*

She contemplated the proposals of Columbus in their true light; and refusing to hearken any longer to the suggestions of cold and timid counsellors, she gave way to the natural impulses of her own noble and generous heart.

'I will assume the undertaking,' said she, 'for my own crown of Castile, and am ready to pawn my jewels to defray the expenses of it, if the funds in the treasury shall be found inadequate.'

The treasury had been reduced to the lowest ebb by the late war; but the receiver, St. Angel, advanced the sums required....

SOURCE: William H. Prescott, *History of the Reign of Ferdinand and Isabella the Catholic*, 1837.

CONSTANTINE (288?–337), Emperor of Rome; called the Great.

The Cross in the sky

Constantine was proclaimed Emperor at York. Just before the battle of the Milvian Bridge (312), which gave Constantine the mastery of the West, he saw in the sky a cross, with the words:

In hoc signo vinces
(In this sign thou shalt conquer)

SOURCE: Eusebius, *Life of Constantine*, i, 28.

Constantine subsequently proclaimed religious toleration through the Edict of Milan and, later in life, was himself converted to Christianity.

The Constantine Cross is a monogram of the first letters in the Greek name for Christ. There have been a number of other claims in history for the vision of a cross in the sky, including the Cross of St. Andrew which appeared to the King of the Scots before his victory over Athelstan and which thereupon, according to the tradition, became the national emblem of Scotland. That the phenomenon is not unknown to modern times is shown from an 1889 newspaper account:

The inhabitants of Dakota were treated to a sublime . . . display on the morning of January 9, 1889 at nearly the time of sunrise. Three gorgeous prismatic columns . . . shot up from the verge of the prairie into the heavens in intense brilliancy, equalling the light of the sun itself. . . . These prismatic columns extended one-third of the way to the zenith, and at the upper end, gradually blended with the sky.

What made the phenomenon remarkably striking was that the centre column assumed the form of a cross, from a small cloud which hung directly athwart the centre, and was illuminated by the light of the sun, still below the horizon, and forming the transept of the figure of the cross.

SOURCE: *Leeds Mercury*; quoted *Notes and Queries*, Jan. 22, 1889, and Brewer, *The Historic Note-Book*, 1891, p. 202.

CONVERSION OF THE ENGLISH: the sending of missionaries, headed by Augustine, by Pope Gregory (540–604).

'Not Angles, but angels'

It is reported that some merchants, having just arrived at Rome on a certain day, exposed many things for sale in the market place, and abundance of people resorted thither to buy. Gregory himself went with the rest, and, among other things, some boys were set to sale, their bodies white, their countenances beautiful, and their hair very fine. Having viewed them, he asked, as is said, from what country or nation they were brought? and was told, from the island of Britain, whose inhabitants were of such personal appearance. He again inquired whether those islanders were Christians, or still involved in the errors of paganism, and was informed that they were pagans.

Then, fetching a deep sigh from the bottom of his heart:

'Alas! what pity,' said he, 'that the author of darkness is possessed of men of such fair countenances that, being remarkable for such graceful aspects, their minds should be void of inward grace.'

He therefore again asked what was the name of that nation, and was answered that they were called Angles.

'Right,' said he, 'for they have an Angelic face, and it becomes such to be co-heirs with the Angels in heaven.'

SOURCE: The Venerable Bede, *Historia Ecclesiastica* (first pub. Strasburg, *c.* 1475), Everyman's Library, J. M. Dent & Sons, 1910, pp. 64.

Note: the traditional quotation is *Non Angli sed Angeli*—'Not Angles, but Angels.'

See also EDWIN, KING OF NORTHUMBRIA (585?–633).

COOLIDGE, CALVIN (1872–1933), 30th President of the United States of America; noted for his lack of ostentation and taciturnity, and known as 'Silent Cal'.

A lost bet

Calvin Coolidge was noted for his terse replies and his dry humour. On one occasion when he found himself seated next to an attractive young woman at dinner, she turned to him and said frankly:

'Mr. President, I have made a bet which I hope you will help me win.'

The President looked at her and said nothing.

'It is that I will engage you in conversation for at least five minutes,' she continued.

Another silence.

'You lose,' said Mr. Coolidge.

SOURCE: Frances Cavanah and Lloyd E. Smith, *I am an American*, Whitman Publishing Co., Racine, Wisconsin, 1940, p. 125.

Probably Coolidge's most celebrated remark was his reply to his wife when he had returned from hearing a sermon on the subject of sin. When asked what the preacher said, the President said: 'He was against it.'

COPENHAGEN, BATTLE OF (April 2, 1801): known also as the Battle of the Baltic. The battle broke up the northern coalition against Britain which Napoleon had worked hard for. After several ships had gone aground in the narrow King's Channel, Nelson, in the *Elephant*, took a new course and led the fleet in. After about three hours' action, which threatened to be indecisive, Sir Hyde Parker made the recall signal, apparently in a generous effort to save Nelson, though he knew his own reputation would suffer.

Nelson's blind eye

'I will make the signal of recall,' said he to his captain, for Nelson's sake. If he is in a condition to continue the action successfully, he will disregard it; if he is not, it will be an excuse for his retreat, and no blame can be imputed to him.' . . .

'Do you know,' said he [Nelson] to Mr. Ferguson, 'what is shown on board the commander-in-chief? No. 39!'

Mr. Ferguson asked what that meant.

'Why, to leave off action!'

Then, shrugging up his shoulders, he repeated the words,

'Leave off action? Now damn me if I do! You know, Foley,' turning to the captain, 'I have only one eye—I have a right to be blind sometimes': and then, putting the glass to his blind eye, in that mood of mind which sports with bitterness, he exclaimed,

'I really do not see the signal!'

SOURCE: Robert Southey, *The Life of Nelson*, 1813, Hutchinson's Library of Standard Lives, p. 240. Later versions do not always put Sir Hyde Parker in such a good light. But Southey's statement that, in ordering the retreat, Parker 'was aware of the consequences to his own reputation, but it would be cowardly for him to leave Nelson to bear the whole shame of failure, if shame it should be deemed', he says he made 'upon the highest and most unquestionable authority'.

COUNTRY-FOLK, WISDOM OF THE (12th Century).

i. *'Let's ask the country-folk'*

'Sustine modicum: ruricolae melius hoc norunt.'

'Wait a bit: let us ask the country folk'—as the senior clerk said to his junior in the exchequer in 1177, when he asked him a tricky question.

SOURCE: *Representation in Mediaeval England*, in *History*, February 1953; quoted George Ewart Evans (and taken as his book title), *Ask the Fellows Who Cut the Hay*, Faber & Faber, 1956.

ii. *'Large books unclasped'*

We old men are old chronicles, and when our tongues go they are not clocks to tell only the time present, but large books unclasped; and our speeches, like leaves turned over and over, discover wonders that are long since past.

SOURCE: *The Great Frost . . . with News out of the Country,* 1608.

CRANMER, THOMAS (1489–1556), Archbishop of Canterbury; burnt at the stake, March 21, 1556.

i. *Cranmer thrusts in his right hand first*

Under severe pressure and constant examination, Cranmer made recantations acknowledging the supremacy of the Pope and the truth of Roman Catholic doctrine; but finally courageously repudiated his recantations. The 'unworthy right hand' was the one he used to sign his recantations.

Then was an iron chain tied about Cranmer, whom, when they perceived to be more steadfast than that he could be moved from his sentence, they commanded the fire to be set unto him.

And when the wood was kindled, and the fire began to burn near him, stretching out his arm, he put his right hand into the flame, which he held so steadfast and immovable (saving that once with the same hand he wiped his face) that all men might see his hand burned before his body was touched. His body did so abide the burning of the flame with such constancy and steadfastness that, standing always in one place, without moving his body, he seemed to move no more than the stake to which he was bound; his eyes were lifted up into heaven, and oftentimes he repeated:

'My unworthy right hand!' so long as his voice would suffer him; and using often the words of Stephen, 'Lord Jesus, receive my spirit,' in the greatness of the flame he gave up the ghost.

SOURCE: John Foxe, *The Actes and Monuments of the Church,* 1563, popularly known as *The Book of Martyrs*: Rev. John Cumming's edition, Chatto & Windus, 1875, Vol. iii, pp. 685–686.

ii. *The charity of Cranmer*

Ever would he plead for those condemned. He uniformly forgave his enemies, and confided in his friends with a childish simplicity.

'Do my lord of Canterbury an ill turn, and he is your friend for ever,' was the world's testimony of him.

When he was informed of their treachery and ingratitude, he led aside Thornden and Barber* into his garden, and told them that some whom he trusted had disclosed his secrets and accused him of heresy, and asked them how they thought such persons ought to be treated. They were loud in expressing their indignation, and declared that such traitors deserved to die.

'Know ye these letters, my masters?' said the primate, and shewed them the proof of their own falsehood. The two offenders fell upon their knees to implore forgiveness; for it was evident that their lives were in his power, but all the revenge he took was to bid them ask God's forgiveness.

SOURCE: *A Book of Days* (edit. R. Chambers), 1864, Vol. I, p. 402.

CRÉCY, AND POITIERS, BATTLES OF (August 26, 1346 and September 19, 1356); the two greatest English victories of the Hundred years War.

i. *The Black Prince wins his spurs*

At one point in the battle, the Prince was so hard pressed that a knight was dispatched to seek reinforcements from the King, who was watching the progress of events from a small hill on which stood a windmill.

The king replied:

'Is my son dead, unhorsed, or so badly wounded that he cannot support himself?'

'Nothing of the sort, thank God,' rejoined the knight, 'but he is in so hot an engagement that he has great need of your help.'

* Two conspirators who involved Cranmer in charges of heresy, 1543.

The King answered:

'Now, Sir Thomas, return back to those that sent you, and tell them from me, not to send again for me this day, or expect that I shall come, let what will happen, as long as my son has life; and say, that I command them to let the boy win his spurs; for I am determined, if it please God, that all the glory and honour of this day shall be given to him, and to those into whose care I have intrusted him.'

SOURCE: Sir John Froissart, *Chronicles of England, France, Spain, . . . from the Latter Part of the Reign of Edward II to the Coronation of Henry IV.* Thomas Johnes's trans. (3rd edition), 1806, Vol. II, p. 167.

ii. *The four squires of Sir James Audley*

Sir James Audley (1316?–1386), a founder-knight of the Order of the Garter and one of the most gallant soldiers of the Hundred Years War, had four famous squires from Cheshire, whom he rewarded after the Battle of Poitiers. Their names were Dutton of Dutton, Delves of Doddington, Fulleshurst of Barthomley and Hawkestone of Wrinehill.

The prince [i.e. the Black Prince], demanded of the knights that were about him for the Lord Audley, if any knew anything of him. Some knights that were there answered and said:

'Sir, he is sore hurt and lieth in a litter here beside.'

'By my faith,' said the prince, 'of his hurts I am right sorry. Go and know if he may be brought hither, or else I will go and see him there as he is.'

Then two knights came to the Lord Audley, and said:

'Sir, the prince desireth greatly to see you. Either ye must go to him, or else he will come to you.'

'Ah, sir,' said the knight, 'I thank the prince when he thinketh on so poor a knight as I am.'

Then he called to eight of his servants, and caused them to bear him in his litter to the place where the prince was. Then the prince took him in his arms and kissed him and made him great cheer, and said:

'Sir James, I ought greatly to honour you; for by your

valiance ye have this day achieved the grace and renown of us all, and ye are reputed for the most valiant of all other.'

'Ah, sir,' said the knight, 'ye say as it pleaseth you. I would it were so, and if I have this day anything advanced myself to serve you, and to accomplish the vow that I made, it ought not to be reputed to me any prowess.'

'Sir James,' said the prince, 'I and all ours take you in this journey for the best doer in arms, and to the intent to furnish you better to pursue the wars, I retain you for ever to be my knight, with five hundred marks of yearly revenues, the which I shall assign you on mine heritage in England.'

'Sir,' said the knight, 'God grant me to deserve the great goodness that ye shew me'; and so he took his leave of the prince, for he was right feeble, and so his servants brought him to his lodging.

... and then he called before them his four squires that had served him that day well and truly. Then he said ... :

'Sirs, it hath pleased my lord the prince to give me five hundred marks of revenues by year in heritage, for the which gift I have done him but small service with my body. Sirs, behold here these four squires, who hath always served me truly, and especially this day. That honour that I have is by their valiantness, wherefor I would reward them. I give and resign into their hands the gift that my lord the prince hath given me of five hundred marks of yearly revenues to them and to their heirs for ever.'

... The lords and others that were there, every man beheld the other, and said among themselves:

'It cometh of a great nobleness to give this gift.'

They answered him with one voice:

'Sir, be it as God will. We shall bear witness in this behalf wheresoever we become.'

SOURCE: Sir John Froissart, *Cronycles of Englande, Fraunce, Spayne, Portyngale, Scotlande, Bretaine, Flaunders: and other places adjoynynge,* trans. by John Bouchier, Lord Berners, 1523–1525, folios lxxxiii and lxxxiv. (When the Black Prince heard of Audley's generous gesture, he not only ratified the gift to the squires but gave Sir James a further revenue of 500 marks in its place.)

iii. *The blind king John of Bohemia falls in the front of the battle*

The valiant king of Bohemia was slain there. . . . The king said:

'Gentlemen, you are all my people, my friends and brethren at arms this day: therefore, as I am blind, I request of you to lead me so far into the engagement that I may strike one stroke with my sword.'

The knights replied they would directly lead him forward; and, in order that they might not lose him in the crowd, they fastened all the reins of their horses together, and put the king at their head, that he might gratify his wish, and advanced towards the enemy. . . .

The king . . . rode in among the enemy and made good use of his sword; for he and his companions had fought most gallantly. They had advanced so far that they were all slain; and on the morrow they were found on the ground, with their horses all tied together.

SOURCE: Sir John Froissart, *Chronicles of England, France, Spain,* etc., Thomas Johnes's trans., 1806, Vol. II, pp. 164–165.

See also HUNDRED YEARS WAR.

CROMPTON, SAMUEL (1753–1827), inventor of the spinning mule. Since he had received so little personal benefit from this important invention, Parliament granted Crompton £5000 in 1812. Spencer Perceval intended to propose a grant of £20,000, which would probably have been carried, but was assassinated before he could do so.

i. *The Hall-in-the-Wood Wheel*

Crompton's youth was spent in a rambling mansion called Hall-in-the-Wood, a mile from Bolton, belonging to his uncle Alexander, who owned a loom. Samuel found Hargreaves's 'spinning jenny' so imperfect that he determined to improve on it.

Five years—from his twenty-first year, in 1774, to his twenty-sixth in 1779—were spent in the construction of the mule.

'My mind,' he relates, 'was in a continual endeavour to realise a more perfect principle of spinning; and, though often baffled, I as often renewed the attempt, and at last succeeded in my utmost desire, at the expense of every shilling I had in the world.' He was, of course, only able to work at the mule in the leisure left after each day's task of spinning, and often in hours stolen from sleep. The purchase of tools and materials absorbed all his spare cash; and when the Bolton theatre was open, he was glad to earn eighteen-pence a night by playing the violin in the orchestra. The first mule was made, for the most part, of wood, and to a small roadside smithy he used to resort 'to file his bits o' things'.

Crompton proceeded very silently with his invention. Even the family at Hall-in-the-Wood knew little of what he was about, until his lights and noise, while at work in the night-time, excited their curiosity. . . .

SOURCE: *The Book of Days* (edit. R. Chambers), 1864, p. 649.

ii. *The machine succeeds*
Meanwhile, he created much surprise in the market by the production of yarn, which, alike in fineness and firmness, surpassed any that had ever been seen. It immediately became the universal question in the trade, 'How does Crompton make that yarn?' . . .

Hall-in-the-Wood became besieged with manufacturers praying for supplies of the precious yarn, and burning with desire to penetrate the secret of its production. All kinds of stratagems were practised to gain admission to the house. Some climbed up to the windows of the workroom and peeped in. Crompton set up a screen to hide himself, but even that was not sufficient. One inquisitive adventurer is said to have hid himself for some days in the loft, and to have watched Crompton at work through a gimlet hole in the ceiling.

SOURCE: ibid., p. 649.

Eventually Crompon was so badgered that, faced with the choice of destroying his beloved machine in self-defence or, since he could not afford to patent it, giving it to the public, he adopted the second course. He was given little credit and little financial return. A group of tradesmen, just over 80 in number, promised subscriptions totalling only £67 6s. 6d., and even then many of them did not pay up. In Crompton's own words:

Many subscribers would not pay the sums they had set opposite their names. When I applied for them, I got nothing but abusive language to drive me from them, which was easily done; for I never till then could think it possible that any man could pretend one thing and act the direct opposite.

CROMWELL, SIR OLIVER (d. 1654), the Protector's uncle and god-father.

Godfather to the Protector

... the oldest gentleman in England who was a knight, though not the oldest knight who was a gentleman.

SOURCE: Thomas Fuller, *The Worthies of England*, 1662. Fuller tells us that the Protector's namesake regarded the activities of his nephew 'with hatred and contempt'. His sons fought for the King against their cousin.

CROMWELL, OLIVER (1599–1658), Lord Protector.

i. *After Marston Moor*, July 2, 1644

Cromwell has a warm reception at the hands of Lady Ingleby.

After the battle of Marston Moor, Cromwell, returning from the pursuit of a party of royalists, purposed to stop at Ripley, the seat of Sir William Ingelby; and having an officer of his troop, a relation of Sir William's, he sent him to announce his arrival. Having sent in his name and obtained an audience, he was answered by the Lady that no such person should be admitted there; adding that she had sufficient force to defend herself and that house against all rebels. The officer, on his part, represented the extreme folly of making any resistance, and that the safest way would be to admit the general peaceably.

After much persuasion, the Lady took the advice of her kinsman, and received Cromwell at the gate of the lodge, with a pair
of pistols stuck in her apron-strings; and having told him she
expected that neither he nor his soldiers would behave im-
properly, led the way to the hall, where, sitting on a sofa, she
passed the whole night.

At his departure in the morning, the lady observed:

'It is well that he behaved in so peacable a manner; for, if
had been otherwise, he should not have left this house alive.'

SOURCE: W. D. Fellowes, *Historical Sketches of Charles I, Cromwell
. . . and the Principal Personages of that Period*, 1828, p. 243.

ii. *Prince Charles's carte-blanche to Cromwell*

One of the most moving and eloquent documents in English
history is, in fact, a blank sheet of paper. It bears, at the foot, only
the signature 'Charles P.' and his seal. It was sent from Holland
by Prince Charles, by the hand of a relative of Cromwell's, for
Oliver to write in his own terms, without restriction, for saving
Charles I's life.

Here Cromwell paused, and seemed to reflect with himself,
and then said:

'Cousin, I desire you will give me till night to consider of it,
and do you go to your inn and not to bed, till you hear from
me.'

This the Colonel [Colonel John Cromwell] observed, and
about one o'clock after midnight, a messenger came and told
him he might go to rest, and expect no other answer to carry
to the Prince, for the council of officers had been seeking God,
as he had also done the same, and it was resolved by them that
the King must dye.

SOURCE: Laurence Echard (1670?–1730) who collected together,
and translated from the French, much of the history of the 17th
Century. Prince Charles's *carte-blanche*, which was part of the
magnificent collection of books and documents formed by Robert
Harley, first Earl of Oxford (1661–1724), is in the British Museum
(Harleian MSS. 6988).

iii. *Cromwell daubs Ireton's face with ink*

Henry Ireton (1611–1651), held many high offices under Cromwell and married his eldest daughter, Bridget. He was one of the signatories of the warrant for Charles I's execution.

I believe it is Ludlow [one of the King's judges and another signer of the execution warrant] that relates an anecdote in his Memoirs, of Oliver Cromwell and Ireton standing at one of the windows of the Painted Chamber, as King Charles passed through it, on his way from Cotton Garden to Westminster Hall.

They stood with their backs to his Majesty and, as soon as he had passed, Oliver Cromwell drew the pen across Ireton's face, and inked it, in his joy at having the moment before procured the signatures of all the parties who signed the death-warrant, then lying on the table.

SOURCE: W. D. Fellowes, *Historical Sketches of Charles I, Cromwell . . . and the Principal Personages of that Period, including the King's Trial and Execution*, 1828, p. 388.

iv. *Cromwell allows himself to be preached at*

The following tradition, concerning Cromwell, is preserved by an uncommonly direct line of traditional evidence; being related (as I am informed) by the grandson of an eyewitness. When Cromwell, in 1650, entered Glasgow, he attended divine service in the High Church; but the Presbyterian divine who officiated, poured forth with more zeal than prudence, the vial of his indignation upon the person, principles, and cause of the Independent General. One of Cromwell's officers rose, and whispered to his commander; who seemed to give him a short and stern answer, and the sermon was concluded without interruption. . . .

'He proposed,' said Cromwell [in conversation afterwards], 'to pull forth the minister by the ears; and I answered that the preacher was one fool and he another.'

SOURCE: Sir Walter Scott, *Minstrelsy of the Scottish Border . . .*, 1802–1803.

v. *Cromwell dismisses Parliament*, April 20, 1653

... the General stept into the midst of the House, where, continuing his distracted language, he said:

'Come, come! I will put an end to your prating.' Then, walking up and down the House like a mad-man, and kicking the ground with his feet, he cried out:

'You are no Parliament! I say you are no Parliament! I will put an end to your sitting. Call them in! Call them in!'

Whereupon the Sergeant attending the Parliament opened the doors, and Lieutenant Colonel Worsley with two files of musqueteers entered the House; which, Sir Henry Vane, observing from his place, said:

'This is not honest; yea, it is against morality and common honesty.'

Then Cromwell fell a-railing at him, crying out with a loud voice:

'O! Sir Henry Vane, Sir Henry Vane! The Lord deliver me from Sir Henry Vane!'

Then . . . he commanded the Mace to be taken away, saying:

'What shall we do with this bauble? Here, take it away!'

SOURCE: *Memoirs of Edmund Ludlow, Esq., Lieutenant General of the Horse* . . . , published in Switzerland, 1698, Vol. II, pp. 456–457.

vi. *Cromwell's Secret Service*

There was not the smallest accident that befell King Charles II in his exile but he [Cromwell] knew it perfectly well; insomuch that, having given leave to an English nobleman to travel upon condition that he should not see Charles Stuart, he asked at his return if he had punctually obeyed his commands. Which, the other affirming he had, Cromwell replied:

'It's true you did not see him; for, to keep your word with me, you agreed to meet him in the dark, the candles being put out for that end'; and withal told him all the particulars that passed in conversation betwixt the King and him at their meeting.

SOURCE: James Welwood, *Memoirs of the most material Transactions in England . . . preceding the Revolution in 1688*, 1700; inc. in W. D. Fellowes, *Historical Sketches of Charles I, Cromwell, Charles II . . . and the Principal Personages of that Period*, 1828, pp. 251–252.

vii. *Cromwell's courtesy to a cavalier*

Sir William Smyth . . . was governor, or commander of the king's garrison at Hillesden House, near Newport Pagnell, when it was beseiged and taken by Cromwell, in 1643. The garrison, however, had capitulated to march out with their arms, baggage, etc., unmolested. But as soon as they were out of the gate, one of Cromwell's soldiers snatched off Sir William Smyth's hat. He immediately complained to Cromwell of the man's insolence, and breach of the capitulation.

'Sir,' said Cromwell, 'if you can point out the man, or I can discover him, I promise you he shall not go unpunished. In the meantime' (taking off a new beaver which he had on his own head) 'be pleased to accept of this hat instead of your own.'

SOURCE: Dr. William King, *Anecdotes of his Own Times*; quoted R. Chambers, *A Book of Days*, 1864.

viii. *Warts and all*

The Protector's instructions to the painter Sir Peter Lely, when he was about to sit for his protrait:

'Mr. Lilly, I desire you would use all your skill to paint my picture truly like me and not flatter me at all. But,' pointing to his own face, 'remark all these roughnesses, pimples, warts and everything as you see me; otherwise I will never pay a farthing for it.'

SOURCE: George Vertue, *Notebooks* and Horace Walpole, *Anecdotes of Painting*, Ch. 12.

ix. *'England's plague for five years'*

The Parish Register of the year 1599, has an entry of baptism of the deepest interest. It is in these words:

'In the year of our Lord, 1599, Oliver, son of Robert Cromwell, gent., and Elizabeth his wife, born 25th of April, and baptized 29th of the same month.'

Just between the date of the year and the name of the child, this line has been inserted:
'England's plague for five years.'
An effort has been made to erase it, but the words can still be easily read.

SOURCE: Sir Bernard Burke, *The Rise of Great Families*, 1873, p. 328.
See also CIVIL WAR; HAMPDEN, JOHN, etc.

CROMWELL, RICHARD (1626–1712); third son of Oliver, and proclaimed Protector in his place. After being recognized by Parliament in 1659, he was soon virtually deposed by Parliament and the army and retired to the Continent, where he lived for 20 years under the name of John Clarke. He later returned to England and lived in retirement till the age of 86.

i. *Richard hears himself appraised*
After Richard had quitted the Protectorship, he made a voyage to France, where, being one day at Montpellier, the Prince of Conti, brother of the great Condé, discoursing with him without knowing who he was, observed:
'Oliver Cromwell was a great man, but his son Richard is a poor wretch, not to know how to enjoy the fruits of his father's crimes.'

SOURCE: from Voltaire; inc. in *The Works of M. de Voltaire translated into English*, 1761–1769, to which Smollett allowed his name to be put as translator, though he probably had very little to do with it. Richard Cromwell seems to have laid down his high office with relief, so that Conti was wide of the mark. When Richard's followers wanted him to meet force with force, he replied:
'I will not have a drop of blood spilt for the preservation of my greatness, which is a burden to me.'

ii. *Richard revisits the scene of his greatness*
Richard Cromwell, when nearly eighty years of age, was brought to London as a witness in a civil suit, tried at Westminster Hall. After the trial was over, he had the curiosity to go into the House of Lords, which was then sitting. While he stood at the bar it was whispered about that the once supreme head

of the state was present, on which Lord Bathurst went to the bar and conversed freely with the ex-protector of the commonwealth for some time. Among other things, he asked Mr. Cromwell how long it was since he had been in that house?

'Never, my lord,' answered Richard, 'since I sat in that chair,' pointing to the throne.

SOURCE: Thomas Byerley and Joseph Clinton Robertson, *The Percy Anecdotes*, 1820–1823.

CROMWELL, THOMAS (1485?–1540), statesman; one of the commissioners appointed to inquire into the smaller monasteries; secretary to Wolsey, Chancellor of the Exchequer, Lord Great Chamberlain, etc.

i. *'I will either make or mar'*

It chanced me upon All-hallown day to come into the great chamber at Asher, in the morning, to give mine attendance, where I found Master Cromwell leaning in the great window, with a primer in his hand, saying of our Lady mattins. He prayed not more earnestly than the tears distilled from his eyes. Whom I bade good morrow. And with that I perceived the tears upon his cheeks. To whom I said:

'Why, master Cromwell, what meaneth all this your sorrow? Is my lord in any danger, for whom ye lament thus? Or is it for any loss that ye have sustained by any misadventure?'

'Nay, nay,' quoth he, 'it is my unhappy adventure which am like to lose all that I have travailed for all the days of my life, for doing of my master true and diligent service . . . and this I understand right well, that I am in disdain with most men for my master's sake; and surely without just cause, howbeit, an ill name once gotten will not lightly be put away. . . . And thus much will I say to you, that I intend, God willing, this afternoon, when my Lord hath dined, to ride to London, and so to the Court, where I will either make or mar. . . .'

SOURCE: George Cavendish, *Life of Cardinal Wolsey*, first published, imperfectly, 1641 and several times subsequently; first accurate edition, 1815.

ii. *Cromwell causes a house to be moved bodily*

On the south side and at the west end of this Church [Church of the Augustine Friars, London] many fair houses are builded, namely in Throgmorton Street; one very large and spacious, builded in the place of old and small tenements by Thomas Cromwell. . . . This House being finished, and having some reasonable plot of ground left for a garden, he caused the pales of the gardens adjoining to the north part thereof on a sudden to be taken down, twenty-two foot to be measured right into the north of every man's ground, a line there to be drawn, a trench to be cast, a foundation laid, and a high brick wall to be builded.

My father had a garden there, and an house standing close to his [Cromwell's] south pale. This house they loosed from the ground, and bare upon rollers into my father's garden twenty-two foot, ere my father heard thereof, no warning was given him, nor other answer, when he spake to the surveyors of that work, but that their master Sir Thomas commanded them to so do; no man durst go to argue the matter, but each man lost his land, and my father paid his whole rent, which was vi^s viii^d the year for that half which was left.

SOURCE: John Stowe, quoted Henry Ellis, *Original Letters Illustrative of English History*, 2nd series, Vol. II, 1827, p. 124.

CUBAN INDEPENDENCE. Cuba, which had for centuries been in Spanish hands, was declared by the U.S. Congress, on April 19, 1898, to be independent. The resolution demanded that Spain withdraw and gave President McKinley power to use the whole resources of the army and navy. The subsequent Spanish-American War lasted about three months and ended in Spain relinquishing the island. Losses of life in battle were light, but for every man killed thirteen died of disease. One of the men chiefly responsible for urging America into the war was the newspaper proprietor William Randolph Hearst and his paper the *New York Journal*.

Hearst supplies the war

When General Weyler [Spanish leader] expelled his correspondents, Hearst sent down others with orders to manufacture news if they were not allowed near the front. One of these special correspondents was Frederic Remington, a popular artist who obliged by providing fanciful sketches of Spanish 'frightfulness'. After a few weeks of idleness, Remington sent Hearst a telegram:

'Everything is quiet. There will be no war. I wish to return.'

Hearst is said to have replied:

'Please remain. You furnish the pictures and I'll furnish the war.'

Whether he actually did send such a telegram, the words quoted certainly represent his attitude and his hopes.

SOURCE: *History Today*, June 1961, p. 375; Arnold Whitridge, *Cuba's Rôle in American History*.

DAMPIER, WILLIAM (1652–1715), pirate, hydrographer and circumnavigator.

Poor fare for mutineers

Till this time [August, 1685] I had been with Captain Davis, but now left him and went aboard of Captain Swan. It was not from any dislike to my old captain, but to get some knowledge of the northern parts of this continent of Mexico; and I knew that Captain Swan determined to coast it as far north as he thought convenient, and then pass over for the East Indies, which was a way very agreeable to my inclination. . . .

Many were well pleased with the voyage, but some thought, such was their ignorance, that he would carry them out of the world. . . . It was well for Captain Swan that we got sight of it [Guam, May 20, 1686] before our provision was spent, of which we had but enough for three days more; for as I was afterwards informed, the men had contrived first to kill Captain Swan and eat him when the victuals was gone, and after him all of us who were accessory in promoting the undertaking this voyage. This made Captain Swan say to me after our arrival at Guam:

'Ah! Dampier, you would have made them but a poor meal'; for I was as lean as the captain was lusty and fleshy.

SOURCE: William Dampier, *Voyage Round the World*, 1697.

DAVENANT, JOHN (1576–1641), Master of Queen's College, Cambridge; Bishop of Salisbury.

The calling with great temptations

Taking leave of his college, and of one John Rolfe, an ancient servant thereof, he desired him to pray for him, and when the other modestly returned that he rather needed his lordship's prayers:

'Yea, John,' said he, 'and I need thine too, being now to enter into a calling wherein I shall meet with many and great temptations.'

SOURCE: Thomas Fuller, *The English Worthies*, 1662, 1952 edition, George Allen & Unwin, p. 371.

DAVY, SIR HUMPHRY (1778–1829), scientist and natural philosopher; invented miners' safety lamp.

i. *Lectures from an 8-year-old*

Numerous anecdotes show that he was a precocious boy. He possessed a remarkable memory, and was singularly rapid in acquiring knowledge of books. He was especially attracted by the 'Pilgrim's Progress', and he delighted in reading history. When but eight years of age he would collect a number of boys, and standing on a cart in the market-place address them on the subject of his latest reading.

SOURCE: Robert Hunt, *Dictionary of National Biography*, 1888.

ii. *Davy anaesthetizes himself*

In another letter written to Davies Gilbert on 10 April [1799] he informs him: 'I made a discovery yesterday which proves how necessary it is to repeat experiments. The gaseous oxide of azote (laughing gas) is perfectly respirable when pure. It is never deleterious but when it contains nitrous gas. I have found a mode of making it pure.' He then says that he breathed six-teen quarts of it for nearly seven minutes, and that 'it absolutely intoxicated me'. . . .

In 1800 Davy informed Davies Gilbert that he had been 'repeating the galvanic experiments with success' in the intervals of experiments on the gases, which 'almost incessantly occupied him from January to April'. In these experiments Davy ran considerable risks. The respiration of nitrous oxide led, by its union with common air in the mouth, to the forma-tion of nitrous acid, which severely injured the mucous mem-brane, and in his attempt to breathe carburetted hydrogen gas he 'seemed sinking into annihilation'.

On being removed into the open air he faintly articulated, 'I do not think I shall die,' but some hours elapsed before the painful symptoms ceased.

SOURCE: Robert Hunt, *Dictionary of National Biography, 1888.*

DEMOSTHENES (384?–322 B.C.), Athenian orator.

i. *Demosthenes keeps himself indoors*

Upon this he built himself a subterranean study. . . . Thither he repaired every day to form his action and exercise his voice; and he would often stay there two or three months together, shaving one side of his head, that, if he should happen to be ever so desirous of going abroad, the shame of appearing in that condition might keep him in.

SOURCE: Plutarch's *Lives*, trans. J. and W. Langhorne, 1821.

ii. *Demosthenes overcomes his defects*

The hesitation and stammering of his tongue he corrected by practising to speak with pebbles in his mouth; and he strength-ened his voice by running or walking up hill, and pronouncing some passage in an oration or a poem, during the difficulty of breath which that caused. He had, moreover, a looking-glass in his house, before which he used to declaim, and adjust all his motions.

SOURCE: ibid.

DENHAM, SIR JOHN (1615–1669), poet.

The second-worst poet

He [George Withers, Puritan poet] was once taken prisoner by the Royalists, and about to be put to death as a traitor; but Sir John Denham begged his life, saying to the king:

'If your Majesty kills Withers, I will then be the worst poet in England.'

SOURCE: quoted R. Chambers, *A Book of Days*, 1864.

DE RUYTER, MICHAEL (1607–1676), Dutch admiral. Brought his ships up the Medway and the Thames, 1667, towing off the flagship *Royal Charles* and inflicting other heavy losses in ships and morale.

i. *The trembling Admiral*

He was naturally healthy, but in his youth he had once been accidentally poisoned through eating bad fish; this had resulted in a slight trembling in all his limbs, which lasted to the end of his life.

SOURCE: Gerard Brandt, who knew him. His life of de Ruyter was translated into French, 1698, as *La Vie du L'Amiral de Ruiter*.

ii. *The English sailors on the Dutch ships*

This was one of the low-water marks in English history, with the sailors in such poor heart, their wages far in arrears and with too little food, that a number were serving with de Ruyter.

But that that he [Mr. Wilson] . . . tells me of worse consequence is, that he himself, I think he said, did hear many Englishmen on board the Dutch ships speaking to one another in English; and that they did cry and say:

'We did heretofore fight for tickets; now we fight for dollars!' and did ask how such and such a one did, and would commend themselves to them.

SOURCE: Samuel Pepys's *Diary*, June 14, 1667.

DETTINGEN, BATTLE OF (June 27, 1743): in the War of the Austrian Succession, the French under Noailles being defeated by the English under Lord Stair and George II. It was the last battle in which an English king fought in person.

The King saves himself from running away

The King was on horseback, and rode forward to reconnoitre the enemy. His horse, frightened at the cannonading, ran away with his Majesty, and nearly carried him into the midst of the French lines. Fortunately one of his attendants succeeded in stopping him. General Cyrus Trapaud, then an ensign, by seizing the horse's bridle, enabled his Majesty to dismount in safety.

'Now that I am once more on my legs,' said he, 'I am sure I shall not run away.'

SOURCE: Frederick the Great, *Histoire de mon Temps*; inc. in John Timbs, *A Century of Anecdote* (Chandos Classics), Frederick Warne & Co., p. 11.

DEVEREUX, ROBERT, second **EARL OF ESSEX** (1567–1601), favourite of Queen Elizabeth.

Essex gets a lesson in manners

Essex's boyish vanity was hurt by the favour shown to Charles Blount* . . . on his first appearance at court. He noticed that Blount wore about his arm a gold chess-queen which the queen

---

* Charles Blount, Earl of Devonshire and Baron Mountjoy (1563–1606), later implicated in Essex's conspiracy.

had given him, and he remarked at the sight of it, 'Now I perceive every fool must wear a favour.' Blount was informed of
the expression, and a duel took place in Marylebone Park, in
which Essex was disarmed and slightly wounded. Both courtiers
were reprimanded by Elizabeth, and became good friends
afterwards.

'By God's death,' Elizabeth truly said of Essex. 'it were
fitting some one should take him down and teach him better
manners, or there were no rule with him.'

SOURCE: S. L. Lee, *Dictionary of National Biography*, 1888.

DIOGENES (*c.* 412–323 B.C.), Greek philosopher. Diogenes of
Sinope belonged to the Cynic school of philosophers, 'Cynic' in
Greek meaning 'doggish'. The Cynics held that men would be
happier if they renounced the social conventions that bound them,
and the luxuries of soft living, and returned to a life of extreme
simplicity, e.g. of 'dogs'. Popular tradition says that Diogenes
lived in a tub; but, if he ever adopted this sort of dwelling, instead
of the public bath-houses or temple porticoes which provided the
only home for many of them, it is more likely to have been one
of the huge earthenware jars used for storing grain, oil or water.

i. *Diogenes sees land*

I have often admired a humorous saying of Diogenes, who,
reading a dull author to several of his friends, when every one
began to be tired, finding he was almost come to a blank leaf
at the end of it, cried:

'Courage, lads! I see land.'

SOURCE: Joseph Addision, *The Spectator*, No. 582, August 18,
1714.

ii. *Answer to a slander*

Diogenes was still more severe [than Aristotle] on one who
spoke ill of him:

'Nobody will believe you when you speak ill of me, any more
than they would believe me should I speak well of you.'

SOURCE: Joseph Addison, *The Guardian*, No. 135, August 15, 1713.

K

iii. *The Emperor who blocked the sunlight*

Diogenes happened to be lying in the sun; and at the approach of so many people, he raised himself up a little, and fixed his eyes on Alexander. The king addressed him in an obliging manner, and asked him if there was anything he could serve him in.

'Only stand a little out of my sunshine,' said Diogenes.

Alexander, we are told, was struck with such surprise at finding himself so little regarded ... that, while his courtiers were ridiculing the philosopher as a monster, he said:

'If I were not Alexander, I should wish to be Diogenes.'

SOURCE: Plutarch's *Lives*, trans. J. and W. Langhorne, 1821.

DISRAELI, BENJAMIN, first EARL OF BEACONSFIELD (1804–1881), statesman and writer.

i. *Disraeli on Gladstone*

... a sophistical rhetorician, inebriated with the exuberance of his own verbosity, and gifted with an egotistical imagination that can at all times command an interminable and inconsistent series of arguments to malign an opponent and to glorify himself.

SOURCE: Speech at a banquet, July 27, 1878, in the Riding School, Knightsbridge.

ii.

Gladstone ... had he been present, would not have laughed at the Prime Minister's reply to someone who asked him to define the difference between the words 'misfortune' and 'calamity'.

'Well,' said Dizzy, 'if Mr. Gladstone fell into the Thames, it would be a misfortune; but, if someone pulled him out, it would be a calamity.'

SOURCE: Hesketh Pearson, *Lives of the Wits*, Heinemann, 1962, p. 160.

iii. *Disraeli on flattery*

In the last year of his life he said to Mr. Matthew Arnold, in a strange burst of confidence which showed how completely he realised that his fall from power was final:

'You have heard me accused of being a flatterer. It is true. I am a flatterer. I have found it useful. Every one likes flattery; and when it comes to Royalty you should lay it on with a trowel.'

SOURCE: George W. E. Russell, *Collections and Recollections*, Smith Elder & Co., 1903, Ch. XXIII.

iv. *Disraeli on Lord John Russell*

If a traveller were informed that such a man [Lord John Russell] was leader of the House of Commons, he may well begin to comprehend how the Egyptians worshipped an insect.

SOURCE: attributed. *Penguin Dictionary of Quotations*, etc.

v. *Disraeli on the Opposition Bench*

As I sat opposite the Treasury Bench, the ministers reminded me of one of those marine landscapes not very unusual on the coasts of South America. You behold a range of exhausted volcanoes.

SOURCE: Speech in Manchester, April 3, 1872.

vi. *Edward VII on Disraeli*

The only indisputable humbug who was also a great man. Personally I couldn't stand him; but I could never ask for a greater Prime Minister, and I would never see one half as great.

SOURCE: Edward VII; quoted *The Whispering Gallery, being Leaves from a Diplomat's Diary*, John Lane, 1926, p. 51.

vii. *Disraeli on Disraeli?*

A man may speak very well in the House of Commons and fail completely in the House of Lords. There are two distinct styles requisite. I intend in the course of my career, if I have time, to give a specimen of both.

SOURCE: *The Young Duke*, Book V, Ch. 6.

viii. *Did Disraeli really like primroses?*

The primrose is now generally supposed to have been Lord Beaconsfield's favourite flower, but I cannot say for certain that I ever heard him express any particular partiality for it, though I dare say he may have done so.

As a matter of fact, I believe that Queen Victoria at the proper season invariably sent Lord Beaconsfield primroses from the slopes at Windsor, and it is probable that, having expressed to someone his warm appreciation of these flowers, it was in consequence assumed that the great statesman had a strong partiality for the primrose.

I sat next Mr. Gladstone at a dinner some time after Lord Beaconsfield's death, and in the course of conversation he suddenly said:

'Tell me, Lady Dorothy, upon your honour, have you ever heard Lord Beaconsfield express any particular fondness for the primrose?'

I was compelled to admit that I had not. . . .

SOURCE: *Reminiscences of Lady Dorothy Nevill* (edit. Ralph Nevill), Thomas Nelson & Sons, 1906.

DOD, JOHN (1549?–1645). Puritan divine. Called 'Decalogue Dod' from his exposition of the Ten Commandments.

Impromptu sermon

Mr. Dodd was a Gentleman that lived within a few miles of Cambridge and had been preaching against Drunkenness for some time. This affronted some of the Oxford scholars, who thought he reflected on them. As they were on a journey one day they happened to meet Mr. Dodd; and when they saw him at a distance, they said one to the other:

'Here is Father Dodd coming. We will ask him to preach us a Sermon.'

So, meeting him, they complimented him with:

'Your Servant, Sir.' He replied:

'Yours, Gentlemen.' They said:

'We have a favour to ask, which must be granted.' He asked them what is was. They replied it was to preach them a sermon from a text they should choose, adding:

'We hear you have been preaching against drunkenness this half year past,' asking him if it was not so. He answered it was.

'And if you please,' said he, 'to appoint the time and place, I will preach you a sermon.'

They told him the time was present and the place, 'that hollow tree', pointing to one near them. The good man said it was an imposition, for that he ought to have a little consideration before preaching: but they said if he refused they would put him into the tree. He therefore went into it, asking them what was to be his text. So they told him the word was MALT.

He then began as follows:

'Beloved, let me crave your attention. I am a little man, come at short warning to preach a short sermon from a small subject to a thin congregation and in an unworthy pulpit. Beloved, my text is "MALT", I cannot divide it into syllables, it being but one; therefore I must necessarily divide it into Letters, which I find in my text to be four, M—A—L—T.

M, my beloved, is Moral.

A, is Allegorical.

L, is Literal.

T, is Theological.

The Allegorical is when one thing is spoken, and another meant.

The Moral is set forth to teach you drunkards good manners; therefore:

M, my Masters,

A, all of you,

L, listen,

T, to my text.

The Allegorical is when one thing is spoken, and another meant. The thing spoken of is MALT, the thing meant is the Oil of Malt, which you rustics make:

M, your Meat

A, your Apparel
L, your Liberty
T, your Trust.

The Literal is according to the Letter.
M, much
A, ale,
L, little
T, thrift.

The Theological is according to the effects it works and those I find to be of two kinds; the first in this world, the second in the world to come. The effects in this world are, in some:
M, mischief and murder
A, adultery
L, in all, Looseness of Life and in some
T, Treason.

Secondly, in the world to come:
M, Misery
A, Anguish
L, Lamentation and
T, Torment.
And so much for this time and text.

First, I shall improve by way of reflection and
M, my Masters,
A, all of you,
L, leave off
T, tippling.

Secondly, by way of commination*
M, my Masters,
A, all of you,
L, look for
T, torment.

Thirdly, by way of caution, take this:
A drunkard is the annoyance of modesty, the spoiler of civility, the destroyer of nature and reason, the brewer's agent, the ale house benefactor, his wife's sorrow, his children's

* i.e., threat or warning of punishment.

trouble, his own shame, his neighbour's scoff, a walking swill-tub, the picture of a beast and the monster of a man.'

SOURCE: Manuscript copy in possession of author.

DODSLEY, ROBERT (1703–1764), bookseller and publisher. The most famous of 18th Century booksellers, Dodsley published for, among other great literary figures, Johnson and Pope. He suggested to the former the plan for an English Dictionary.

The source of a quotation
> *He that fights and runs away*
> *May live to fight another day*

These lines are almost universally supposed to form part of *Hudibras* [the rhyming political satire by Samuel Butler]; and so confident have even scholars been on the subject that, in 1784, a wager was made at Bootle's of twenty to one that they were to be found in that inimitable poem. Dodsley [the well-known bookseller and publisher] was referred to as the arbiter, when he ridiculed the idea of consulting him on the subject, saying:
'Every fool knows they are in Hudibras.'
George Selwyn, who was present, said to Dodsley:
'Pray, sir, will you be good enough, then, to inform an old fool who is, at the same time your wise worship's very humble servant, in what canto they are to be found?'
Dodsley took down the volume, but he could not find the passage. The next day came with no better success, and the sage bibliophile was obliged to confess 'that a man might be ignorant of the author of this well-known couplet, without being absolutely a fool'.

SOURCE: Stephen Collet, *Relics of Literature*, 1823, p. 185. The couplet, in fact, occurs in *Musarum Deliciae*, collected by Sir John Mennes and Dr. James Smith, 1656. The additional couplet—
> *But he who is in battle slain*
> *Can never rise and fight again*
occurs in *Art of Poetry on a New Plan*, written by John Newbery (1713–1767) and revised by Goldsmith.

DOUGLAS, SIR JAMES (1286?–1330), called 'the Good'. Deprived of his inheritance by Edward I and three times attacked his own castle, which became known as 'the Perilous Castle of Douglas'. At the third attack, Douglas destroyed his own ancestral home to prevent it any more being garrisoned by the English.

i. *The end of Castle Perilous*

Sir James, taking along with him a body of armed men, gained the neighbourhood undiscovered, where himself and the greater number immediately planted themselves in ambuscade, as near as possible to the gate of the castle. Fourteen of his best men he directed to disguise themselves as peasants wearing smock-frocks, under which their arms might conveniently be concealed, and having sacks filled with grass laid across their horses, who in this guise were to pass within view of the castle, as if they had been countrymen carrying corn for sale to Lanark fair. The stratagem had the desired effect; for the garrison being then scarce of provisions, had no mind to let pass so favourable an opportunity, as it appeared to them, of supplying themselves; wherefore, the greater part, with the governor . . . at their head, issued out in great haste to overtake and plunder the supposed peasants.

These, finding themselves pursued, hurried onward with what speed they could muster, till, ascertaining that the unwary Englishmen had passed the ambush, they suddenly threw down their sacks, stripped off the frocks which concealed their armour, mounted their horses, and, raising a loud shout, seemed determined in turn to become the assailants. Douglas and his concealed followers no sooner heard the shouts of their companions, which was the concerted signal of onset, than, starting into view in the rear of the English party, these found themselves . . . unexpectedly and furiously attacked from two opposite quarters. In this desperate encounter their retreat to the castle being effectually cut off, Wilton and his whole party are reported to have been slain.

When this successful exploit was ended, Sir James . . . razed the fortress of his ancestors to the ground that it might on no future occasion afford protection to the enemies of his country and the usurpers of his patrimony.

SOURCE: John Barbour, *Brus*; Robert Chambers, *A Biographical Dictionary of Eminent Scotsmen*, 1837, Vol. II, p. 103.

ii. *The heart of Robert Bruce*

After Bruce had died of leprosy in 1329, Douglas set out to carry his heart to Jerusalem, to which the King had always wished to make pilgrimage. On the way he was inveigled into a battle against the Moors in Andalusia.

The Moors, not long able to withstand the furious encounter of their assailants, betook themselves to flight. Douglas . . . followed hard after the fugitives until, finding himself almost deserted by his followers, he turned his horse with the intention of rejoining the main body. Just then, however, observing a knight of his own company to be surrounded by a body of Moors, who had suddenly rallied, 'Alas!' said he, 'yonder worthy knight shall perish but for present help'; and with the few who now attended him, amounting to no more than ten men, he turned hastily to attempt his rescue. He soon found himself hard pressed by the numbers who thronged upon him. Taking from his neck the silver casquet which contained the heart of Bruce, he threw it before him among the thickest of the enemy, saying:

'Now pass thou onward before us, as thou wert wont, and I will follow thee or die.'

Douglas, and almost the whole of the brave men who fought by his side were here slain. His body and the casquet . . . were found together upon the field; and were, by his companions, conveyed with great care and reverence into Scotland . . . and the heart of Bruce solemnly interred by Moray, the regent, under the high altar in Melrose Abbey.

SOURCE: ibid., pp. 111–112.

DRAKE, SIR FRANCIS (1540?–1596), admiral and circum-navigator.

i. *The King of Spain's beard*

In 1587, Drake carried out an enterprise on Cadiz and other Spanish possessions when preparations for the Armada were in full swing. 'At Cadiz, ringed about with castles and fortresses, lay the principal galley fleet in the world; a fleet similar to that which had won Lepanto; a fleet which yearned to match its guns and rams with the insolent armed merchantmen of Drake' (Sir Geoffrey Callender). Drake destroyed between 50 and 60 ships, then sailed to Cape St. Vincent and sank or burnt something like 100 more of various tonnages.

I remember Drake, in the vaunting style of a soldier, would call the Enterprise the singeing of the King of Spain's Beard.

SOURCE: Sir Francis Bacon, *Considerations touching a War with Spain*, Harleian Miscellany, 1745, Vol. V, p. 85.

ii. *Communion before execution*

During his voyage round the world, 1577–1581, Drake executed one of his officers, Thomas Doughty, on charges of conspiracy and mutiny.

In this port [Saint Julian] our General* began to enquire diligently of the actions of Mr. Thomas Doughty, and found them not to be such as he looked for, but tending rather to contention or mutiny, or some other disorder, whereby . . . the success of the voyage might greatly have been hazarded; whereupon the company was called together and made acquainted with the particulars of the cause, which were found, partly by Mr. Doughty's own confession, and partly by the evidence of the fact, to be true; . . . so that the cause being thoroughly heard, and all things done in good order, as near as might be to the course of our laws in England, it was concluded that Mr. Doughty should receive punishment according to the quality of the offence; and he, seeing no remedy but patience for himself, desired before his death to receive the communion,

---

* 'General' was frequently used at this time for the commander-in-chief at sea. In the next century we find a famous triumvirate of 'Generals at Sea', Edward Popham, Richard Deane and Robert Blake.

which he did at the hands of Mr. Fletcher, our minister, and our General himself accompanied him in that holy action; which being done, and the place of execution made ready, he having embraced our General, and taken leave of all the company, with prayer for the Queen's Majesty and our realm, in quiet sort laid his head to the block, where he ended his life.

SOURCE: Richard Hakluyt, *Principall Navigations, Voiages, and Discoveries of the English Nation*, first issued 1589 and, much enlarged, 1598–1600.

iii. *Drake refuses class distinction on his ships*

'I must have the gentleman to haul and draw with the mariner, and the mariner with the gentleman ... I would know him that would refuse to set his hand to a rope—but I know there is not any such here.'

SOURCE: Julian Corbett, *Sir Francis Drake*, Macmillan, 1901, p. 75, and *Drake and the Tudor Navy*, i. p. 249.
   Drake's words were spoken some weeks after the trial and execution of Doughty for treason and mutiny, when there was great tension between the 'gentlemen' and the 'mariners'. Drake called the companies ashore at Port St. Julian and told the chaplain he would preach the sermon. Afterwards, he dismissed in a rage every officer in the ships; but afterwards, his supremacy established beyond question, reinstated them all and 'with cheery words of hope and kindliness he dismissed them to their duty. From that moment his reputation as a disciplinarian was unrivalled. The state of his ships was a wonder to all who saw them' (Corbett).

See also ARMADA, SPANISH.

DU GUESCLIN, BERTRAND (1320?–1380), Constable of France; the most famous French soldier of the Hundred Years War.

The Death of Bertrand du Guesclin (1320–1380), Constable of France.

i. '*Soiez bonne gent*'

... he smiled and looked at those who were gathered about him in his tent. Bretons there were, and French, and English—

men of different nationalities, enemies. Yet he saw no hatred in
them, no difference between them; saw only honest fighting
men, doing each his duty as he saw it. Bretons, and English,
and French—he looked from face to face, and smiled.

'Soiez bonne gent,' he said, 'Be good fellows.'

Then once again he spoke, saying:

'Good-bye, my companions! And remember, wherever you
make war, that women, children, church-folk, and the poor,
are not your enemies.'

SOURCE: Du Guesclin's last 'splendid injunction to humanity' is
well known. This version is from M. Coryn, *Black Mastiff*, Arthur
Barker Ltd., 1932, p. 283.

ii. *Tribute from an enemy*

Du Guesclin's last siege was of the Chateauneuf de Randon, in the
seneschalry of Beaucaire, held by the English, whose captain
promised to capitulate, and gave hostages to this effect, if relief
did not reach him by July 12. On July 13, de Guesclin, stricken
with a malignant fever, died in his tent and, by military conven-
tion, the English captain was thereby freed from his promise to
yield up the keys. But he made one of the great gestures of
history:

The French army was waiting for him, with flags waving in
the wind, and their weapons upright. Under the tent Bertrand
du Guesclin was resting, his hands exactly joined, in full
armour, with the Constable's sword, naked, at his feet on a
cushion of mauve velvet covered with gold fleur-de-lis.

The English captain and his officers knelt for a short prayer;
then, rising, the governor gently placed the bunch of huge keys
on the dead man's knees. As they went away, the English wept
like the French, because he was the most valiant man in the
world, because he waged the best war that had ever been, and
because he ransomed them with courtesy and had always
shown himself trustworthy in his promises of peace or truce.

SOURCE: Another celebrated episode in the du Guesclin story,
which sometimes has it that the Constable took the keys in his
hands, which had been folded as though in prayer, just *before* he

died. But the essentials are the same. This version is from Roger
Vercel, *Bertrand of Brittany*, George Routledge & Sons, 1934,
p. 242.

DUVAL, CLAUDE (1643–1670), highwayman.

Duval dances a coranto

Yet, to do him right, one story there is that savours of gallantry,
and I should not be an honest historian, if I should conceal it.
He with his squadron overtakes a coach . . . having intelligence
of a booty of four-hundred pounds in it. In the coach was a
knight, his lady, and only one serving-maid, who, perceiving
five horsemen making up to them, presently imagined they
were beset; and they were confirmed in this apprehension, by
seeing them whisper to one another, and ride backwards and
forwards: the lady to shew she was not afraid, takes a flageolet
out of her pocket and plays. Du Vall takes the hint, plays also,
and excellently well, upon a flageolet of his own; and, in this
posture, he rides up to the coach-side.

'Sir,' says he to the person in the coach, 'Your lady plays
excellently, and I doubt not but that she dances as well; will
you please to walk out of the coach, and let me have the honour
to dance one currant [i.e. *courant* or *coranto*, a rapid dance with
a running or gliding step] with her upon the heath.'

'Sir,' said the person in the coach, 'I dare not deny any thing
to one of your quality and good mind; and you seem a gentleman, and your request is very reasonable.'

Which said, the lacquey opens the boot; out comes the
knight, Du Vall leaps lightly off his horse, and hands the lady
out of the coach. They danced, and here it was that Du Vall
performed marvels; the best master in London, except those
that are French, not being able to shew such footing as he did
in his great French riding boots. The dancing being over, he
waits on the lady to her coach: as the knight was going in, says
Du Vall to him:

'Sir, you have forgot to pay the musick.'

'No, I have not,' replies the knight, and, putting his hand

under the seat of the coach, pulls out an hundred pounds in a
bag, and delivers it to him; which Du Vall took with a very
good grace, and courteously answered:

'Sir, you are liberal, and shall have no cause to repent your
being so; this liberality of yours shall excuse you the other three
hundred pounds.'

SOURCE: *The Memoirs of Monsieur Du Vall* . . . 1670 (Harleian
Miscellany).

EDEN, ANTHONY, LORD AVON (b. 1897), statesman.

Modern communications

It is not so long since the most sophisticated bit of gadgetry in
the private office at No. 10 was a direct line to the President of
the United States. This was considerably in use during the life-
time of the late President Kennedy. A future historian may
observe, without irony, that since its installation the 'special
relationship' has steadily become less special.

Now there is to be a teletype machine for instant communications between the Prime Minister and the Kremlin.

All will wish it well. But some will also remember the aphor-
ism of Lord Avon when he was Foreign Secretary:

'Modern communications corrupt good manners.'

SOURCE: *Daily Telegraph*, February 14, 1967.

EDGEHILL, BATTLE OF (October 23, 1642).

The remarkable survival of Sir Gervase Scroop

Amongst those who fell on the king's side, and were left on the
field as dead, was Sir Gervase Scroop, who had fallen covered
with wounds about three o'clock on Sunday afternoon.

It was not till Tuesday evening that his son, who was also in
the king's forces, was able to return to the battle-field to search
for the body of his father. When he found it, it was perfectly
naked, having been stripped, like the rest of the slain, on
Sunday evening, by camp-plunderers. In this state it had lain

all Sunday night, all Monday, and Monday night, and was apparently dead, having received no less than sixteen severe wounds. Monday night, it ought to be stated, had been remarkably cold and frosty.

Sir Gervase's son carried him to a lodging near at hand, and fancied he felt in the body some degree of heat. 'That heat,' says Fuller, 'was, with rubbing, within few minutes, improved into motion; that motion, within some hours, into sense; that sense, within a day, into speech; that speech, within certain weeks, into a perfect recovery; living more than ten years after, a monument of God's mercy and his son's affection. The effect of this story I received from his own mouth.'

SOURCE: Thomas Fuller, *Worthies of Leicestershire*; *The Book of Days* (edit. R. Chambers), 1864, Vol. II, p. 488.

EDINGTON, WILLIAM (d. 1366), Bishop of Winchester and Chancellor. Refused the Archbishopric of Canterbury, ostensibly on the grounds of ill-health.

The better manger

'Canterbury is the higher rack, but Winchester is the better manger'

W. Edington, bishop of Winchester, was the author of this expression, rendering this the reason of his refusal to be removed to Canterbury, though chosen thereunto. Indeed, though Canterbury be graced with a higher honour, the revenues of Winchester . . . are more advantageous to gather riches thereon. The proverb is applicable to such who prefer a wealthy privacy before a less profitable dignity.

SOURCE: Thomas Fuller, *The Worthies of England*, 1662, 1952 edition, George Allen & Unwin, p. 202.

EDUCATION, GLIMPSES OF.

i. *A schoolmaster in America, c.* 1765 (an Englishman, Mr. Dove, in Philadelphia)

He had another contrivance for boys who were late in their morning attendance. This was to dispatch a committee of five or six scholars for them, with a bell and lighted lantern; and in this odd equipage, in broad daylight, the bell all the time tingling, were they escorted through the streets to school. As Dove affected a strict regard to justice in his dispensations of punishment, and always professed a willingness to have an equal measure of it meted out to himself in case of his transgressing, the boys took him at his word; and one morning, when he had overstaid his time, he found himself waited on in the usual form. He immediately admitted the justice of the procedure, and, putting himself behind the lantern and bell, marched with great solemnity to school, to the no small gratification of the boys and entertainment of the spectators.

SOURCE: Alexander Graydon's reminiscences; quoted Clifton Johnson, *Old-Time Schools and School-Books*, 1904, Dover Publications edition, 1963, pp. 41–42.

ii. *Another schoolmaster in America, c.* 1770 (a Scotsman, Mr. Beveridge)

He was diligent and laborious in his attention to his school; and had he possessed the faculty of making himself beloved by his scholars, and of exciting their emulation and exertion, nothing would have been wanting in him to an entire qualification for his office. . . .

Various were the rogueries that were played upon him; but, the most audacious of all was the following. At the hour of convening in the afternoon (that being the most convenient, from the circumstance of Mr. Beveridge being usually a little beyond the time) the bell having rung, the ushers being at their posts, and the scholars arranged in their classes, three or four of the conspirators conceal themselves without, for the purpose of observing the motions of their victim. He arrives, enters the school, and is permitted to proceed until he is supposed to have nearly reached his chair at the upper end of the room, when instantly the door and every window-shutter is closed. Now, shrouded in utter darkness, the most hideous yells that can be conceived are sent forth from at least three score of throats; and Ovids and Virgils and Horaces, together with the more heavy metal of dictionaries, are hurled without remorse at the astonished preceptor, who, groping and crawling under cover of the forms, makes the best of his way to the door. When attained, and light restored, a death-like silence ensues. Every boy is at his lesson: no-one has had a hand or a voice in the recent atrocity. What, then, is to be done? and who shall be chastised?

SOURCE: ibid., pp. 42–43.

iii. *A barring-out in New Hampshire, c.* 1820

At the close of the morning session of the first of January, and perhaps on some other day that the big boys chose to consider or make a holiday, the moment the master left the house in quest of his dinner, the little ones were started homeward, the doors and windows suddenly and securely barricaded, and the older pupils, thus fortified against intrusion, proceeded to spend the afternoon in play and hilarity. I have known a master to make a desperate struggle for admission, but the odds were too great. If he appealed to the neighboring fathers, they were apt to advise him to desist, and let matters take their course. I recollect one instance, however, where a youth was shut out who, procuring a piece of board, mounted from a fence to the roof of the schoolhouse and covered the top of the chimney nicely with his board. Ten minutes thereafter, the house was filled with smoke, and its inmates, opening the doors and windows, were glad to make terms with the outsider.

SOURCE: Horace Greeley's reminiscences; quoted ibid., pp. 125–126.

iv. *A text-book inscription*

> *If there should be another flood,*
> *Then to this book I'd fly;*
> *If all the earth should be submerged*
> *This book would still be dry.*

SOURCE: quoted from some early American text-books, Clifton Johnson, *Old-Time Schools and School-Books*, 1904, Dover Publications edition, 1963, p. 157.

L

v. *The omnibus relative*

The discipline at Christ's Hospital in my time was ultra-Spartan; all domestic ties were to be put aside.

'Boy!' I remember Bowyer saying to me once when I was crying the first day of my return after the holidays, 'Boy! the school is your father! Boy! the school is your mother! Boy! the school is your brother! the school is your sister! the school is your first-cousin, and your second-cousin, and all the rest of your relations! Let's have no more crying!'

SOURCE: Samuel Taylor Coleridge, *Table Talk*, August 16, 1832.

iv. *Behaviour for the young,* 1773

Some precepts from the note-book of a boy of good family.

Of Behaviour at Home to your Parents

1. Having come softly up to the Door, and knocked at it once, and not too loud, as soon as it is opened go in.
2. Take off your Hat as soon as you are entered, and don't touch it again till you are going out.
3. As soon as you come into the Room to your Parents and Relations, bow, and stand near the Door till you are told where to sit.
4. When any one calls to you, go up to him without running; when you are come near him, stand still, & fixing your Eyes modestly on his Face, wait till he is pleased to speak to you.
5. Never sit down till you are desired; and then not till you have bowed, and answered what was asked you.
6. Be careful how you speak to those who have not spoken to you.
7. Never speak to any one while he is talking with another nor while he is reading, nor when he is busy.

10. Begin what you would say with Sir or Madam, and when you have spoken, wait patiently for an Answer.
11. Before you speak, make a bow, or Curtsey, and when you have received your Answer, make another, but with Discretion.

12. You may be sure that whatever your Parents bid you to do is right; therefore do it with good Will and Readiness.

14. When in the room with your parents or Relations never slip out privately, for that is mean and unhandsome.

SOURCE: manuscript note-book of Richard Hickman, 1773, in editor's collection.

vii. *The penalty of false spelling*

I must tell you that orthography, in the true sense of the word, is so absolutely necessary for a man of letters, or a gentleman, that one false spelling may fix a ridicule upon him for the rest of his life. And I know a man of quality who never recovered the ridicule of having spelled *wholesome* without the *w*.

SOURCE: Lord Chesterfield to his son, 1750.

viii. *A happy childhood, c.* 1785

Lady Jane Grey speaks of the severities to which she was subjected by her noble parents.* I had neither nips, nor bobs, nor pinches; but I experienced what I thought much worse. It was the fashion then for children to wear iron collars round the neck, with a backboard strapped over the shoulders: to one of these I was subjected from my sixth to my thirteenth year. It was put on in the morning, and seldom taken off till late in the evening; and I generally did my lessons standing in stocks, with this stiff collar round my neck. At the same time I had the plainest possible food, such as dry bread and cold milk. I never sat on a chair in my mother's presence. Yet I was a very happy child; and when relieved from my collar, I not unseldom manifested my delight by starting from our hall door, and taking a run for at least half a mile through the woods which adjoined our pleasure-grounds.

SOURCE: Sophia Kelly (edit.), *The Life of Mrs. Sherwood* . . . 1854, p. 39.

* See entry for GREY, LADY JANE,

ix. *The most impressive sight in America*

Mr. Matthew Arnold was greatly struck by this democratic government of our reading-room when he was in Boston. He came in here one day and saw a little barefooted newsboy sitting in one of the best chairs in the reading-room, enjoying himself apparently for dear life. The great essayist was completely astounded.

'Do you let bare footed boys in this reading-room?' he asked. 'You would never see such a sight as that in Europe. I do not believe there is a reading-room in all Europe in which that boy, dressed as he is, would enter.'

Then Mr. Arnold went over to the boy, engaged him in conversation, and found that he was reading the *Life of Washington*, that he was a young gentleman of decidedly anti-British tendencies, and, for his age, remarkably well informed. Mr. Arnold remained talking with the youngster for some time, and, as he came back to our desk, the great Englishman said:

'I do not think I have been so impressed with anything that I have seen since arriving in this country as I am now with meeting that barefooted boy in this reading-room.'

SOURCE: the Librarian of the Boston Public Library, *Book-Lore*, September 1887.

EDWARD, called **THE CONFESSOR** (d. 1066). A pious king who, an early chronicler says, 'used to stand with lamb-like meekness and tranquil mind at the holy offices of the divine mysteries and masses', taking no notice of anyone unless directly addressed, and very simply dressed. It was only on special occasions, and prompted by his queen (Edith, daughter of Earl Godwin) that he would dress up in all his royal finery.

i. *The simple suit*

When a simple religious man, seeing him meanly attired, wondering thereat, asked him why he, being so potent a Prince, wore so simple a suit, he answered:

'Father, father, you know how God regardeth garments. What can I do more in royal robes than in this my gaberdine?'

SOURCE: William Camden, *Remains Concerning Britain*, 7th impression 1674, p. 281.

Note: 'gaberdine' is an interesting word. Often used today for school mackintoshes, in the Middle Ages it was a long coarse cloak or gown, and originally meant a pilgrim's frock.

ii. *Edward the Confessor's crucifix*

On June 11, 1685, a plank fell on Edward the Confessor's shrine in Westminster Abbey and broke away some of the stone. A singing-man named Charles Taylor put his hand in the shrine and, after fumbling about, drew out 'a Crucifix richly adorned and enamelled, and a gold chain twenty-four inches long the which I immediately showed to my friends'. Several weeks later Taylor had an interview with James II and handed over his treasure.

'... and being no sooner introduced to his Majesty's closet (when I had the honour to kiss his Royal hand) but upon my knees I delivered them with my own hands to him, which his Most Sacred Majesty was pleased to accept with much satisfaction.'

SOURCE: Evelyn's *Diary; Autobiography of Bishop Patrick*, 1839; *A House of Kings* (edit. Edward Carpenter, John Baker, 1966, p. 193.

EDWARD I (1239–1307), King of England; nicknamed 'Longshanks'. Edward was 6 feet 2 inches tall, much above the average for his time. He could leap fully armed into the saddle without the aid of stirrups and was immensely strong.

i. *The poisoned dagger*

Eleanor, wife to King Edward the first, a most vertuous and wise woman, when he took his long and dangerous journey into the Holy Land, would not be dissuaded to tarry at home, but would needs accompany him, saying:

'Nothing must part them whom God hath joined, and the way to Heaven is as near in the Holy Land (if not nearer) as in England or Spain.'

When King Edward the First was in the Holy Land, he was stabbed with a poisoned dagger by a Saracen, and through the rancour of the poison the wound was judged incurable by his physicians. This good Queen Eleanor, his wife, who had accompanied him in that journey, endangering her own life, in loving affection saved his life and eternised her own honour; for she daily and nightly sucked out the rank poison, which love made sweet to her, and thereby effected that which no art durst attempt, to his safety, her joy, and the comfort of all England.

SOURCE: Ptolemy of Lucca's *Ecclesiastical History*; this version from William Camden, *Remains Concerning Britain*, 7th impression, 1674, p. 283. Doubts have been cast upon the authenticity of this very popular—and very early—story. The attempted assassination was probably genuine enough, but there are grounds for thinking it was Edward's friend and secretary, Otto de Grandison, who sucked the poison. Another version, with a respectable ancestry, has it that the flesh was cut from the poisoned arm and that Queen Eleanor had to be carried protesting from the tent, so that she should not see the doctor at work. This is the version accepted by Philip Lindsay in *Kings of Merry England*, 1935:

In warding off the blow he had gashed his arm on the dagger point, and within a few days the poison had swollen and blackened the flesh, and Edward was so certain of death that he signed his will.

'What are you whispering about?' he demanded of the surgeons, as with solemn faces they consulted; 'can I not be cured? Tell me, do not be afraid.'

An English surgeon answered:

'You can be cured, but only with immense pain.'

'Are you certain of the cure if I submit?' asked Edward, and the surgeon told him:

'I will answer for it.'

Edward immediately gave himself wholly to their skill, but first he was asked if he had any with him whom he could trust, and on his remarking that he had several, including his brother Edmund, they were told:

'Then take this lady away and do not let her see her lord again until I say.'

Weeping and half-refusing to go, the lady, Eleanor, was led outside.

'It is better, lady,' she was told, 'that you should weep than the whole of England.'

ii. The King is 'lifted' at Easter

In Lancashire, Staffordshire, Warwickshire, and some other parts of England there prevails this custom of *heaving* or *lifting* at Easter-tide. This is performed mostly in the open street, though sometimes it is insisted on and submitted to inside the house. People form into parties . . . and from everyone *lifted* or *heaved* they extort a contribution.

The late Mr. Lysons [Samuel Lysons, keeper of the Tower of London records] read to the Society of Antiquaries an extract from a roll in his custody . . . which contains a payment to certain ladies and maids of honour for taking Edward I in his bed at Easter; from whence it has been presumed that he was *lifted* on the authority of that custom, which is said to have prevailed among all ranks throughout the kingdom. The usage is a vulgar commemoration of the resurrection which the festival of Easter celebrates.

SOURCE: William Hone, *The Every-day Book*, 1830, Vol. 1.

iii. The King's son is treated with red cloth for small-pox

Let scarlet cloth be taken, and let him who is suffering small-pox be entirely wrapped in it or in some other red cloth. I did this when the son of the illustrious King of England suffered from small-pox; I took care that all about his bed should be red, and that cure succeeded very well.

SOURCE: John of Gaddesden (1280?–1361), *Rosa Anglica*, first printed Pavia, 1492; Augsburg, 1595, lib. ii, p. 1050. J. J. Jusserand, who quoted this with a smile in *English Wayfaring Life in the Middle Ages*, adds a footnote (13th impression, 1929, p.186):

'To which Gaddesden, I now make humble apologies: for . . . modern discoveries, those especially of Niels Finsen, of Copenhagen, a man of the truest worth, whom I saw at work, have justified him. Red light, it has been found, really has an influence on the healing of the scars left by small-pox, and even of the disease itself.'

iv. *The first Prince of Wales—destruction of an anecdote*

Still more frequently repeated is the myth that Edward I presented his infant son to the Welsh chieftains as their prince at Caernarvon Castle in 1284. The future Edward II was certainly born in the unfinished castle, but this was of no particular significance, as Edward I and the Queen had lived much in Wales and the border counties in the previous two years. Edward II was, in fact, the fourth son of Edward I, and at the time of his birth his elder brother, Alfonso, was still alive. It was Alfonso's death later in the year which made Edward heir to the throne. He was not created Prince of Wales until 1301 [when he was about 17 years old] and this was not done at Caernarvon but at Lincoln. Moreover it was to Chester that the Welsh chieftains came to pay homage to their new prince.

SOURCE: *Common Errors in History*, Historical Association, 1946, p. 4.

EDWARD III (1312–1377), King of England.

i. *King Edward III gives his charter to a hanged man*

About this time [i.e. 1363] one Walter Winkeburne was for some capital crime or other so violently prosecuted by one of the Knights Hospitallers that, whether guilty or no, he received judgment to be hanged, and hanged he was. Being after such a time cut down, as he was carried for dead to be laid on the church-yard of St. Sepulchre at Leicester, he began to revive in the cart, and being thereupon carried for safeguard into the church, was there perfectly recovered, and carefully watched by the clergy of Leicester, lest the Sheriff should take him away to hang him again; while some were sent to tell the King, who was then in those parts, of the adventure, and to beg his charter of pardon, since the person had in a manner satisfied the law, and that his miraculous recovery might seem no bad argument of his innocency.

Accordingly, King Edward presently after granted him his charter in the Abbey of Leicester, saying these words:

'Since God hath given him life, I'll give him my charter.'

SOURCE: Joshua Barnes, *The History of that Most Victorious Monarch Edward III . . .*, 1688, p. 632.

ii. *Queen Philippa saves the burghers of Calais*, 1347

Doubts have been cast on the truth of this incident, related by Froissart only a few years after the event, on the grounds that no other contemporary chronicler mentions it. But Froissart, in fact, had it from Jehan le Bel, writing about half a century before, soon after the event. Another version has it that Edward III kept as prisoners the governor, 15 knights and a number of citizens, and loaded them with presents before sending them to England. The king demanded the unconditional surrender of Calais and its citizens to do whatever he wished with. Many of his followers suggested he should be more merciful, including the gallant Sir Walter Manny.

Upon which the king replied:

'Gentleman, I am not so obstinate as to hold my opinion alone against you all. Sir Walter, you will inform the governor of Calais that the only grace he must expect of me is that six of the principal citizens of Calais march out of the town, with bare heads and feet, with ropes round their necks, and the keys of the town and castle in their hands. These six persons shall be at my absolute disposal, and the remainder of the inhabitants pardoned.'

Sir Walter returned to the lord de Vienne, who was waiting for him on the battlements, and told him all that he had been able to gain from the king. . . . This information caused the greatest lamentations and despair; so that the hardest heart would have had compassion on them; even the lord de Vienne wept bitterly.

After a short time, the most wealthy citizen of the town, by name Eustace de St. Pierre, rose up and said:

'Gentlemen, both high and low, it would be a very great pity to suffer so many people to die through famine, if any means could be found to prevent it; and it would be highly meritorious in the eyes of our Saviour if such misery could be averted. I have such faith and trust in finding grace before God if I die to save my townsmen, that I name myself as first of the six.'

... Another citizen, very rich and respected, rose up and said he would be second to his companion Eustace; his name was John Daire. After him, James Wisant, who was very rich in merchandize and lands, offered himself as companions to his two cousins, as did Peter Wisant, his brother. Two others then named themselves, which completed the number demanded by the king of England. ...

When Sir Walter Manny had presented these six citizens to the king, they fell upon their knees and, with uplifted hands, said:

'Most gallant king, see before you six citizens of Calais, who have been capital merchants, and who bring you the keys of the castle and of the town. We surrender ourselves to your absolute will and pleasure, in order to save the remainder of the inhabitants of Calais, who have suffered much distress and misery. Condescend, therefore, out of the nobleness of your mind, to have mercy and compassion upon us.'

The king eyed them with angry looks (for he hated much the people of Calais for the great losses he had formerly suffered from them at sea) and ordered their heads to be stricken off. All present intreated the king that he would be more merciful to them, but he would not listen to them. ... The queen of England, who at that time was very big with child, fell on her knees and, with tears, said:

'Ah, gentle sir, since I have crossed the sea with very great danger to see you, I have never asked you one favour. Now, I most humbly ask as a gift, for the sake of the Son of the blessed Mary, and for your love to me, that you will be merciful to these six men.'

The king looked at her for some time in silence, and then said:

'Ah, lady, I wish you had been anywhere else than here. You have entreated in such a manner that I cannot refuse you. I therefore give them to you, to do as you please with them.'

The queen conducted the six citizens to her apartments, and

had the halters taken from round their necks, after which she
new clothed them and served them with a plentiful dinner.

SOURCE: Sir John Froissart's *Chronicles of England, France, Spain* . . .
   and other places adjoining, first translated into English by John
   Bouchier, Lord Berners, 1525; this version from Thomas Johnes's
   translation, 1806, Vol. ii, pp. 223–227.

iii. *A grand-stand collapses under Queen Philippa*

In 1329, a great tournament was held in Cheapside, London,
'where the stony street was well cover'd with sand', when,
prompted by Edward III, thirteen knights offered 'for three days
together, to perform feats of arms against all comers whatsoever'.
A great wooden scaffold, or grand-stand, designed like a tower,
had been erected across the street, for Queen Philippa and the
other distinguished ladies from all over the realm.

But in the height of this recreation, there happened an accident
which had like to have proved tragical. For the stage whereon
the Queen and her ladies were placed, suddenly brake under
them, to the great affrightment of all the company; though,
by the wonderful goodness of God, it happened that no harm
at all was done.

But the King was thereby so incensed at the master workmen, that it would have proved very difficult for them to have
avoided a severe punishment, had not the noble-minded Queen
herself upon her knees requested their pardon; which be sure
the King would never have granted on any other consideration
to those who had occasioned the hazard of a lady so dear to
him.

SOURCE: Joshua Barnes, *The History of that Most Victorious Monarch
   Edward III* . . . , 1688, p. 38.

iv. *Edward III's epitaph*

> Here lies the glory of England,
> the flower of past kings and
> the pattern for those to come.
>
> (Tomb in Westminster Abbey)

See also CRÉCY and HUNDRED YEARS WAR.

EDWARD IV (1442–1483), King of England.

i. *Forty pounds for a kiss*

Edward IV was fond of extracting money from his subjects. One observer said the king was always careful to owe the leading citizens of London some 300,000 or 400,000 crowns, so that they would be anxious to ensure his life and prosperity.

He sent, among others, for an old rich widow, and asked her, with a smile, what she would give towards the prosecution of the war.

'For thy lovely face,' says she, 'thou shalt have twenty pounds.'

This being twice as much as the King expected, he gave her thanks and a kiss. Perhaps a kiss of any sort had not come near her lips for many years, but she was so delighted with the royal one that she doubled her offer and gave him forty.

SOURCE: based on Holinshed's *Chronicles*; W. Hutton, *The Battle of Bosworth Field*, 1788, Intro. li.

ii. *The King alters his views on the giving of quarter*

a. It is the custom in England, when a battle is won, to give quarter, and no man is killed, especially of the common soldiers ... King Edward told me that, in all the battles he had gained, his way was, when the victory was on his side, to mount on horse-back and cry out to save the common people and put the gentlemen to the sword, by which means none, or very few of them, escaped.

b. (At the Battle of Barnet, 1471, after Edward's return from exile in Flanders.) King Edward had resolved, at his departure from Flanders, to call out no more to spare the common soldiers and kill only the gentlemen, as he had formerly done; for he had conceived a mortal hatred against the commons of England, for having favoured the Earl of Warwick so much, and for other reasons besides, so that he spared none of them at that time.

SOURCE: *Memoirs of Philip de Commines, Lord of Argenton*, first pub. 1524.

iii. The Queen refuses to come out of Sanctuary

Elizabeth Woodville, queen of Edward IV, went into sanctuary at Westminster when Edward IV fled the country in 1470, and again in 1483, after the king's death. (See SANCTUARY for further information.) Elizabeth's son, Edward V, was born in the sanctuary of Westminster, from which Richard III made a number of efforts, at first unsuccessful, to tempt her to emerge.

'In what place could I reckon him sure [i.e. reckon the young prince safe], if he be not sure in this the sanctuary, whereof there was never tyrant yet so devilish, that durst presume to break. . . . For sooth [in truth] he hath found a goodly glose [to glose was to speak temptingly or coaxingly], by which that place that may defend a thief may not save an innocent.'

SOURCE: *The History of King Richard the Thirde, writen by Master Thomas More . . . about the yeare of our Lorde, 1513.*

iv. The Lady who danced at Edward IV's wedding

1 Aug. 1742. My Lord Bishop John Hough, Bishop of Worcester said he was told by my Lord Burlington, son to the Earl of Cork . . . that he had seen the Countess of Desmond who lived to 150, at his father's house, about seven miles from her own, where she had walked most of the way that morning, and observing her petticoat, told her it was mighty fine.

'Well, Mr. Two-shoes, I suppose you mean by that 'tis very old-fashioned; and I can tell you,' says she, 'that I danced in it at King Edward the Fourth's Wedding.'

SOURCE: *Collecteana*, 2nd series, Oxford Historical Society; quoted Hedley Hope-Nicholson, *The Mindes Delight*, Cayme Press, 1928, p. 220. Edward IV was married secretly to Elizabeth Grey in 1464 in the presence only of her mother, two gentlewomen, a priest and a boy 'who helped the priest to sing', so that the Countess of Desmond was perhaps referring to the celebrations when the wedding was later made public. For another example of a small number of lives spanning long periods of time, see FLODDEN, BATTLE OF.

EDWARD VI (1537–1553), King of England. Edward succeeded
to the throne when he was only nine years old, on the death of
Henry VIII, and died at the age of fifteen. Like the rest of the
Tudor children, he was a ready scholar, and was competent in
Latin, Greek and French, as well as being a musician and some-
thing of an astronomer.

i. *Edward VI's homework*

The British Museum has a manuscript consisting of a number of
questions 'in History and Policy for his improvement' submitted
for the king's study by William Thomas, clerk of the Council. In
all, there were 85 subjects for the young king to work at. Six are
given as a sample:

14. Whether the people commonly desire the destruction of
    him that is in authority, and what moveth them so to do?
42. What is the cause of war?
45. Whether they that fight for their own glory are good and
    faithful soldiers?
63. Whether ought more to be esteemed footmen or horsemen?
67. Whether is more to be esteemed a good Captain with a
    weak army, or a strong army with a weak Captain?
82. Whether promises made by force ought to be observed?

SOURCE: British Museum, Cottonian MSS.; whole document inc.
in Henry Ellis, *Original Letters Illustrative of English History*, 2nd
series, 1827, Vol. ii, pp. 189–195. Thomas finishes up by asking
that the questions should be kept secret, since it is better 'to keep
the principal things of wisdom secret till occasions require the
utterance'.

ii. *King Edward's perfume*

Take twelve spoonfuls of right red Rose water, the weight of
sixpence in fine powder of Sugar, and boyl it on hot Embers and
Coals softly, and the house will smell as though it were full of
Roses; but you must burn the sweet Cypress wood before, to
take away the gross air.

SOURCE: *A Queens Delight, or, The Art of Preserving, Conserving, and
Candying, as also, A Right Knowledge of making of Perfumes* . . . , 1679,
p. 78.

EDWARD VII (1841–1910), King of Great Britain.

i. *The King on parents and children*

'One of the saddest things in life,' he once said to me, 'is that nearly every man is cut off, by differences in outlook and temperament, from his parents and children. I was as fond of my father as he allowed me to be. We didn't understand one another. My mother, whom I greatly admired, hated me, because she imagined that I had hastened my father's death. I never in my life had a real heart-to-heart talk with her. Whenever we were together, either she was upbraiding me or I was chafing under her total inability to understand me and her refusal to trust me, which of course she construed into a fit of the sulks. Towards the end of her life we were mutually obnoxious, and I never left her presence without a sigh of relief.'

SOURCE: (anon.) *The Whispering Gallery, Leaves from a Diplomat's Diary*, John Lane, 1926, p. 49.

ii. *Lord Northcliffe on the King*

The greatest monarch we've ever had—on a race-course.

SOURCE: Lord Northcliffe; quoted ibid., p. 6.

iii. *The King's interest in hospitals and medicine*

He cared a great deal about the alleviation of pain and suffering. His patronage of hospitals was something which he understood not as a mere Royal duty, nor for that matter as a fad or personal fancy; it was the expression of a deeply felt attitude to life, a spontaneous and generous sympathy with suffering in all its forms. . . . I can hear the very inflexion in his voice as he said . . . about certain diseases which doctors describe as preventable:

'If preventable, why not prevented?'

SOURCE: *The Memoirs of Aga Khan*, Cassell & Co., 1954, p. 48.

EDWARD AUGUSTUS, DUKE OF KENT AND STRATH-EARN (1767–1820), fourth son of George III.

George III loses a clock

Edward, exasperated on one occasion by George III, deliberately smashed a clock much prized by the King. When the culprit was discovered, the following conversation took place:
'I did it.'
'But your Royal Highness did it by accident?'
'No, I did it intentionally.'
'But your Royal Highness regrets what you have done?'
'No, not at all.'

SOURCE: told by Doctor John Fisher, tutor to the Prince. Fisher was successively Bishop of Exeter and Salisbury, and was called by the royal children 'the great U.P.'

EDWIN, KING OF NORTHUMBRIA (585?–633), Conversion of: by Paulinus (d. 644). Paulinus was a Roman who joined Augustine in Kent and was later ordained Bishop of York. In A.D. 627, Edwin held a counsel with his chief men about embracing Christianity. His chief priest was named Coifi.

The flight of the sparrow

... Coifi immediately answered:
'O king, consider what this is which is now preached to us; for I verily declare to you, that the religion which we have hitherto professed has, as far as I can learn, no virtue in it. . . . It remains, therefore, that if upon examination you find these new doctrines, which are now preached to us, better and more efficacious, we immediately receive them without any delay.'

Another of the king's chief men, approving of his words and exhortations, presently added:
'The present life of man, O king, seems to me, in comparison of that time which is unknown to us, like to the swift flight of a sparrow through the room wherein you sit at supper in winter, with your commanders and ministers, and a good fire in the midst, whilst the storms of rain and snow prevail abroad; the sparrow, I say, flying in at one door, and immediately out at another, whilst he is within, is safe from the wintry storm; but

after a short space of fair weather, he immediately vanishes out of your sight, into the dark winter from which he had emerged. So this life of man appears for a short space, but of what went before, or what is to follow, we are utterly ignorant. If, therefore, this new doctrine contains something more certain, it seems justly to deserve to be followed.'

SOURCE: The Venerable Bede, *Historia Ecclesiastica* (first pub. Strasburg, *c.* 1475), Everyman's Library, J. M. Dent & Sons, 1910, pp. 90–91.

ELECTIONS

i. *A 1649 election*
If we must chuse a knight, let him not be a lord. We do not read in all of the Scripture of any lord was ever chosen knight of the shire for Berkshire.

SOURCE: part of an election speech by 'a well-affected tanner', standing in opposition to Philip Herbert, Lord Pembroke, at an election for a knight of the shire in April 1649; noted in Stephen Collet, *Relics of Literature*, 1823. Pembroke's reply included the sentence: 'I hate any thing that's old, except it be an old man; for Adam was an old man, and so am I, and I hate myself for being an old man; and, therefore, will love you if you'll make me a new knight.'

ii. *The King canvasses in person*
In 1780 King George III personally canvassed the Borough of Windsor against the Whig candidate, Admiral Keppel, and propitiated a silk-mercer by calling at his shop and saying,
'The Queen wants a gown—wants a gown. No Keppel! No Keppel!'

SOURCE: George W. E. Russell, *Collections and Recollections*, Smith, Elder & Co., 1903, Ch. X.

iii. *A highwaymen is enlisted to aid the Whigs*
A by-election was impending in Yorkshire, and Pitt, paying a social visit to the famous Mrs. B——, one of the Whig Queens of the West Riding—said banteringly:

M

'Well, the election is all right for us. Ten thousand guineas for the use of our side go down to Yorkshire to-night by a sure hand.'

'The devil they do!' responded Mrs. B., and that night the bearer of the precious burden was stopped by a highwayman on the Great North Road, and the ten thousand guineas were used to procure the return of the Whig candidate.

SOURCE: George W. E. Russell, *Collections and Recollections*, Smith, Elder & Co., 1903, Ch. X.

iv. *Pitt comes to Parliament*

The election of William Pitt provides a good example of the unashamed and, sometimes, almost casual patronage that could bring a man to the House.

During the Autumn of the year 1780, the Duke [of Rutland] dispatched Kirkpatrick from his house in Arlington-street to Sir James Lowther, who resided in Charles-street, Berkeley-square, with a verbal request that Sir James would do him the favour, if possible, to reserve a seat among his Boroughs for a friend of the Duke's, Mr. William Pitt, a younger son of the Earl of Chatham.

Kirkpatrick has often related to me the particulars of his interview and conversation with Sir James Lowther, whom he found in the act of shaving himself.

'Well, Kirk, what may be your business?'

'I am come from Arlington-street,' answered he, 'with a message to you from the Duke.'

'What are his commands?' replied Sir James.

'He requests that you will oblige him by reserving a seat for a friend of his, Mr. Pitt . . . a young gentleman of vast abilities, whom the Duke wishes to bring into Parliament.'

'I wish he had sent sooner to me,' returned he. 'Is he very anxious about it, Kirk?'

'Exceedingly so, you may be assured.'

'Then go back to the Duke,' was the reply, 'and tell him that I will see him in the course of this day, and we will talk the matter over together.'

SOURCE: Sir N. William Wraxall, *Historical Memoirs of My Own Time*, 1815, Vol. II, pp. 69–70.

As a result of the promised conversation, Pitt was returned for Appleby, in Westmorland. After a silence of some five weeks, he immediately claimed the attention of the House in his first speech, and Burke remarked: 'He's not merely a chip of the old block, but the old block itself.'

v. *Exertions of a Duchess*

The personal exertions made by the Duchess of Devonshire in favour of Charles Fox, during the contested election for Westminster, in 1784, are well known. Accompanied by her sister, Lady Duncannon, she visited the abodes of the humblest amongst the electors; she dazzled and enslaved them by the fascination of her manners, the power of her beauty, and the influence of her high rank; and is known, on more than one occasion, to have carried with her the meanest one, drunk, to the hustings in her carriage.

The fact of her having purchased the vote of a stubborn butcher by a kiss, is, we believe, undoubted. It was during these scenes that the Irish mechanic paid Her Grace the well-known compliment: gazing with admiration at her beautiful countenance, he said:

'I could light my pipe at her eyes.'

SOURCE: John Timbs, *A Century of Anecdote, 1760–1860.*

vi. *One day's election expenses*, 1813

Charges of ONE DAY'S EXPENSES at a small POT HOUSE at Ilchester, in the contest for the county of Somerset, in 1813.

353 bottles rum and gin	at 6s.	£105	18	0
57 bottles French brandy	at 10s. 6	29	18	6
514 gallons beer . .	at 2s. 8	68	18	8
792 dinners . . .	at 2s. 6	99	0	0
		£304	17	2

SOURCE: quoted, *The Percy Anecdotes, 1820–1823.*

vii. *The ablest man on a canvas*

When a report was circulated that Sir Joshua Reynolds [portrait painter] was to stand for the borough of Plympton on the next occasion of an election, the . . . club-men and gentlemen generally laughed at the idea of an artist, or of a literary man, presuming to have a chance to get into the House of Commons.

'He is not to be laughed at, however,' said Selwyn; 'he may very well succeed in being elected, for Sir Joshua is the ablest man I know on a canvas.'*

SOURCE: John Timbs, *A Century of Anecdote, 1760–1860.*

viii. *Captain R. H. Gronow's Election for Stafford,* 1832

I had plenty of money in those days, and was determined that no-one should outbid me for the support of these worthy and independent gentlemen, so I set to work to bribe every man, woman and child in the ancient borough of Stafford. I engaged numerous agents, opened all the public houses which were not already taken by my opponents, gave suppers every night to my supporters, kissed all their wives and children, drank their health in every sort of abominable mixture, and secured my return against great local interest.

SOURCE: *The Reminiscences and Recollections of Captain Gronow,* 1892, abridged edition by John Raymond, Bodley Head, 1964, p. 214.

ix. *The candidate who was worn away*

His [Lord John Russell's] massive head and shoulders gave him when he sate the appearance of greater size, and when he rose to his feet the diminutive stature caused a feeling of surprise. Sydney Smith declared that when Lord John first contested Devonshire, the burly electors were disappointed by the exiguity of their candidate, but were satisfied when it was explained to them that he had once been much larger, but was

* George Selwyn's pun raises an interesting etymological point. The verb 'to canvass', meaning to seek votes, really means to 'sift through canvas', i.e. to sift the votes.

worn away by the anxieties and struggles of the Reform Bill of 1832.

SOURCE: George W. E. Russell, *Collections and Recollections*, Smith, Elder & Co., 1903, Ch. II.

x. *Trouble in Tottenham*

An election meeting with Charles Bradlaugh (1833–1891). Bradlaugh was a free-thinker who, on election to Parliament, several times refused to swear on the Bible and was on different occasions unseated, ejected, expelled and excluded. He was finally allowed to take his seat in 1886.

... I had a most amusing encounter with Mr. Bradlaugh at Tottenham. Bradlaugh lived there and was a considerable power amongst the extremists. He had been heavily defeated in a Parliamentary contest at Northampton a day or two before our meeting. This defeat did not improve his temper or that of his followers. As soon as I had spoken, he came from the far end of the hall, where his followers were concentrated, close up to the platform, and he began in a loud and hectoring manner to put to me the catch Radical catechism. Suddenly a man, as much bigger than Bradlaugh as Bradlaugh was than myself, got up with a huge club and said:

'Give me the signal, my lord, and I will crack this infernal scoundrel's skull.'

A perfect pandemonium ensued. Bradlaugh's people tried to come to their hero's rescue, my people keeping them back. Bradlaugh and the big man both remained immovable, but Bradlaugh was furtively watching out of the corner of his eye the big club over his head, and the holder of it was watching intently for me to give the signal for an onslaught. The tension was broken by a big Irish parson who was Rector of Tottenham, and who had had many an encounter with Bradlaugh. He jumped up and began to exorcise Bradlaugh with tongue and fists as if he were the devil. I was afraid he would strike Bradlaugh, so I got hold of one end of the very long tails of the orthodox parson's frock-coat. One of my uncles seized the end of the other tail, and the result of our combined effort was that the coat split right to the neck, leaving us each with a coat-tail in our hands.

SOURCE: Lord George Hamilton, *Parliamentary Reminiscences and Reflections, 1868–1885*, John Murray, 1917.

ELIOT, JOHN (1604–1690), called the 'Indian Apostle'; emigrated to America, 1631; preached to the Indians in their own tongue and translated books, including the Bible, into the dialect of the Massachusetts Indians.

A call to the unconverted

WEHKOMAONGANOO ASQUAM PEANTOGIG
KAH ASQUAM QUINNUPPEGIG TOKONOGQUF
MA HCHE WOSKECHE PEANTAMWOG
ONK WOH SAMPWUTTEAHAE PEANTAMWOG
   WUTANAKAUFUONK
WUNNETU NOH NOH NOHTOMPEANTOG
USSOWESO MR RICHARD BAXTER

SOURCE: Title of Eliot's Red Indian translation of Richard Baxter's *Call to the Unconverted*, 1657.

ELIZABETH I (1558–1603), Queen of England.

i. *Elizabeth, Prisoner*

At the beginning of Mary's reign, the young Princess Elizabeth was confined first in the Tower, then at Woodstock Palace, Oxfordshire, on suspicion of complicity in Thomas Wyatt's rebellion. While there, she scratched the following inscription on a window pane with a diamond:

> *Much suspected, of me*
> *nothing proved can be,*
> *Quoth Elizabeth, Prisoner.*

SOURCE: quoted Ian Dunlop, *Palaces & Progresses of Elizabeth I*, Jonathan Cape, 1962, p. 15.

ii. *Essex gets a box on the ear*

The Queen deals with the insolence of Robert Devereux, second Earl of Essex.

There followed . . . a pretty warm dispute between the Queen and Essex, about the choice of some fit and able persons to superintend the affairs of Ireland. . . . The Queen looked upon Sir William Knollys, uncle to Essex, as the most proper person for that charge; and Essex contended, on the other side, that Sir George Carew would much better become that post . . .: and when the Queen could by no means be persuaded to approve his choice, he quite forgot himself and his duty, and turned his back upon his Sovereign in a kind of contempt. The Queen was not able to bear this insolence, and so bestowed on him a box on the ear, and bade him 'go and be hanged'.

He immediately clapped his hand on his sword, and the Lord Admiral stepping in between, he swore a great oath that he neither could nor would put up with an affront of that nature, nor would he have taken it at the hands of Henry the Eighth himself; and, in a great passion, he immediately withdrew from the Court.

SOURCE: William Camden, *Annals of the Reign of Queen Elizabeth*, pub. 1615 and 1628; David Jardine, *Criminal Trials*, 1832, pp. 293-294.

iii. *The silk-knit stockings*

Queen Elizabeth, in 1561, was presented with a pair of black silk knit stockings by her silk-woman, Mrs. Montague, and thenceforth she never wore cloth hose any more.

SOURCE: William Howell, *An Institution of General History . . .* , 1661; quoted *A Book of Days* (edit. R. Chambers,) 1864.

The silk knit stockings were one of the innumerable gifts to the Queen at the New Year, when everyone, from the highest ministers and courtiers to the lowliest employee, gave a present according to their means and ability. The gifts were annually recorded on a great roll, signed by the Queen and her chief officers, and her gifts to others were likewise entered.

The 1596/7 roll contained, at one end of the scale, a magnificently jewelled pair of gold bracelets from the Earl of Essex, a cloak of

'black Velvett the grounde gold with a flatte lace of Venis silver
about yt' from Lord Bacon; and, at the other, some preserved
plums, a box of lozenges, and, from the Master Cook, a confection
of marchpane [marzipan]. The Queen's gifts in this roll consisted
entirely of gilt plate, whose weight varied according to the status
of the recipient.

The 1596/7 roll measures 13 feet by 15½ inches and was sold by
auction in London in 1967. They are known to have been compiled for over 100 years, but very few have survived.

iv. *Queen Elizabeth admonishes the preacher*

Preachers who overstepped discretion, sometimes found themselves sharply pulled up. Nowell, Dean of St. Paul's, preaching
a Lenten sermon before a large congregation at Court in 1565,
inveighed against a recent Catholic book dedicated to the
Queen, and went on to attack images and idolatry, an attack
which in the circumstances was palpably meant for the crucifix
in the royal Chapel.

'Do not talk about that!' Elizabeth called out; and as he went
on, not hearing her:

'Leave that!' she cried, raising her voice, 'it has nothing to
do with your subject, and the matter is now threadbare.'

SOURCE: J. E. Neale, *Queen Elizabeth*, Jonathan Cape, 1934, p.
216.

v. *Queen Elizabeth rebukes an Archbishop's wife*

Queen Elizabeth did not approve of married clergy. On one
occasion she found it necessary to thank the wife of Matthew
Parker (1504–1575), Archbishop of Canterbury, and said:

'Madam I may not call you; mistress I am ashamed to call
you; and so I know not what to call you; but, howsoever, I
thank you.'

SOURCE: Sir John Harington, *A briefe View of the State of the
Church of England* ... 1653. Parker married Margaret Harlestone
of Mattishall, Norfolk, to whom he was betrothed for seven years,
when the law against the clergy marrying was amended by the
Lower House of Convocation. Margaret was an admirable wife—
so much so that another Bishop inquired whether she had a sister!

vi. *Sir John Harington describes the Queen*

... when she smiled it was pure sunshine, that everyone did choose to bask in, if they could: but anon came a storm from a sudden gathering of clouds, and the thunder fell in wondrous manner on all alike.

SOURCE: Sir John Harington, *Nugae Antiquae* (first pub., 1769). Harington was Queen Elizabeth's godson.

vii. *The heart and stomach of a King*

Let tyrants fear. I have always so behaved myself that, under God, I have placed my chiefest strength and safeguard in the loyal hearts and good will of my subjects; and therefore I am come amongst you, as you see, at this time, not for my recreation and disport, but being resolved, in the midst and heat of the battle, to live or die amongst you all, to lay down for my God, and for my kingdom, and for my people, my honour and my blood, even in the dust. I know I have the body of a weak and feeble woman, but I have the heart and stomach of a king, and of a king of England, too.

SOURCE: speech to the army at Tilbury, August 8, 1588, on the approach of the Armada.

viii. *The Queen lectures the Polish Ambassador in Latin*

In 1597 Sigismund of Poland sent an ambassador whose arrogant demeanour roused Elizabeth to an extempore display of her scholarship.

He was brought in attired in a long robe of black velvet, well jewelled and buttoned, and came to kiss her Majesty's hands ... he straight retired, ten yards off, and then began his oration aloud in Latin, with such a gallant countenance as in my life I never beheld.

The ambassador complained that, whereas the king of Poland had always received Elizabeth's merchants and subjects with friendship, she permitted his 'to be spoiled without restitution, not for lack of knowledge of the violences, but out of mere injustice'. He concluded that 'if her Majesty would not reform it, he would'.

To this I sweare by the living God that her Majesty made one
of the best answers extempore in Latin that ever I heard, being
much moved to be so challenged in public:

'Is this the business your King hath sent you about? Surely I
can hardly believe that, if the King himself were present, he
would have used such a language; for if he should I must have
thought that his being a King of not many years . . . may
haply leave him uninformed of that course which his father and
ancestors have taken with us, and which peradventure shall be
observed by those that shall live to come after him.

'And as for you, although I perceive you have read many
books to fortify your arguments in this case, yet I am apt to
believe that you have not lighted upon the chapter that
prescribeth the form to be used between Kings and Princes.'

SOURCE: letter from Sir Robert Cecil to the Earl of Essex, July 26,
1597. British Museum, Lansdowne MSS. Inc. in Henry Ellis,
Original Letters, Illustrative of English History, 1825, vol. iii, pp.
43–45.

Speed records that, when the Queen had finished, she turned
round to her attendants and said:

'God's death, my Lords, I have been enforced this day to scour
up my old Latin, that hath lain long in rusting.'

ix. *Tribute from the King of France*

She only is a king! She only knows how to rule!

SOURCE: Henry IV of France; quoted J. E. Neale, *Queen Elizabeth*,
Jonathan Cape, 1934, p. 376.

x. *The sword in the arras*

. . . she is quite disfavoured, and unattired, and these troubles
waste her much. . . . The many evil plots and designs have
overcome all her Highness' sweet temper. She walks much in her
Privy Chamber, and stamps with her feet at ill news, and thrusts
her rusty sword at times into the arras in great rage. . . . The
dangers are over, and yet she always keeps a sword by her table.

SOURCE: the Queen's godson, Sir John Harington; quoted ibid.,
p. 379. The things that had chiefly upset the Queen were the Irish
troubles, and the insurrection and execution of the Earl of Essex.

xi. *The 'Golden Speech'*

... though God hath raised me high, yet this I account the glory of my crown, that I have reigned with your loves. ... It is not my desire to live or reign longer than my life and reign shall be for your good. And though you have had, and may have, many mightier and wiser princes sitting in this seat, yet you never had, nor shall have, any that will love you better.

SOURCE: speech to her last Parliament, November 30, 1601.

xii. *The Queen's legacy*

She made no will, nor gave anything away, so that they which come after shall find a well-stored jewel house and a rich wardrobe of more than 2000 gowns with all things else answerable.

SOURCE: John Chamberlain in a letter to Dudley Carleton, March 30, 1603.

xiii. *The aged Queen looks in a mirror*

It is credibly reported that not long before her death she had a great apprehension of her own age and declination by seeing her face (then lean and full of wrinkles) truly represented to her in a glass, which she a good while very earnestly beheld: perceiving thereby how often she had been abused by flatterers (whom she held in too great estimation) that had informed her the contrary.

SOURCE: Sloane MSS., British Museum; inc. in Henry Ellis, *Original Letters Illustrative of English History*, 1827, 2nd. series, Vol. III, pp. 193-194.
See also BACON, SIR NICHOLAS; CAREY, SIR ROBERT; CECIL, WILLIAM; DEVEREUX, ROBERT; and RALEGH, SIR WALTER.

ELIZABETH, PRINCESS (1618–1680), daughter of Frederick V, Elector Palatine and Elizabeth, daughter of James I.

The red-nosed Princess

My sister, who was called Madame Elizabeth, had black hair, a dazzling complexion, a well-shaped forehead, beautiful cherry lips, and a sharp aquiline nose, which was apt to turn red. She loved study, but all her philosophy could not save her from vexation when her nose was red. At such times she hid herself from the world. I remember that my sister, Princess Louise, who was not so sensitive, asked her on one such unlucky occasion to come upstairs to the Queen, as it was the usual hour for visiting her. Princess Elizabeth said:

'Would you have me go with this nose?'

The other replied:

'Will you wait till you get another?'

SOURCE: Elizabeth's sister, Sophia, Electress of Hanover, *Memoirs*, 1888.

ELIZABETHAN LONDON.

A school for pickpockets in London, 1585

Fagin's school for pickpockets in Dickens's *Oliver Twist* was no new development. Lord Treasurer Burghley received a very full account of one from William Fleetwood, Recorder of London, in 1585.

Amongst our travels this one tumbled out by the way, that one Wotton, a gentleman born, and sometime a merchant of good credit, who falling by time into decay, kept an ale-house at Smart's Key [Quay] near Billingsgate, and after, for some misdemeanour being put down, he reared up a new trade of life, and in the same house he procured all the cut-purses about this city to repair to his said house.

There, was a school house set up to learn young boys to cut purses. There were hung up two devices, the one was a pocket, the other was a purse. The pocket had in it certain counters and was hung about with hawk's bells, and over the top did hang a little sacring [=sanctus] bell; and he that could take out a counter without any noise was allowed to be a *public foyster* [see below]: and he that could take a piece of silver out of the purse without the noise of any of the bells, he was adjudged a *judicial nipper* [see below].

SOURCE: British Museum, Landsdowne MSS.; Henry Ellis, *Original Letters Illustrative of English History*, 1825, Vol. ii, pp. 297–298.

The manuscript also contains an interesting note on Elizabethan thieves' slang. To *foyste* was to cut a pocket; to *nip* was to cut a purse; to *lift* was to rob a shop (cf. the modern term *shoplifter*) or a gentleman's chamber; to *shave* was to steal a cloak, a sword, a silver spoon, etc., 'that is negligently looked unto'.

ERNEST AUGUSTUS, DUKE OF CUMBERLAND (1771–1851), fifth son of George III; King of Hanover from 1837.

i. *The Duke on the decline in status of Bishops*

I maintain that the first change and shock in the ecclesiastical habits was the bishops being allowed to lay aside their wigs, their purple coats, short cassocks, and stockings, and cocked hats, when appearing in public. . . . The present Bishop of Oxford was the first who persuaded George IV to be allowed to lay aside his wig, because his wife found him better-looking without it. I recollect full well . . . the Bishop of London who succeeded Bishop Porteous . . . coming to St. James's to do homage to my father . . . when Lord Sidmouth was Secretary of State, and he came into the closet, where I was at the time, and informed his majesty that the bishop was there, but that he had refused to introduce him, as he had not on a wig. Upon which I remember full well, as if it were to-day, that the king replied:

'You were perfectly right, my lord, and tell the bishop from me that until he has shaven his head, and has provided himself with a wig suitable to his garb, I shall not admit him into my presence. . . .'

Now, you will laugh at this anecdote; but you may depend upon it that nothing has contributed to the lowering of respect for the bishops from the vulgar than this change. . . . Times are so changed that I have myself seen the present Bishop of

London attend the committee-room in the House of Lords in a black Wellington coat, with top-boots, and coming in with a hat like a butcher or coach-master.

SOURCE: letter to Lord Strangford; de Fonblanque's *Lives of the Lords Strangford*; quoted Percy Fitzgerald, *The Royal Dukes and Princesses* . . . , 1882, Vol. II.

ii. *On a lowly-born Archbishop*

Conceive! the newly-appointed Archbishop of York's father was a taylor and measured Wilkinson here and made his breeches; consequently you will agree with me he is neither born or bred a gentleman, and cannot know what thereunto belongs. . . . Westmoreland confirms this information, and also employed him as a breeches maker! Now, I ask you, is that a man fit to sit upon the bench?

SOURCE: ibid.

ETON COLLEGE. Founded by Henry VI in 1440, when he was eighteen years old: '. . . it has become a fixed purpose in our heart to found a college, in honour and in support of that our [Holy] Mother, who is so great and so holy, in the parochial church of Eton near Windsor, not far from our birthplace.'

i. *Young Paston wants his wardrobe replenished,* 1478

Also I beseech you to send me a hose cloth, one for the holy-days of some colour, and another for the working days how coarse soever it be maketh no matter, and a stomacher, and two shirts, and a pair of slippers; and if it like you that I may come with Alweder by water, and sport me with you at London a day or two this term time, then ye may let all this be till the time that I come, and then I will tell you when I shall be ready to come from Eton by the grace of God.

SOURCE: The Paston Letters, first pub. 1787–1823. William Paston is the first known 'oppidan', i.e. boarder in the town, of whom records exist.

ii. *The Sixth Form in revolt*

When I was at Eton, a circumstance occurred that threw the school first into confusion, and then into a rebellion. A boy in the sixth form, named Pigot, for some trifling offence given to Dr. Foster, was flogged. This ignominious chastisement to one so high in scholastic rank, was deemed a perfect profanation; and the flame of discontent ran like lightning through the school. I can never forget the explosion of this diminutive rebellion; when, about two hundred boys, instead of marching into school, desperately rushed into the playing fields, and thence, threw about two hundred Homers into the Thames. It was the work of an instant, done as by the motion of the manual exercise; and never before did the greatest capacity imbibe Greek half so rapidly, as old Father Thames!

Having performed this noble feat, the two hundred rebels marched to the inn at Salthill, to refresh themselves, after their fatigues. The landlord seemed astonished at such a visitation; but did what he could to provide for his guests. For myself, and forty others of the lower boys, accommodation was easily found, as we slept on the floor. In the morning, the reckoning came to one hundred and fifty pounds; but, this circumstance affected not me, for the best of all possible reasons—I had not a farthing. Recourse was, therefore, had to the late Duke of Rutland, and other boys of elevated rank, who, accordingly, suffered for their wealth. The result of the affair was that five of the ringleaders were expelled, and the rest returned home, to make peace with their parents.

SOURCE: Edward Topham; quoted *The Life and Times of Frederick Reynolds, Written by himself*, 1826.

iii. *Things unprofitable and dangerous*

No Fellow, Chaplain, Clerk, Scholar or Chorister shall grow long hair or a beard, or wear peaked shoes, or red, green or white hose. They shall not carry swords, long knives or other arms, or frequent taverns or playhouses. They shall not keep among themselves, or in the College, hounds, nets, ferrets, sparrow-hawks, or goshawks, for sport, or a monkey, a bear, a fox, a hart, a hound, a doe, or a badger, or any other strange beast that would be unprofitable or dangerous to the College.

SOURCE: Henry VI's statutes for the governance of Eton; quoted Christopher Hollis, *Eton*, Hollis & Carter, 1960, p. 6.

iv. *'Don't ever be late again'*

With the death of Mr. H. K. Marsden in his 80th year, Eton has lost one of the most engagingly eccentric and dedicated of its worthies.

I like to recall the story of the boy in his house who had a family connection with the Royal Household and was asked to tea at Windsor Castle with the King and Queen. Unfortunately he was late in arriving back at Eton and was sent for by Marsden.

Great names meant nothing to him—and schoolboy excuses even less. So the wretched boy was sent up to the Castle the next day to produce written proof that he had been where he claimed.

King George VI entered into the spirit of the game and, much amused, wrote on a piece of Windsor Castle writing paper the following note:

'Please excuse ——. He was having tea with me and it was my fault that he was late returning to Eton.

George, R.I.'

The boy took the note to Marsden, who glanced at it and said sternly: 'Don't ever be late again.'

Then he tore the note into little pieces and threw them into the waste-paper basket.

SOURCE: 'Albany', *Sunday Telegraph*, January 22, 1967.

EUGÉNIE, EMPRESS (1826–1920), wife of Napoleon III.

The visitor to the Tuileries

When my wife, Victoria, and I were staying at the hotel at Cap Martin we were invited to luncheon by the Empress Eugénie at her villa, which was close by. When we arrived, I attempted to kiss the Empress's hand, but she gently stopped me, saying: 'Non, non. Point de révérences. Le temps pour cela est passe depuis longtemps.' (*No obeisances. The time for that was over a long time ago. ...*)

The Empress's lady-in-waiting, who was also her friend and had been with her for many years, told me that when H.M. passed through Paris, she often sat on a chair in the Tuileries gardens and paid her *sou* like anyone else. I thought what a wonderful experience it must be for her who, when Empress of the French, had lived in great splendour in the Tuileries Palace, and had doubtless walked many times through those very gardens. But perhaps—who knows?—H.M. was happier sitting on a chair for which she had paid a *sou* than when she sat on the Throne.

SOURCE: The Duke of Portland, *Men, Women and Things*, Faber & Faber, 1937, p. 284.

FAIRFAX, THOMAS, third BARON FAIRFAX OF CAMERON
(1612–1671), Parliamentary General.

The General sets an example

During the operations before Naseby Fairfax had given orders that each regiment in turn was to form the rearguard. When it came to the turn of his own, the men claimed exemption on the ground that they formed the General's guard. They were as ready to fight as others, and no doubt disposed to agree that it was their part to fight better; but they held, and the military ideas of the time bore them out, that they were not to be expected to do dirty and disagreeable work, such as marching over ground which had been trampled into mud by all the rest of the army and the waggons.

Fairfax brought them to order by dismounting and placing himself at their head. They could not refuse to do what their General and Colonel was prepared to do with them.

When one remembers what the weight of the riding boots worn in those times was, and that it must have been heavy

N

marching over the roadless country much cut up by the passage of troops, it must be allowed that the General of the Parliament did not spare himself.

SOURCE: David Hannay, *The Point of Honour*; in *Ships and Men*, William Blackwood & Sons, 1910, p. 270.

FEMALE SOLDIERS AND SAILORS. There have been a number of instances of women serving undetected as soldiers and sailors for considerable periods. Among the best-known were Christian Davies (1667–1739), who enlisted under the name of Christopher Welsh in about 1693, fought at the battle of Blenheim and was wounded at Ramillies; Phoebe Hessel, who lived to be 108, and who received a bayonet wound in the arm at Fontenoy; and Hannah Snell (1723–1792) who received a pension for wounds sustained at Pondicherry.

i. *Phoebe Hessel—the oldest soldier*

Subsequently she entered the Brighton poor-house, but quitted it in 1808, when the Prince of Wales settled on her a small annuity. She obtained leave to sit at the corner of The Steine and the Marine Parade with a little basket containing sweets, pin-cushions and toys. . . . It was a point of honour among most visitors to patronise the old woman; and when a grand *fête* was organised at Brighton to celebrate the victory at Waterloo, the ex-soldier, then one hundred and two years old, was seated, as the town's oldest inhabitant, at the Vicar's right hand.

SOURCE: Lewis Melville, *Brighton: its History, its Follies, and its Fashions*, Chapman & Hall, 1909, p. 83.

ii. *Parson Woodforde goes to see Hannah Snell*

We all breakfasted, dined and slept again at Weston. I walked up to the White Hart [at Weston Longeville, Norfolk] with Mr. Lewis and Bill to see a famous Woman in Men's Clothes, by name Hannah Snell, who was 21 years as a common soldier in the Army, and not discovered by any as a woman. She went in the Army by the name of John Gray. She has a Pension from the Crown now of £18.5.0. per annum, and the liberty of wearing Men's Clothes and also a cockade in her Hat, which she still wears. . . . The forefinger of her right hand was cut off by a sword at the taking of Pondicherry

SOURCE: Rev. James Woodforde, *Diary of a Country Parson* (May 21, 1778).

Hannah also served as a sailor and marine. On one occasion, to avoid detection, she had to remove a bullet from her body herself.

iii. *The female 'powder-monkey'*

One 'powder-monkey' on board the *Victory* . . . was a woman, as came out later. She was married, and her husband was on board the ship as one of the Maltese seamen; but her sex was unknown to the rest of the crew, as she wore man's dress. She was alive in 1841, being then, we are told, 'a sturdy woman of 70'.

SOURCE: Edward Fraser, *The Sailors Whom Nelson Led*, Methuen 1913, pp. 243–244.

iv. *A baby receives the Naval General Service Medal*

It is certain that there were one or two women on board the British ships at Trafalgar. It had been so at the Glorious First of June [June 1, 1794] when a woman in H.M.S. *Tremendous* had recently become a mother. Her son, Daniel Tremendous Mackenzie, duly received the Naval General Service Medal, with the appropriate clasp, when it was issued in 1848. . . .

SOURCE: Oliver Warner, *Trafalgar*, Batsford, 1959, p. 136.

A letter on this subject appeared recently in the press:

Few of your readers may know that a Government war medal was actually awarded to a baby, and so named on the award.

Anomalous as this may seem, one Daniel Tremendous McKenzie was allotted the Naval General Service medal with bar '1st June 1794', rating 'baby', he having been on board H.M.S. *Tremendous* at the time. Yet another is recorded, that of Jane Townshend on board H.M.S. *Defiance*, with the bar 'Trafalgar'.

SOURCE: A. J. Newnham, letter in *Daily Telegraph*, 1966.

v. *'A little female tar'*

Yet there were some real cases. The Annual Register of 1807 (p. 496) records one which came out during a court martial on a certain Lieutenant Berry:

'One of the witnesses in this awful and horrible trial was a little female tar, Elizabeth Bowden, who has been on board the *Hazard* these eight months. She appeared in court in a long jacket and blue trousers.'

She masqueraded, presumably, as a Boy.* But there was certainly one who did not, and who must hold an easy record for length of deception. 'William Brown' was proved in 1815 to have served in the *Queen Charlotte* for eleven years. 'He' was a Negress and, by all accounts, a very prime seaman, successfully filling for many years the rating of Captain of the Main Top, a post given only to the most skilled and agile members of the crew.

SOURCE: Michael Lewis, *A Social History of the Navy*, George Allen & Unwin, 1960, p. 286.

FIRE-CROSS, HIGHLAND.

Call to arms

And this is the cross (as I have heard some say) of two brands' ends carried across upon spears' points, with proclamation of the time and place when and whither they shall come, with how much provision of victual. Some others say, it is a cross, painted all red, and set for certain days in the fields of that barony, whereof they will have the people to come, whereby all between sixty and sixteen, are peremptorily summoned: that if they come not with their victual, according to the time and place then appointed, all the land there is forfeited straight to the king's use. . . .

SOURCE: William Patin (Patten) (fl. 1548–1580). The method was in use by the government as late as the 17th Century, for the Diary of Lord Fountainhall (1646–1722) records: 'The fire-cross,

* 'Boy' was an official naval rating after 1794, and has little to do with age.

by order of council, is sent through the west of Fife and Kinross, as nearest Stirling, that all between sixteen and sixty might rise and oppose Argyle.'

FISHER, JOHN ARBUTHNOT, first **BARON FISHER** (1841–1920), Admiral of the Fleet; one of the greatest administrators in British naval history. His programme of reforms split the navy sharply, his own supporters being described by his opponents as in the 'Fishpond', and by himself as in the 'Blue Water school'; while he called the opposition members the 'Blue Funk school' and the 'Yellow Admirals'.

One of Fisher's chief critics was Admiral Lord Charles Beresford; one of his great supporters was Admiral Sir Percy Scott.

The 'Paintwork' quarrel

In April 1907 Beresford took up the appointment of commander-in-chief, Channel fleet. . . . In November occurred the famous 'paintwork' incident. On the fourth of that month Beresford ordered the Channel fleet to curtail its exercises and to paint ship in preparation for a forthcoming inspection by the German emperor. The cruiser *Roxburgh*, engaged in gunnery practice, sent a signal to the rear-admiral, first cruiser squadron, Percy Scott, requesting permission to continue her practice. Scott, who was well known to be in the 'Fishpond', replied by signal:

'Paintwork appears to be more in demand than gunnery, so you had better come in in time to make yourself look pretty by the 8th.'

Beresford was furious, sent for Scott, and publicly reprimanded him on the flagship's quarterdeck in front of all the officers. The Admiralty [i.e. Fisher] refused his demand for Scott to be superseded.

SOURCE: P. K. Kemp, in *Edwardian England* (edit. Simon Nowell-Smith), O.U.P., 1964, pp. 511–512.

FLODDEN, BATTLE OF (September 9, 1513).

The boy who carried arrows at Flodden Field

King William IV had spoken to a butcher at Windsor who had conversed with Charles II. What is still more remarkable, a person living in 1847, aged then about sixty-one, was frequently assured by his father that, in 1786, he repeatedly saw one Peter Garden, who died in that year at the age of 127 years; and who, when a boy, heard Henry Jenkins give evidence in a court of justice at York, to the effect that, when a boy, he was employed in carrying arrows up the hill before the battle of Flodden Field.

This battle was fought in		1513
Henry Jenkins died in 1670, at the age of	169	
Deduct for his age at the time of the battle of Flodden Field	12	
	—	
		157
Peter Garden, the man who heard Jenkins give his evidence, died at	127	
Deduct for his age when he saw Jenkins	11	
	—	
		116
The person whose father knew Peter Garden was born shortly before 1786, or 70 years since		70
		—
	A.D.	1856

In this year, 1856, Mr. Sidney Gibson, F.S.A., showed, as above, that a person living in 1786, conversed with a man that fought at Flodden Field.

SOURCE: John Timbs, *Nooks and Corners of English Life*, 1867, pp. 294–295. The *Dictionary of National Biography* records Henry Jenkins, who died in 1670. He was born at Ellerton-upon-Swale and claimed to have been born in 1501.

The parish registers of Llanmaes, near Cowbridge, Glamorganshire, contain an entry concerning the death in July 1621 of Ivan Yorath, who was about 180 years of age, and who had been a soldier at the Battle of Bosworth (1485).

FONTENOY, BATTLE OF (May 11, 1745). Fought during the War of the Austrian Succession, between Soult's troops, besieging Tournay, and a miscellaneous Allied army under the young Duke of Cumberland. After some initial success, the Allies were repulsed, the losses being very heavy on both sides.

A toast to the enemy

At last the crest of the ridge was gained and the ranks of the French battalions came suddenly into view little more than a hundred yards distant.... Closer and closer came the British, still with arms shouldered, always silent, always with the same slow, measured tread, till they advanced to within fifty yards of the French.

Then at length Lord Charles Hay of the First Guards stepped forward with flask in hand, and doffing his hat drank politely to his enemies.

'I hope, gentlemen,' he shouted, 'that you are going to wait for us to-day and not swim the Scheldt as you swam the Main at Dettingen.'

SOURCE: Sir John Fortescue, *History of the British Army*, Vol. II.

FORD, HENRY (1863–1947), American motor manufacturer.

i. *Ford makes history*

Early one morning in the winter of 1906–1907, Henry Ford dropped in at the pattern department of the Piquette Avenue plant to see me.

'Come with me, Charlie,' he said. 'I want to show you something.'

I followed him to the third floor and its north end, which was not fully occupied for assembly work. He looked about and said, 'Charlie, I'd like to have a room finished off right here in this space. Put up a wall with a door in big enough to run a car in and out. Get a good lock for the door, and when you're ready, we'll have Joe Galamb come up in here. We're going to start a completely new job.'

The room he had in mind became the maternity ward for Model T. . . .

By March, 1908, we were ready to announce the Model T, but not to produce it. On October 1 of that year the first car was introduced to the public. . . . In the next eighteen years, out of Piquette Avenue, Highland Park, River Rouge, and from assembly plants all over the United States, came 15,000,000 more.

SOURCE: Charles E. Sorensen, *My Forty Years with Ford*, W. W. Norton & Company, Inc., 1956.

ii. *Ford defines history*

History is bunk.

SOURCE: Henry Ford in the witness box during a libel suit against the *Chicago Tribune*, July 1919.

FOX, CHARLES JAMES (1749–1806), statesman.

i. *Guide to speech-making*

Charles Fox used to say as to quotation [in speeches]:

'No Greek; as much Latin as you like; and never French under any circumstances.'

SOURCE: Lord Grey, describing former Parliamentary conventions; George W. E. Russell, *Collections and Recollections*, Smith, Elder & Co., 1903, Ch. XI.

ii. *Fox the gambler*

He was an unlucky gambler, and it is said that during one memorable sitting, when he played continuously for nearly twenty-four hours, his 'most infernal luck', to use his own expression, made him lose at the rate of five hundred guineas an hour; while in the course of a very few years he squandered at the gaming-table an ample fortune, amounting to about £140,000.

Yet when the crash came Fox took it like a man; and when

his friend Beauclerk went round to see him immediately after he had lost everything, he found him sitting before a roaring wood fire and reading Herodotus with evident enjoyment. When his would-be consoler murmured some discreet and conventional words of sympathy, and expressed wonder that the ruined man could bring his mind to read Greek, Fox laughed aside the idea.

'What is a man to do?' he asked. 'When he is miserable, egad, he must keep good company!'

SOURCE: A. J. Ireland, *English Life in the Eighteenth Century*, in *Universal History of the World* (edit. J. A. Hammerton), Amalgamated Press.

iii. *Fox has his pocket picked*

I saw Lunardi make the first ascent in a balloon which had been witnessed in England. It was from the Artillery-ground. Fox was there with his brother, General F.* The crowd was immense. Fox, happening to put his hand down to his watch, found another hand upon it, which he immediately seized.

'My friend,' said he to the owner of the strange hand, 'you have chosen an occupation which will be your ruin at last.'

'O, Mr. Fox,' was the reply, 'forgive me, and let me go! I have been driven to this course by necessity alone; my wife and children are starving at home.'

Fox, always tender-hearted, slipped a guinea into the hand, and then released it. On the conclusion of the show Fox was proceeding to look what o'clock it was.

'Good G-d,' cried he, 'my watch is gone!'

'Yes,' answered General F, 'I know it is; I saw your friend take it.'

'Saw him take it! and you made no attempt to stop him?'

'Really, you and he appeared to be on such good terms with each other that I did not choose to interfere.'

SOURCE: Samuel Rogers, *Recollections*; John Timbs, *A Century of Anecdote, 1760–1860*.

* General Henry Edward Fox (1755–1811).

FOX, HENRY, first **BARON HOLLAND** (1705–1774), politician; Surveyor-General of Works, Secretary of State, Paymaster General, etc.; amassed a large fortune and achieved ends by large-scale bribery.

Reminder of the Gunpowder Plot

The Earl of Bath,* inveighing in strong terms, in the House of Lords, against the administration of Fox, afterwards Lord Holland, and Pitt (Earl of Chatham), was reminded that the latter was about to be dismissed and that Fox only would remain in office.

'This half measure,' said his Lordship, 'is the worst of all, and reminds me of the Gunpowder Plot. The Lord Chamberlain was sent to examine the vaults underneath the Parliament House, and returned with the report that he had found five-and-twenty barrels of gunpowder, but that he had removed ten of them, and hoped the remainder would do no harm!'

SOURCE: Thomas Byerley and Joseph Clinton Robertson, *The Percy Anecdotes*, 1820–1823.

FOX, JOHN (fl. 1560–1580).

The gunner who delivered 266 captives

John Fox, gunner of the *Three Half Moons*, was taken prisoner by Turkish galleys near the Straits of Gibraltar in 1563 and carried off to captivity in Alexandria where he found more than 260 other Christian prisoners, from sixteen different nations. After thirteen or fourteen years, with six companions, he planned an escape.

In the mean season, the other seven had provided them of such weapons as they could get in that house: and John Fox took him to an old rusty sword blade, without either hilt or pommel; which he made to serve his turn, in bending the hand end of the sword, instead of a pommel: and the others had got such spits and glaives as they found in the house.

---

* Sir William Pulteney, Earl of Bath (1684–1764) was a considerable orator. Sir Robert Walpole, himself no mean protagonist, said he feared Pulteney's tongue more than another man's sword.

The Keeper now being come into the house, and perceiving no light, nor hearing any noise, straightway suspected the matter: and returning backward, John Fox, standing behind the corner of the house stepped forth unto him; who perceiving it to be John Fox said:

'O Fox! what have I deserved of thee, that thou shouldest seek my death?'

'Thou villain,' quoth Fox, 'Hast been a bloodsucker of many a Christian's blood; and now thou shalt know what thou hast deserved at my hands.'

Wherewith he lifted up his bright shining sword of ten years' rust, and stroke him so main a blow . . . that he fell stark dead to the ground. . . .

Then marched they toward the road, whereinto they entered softly; where were six warders, one of whom asked, saying 'Who was there?' Quoth Fox and his company 'All friends'. Which was when they were all within proved contrary; for, quoth Fox:

'My masters, here is not to every man, a man; wherefore look you play your parts.' Who so behaved themselves indeed, that they had despatched these six quickly. Then John Fox, intending not to be barred of his enterprise, and minding to work surely in that which he went about, barred the gate surely and planted a cannon against it.

Then entered they into the Gaoler's lodge, where they found the keys of the fortress and prison by his bedside; and there had they all better weapons. In this chamber was a chest, wherein was a rich treasure, and all in ducats; which . . . Peter Unticaro and two more, opening, stuffed themselves so full as they could between their shirts and their skin: which John Fox would not once touch, and said that it was his and their liberty whether he sought for, to the honour of his God; and not to make a mart of the wicked treasure of the infidels. . . .

Now these eight being armed with such weapons as they thought well of, thinking themselves sufficient champions to encounter a stronger enemy, and coming into the prison, Fox opened the gates and doors thereof, and called forth all the prisoners: whom he set, some to ramming up the gate, some to the dressing up of a certain galley, which was the best in all the road, and was called the *Captain of Alexandria*; whereinto some carried masts, sails, oars, and other such furniture as doth belong to a galley.

(The galley, worked by willing hands, got safely out of Alexandria, undamaged by the Turkish shot that whistled about their ears, and undeterred by the rough weather which made the enemy galleys reluctant to pursue them. On the 29th day after leaving Alexandria, the escaped prisoners landed at Gallipoli, and were hospitably received by the monks there. At Tarento they sold the galley and divided the proceeds. John Fox, after a sojourn in Rome and in Spain, where the King gave him twenty pence a day for his valour, arrived back in England in 1579. His rusty sword, at the supplication of the monks, was left behind in the friendly monastery at Gallipoli.)

The copy of the certificate for John Fox and
his company, made by the Prior and the
brethren of Gallipoli; where they
first landed.

We the Prior and Fathers of the Convent of the Amerciates, of the city of Gallipoli, of the Order of Preachers, do testify that upon the 29th of January last past, 1577, there came into the said city a certain galley from Alexandria, taken from the Turks, with two hundred and fifty and eight Christians: whereof was principal, master John Fox, an Englishman, Gunner; and one of the chiefest that did accomplish that great work, whereby so many Christians have recovered their liberties. In token and remembrance whereof, upon our earnest request to the same John Fox, he hath left an old sword wherewith he slew the Keeper of the prison: which sword we do as a monument and memorial of so worthy a deed, hang up in the chief of our Convent house. And for because all things aforesaid are such as we will testify to be true, as they are orderly passed and have therefore good credit, that so much as is above expressed is true; and for the more faith thereof, we the Prior and Fathers aforesaid have ratified and subscribed these presents. Given in Gallipoli the third of February, 1577.

SOURCE: Richard Hakluyt, *Principall Navigations, Voiages, and Discoveries of the English Nation*, 1589.

FRANCO-GERMAN WAR, July 1870–March 1871.

Clanricarde clincher

The celebrated Lady Clanricarde, daughter of George Canning, was talking during the Franco-German War of 1870 to the French Ambassador, who complained bitterly that England had not intervened on behalf of France.

'But, after all,' he said, 'it is only what we might have expected. We always believed that you were a nation of shop-keepers, and now we know you are.'

'And we,' replied Lady Clanricarde, 'always believed that you were a nation of soldiers, and now we know that you are not.'

SOURCE: George W. E. Russell, *Collections and Recollections*, Smith, Elder & Co., 1903, Ch. XIX.

FREDERICK II (1712–1786), King of Prussia; called 'the Great.'

i. *The miller of Potsdam*

When Frederick built the palace of Sans Souci, there happened to be a mill which greatly straitened him in the execution of his plan, and he desired to know how much the miller would take for it. The miller replied that, for a long series of years, his family possessed the mill from father to son, and that he would not sell it.

The king employed solicitations, offered to build him a mill in a better place, besides paying any sum which he might demand. The obstinate miller persisted in his determinations to preserve the inheritance of his ancestors. The king, irritated at this resistance, sent for him and said to him angrily:

'Why do you refuse to sell your mill, notwithstanding all the advantages which I have offered to you.'

The miller repeated all his reasons.

'Do you know,' continued the king, 'that I could take it without giving you a farthing?'

'Yes,' replied the miller, 'if it was not for the Chamber of Justice at Berlin.'

The king was extremely flattered with this answer, which shewed that he was incapable of an act of injustice. He acquiesced in the miller's refusal, and changed the plan of his gardens.

SOURCE: Mr. Addison (pseud.) *Interesting Anecdotes, Memoirs,* etc. ... 1804.

A similar story is told about another miller, the Miller Arnold. On both incidents, Harold Nicolson comments:

One of the peculiarities of this highly gifted king was that he possessed a talent for propaganda unusual in monarchs and was able to project, both to his own subjects and to foreign opinion, an idealised picture of himself. He was not a cleanly man and persuaded people that his dirty clothes were evidence of commendable austerity. He would in public feed on beer and sausages, whereas in his private supper-room at Sans Souci the most exquisite French cuisine and wines were provided.

In was ingenious of him to secure such wide publicity for the story of Miller Arnold, whose livelihood had been affected by the construction in the mill-stream of a pleasure pond for some riparian noble. The judges of Custrin had decided against Arnold, whose wife was an obstinate and litigious shrew, who managed by her persistence to attract the King's attention, to have the judgement reversed, and the unjust judges cast into prison. It is true that on King Frederick's death the case was revised and the judges exonerated. It is also true that in strict liberal theory the Monarchy had no right to interfere with the judiciary. Yet the Miller Arnold legend spread throughout Europe and seemed to justify the despot's claim to be 'the advocate of the poor.'

Another such sentimental story was the tale of another miller, who refused to sell his mill at Potsdam to provide for an extension of the terrace at Sans Souci.

'Do you not realise,' thundered the King's land agent at the obstinate miller, 'that the King can confiscate your property?'

'But haven't we,' the man replied, 'the Court of Justice . . .?'

So he kept his mill, the stump of which, to this day, is pointed out to tourists by the Potsdam guides as 'the historic mill'.

SOURCE: Harold Nicolson, *Monarchy*, Weidenfeld & Nicolson, 1962, pp. 258–259.

ii. *The King of Prussia prescribes his own medicines, with poor results*

The King of Prussia's indisposition proved more serious than was apprehended . . .; but that monarch is now thought out of all danger, into which he had thrown himself by taking some medicines of his own prescription, and by what I have heard was in more danger from the medicines than from the distempers.

SOURCE: letter from Sir Andrew Mitchell to Lord Rochford, March 31, 1770. British Museum, Mitchell Papers. Inc. in Henry Ellis, *Original Letters, Illustrative of English History*, 2nd series, 1827, Vol. iv, p. 527.

FREDERICK AUGUSTUS, DUKE OF YORK AND ALBANY
(1763–1827), second son of George III; Commander-in-Chief.

i. *Dan impersonates the Commander-in-Chief*

Colonel Mackinnon, commonly called 'Dan' . . . was famous for practical jokes; which were, however, always played in a gentlemanly way. Before landing at St. Andero's, with some other officers who had been on leave in England, he agreed to personate the Duke of York, and make the Spaniards believe that his Royal Highness was amongst them. On nearing the shore, a royal standard was hoisted at the masthead, and Mackinnon disembarked, wearing the star of his shako on his left breast, and accompanied by his friends, who agreed to play the part of aides-de-camp to royalty. The Spanish authorities were soon informed of the arrival of the Royal Commander-in-Chief of the British army; so they received Mackinnon with the usual pomp and circumstance attending such occasions. The mayor of the place, in honour of the illustrious arrival, gave a grand banquet, which terminated with the appearance of a huge bowl of punch. Whereupon Dan, thinking that the joke had gone far enough, suddenly dived his head into the porcelain vase, and threw his heels in the air.

SOURCE: *The Reminiscences and Recollections of Captain Gronow*, 1861–1866; abridged edition by John Raymond, Bodley Head, 1964, pp. 63–64.

ii. *Case for reform*

A picture of the method of appointing officers, before the reforms instituted by Frederick, Duke of York when commander-in-chief.

No science was required, no service, no previous experience whatsoever; the boy, let loose from school the last week, might in the course of a month be a field officer, if his friends were disposed to be liberal of money and influence. It was no uncommon thing for a commission to be obtained for a child in the cradle; and when he came from college, the fortunate youth was at least a lieutenant of some standing by dint of fair promotion. To sum up this catalogue of abuses, commissions were in some instances bestowed upon young ladies, when pensions could not be had. We know one fair dame who drew the pay of a captain in the Dragoons, and was probably not much less fit for the service than some who did actual duty.

SOURCE: Sir Walter Scott; quoted Percy Fitzgerald, *The Royal Dukes and Princesses of the Family of George III*, 1882, pp. 129–130.

FREDERICK HENRY (1614–1629), Count Palatine of the Rhine; eldest son of Elizabeth and the Elector Palatine; grandson of James I.

The young prince reports his educational progress to James I
Sr,
    I kisse your hand. I would faine see Yo^r Ma. I can say Nominative hic, haec, hoc, and all 5 declensons, and a part of pronomen and a part of verbum. I have two horses alive, that

can goe up my staires, a blacke horse, and a Chestnut horse. I
pray God to blesse Your Matie

Yo^r. Maties.

obedient Grand-child

Friderick Henry

SOURCE: William Basevi Sanders, *Specimens of Facsimiles of
National Manuscripts of Great Britain and Ireland.*

FREDERICK LOUIS, PRINCE OF WALES (1707–1751). Father
of George III. Alienated from George II and Queen Caroline.
Led the opposition to the government.

i. *Epitaph for a Prince*

> *Here lies Fred,*
> *Who was alive and is dead:*
> *Had it been his father,*
> *I had much rather;*
> *Had it been his brother,*
> *Better than another;*
> *Had it been his sister,*
> *No one would have missed her;*
> *Had it been the whole generation,*
> *Better for the nation:*
> *But since 'tis only Fred,*
> *Who was alive and is dead—*
> *There's no more to be said.*

SOURCE: Horace Walpole, *Memoirs of George II*, 1847, Vol. i,
p. 436.

ii. *Inscription for a dog-collar*

> *I am his Highness's dog at Kew;*
> *Pray tell me, sir, whose dog are you?*

SOURCE: inscription by Alexander Pope on the collar of a dog
which he gave to the Prince of Wales. Prince Frederick Louis
obtained a lease of Kew House in 1730 and developed a collection
of exotic plants. A former Keeper of the Herbarium and Library
at the Royal Botanic Gardens said that 'It is possible that the

o

establishment of a botanic garden at Kew, from which developed the present Royal Botanic Gardens, owes more to Frederick than is generally acknowledged'.

iii. *The Prince's bride*

Augusta of Saxe-Gotha, a German princess, was selected as a bride for Frederick as being a reasonably well-balanced sort of person. A number of other possible candidates had a strain of madness in their families.

I did not think ingrafting my half-witted coxcomb upon a madwoman would mend the breed.

SOURCE: George II's comment on the rejection of some other candidates.

iv. *His mother's opinion of her son*

My dear first-born is the greatest ass, and the greatest liar, and the greatest *canaille*, and the greatest beast in the whole world, and I most heartily wish he was out of it.

SOURCE: Queen Augusta, wife of George II; a remark reported by Lord Hervey, *Memoirs of the Reign of George II*.

FRENCH REVOLUTION, THE.

i. *The Three Estates*

There was an old saying in France that the commons paid in goods, the nobles in blood and the clergy in prayer. The States-General, or National Assembly, made up of the three orders, of which the commons were the third, had not met since 1614.

The Abbe Siéyès, in a famous brochure which examined the questions everywhere being asked, said, 'What is the third order?—The nation. What is the nation?—Nothing. What must it become?—Everything.' Thus to the saying of Louis XIV, 'L'Etat c'est moi,' Siéyès replied, 'L'Etat c'est nous.'

SOURCE: Victor Duruy, *A Short History of France*, Everyman's Library edition, J. M. Dent & Sons, Vol. II.

It may be recalled here that Burke on one occasion, pointing to the Press Gallery in Parliament, said: 'Yon dersits the Fourth Estate, more powerful than them all.'

ii. *Breaks for meals during insurrections*

Here I will make one remark. During the frequent insurrections which took place in Paris in the course of the Revolution, it has been observed that the people always dispersed at meal-times. The same characteristic was observed in the previous century by the Cardinal de Retz who, on receiving the order to disperse the crowd on the first day of the Fronde rebellion, replied:

'That will not give me much trouble. It will soon be supper-time.'

SOURCE: Helen Maria Williams, *Letters containing a sketch of the politics of France* . . . , London, 1795. Helen Williams was an eye-witness of many of the events of the Revolution.

iii. *Burke recalls a glimpse of Marie Antoinette*

It is now sixteen or seventeen years since I saw the Queen of France, then the Dauphiness, at Versailles; and surely never lighted on this orb, which she hardly seemed to touch, a more delightful vision. I saw her just above the horizon, decorating and cheering the elevated sphere she just began to move in— glittering like the morning star, full of life, and splendour, and joy. . . . Little did I dream that I should have lived to see disasters fallen upon her in a nation of gallant men, in a nation of men of honour, and of cavaliers. I thought ten thousand swords must have leaped from their scabbards to avenge even a look that threatened her with insult. But the age of chivalry is gone.

SOURCE: Edmund Burke, *Reflections on the Revolution in France.*

iv. *A French aristocrat finds better servants*

The Duc de la Rochefoucauld Liancourt, whom he [Isaac Weld, traveller] met in America in 1795, was speaking of his altered circumstances.

'When I was in France,' said the Duc, 'I had sixteen servants to wait on me. Now that I have only two, I am better attended than ever I was. And here,' he added, holding up his two hands, 'are those two servants.'

SOURCE: Isaac Weld, *Travels*, 1799; Sir Bernard Burke, *The Rise of Great Families*, 1873, p. 56.

v. *'You cannot help leaving us the stars'*

During the French Revolution, Jean Bon St. André, the Vendean leader, said to a peasant:

'I will have all your steeples pulled down, that you may no longer have any objects by which you may be reminded of your old superstititions.'

'You cannot help leaving us the stars,' replied the peasant, 'and we can see them further off than our steeples.'

SOURCE: John Timbs, *A Century of Anecdote, 1760–1860.*

vi. *The baker comes to Paris*

In 1789, Paris was in the grip of famine. Louis XVI was at Versailles, and the mob demanded his return, apparently thinking that his presence would ensure a plentiful supply of bread. He was accompanied by the Queen and their children.

A deputation of one hundred members was . . . appointed to accompany the king to Paris. . . . It was two o'clock in the afternoon before the procession set out. During the progress all was gaiety and joy among the soldiers and the spectators; and such was the respect in which the French nation still held the name and the person of their king, that the multitude were superstitiously persuaded that the royal presence would actually put an end to the famine.

The popular exclamation was, as they proceeded along:

'We are bringing the baker, the baker's wife, and the little journeyman.'

SOURCE: *An Impartial History of the War* . . . (anon.), Manchester, 1811.

vii. *The King puts on the revolutionary cockade*, June, 1792

An immense crowd . . . had, by this time, collected round the palace and the garden of the Tuileries. . . . Having pointed four cannon, under the vestibule, two on the side of the garden, and two on the side of the court, they entered the palace at the moment when the Royal Family were at dinner. They threatened to burn it, if the doors were not opened. On their attempting to break open the door of the apartment where the

King was, he rose, and prevented the guards from resisting, saying, calmly:

'I will go to them—I will prevent them from breaking open the door.'

On the instant the door opened, a pike, which had been thrust against it to force it open, would have killed the King, had not a chasseur, with his hand, put it aside. The party having thus entered the King's private room, a man in a red bonnet, with a pike and pistols at his girdle, made the King sit down in an arm chair . . . and interrogated his Majesty. He next insisted that the King should wear his cap, which was the ensign of the Jacobins. . . . The King asked three days' consideration. The mob replied that they would not depart without a satisfactory promise. His Majesty promised them and took the national cockade. He was then led with the red bonnet on his head, and coloured ribbons on his arms, to the window, and shewn in this equipage to the mob. He was next presented with a bottle, and desired to drink the health of the nation. Some of the attendants offered to bring a glass; but the Sovereign refused the offer, and immediately drank out of the bottle.

SOURCE: ibid.

GANDHI, MAHATMA (1869–1948), Indian leader; organizer of passive resistance to British rule. His real name was Mohandas, but he became universally known as Mahatma, or Holy One.

i. *'The Mickey Mouse of History'*

Gandhi celebrated his sixty-second birthday on October 2, 1931. . . . I received an invitation to his birthday party, which was held in the Student Movement House. Gandhi sat among us at a flower-decked table with a pile of presents from the Indian students in front of him, not sumptuous gifts, just bananas, oranges, and some mangoes.

Mrs. Naidu was the principal speaker.

'Look at him,' she said. 'How shall I describe him? He looks to me like the Mickey Mouse of history!'

Gandhi burst into laughter so loud that his few remaining teeth almost fell out of his head.

SOURCE: Emery Kelen, *Peace in Their Time*, Victor Gollancz, 1964, p. 258.

ii. *Saint or politician?*

People were always thinking up names for Gandhi. Lady Astor called him the 'wild man of God'. Churchill called him the 'naked fakir'. To his disciple, Umar Sobani, he was 'beloved slave driver'. He didn't care what anyone called him as long as they didn't call him a saint.

'They say I am a saint trying to be a politician,' he said. 'But I am only a politician trying to be a saint.'

SOURCE: ibid., p. 259.

iii. *The cost of keeping a man poor*

He winked an eye now and then at his vow of poverty. He lived like the poorest, always travelled third class, ate mostly fruit. But he raised no outcry when a costly ventilation system was installed in his third-class compartment, or when his followers presented him with rare, expensive fruits.

'People have no idea,' remarked Mrs. Naidu, 'how much it costs to keep the Mahatma poor.'

SOURCE: ibid., p. 261.

GEORGE I (1660–1727), King of Great Britain.

i. *No preferment for the Pope*

Dean Lockyer, a great favourite of George I, after a visit which he paid to Rome, was asked by His Majesty, in a jocular manner, as they sat over their bowl of punch, whether he had succeeded in converting the Pope.

'No, your Majesty,' replied the Dean; 'His Holiness has most excellent Church preferment, and a most desirable bishopric, and I had nothing better to offer him.'

SOURCE: *The Reminiscences and Recollections of Captain Gronow*, 1892, abridged edition by John Raymond, Bodley Head, 1964, p. 281.

ii. *The King's dislikes*
'I hate all Boets and Bainters.'

SOURCE: Campbell, *Lives of the Chief Justices*, Ch. 30.

GEORGE II (1683–1760), King of Great Britain.

i. *The Princess and the baboon*
The marriage of Anne, Princess Royal, daughter of George II, to William Charles Henry, Prince of Orange, March 14, 1734.

... the Mars who was locked in the arms of this Venus, was a monster so deformed, that when the King had chosen him for a son-in-law, he could not help, in the honesty of his heart, and the coarseness of his expression, telling the Princess how hideous a bridegroom she was to expect, and even gave her permission to refuse.

She replied, she would marry him if he was a baboon.

'Well then,' said the King, 'there is baboon enough for you!'

SOURCE: Horace Walpole, *Memoirs of the Reign of King George the Second*, edit. Lord Holland, 1847, Vol. 1, pp. 206–207.

ii. *The royal physician*
About forty years ago, a very worthy man went to St. James's Palace, whose apartment was two pair of stairs high. He drank tea there, took his leave, and stepping back unadvisedly (on his friend's shutting the door after him) he half slipped, and half tumbled, down a whole flight of steps, and, with his head, burst open a closet door. The unlucky visitor was completely stunned with the fall; and, on his recovery, found himself sitting on the floor of a small room, and most kindly attended by a neat little old gentleman, who was carefully washing his head with a

towel, and fitting with great exactness, pieces of sticking plaster to the variegated cuts which the accident had conferred on the abrupt visitor's unwigged pate.

For some time his surprize kept him silent; but, finding that the kind physician had completed his task, and had even picked up his wig and replaced it on his head, he rose from the floor, and limping towards his benefactor, was going to utter a profusion of thanks for the succour he had received. These were, however, instantly checked by an intelligent frown, and by a significant wave of the hand toward the door of the closet. The patient understood the hint, and retired, wondering how so much humanity, and so much unsociableness, could dwell in the same breast. His wonder ceased when he found, on describing to a friend the situation of the closet, that he had owed the kind assistance he had received to the first man in the kingdom.

SOURCE: Mr. Addison (pseud.) *Interesting Anecdotes, Memoirs . . . ,* etc., 1794.

See WOLFE, GENERAL; DETTINGEN; FREDERICK LOUIS.

GEORGE III (1738–1820), King of Great Britain.

i. *The solitary harvester*

Once at harvest time when passing a field where only one woman was at work he stopped to ask her where the other labourers were. The woman said they had gone to see the King and added:

'I wouldn't give a pin to see him. Besides the fools will lose a day's work by it, and that is more than I can afford to do. I have five children to work for.'

'Well, then,' said the King, putting some money in her hands, 'you may tell your companions who are gone to see the King, that the King came to see you.'

SOURCE: Lewis Melville, *Farmer George*, 1907; Christopher Hibbert, *The Court at Windsor*, Longmans, 1964, pp. 110–111.

ii. *The King and the coal scuttle*

He was considerate in other ways, too; and the story was told that one evening when the fire was getting low he rang for the page in waiting and asked him to go for some more coal as the scuttle was empty. The page considered this task too menial and rang for an old footman whose job it properly was. Immediately the King picked up the scuttle himself, told the page to show him where the coal was kept, filled the scuttle, went back to the fire, tipped the coal on to it and, handing the empty scuttle to the page, he said:

'Never ask an old man to do what you are so much better able to do yourself.'

SOURCE: J. H. Jesse, *Memoirs of the Life and Reign of George III*; Christopher Hibbert, *The Court at Windsor*, Longmans, 1964, p. 111.

iii. *The best purl in Windsor*

Inside the stables . . . he found the grooms arguing so urgently that they did not notice his arrival. 'I don't care what you say, Robert,' one of them said, 'but everyone else agrees, that the man at the Three Tuns makes the best purl in Windsor.'

'Purl? Purl? Purl?' whispered the King in his quick excited way to Robert who was standing next to him. 'Purl? What's purl, Robert?'

Robert said it was a tankard of warm beer with a glass of gin in it.

'I dare say a very good drink, grooms,' said the King so loudly that they all turned round and recognised him, 'but, grooms, too strong for the morning. Never drink in the morning, grooms.'

He never expected that they would take his advice, and many years later, arriving at the stables much earlier than usual, he found them deserted except for a small lad who did not know him.

'Boy! Boy!' the King asked, 'Boy! Where are the grooms?'

'I don't know, sir, but they'll soon be back because they expect the King.'

'Aha! Then run, boy, run, and say the King expects them. Run to the Three Tuns, boy. They are sure to be there, boy, for the landlord makes the best purl in Windsor.'

SOURCE: Joseph Taylor, *Relics of Royalty*: or *Remarks, Anecdotes and Amusements of George III*, 1820; Christopher Hibbert, *The Court at Windsor*, Longmans, 1964, p. 113.

iv. *The strictness of Court etiquette*

A strict formal etiquette was maintained at the Court of George III. Even his daughters stood when he entered their rooms and did not speak unless asked a question; they left a room only with permission when the King was present and they retired backwards like any other subject. The Queen's Ladies-in-Waiting had to remain on their feet all the time and could not even cross an open doorway if a member of the royal family happened to be inside. The account written by Madame D'Arblay, second Keeper of the Queen's Robes is exaggerated for the sake of humour, but contains a good deal of wry truth:

If you find a cough tickling your throat you must arrest it from making any sound; if you find yourself choking with for-bearance, you must choke—but not cough.

In the second place, you must not sneeze. If you have a vehement cold, you must take no notice of it; if your nose-membranes feel a great irritation, you must hold your breath; if a sneeze still insists upon making its way, you must oppose it, by keeping your teeth grinding together; if the violence of the repulse break some blood-vessel, you must break the blood-vessel—but not sneeze.

In the third place, you must not, upon any account, stir either hand or foot. If, by chance, a black pin runs into your head, you must not take it out. If the pain is very great, you must be sure to bear it without wincing; if it brings tears into your eyes, you must not wipe them off. . . . If, however, the agony is very great, you may, privately, bite the inside of your cheek, or of your lips, for a little relief; taking care, meanwhile, to do it so cautiously as to make no apparent dent outwardly. . . .

SOURCE: letter to her sister-in-law, December 1785; Charlotte Barrett D'Arblay (edit.), *Diary and Letters of Madame D'Arblay*, 1778–1840, 1904.

v. *Nothing new under the grandson*

Walpole, observing that there had existed the same indecision, irresolution, and want of system in the politics of Queen Anne, that now distinguished those of the reign of George III, added:

'But, there is nothing new under the sun.'

'No,' said Selwyn, 'nor under the grandson.'

SOURCE: John Timbs, *A Century of Anecdote, 1760–1860*.

George Selwyn held a number of minor political posts, including those of Paymaster of the Works and Surveyor-General of the Works.

vi. *The King's coach attacked*

Soon after two this day [October 29, 1795] his majesty, attended by the Earl of Westmoreland and myself, set out from St. James's in his state-coach, to open the session of Parliament. The multitude of people in the Park was prodigious. A sullen silence, I observed to myself, prevailed through the whole, very few individuals excepted. No hats, or at least very few, were pulled off; little or no huzzaing, and frequently a cry of 'Give us bread!'—'No war!' and once or twice, 'No king!' with hissing and groaning.

My grandson Cranley, who was upon the king's guard, had told me, just before we set out from St. James's, that the Park was full of people, who seemed discontented and tumultuous, and that he apprehended insult would be offered to the king.

Nothing material however happened, till we got to the narrowest part of the street called St. Margaret's, between the two Palace-yards, when, the moment we had passed the Office of Ordnance, and were just opposite the parlour window of the house adjoining it, a small ball, either of lead or marble, passed through the window glass on the king's right hand, and perforated it, leaving a small hole the bigness of the top of my little finger (which I instantly put through it, to mark the size), and passed through the coach out of the other door, the glass of which was down. We all instantly exclaimed:

'This is a shot!'

The king shewed, and I am persuaded felt, no alarm; much less did he fear, to which indeed he is insensible. We proceeded to the House of Lords, when, on getting out of the coach, I first, and the king immediately afterwards, said to the Lord Chancellor, who was in waiting at the bottom of the stairs, robed:

'My Lord, we have been shot at'; and then, perfectly free from the smallest agitation, read his speech with peculiar correctness, and even less hesitation than usual. . . . And afterwards, on getting into the coach, the first words he said were:

'Well, my Lords, one person is *proposing* this, and another is *supposing* that, forgetting that there is One above us all, who *disposes* of everything, and on whom alone we depend.'

The magnanimity, piety, and good sense of this struck me most forcibly, and I shall never forget the words.

SOURCE: Lord Onslow, in a private letter; quoted Percy Fitz-gerald, *The Royal Dukes and Princesses . . .* , 1882, Vol. I.

vii. *Margaret Nicholson attempts the King's life*, 1786

His carriage had just stopped at the garden-door of St. James's, and he had just alighted from it, when a decently-dressed woman, who had been waiting for him for some time, approached him with a petition. It was rolled up, and had the usual superscription:

'For the King's Most Excellent Majesty.'

She presented it with her right hand; and, at the same moment that the king bent forward to take it, she drew from it, with her left hand, a knife, with which she aimed straight at his heart!

The fortunate awkwardness of taking the instrument with the left hand made her design perceived before it could be executed; the king started back, scarcely believing the testimony of his own eyes; and the woman made a second thrust, which just touched his waistcoat before he had time to prevent her; and at that moment one of the attendants, seeing her horrible intent, wrenched the knife from her hand. . . . While the guards and his own people now surrounded the king, the assassin was seized by the populace, who were tearing her away, no doubt to fall the instant sacrifice of her murtherous purpose, when the king, the only calm and moderate person then present, called aloud to the mob:

'The poor creature is mad! Do not hurt her! She has not hurt me!'

SOURCE: Percy Fitzgerald, *The Royal Dukes and Princesses . . .*, 1882, Vol. I. The attacker, a housemaid named Margaret Nicholson, was certified insane and sent to an asylum.

viii. *The King's industry*

Add to all this the industry, that suffocating industry. He blundered through the lucid years of his reign with a thoroughness approaching genius. He worked early and late, no detail of state business escaping his supervision . . . . A continual procession of messengers hurried through the gates of the royal residence on their way to ministers, each bearing a note or a sheaf of notes written in the King's hand. These notes, meticulously dated 'Queen's House, January 3rd, 1775. 3 min. pt. 9 p.m.,' 'Kew, July 31st, 1779. 59 min. pt. 7 a.m.,' often written in tumbling haste . . . on every conceivable topic, represent an intensive application that almost defies belief. Lord North alone received some eight hundred of them.

SOURCE: John Drinkwater, *Charles James Fox*, Ernest Benn, 1928, pp. 43-44.

ix. *A menagerie arrives for the King*

An odd incident of this early time that deserves record was the arrival of Omar Effendi, the new ambassador for Algiers, who on June 3rd had an audience of the king to deliver his credentials. He brought over, as a present, twenty-four fine horses, a lion, two tigers, and some curious sheep. He was very desirous of having the lions and tigers led before the king in procession, such being the custom he declared, in his own country; his request, however, could not be granted; the fine horses and curious sheep were, however, admitted into the procession. But here he wished that the animals might actually be driven into the presence of the king, that he might report to his master that he had delivered them with his own hands. On being informed that this could not be granted, as the horses could not ascend the stairs, he wished to be informed whether, as the horses could not ascend to the kng, the king could not descend to them. The animals were then driven into the royal gardens, and his majesty viewed them from the window of the palace. The ambassador was then admitted into the royal presence, and he apologised to his majesty for his not being attended with the lions and tigers.

SOURCE: Horace Walpole; quoted Percy Fitzgerald, *The Royal Dukes and Princesses* . . . , 1882, Vol. I.

x. *An English sailor smuggles a letter to the King*

The original spelling is preserved in this remarkable letter from a sailor who had partly forgotten how to 'indight . . . letters in adeascente maner'. The king of Prussia was Frederick the Great.

Sir,

The inscerted comes with my dutyfull seruice to your honered and moast Soveren Mayjesty, hopeing that your Mayesty will pardon my bouldness and exkcapt of these few lines . . . iam a seaman bred and born in Whitewell near York Cetty in Yorkshire. James Richardson is my name: born of powr parrents: served eight years duttyfully to John Besswick of Scareborough in the coasting and marhent service: but not withstanding, my supperyours always gave me agood carrackter.

(Richardson goes on to relate how, on May 20, 1766, he made a shore expedition a few miles from the East Prussian port of Memel, and was forcibly drafted into the Prussian army.)

Blessed be God i am not yoused ill, for when thare own contrymen they flog, brouse, and beat with a stick, they give me a good word; but when iam alone ifreat and cry to that condishon that ilay seick for ten weeks to geather to think that iam stole away from my native land in such amaner, and no hope of geting clear at all. A verry honorowble ould gentleman, a marchant from Ingland hath tould me that it would be the only way for to send your Mayjesty those few lines, being aman born of powr parrants. . . . and for the good your Mayjesty will do for me iam willing to obbay and serve your Mayjesty ather by land or sea, so long as breth remain; as i hope and pray to my macker for your Hieness to forgive and pardon me if i hath written anny thing amiss, for ihath partly fogoten my mothers toungue, and to indight my letters in adeascente maner. This Letter imust smugle awayin toan inglishmans hands that none of the offiscears catsh me with this letter. iam 28 years of agge and 5 foot aleaven in hight. and so no more at prescent, but remain in prays to the Allmighty for your Mayjestys long rean, and in peace with all men

$\qquad$ JAMES RICHARDSON
. . . in Cenesbourg [Koningsberg]
May the 31th.1767
. . . For his Prescent Mayjesty
$\qquad$ King George y^e third
$\qquad$ London.

SOURCE: British Museum, Mitchell Papers, Inc. in Henry Ellis, *Original Letters, Illustrative of English History*, 2nd series, 1827, Vol. iv, pp. 509–512. The letter is postmarked 'Hull' and was apparently forwarded from there by the friend who had smuggled it out of Prussia. It seems to have been taken notice of, for accompanying the sailor's letter is a certificate, also in his hand, saying that he had got his discharge and 'one dallar to bear my expences on my way, and a pass, and macke the best of my way to owld ingland'. It is dated September 18, 1767.

See also EDWARD AUGUSTUS and ELECTIONS.

GEORGE IV (1762–1830), King of Great Britain; Regent during the incapacity of George III.

i. *His tutor's prophecy*
He will become either the most polished gentleman, or the most accomplished blackguard in Europe—possibly both.

SOURCE: Richard Hurd, Bishop of Worcester, tutor to the Prince of Wales.

ii. *The King in kilts*

Although his Most Gracious Majesty George IV visited in 1822, I am not able to relate personally anything about it . . . but I can give a charming anecdote of him told me by Lady Jane Hamilton Dalrymple, a connection of our family, who was with him at the time. The King, it will be remembered, appeared in full Highland costume, and begged the ladies to tell him how he looked. They all assured him nothing could be better. At that moment appeared the portly alderman, Sir Wm. Curtis—also in full Highland costume—a most ridiculous figure. The King bit his lip and said:

'I hope I do not look like that; at all events, that my kilt is not so short.'

Lady Jane made him a low curtsy and said:

'As your Majesty stays so short a time in Scotland, the more we see of you the better.'

SOURCE: Lieut.-Colonel Balcarres D. Wardlaw Ramsey, *Rough Recollections of Military Service and Society*, 1882, Vol. 1, pp. 4–5.

iii. *His Majesty mounts his horse*

The late Sir Francis Head told me he . . . received an order to proceed with a party of sappers to a certain spot on the road to Portobello, and construct a mound of a certain dimension during the night; and himself to be there the next day at a given hour. These orders were executed; and soon after the time appointed, the royal cavalcade was seen approaching—the King in a carriage, with his horse led behind him. On arriving at the mound the King said:

'I think I shall mount my horse here; this mound seems as if it was made on purpose for me'—as indeed it was, for getting on horseback was a matter of extreme difficulty to him then.

SOURCE: ibid., pp. 5–6.

iv. *H.R.H. takes lessons in elocution*

John Kemble [the great Shakespearean actor] had the honour of giving the Prince of Wales some lessons in elocution. According to the vitiated pronunciation of the day, the prince, instead of saying 'oblige', would say 'obleege', upon which Kemble, with much disgust depicted upon his countenance, said:

'Sir, may I beseech your Royal Highness to open your royal jaws, and say "oblige"?'

SOURCE: *Reminiscences and Recollections of Captain Gronow*, 1892, first pub. 1862–1866.

v. *The King's indolence*

The King's indolence is so great that it is next to impossible to get him to do even the most ordinary business . . . . His greatest delight is to make those who have business to transact with him, or to lay papers before him, wait in his anteroom while he is lounging with Mount Charles or anybody, talking of horses or any trivial matter; and when he is told, 'Sir, there is Watson waiting,' &c., he replies, 'Damn Watson; let him wait.' He does it on purpose, and likes it. This account corresponds with all I have before heard, and confirms the opinion I have long had that a more contemptible, cowardly, selfish, unfeeling dog does not exist than this King.

SOURCE: Charles Greville, *The Greville Memoirs*, pub. 1875-1887.

vi. *The Duke deals with a tall story by the King*

The story of George IV talking of his youthful exploits and telling the Duke of Wellington that he had made a body of troops charge down the Devil's Dyke, is very inferior to the story as Mr. Rogers told it to me while we were together at the Dyke.

The King said to the Duke:

'I once galloped down that hill at the head of my regiment.'

'Very steep, sir,' said the Duke.

P

SOURCE: Charles Robert Leslie, *Autobiographical Recollections*, 1860, Vol. I, p. 238. On another occasion the King is said to have described to Wellington his part in the Battle of Waterloo, a story which the Duke received with equal composure.

GEORGE V (1865–1936), King of Great Britain.

i. *The adoption of the surname Windsor*

In the 1914–1918 War, George V was disturbed by reports that some people thought he must be pro-German since he came of German origins. He determined to adopt an undeniably British name.

In fact no one in his family was quite sure what their surname was, and when the College of Heralds was consulted, Mr. Farnham Burke had to admit that he could not be sure either. It was not Stewart; Mr. Burke doubted if it were Guelph; it might be Wipper, but there again it might be Wettin. The King resolved that the problem must be solved by the adoption of a name that was unmistakably British, or at least not obviously German. The Duke of Connaught suggested Tudor or Stewart. Other suggestions were York, Lancaster, Plantagenet, England, Fitzroy, or even D'Este. The proposal of the King's Private Secretary, however, seemed the best. He thought that as Edward III had been known as Edward of Windsor, they need look no further for a name at once undoubtedly English and undeniably appropriate. The suggestion was adopted—and the Kaiser, so it was said, retaliated by ordering a performance of the Merry Wives of Saxe-Coburg and Gotha.

SOURCE: Sir Harold Nicolson, *King George V: His Life and Reign* and Sir George Arthur, *King George V*; Christopher Hibbert, *The Court at Windsor*, Longmans, 1964, p. 262.

ii. *The King's last question*

'How is the Empire?'

'It is all absolutely right, Sir' (Lord Wigram).

GILBERT, SIR HUMPHREY (1539?–1583), explorer and colon-
izer. Gilbert left Plymouth with five ships in an effort to colonize
Newfoundland. He landed at St. John on August 5 and established
the first British colony in North America. After voyaging farther
along the coast he was lost in a storm off the southern Azores.

'We are as near to heaven by sea as by land'

Monday, the ninth of September, in the afternoon, the frigate
was near cast away, oppressed by waves, yet at that time
recovered; and giving forth signs of joy, the General, sitting
abaft with a book in his hand, cried out unto us in the *Hind*, so
oft as we did approach within hearing:

'We are as near to heaven by sea as by land!'; reiterating the
same speech, well beseeming a soldier, resolute in Jesus Christ,
as I can testify he was.

SOURCE: Edward Hayes, *A report of the voyage and success thereof,
attempted in the year of our Lord 1583 by Sir Humphrey Gilbert, Knight
. . .* ; in Richard Hakluyt's *Principall Navigations . . .* , etc., 1589.

GODOY, MANUEL DE (1767–1851), minister and virtual dic-
tator of Spain under Charles IV and Queen Maria Luisa. Known
as 'The Prince of Peace'. In 1808, when thousands of Napoleon's
troops had been infiltrating into Spain, the mob stormed Godoy's
house at Aranjuez, under the impression that the minister intended
to spirit the Spanish royal family out of the country.

i. *The harrying of the Sausage Man*

Between eleven and twelve o'clock [March 17, 1808] a carriage
with the blinds down came out of Godoy's house; it was
escorted, and contained . . . Doña Josepha Tudo. The party
was driving through a crowd of loiterers, and at once the cry
went up that the King and Queen were being spirited away.
The exact sequence of events after this is not easy to determine,
but a shot, probably a pre-arranged signal, was fired, and there
was a general rush towards the minister's residence.

The guards on duty refused to fire, and the mob burst into the building, which they then proceeded to sack, while yelling: 'Death to the sausage man!'*

Godoy first of all tried to escape to the house next door, but, finding this impossible, he hid himself in one of his own attics, rolled up in a mat, and there he remained for thirty-six hours.

SOURCE: Sir Charles Petrie, *The Spanish Royal House*, Geoffrey Bles, 1958, p. 117. Godoy eventually escaped, but with the abdication and exile of Charles, he never recovered power and, after a period of extreme poverty, finished up in Paris living on a small pension from Louis Philippe.

ii. *The umpire in the Palais Royal gardens*

His [Godoy's] great amusement was to sit on a bench in the gardens of the Palais Royal; and there the children of the poor would ask M. Manuel to umpire their games, not knowing that he who watched them had given absolute decisions for the administration of one of the widest empires that history has seen, that he was Grand Admiral of the Fleet which engaged with Nelson at Trafalgar, and treated, as the head of a Great Power, with the invincible Emperor of the French.

SOURCE: R. Sencourt, *Spain's Uncertain Crown*, 1932, p. 114.

GOODWIN SANDS, THE.

The coming of the Goodwin Sands

These treacherous sands occupy land which formerly belonged to Godwin or Godwine, Earl of the West Saxons (d. 1053), father of Harold, king of the English. While there is no reason to doubt the account below, a contributory factor may well have been that the monastery of St. Augustine, Canterbury, to whom the land was given, neglected to keep the sea wall in good repair.

1092—By the high spring tides many towns, castles and woods were drowned, as well in Scotland as in England. After the

* Godoy's home province, Extremadura, was famous for its sausages.

ceasing of the tempest, the lands that sometime were Earl Goodwin's, by violent force and drift of the sea were made a sandbed, and ever since have been called Goodwin's Sands.

SOURCE: Holinshed's *Chronicles*. William Camden puts the event a little later, in 1097, when he says 'in an unusual storm of wind and rain, and a very tempestuous sea, the Goodwin Sands were formed'.

GORDON, CHARLES GEORGE (1833–1885). Called 'Chinese Gordon'. Suppressed Tai-ping rebellion in China. In 1874, appointed governor of the tribes in the Sudan by the Khedive of Egypt, and worked to put down the slave trade. Became Governor-General of the Sudan and Equatorial Provinces, 1877. Sent to Khartoum, 1884, to bring out from the Sudan the garrisons cut off by forces of the Mahdi. Sustained a siege of 317 days and was killed when the city eventually fell.

Dealings with 'Chinese Gordon'

I also met 'Chinese Gordon' in London, who wrote me out a biographical sketch of all the leading spirits in China, foreigners and native, for my information. I found it extremely useful. He hit off the characters of each one of them with marvellous precision. . . .

He also made me a present of a house-boat, told me to fix my own price on a bungalow he had built up country, and offered to lend me a perfect copy of the *Chinese Repository* to read on the voyage.

The house-boat I found he had already given away thrice before I claimed it. The bungalow had been sold and the purchase money remitted to him. The books never reached me.

SOURCE: Sir Edmund Hornby, *An Autobiography*, Constable & Co., 1929, p. 194.

GORDON RIOTS (June 1780): the most formidable popular rising of the 18th Century, sparked off by the passing of the Catholic Relief Act (1778) to ease some of the penal laws against Roman

Catholics. A leader was found in the twenty-eight-year-old Lord George Gordon, son of the third Duke of Gordon. In the course of the riots, the mob stormed the lobby of the House and prevented the conduct of further business, attacked the house of Sir George Savile, broke open several jails and burnt the house and library of Lord Mansfield, Lord Chief Justice. During military action against the rioters, at least 200 were shot dead and 25 were later executed. Gordon was committed to the Tower and brought to trial on a charge of treason, but was acquitted. Eight years later he was imprisoned for libels against the government and died in Newgate.

Covering the prisons of London

A person begging alms of Lord George Gordon said:

'God bless you, my Lord! You and I have been in all the prisons of London.'

'What do you mean?' cried Lord George; 'I never was in any other prison but the Tower.'

'That is true, my Lord,' said the other, 'and I have been in all the rest.'

SOURCE: John Timbs, *A Century of Anecdote* (Chandos Classics), Frederick Warne & Co., p. 127.

GREAT EXHIBITION, THE (1851). Though the idea had been put up earlier, it was not till the Prince Consort sponsored the scheme in 1849 that the plan came to life.

i. *Offer from the Prince Consort*

'Now is the time to prepare for a Great Exhibition, an exhibition worthy of the greatness of this country; not merely national in its scope and benefits, but comprehensive of the whole world; and I offer myself to the public as their leader, if they are willing to assist in the undertaking.'

SOURCE: the Prince Consort, as President of the Society of Arts, 1849.

ii. *'This trumpery show'*

The folly and absurdity of the queen in allowing this trumpery show must strike every sensible and well-thinking mind, and I am astonished the ministers themselves do not insist on her at least going to Osborne during the Exhibition, as no human being can possibly answer for what may occur on the occasion. The idea of permitting 3000 National Guards to come over *en corps*, and parade in London in their side-arms, must shock every honest and well-meaning Englishman. But it seems everything is conspiring to lower us in the eyes of all Europe.

SOURCE: Ernest Augustus, Duke of Cumberland, in a letter to Lord Strangford; de Fonblanque, *Lives of the Lords Strangford*; quoted Percy Fitzgerald, *The Royal Dukes and Princesses . . .*, 1882, Vol. II.

iii. *Solution by the Iron Duke*

'Sparrowhawks, Ma'am.'

SOURCE: reply attributed to the Duke of Wellington, when Queen Victoria asked how the sparrows could be got out of the trees to be enclosed in the great glass pavilion for the 1851 Exhibition.

GREAT SEAL OF ENGLAND, THE. The principal seal, kept by the Lord Chancellor for the authentication of state documents. There have been approximately 100 Great Seals of English sovereigns since the Norman Conquest. Almost all have shown two portraits of the king or queen, one on a throne and the other on horseback.

i. *A fisherman finds the Great Seal*

On the 11th of December [1688] at three o'clock in the morning, attended by Sir Edward Hales and two servants, James withdrew by a private passage from Whitehall, and passed the river in a barge rowed by two watermen, after giving orders to the Duke of Northumberland, who was the lord in waiting, not to mention, until the morning, what he had seen. Some time before he had destroyed the writs for a new parliament, and now threw the great seal into the river. The seal was afterwards found by a fisherman and brought to London; Heaven seeming by this accident to declare, that the laws, the constitution, and the sovereignty of Britain were not to depend upon the frailty of man.

SOURCE: Sir John Dalrymple, *Memoirs of Great Britain and Ireland* ... 2nd edition, 1771, Vol. I, p. 239.

ii. *The Great Seal is stolen*

Lord Thurlow lived, during his Chancellorship, at No. 45, in Great Ormond-street, Queen-square. The Great Seal of England was stolen from his house on the night of 24th March, 1784, the day before the dissolution of Parliament. The thieves got in by scaling the garden-wall, and forcing two iron bars out of the kitchen-window. They then made their way to the Chancellor's study, broke open the drawers of his Lordship's writing-table, ransacked the room, and carried away the Great Seal, rejecting ... the mace as too unwieldy.

SOURCE: John Timbs, *A Century of Anecdote, 1760–1860*. This Great Seal was never recovered, and a good deal of public business had to be held up till a new one was made.

iii. *The Great Seal that was cut in halves*

A pleasant story is related of the damasking* of the Great Seal (the perquisite of the Lord Chancellor) at the demise of George IV. Lord Lyndhurst then held the Great Seal, but Lord Brougham was its Keeper when the Seal of William IV was completed; hence there were two claimants for the damasked Seal, one arguing that it was really a Seal of the preceding reign, and as such vested in him at the death of the Sovereign; the other that it was in full force till it was actually defaced. King William [IV] was appealed to to settle the dispute, and decided that each of the two Lords should have half the old Seal: his Majesty ordered his goldsmith to insert the two halves in two superb silver salvers, which he presented to Lord Lyndhurst and Lord Brougham, recommending them to 'toss up' which should have the obverse and which the reverse of the Seal.

SOURCE: ibid.

* Defacing it as a sign that it was no longer valid.

GRENVILLE, SIR RICHARD (1541?–1591), naval commander.

i. 'That nothing might remain of glory or victory to the Spaniards'

The *Revenge*, of 500 tons, was launched at Deptford in 1577 and was Drake's flag-ship against the Armada, in 1588. In 1591, a squadron of six English ships was lying in wait for the Spaniards off the Azores when they received a message than a great treasure fleet was almost on them, escorted by 53 ships of war. The English commander-in-chief, Lord Thomas Howard, stood out to sea, but asked Grenville to pick up the sick men on shore before joining the rest of the squadron. Before Grenville could do so, the Spanish fleet was between him and the other five English ships. Grenville, whose ship was a fast sailer, could have run before the wind and probably escaped. But he chose to sail straight for the Spanish fleet, hoping to cut through a gap and rejoin Howard. But the enemy ships closed in. The rest is the most heroic action in our naval history. For fifteen hours Grenville held out against 53 ships and 15,000 men, until, mortally wounded, he was carried aboard the Spanish flag-ship, where he was received with great honour.

All the powder of the *Revenge* to the last barrel was now spent, all her pikes broken, forty of her best men slain, and the most part of the rest hurt. In the beginning of the fight she had but one hundred free from sickness . . . a small troop to man such a ship, and a weak garrison to resist so mighty an army. . . . Unto ours there remained no comfort at all, no hope, no supply either of ships, men, or weapons; the masts all beaten overboard, all her tackle cut asunder, her upper work altogether razed. . . Sir Richard, finding himself in this distress and unable any longer to make resistance . . . commanded the master gunner, whom he knew to be a most resolute man, to split and sink the ship; that thereby nothing might remain of glory or victory to the Spaniards. . . . The master gunner readily condescended and divers others; but the Captain and Master were of another opinion. . . .

SOURCE: Sir Walter Raleigh, *Report on the truth of the fight about the Iles of the Azores, this last sommer.* . . . The quotation most often used, 'Sink me the ship, master gunner', is not from the original account, but from Tennyson's poem.

ii. *Sir Richard's last words*

Here die I, Richard Grenville, with a joyful and quiet mind, for that I have ended my life as a true soldier ought to do, that hath fought for his country, Queen, religion and honour, whereby my soul most joyful departeth out of this body, and shall always leave behind it an everlasting fame of a valiant and true soldier, that hath done his duty as he was bound to do.

SOURCE: Jan Huygen van Linschoten (1563–1611), a Dutch traveller who was seventy miles from the Azores when the action was fought, returning home from India. He published an account of his voyage, an English translation of which appeared in 1598.

GREVILLE, FULKE, FIRST BARON BROOKE (1554–1628), statesman and writer; biographer of Sir Philip Sidney (see ZUTPHEN).

Proud epitaph

Greville wrote his own epitaph, which was placed on his monument in Warwick:

> Servant to Queen Elizabeth
> Councillor to King James and
> Friend to Sir Philip Sidney.

GREY, LADY JANE (1537–1554), scholar and Queen of England for nine days. Executed on February 12, 1554, the same day as her husband, Lord Guildford Dudley, she inside the Tower because she was of the blood royal, he outside because he was not.

So sharp and severe parents, and so gentle a schoolmaster

Before I went into Germany, I came to Bradgate, in Leicestershire, to take my leave of that noble Lady Jane Grey, to whom I was exceeding much beholden. Her parents, the Duke and

Duchess, with all the household, Gentlemen and Gentlewomen, were hunting in the Park: I found her, in her chamber, reading *Phaedon Platonis* in Greek. . . . After salutation, and duty done, with some other talk, I asked her why she would lose such pastime in the Park. Smiling she answered me:

'I know all their sport in the Park is but a shadow to that pleasure that I find in Plato. Alas, good folk, they never felt what true pleasure meant.'

'And how came you, Madame,' quoth I, 'to this deep knowledge of pleasure, and what did chiefly allure you?' . . .

'I will tell you,' quoth she, 'and tell you a truth which perchance ye will marvel at. One of the greatest benefits that God ever gave me, is, that he sent me so sharp and severe parents, and so gentle a schoolmaster. For when I am in presence either of father or mother, whether I speak, keep silence, sit, stand, or go, eat, drink, be merry, or sad, be sewing, playing, dancing, or doing anything else, I must do it, as it were, in such weight, measure, and number, even so perfectly as God made the world; or else I am so sharply taunted, so cruelly threatened, yea presently some times with pinches, nips, and bobs [shakes], and other ways, which I will not name for the honour I bear them . . . that I think myself in hell till time come that I must go to Mr. Elmer, * who teacheth me so gently, so pleasantly, with such fair allurements to learning, that I think all the time nothing, whiles I am with him. . . . And thus my book hath been so much my pleasure, and bringeth daily to me more pleasure and more, that in respect of it all other pleasures, in very deed, be but trifles and troubles unto me.'

SOURCE: Roger Ascham, *The Scholemaster*, 1570. (Spelling modernized.)

---

* John Aylmer (1521–1594), later Bishop of London. This is the man of whom Thomas Fuller writes (1662): 'In the reign of Queen Mary he fled over beyond sea, and was little less than miraculously saved from the searchers of the ship by the ingenuity of a merchant, who put him into a great wine-butt, which had a partition in the middle, so that Master Aylmer sate in the hind part, whilst the searchers drank of the wine which they saw drawn out of the head or other end thereof.

GROSSTÊTE (or **GROSSETESTE), ROBERT** (1175–1253). Bishop of Lincoln. Of humble origins, but a great scholar and a priest of courage, humanity and humour.

Penance pontifical

The worthy prelate (Grosstête), who was a special friend of the Franciscans, enjoined on a certain melancholy friar of this order that he should drink a cupful of the best wine for penance; and when he had drunk it up, though most unwillingly, he said to him:

'Dearest brother, if you had frequently such penance, you would certainly have a better-ordered conscience.'

SOURCE: André L. Simon, *The History of the Wine Trade in England*, 1906, Vol. i, p. 119. The story is found in Thomas Eccleston (contemporary with Grosstête) *De Adventu Fratrum Minorum in Angliam*, printed 1858.

GUNPOWDER PLOT (1605).

i. *Money for the conspirators*

May it pleasure your lordship:

I understande by the Post Master of Ware that Mr. Thomas Percy came to London on friday at night with two men with hime, the one a gentlman whose name I cannott learne, the other a servante of his owne. They brought upp with them three Portemantues full of money. Thus much I thought good to certifie your lordship togither with my humble dutie. I humbly take leave

Your lordship's most bownden servant,

Ware this friday
5 a clock at night   Thomas Fotherly.
beinge the 7th of
November 1605.

SOURCE: manuscript letter from Thomas Fotherly, a household officer, to Henry Percy, ninth Earl of Northumberland; original Entry Book of Letters, Alnwick Castle, Northumberland. Thomas Percy was a Steward to the Earl and had absconded with some of the rents to finance the Plot.

ii. *Dangerous disease—desperate remedy*

When he was brought into the King's presence, the King asked him how he could conspire so hideous a treason against his children and so many innocent souls which never offended him? He answered that it was true, but a dangerous disease required a desperate remedy. He told some of the Scots that his intent was to have blown them back into Scotland.

SOURCE: *The True Copy of the Declaration of Guido Fawkes of Nov. 17th.* . . . Reprinted in Harleian Miscellany, 1809 edition, Vol. III.

HAMPDEN, JOHN (1594–1643). Parliamentarian. Opposed levy of Ship Money by Charles I. One of the Five Members whose arrest was attempted by the king.

i. *Hampden's opinion of Cromwell*

When a noble lord, hearing a speech by Oliver Cromwell, enquired blandly:

'Pray, Mr. Hampden, who is that sloven?', Hampden retorted:

'That sloven whom you see before you hath no ornament in his speech; but that sloven I say, if we should ever come to a breach with the King (which God forbid!), in such a case, I say, that sloven will be the greatest man in England.'

SOURCE: quoted Hugh Ross Williamson, *John Hampden, A Life*, Hodder & Stoughton, 1933, p. 288.

ii. *Cromwell's opinion of Hampden*

'I had a very worthy friend then; and he was a very noble person, and I know his memory is very grateful to all. At my first going out into this engagement [i.e. the Civil War] I saw our men were beaten at every hand. I did indeed; and desired him that he would make some additions to my Lord Essex's army, of some new regiments.

' "Your troops," said I, "are most of them old decayed serving men and tapsters and such kind of fellows; and" said I, "their troops are gentlemen's sons, younger sons and persons of quality; do you think that the spirits of such base and mean fellows will ever be able to encounter gentlemen, that have honour and courage and resolution in them? You must get men of spirit: and take it not ill what I say—I know you will not—of a spirit that is likely to go on as far as gentlemen will go—or else you will be beaten still."

'I told him so; I did truly. He was a wise and worthy person; and he did think that I talked a good notion, but an impracticable one.'

SOURCE: quoted Hugh Ross Williamson, *John Hampden, A Life*, Hodder & Stoughton, 1933, p. 309.

HANDEL, GEORGE FREDERICK (1685–1759), musical composer.

i. *Handel deals with critics*

A singer found fault with his method of accompanying, saying that, if he accompanied him in that way, he would jump from the stage into the harpsichord.

'Oh, you will jump, will you?' said Handel. 'Then let me know when you will jump and I will advertise it on the bills; and I shall get more people to see you jump than to hear you sing.'

On another occasion, when a librettist complained that the setting was unsuitable, Handel replied:
'What, sir, you teach me music? The music, sir, is good music. It is your words that are bad. Hear the passage again. There! go you and make words to that music.'

SOURCE: various Handel biographies.

ii. *Handel's sight becomes 'so relaxt'*

In 1751 Handel's sight began to fail him. He was working on his oratorio *Jephtha* and had just set the words 'All hid from mortal sight' when he was forced to lay down his pen, the left eye being 'so relaxt', as he recorded in the margin of his score.

SOURCE: Julian Herbage, *Handel in England*, article in *The Purcell-Handel Festival*, June 1959.

HARVEY, WILLIAM (1578–1657), physician and discoverer of the circulation of the blood.

The physician on the roof

He was much troubled with the gout, and his way of cure was thus: he would then sit with his legs bare, if it were a frost, on the leads of Cockaine House, put them into a pail of water, till he was almost dead with cold, and betake himself to his stove, and so 'twas gone. . . .

SOURCE: John Aubrey, *Brief Lives.*

HASTINGS, BATTLE OF (October 14, 1066).

i. *The landing of Duke William*

Then Duke William came towards England, after Michaelmas Day, and landed at Hastings in a place called Pevensey. In going out of his ship his foot stumbled and he groped in the sand. The knight that was next him cried to him straightway:

'Now that you hold England, my lord, you shall right soon be king!'

Duke William encouraged his men to the battle, and became aware that his habergeon [coat of mail] was turned inside-out; and put this right with a jest, saying:

'The power of an earldom shall turn into a kingdom.'

SOURCE: John of Trevisa, Cotton MS., Lib. VI, cap. 29; inc. in Morris and Skeat, *Specimens of Early English*, Part II, Clarendon Press, 1889, pp. 244 and 246.

ii. *Another version of the same incidents*

William Conqueror, when he invaded this Island, chanced at his arrival to be gravelled, and one of his feet stuck so fast in the sand that he fell to the ground. Wherewithal one of his attendants caught him by the arm, and helped him up, saying:

'Stand up, my liege Lord, and be of good cheer, for now you have taken fast footing in England'; and then, espying that he brought up sand and earth in his hand, added 'Yea, and you have taken livery and seisin of the Country.' For you know that in delivering of livery and seisin a piece of earth is taken.

That morning that he was to join battle with Harold, his Armourer put on his back-piece before, and his breast-plate behind; the which being espied by some that stood by, was taken among them for an ill token, and therefore advised him not to fight that day; to whom the Duke answered:

'. . . If I have any skill in soothsaying (as, in sooth, I have none), it doth prognosticate that I shall change Copy [i.e. pedigree] from a Duke to a King.'

SOURCE: William Camden, *Remains Concerning Britain*, 7th impression, 1674.

iii. *The minstrel Taillefer begins the Battle*

Then Taillefer, who sang right well, rode mounted on a swift horse before the duke, singing of Charlemagne, and of Roland, of Oliver, and the Peers who died in Roncevalles. And when they drew nigh to the English:

'A boon, sire!' cried Taillefer. 'I have long served you, and you owe me for all such service. To-day, so please you, you shall repay it. I ask as my guerdon, and beseech you for it earnestly, that you will allow me to strike the first blow in the battle!'

And the Duke answered:

'I grant it.'

Then Taillefer put his horse to a gallop, charging before all the rest, and struck an Englishman dead, driving his lance below the breast into his body, and stretching him upon the ground. Then he drew his sword, and struck another, crying out:

'Come on, come on! What do ye sirs? Lay on, lay on!'

At the second blow he struck, the English pushed forward, and surrounded and slew him.

SOURCE: Robert Wace (fl. 1170), *Roman de Rou*; quoted Sir Edward Creasy, *The Fifteen Decisive Battles of the World*, 1851 (32nd edition), 1886, pp. 293–294.

iv. *The death of Harold*

The Norman archers with their bows shot thickly upon the
English; but they covered themselves with their shields, so that
the arrows could not reach their bodies, nor do any mischief,
how true soever was their aim, or however well they shot.
Then the Normans determined to shoot their arrows upwards
into the air, so that they might fall on their enemies' heads, and
strike their faces. The archers adopted this scheme, and shot
up in the air towards the English; and the arrows in falling
struck their head and faces, and put out the eyes of many; and
all feared to open their eyes, or leave their faces unguarded.

The arrows now flew thicker than rain before the wind. . . .
Then it was that an arrow, that had been thus shot upwards
struck Harold above his right eye, and put it out. In his agony
he drew the arrow and threw it away, breaking it with his
hands; and the pain to his head was so great, that he leaned upon
his shield.

And now the Normans pressed on so far, that at last they
reached the standard. There Harold had remained, defending
himself to the utmost; but he was sorely wounded in his eye by
the arrow, and suffered grievous pain from the blow. An
armed man came in the throng of the battle, and struck him on
the ventaille of his helmet, and beat him to the ground; and
as he sought to recover himself, a knight beat him down
again. . . .

The standard was beaten down, the golden standard was
taken, and Harold and the best of his friends were slain.

SOURCE: Ibid.

HASTINGS, HENRY, fifth **EARL OF HUNTINGDON** (17th
Century).

'*Your son, my kinsman*'

It happened in the reign of King James, when Henry Earl of
Huntingdon was lieutenant of Leicestershire, that a labourer's

Q

son in that county was pressed into the wars. . . . The old man at Leicester requested his son might be discharged, as being the only staff of his age, who by his industry maintained him and his mother. The earl demanded his name, which the man for a long time was loath to tell, as suspecting it a fault for so poor a man to tell the truth. At last he told his name was Hastings.

'Cousin Hastings,' said the earl, 'we cannot all be top branches of the tree, though we all spring from the same root; your son, my kinsman, shall not be pressed.'

SOURCE: Thomas Fuller, *Worthies of England*, 1662.

HASTINGS, WARREN (1732–1818), Governor-General of India. Impeached for corruption and cruelty in a trial lasting 145 days, 1788–1795, but acquitted, at a cost to him of £70,000.

i. *The pantheon of Warren Hastings*

At the time of the trial of Warren Hastings, it was said that at Benares, the very place in which the acts set forth in the first article of impeachment had been committed, the natives had erected a temple to Hastings; and this story excited a strong sensation in England. Burke's observations . . . were admirable. He saw no reason for astonishment, he said, in the incident which had been represented as so striking. He knew something of the mythology of the Brahmins. He knew that as they worshipped some gods from love, so they worshipped others from fear. He knew that they erected shrines, not only to the benignant deities of light and plenty, but also to the fiends who preside over small-pox and murder; nor did he at all dispute the claim of Mr. Hastings to be admitted into such a pantheon.

SOURCE: John Timbs, *A Century of Anecdote, 1760–1860*, Frederick Warne & Co.

ii. *Tribute to eloquence*

One of the greatest tributes ever paid to eloquence, Mr. Sheridan received from Mr. Pitt, when, after Sheridan had, in opposition to him, advocated the prosecution of Warren Hastings, Pitt moved an adjournment, that 'the House might have time to recover from the overpowering effect of Mr. Sheridan's oratory'.

SOURCE: Ibid.

HAWKER, ROBERT STEPHEN (1803–1875). Eccentric, poet and antiquary. Vicar of Morwenstowe, Cornwall.

i. *The cat that was excommunicated*
He was usually followed to church by nine or ten cats, which entered the chancel with him and careered about it during service. Whilst saying prayers, Mr. Hawker would pat his cats, or scratch them under their chins. Originally ten cats accompanied him to church; but one, having caught, killed and eaten a mouse on Sunday, was excommunicated and from that day not allowed again within the sanctuary.

SOURCE: Rev. Sabine Baring-Gould, 1899.

ii. *And shall Trelawny die?*
Hawker wrote several volumes of poems, the best known of which is *The Song of the Western Men*, with its catchy refrain:

> *And have they fixed the where and when?*
> *And shall Trelawny die?*
> *Here's twenty thousand Cornish men*
> *Will know the reason why!*

This purported to be a 17th Century song raised on behalf of Bishop Jonathan Trelawny, one of the Seven Bishops who were imprisoned by James II in 1688 for refusing to read the Declaration of Indulgence in their churches. The Declaration greatly alleviated the laws against Roman Catholics. Hawker sent the poem anonymously to a Plymouth paper, where it was printed and taken to be an original ballad and was praised as such by Scott, Macaulay and Dickens. Hawker, however, said later that, except for the chorus lines, he composed the whole of it 'under a stag-horned oak in Sir Beville's Walk in Stowe Wood'. In point of fact, Hawker was probably in error in ascribing the 'And shall Trelawny die?' call to the time of the imprisonment of the Bishops. It is likely to go back another 60 years, to the time when Bishop Trelawny's grandfather, Sir John Trelawny, was imprisoned for resisting the election of Sir John Eliot to Parliament for Cornwall in 1628.

HEAD AND HAIR FASHIONS. Wigs, usually worn on the shaven head, were known to early civilizations. In England, they were in common use from the 17th Century to the early years of the 19th, though in some of the professions they continued later.

i. *Curious behaviour of a Lord Chief Justice*

It was observed for a number of years before he [Lord Chief Justice Kenyon, 1732–1802] died that he had two hats and two wigs. Of the hats and the wigs, one was dreadfully old and shabby, the other comparatively spruce. He always carried into court with him the very old hat and the comparatively spruce wig, or the very old wig and the comparatively spruce hat. On the days of the very old hat and the comparatively spruce wig, he shoved his hat under the bench and displayed his wig; but on the days of the very old wig and the comparatively spruce hat, he always continued covered.

SOURCE: John Timbs, *A Century of Anecdote, 1760–1860.*

ii. *A Westmorland clergyman's wife, c. 1827*

... such a devil for ugliness as you never beheld—a regular strolling player in a barn, a cap bolt upright of a yard's length, her hair behind nearly pulled up to the roots to be got into the cap, and in front an amethyst star half mast high. ...

SOURCE: Thomas Creevey, *The Creevey Papers.*

iii. *The most variable thing in nature*

There is not so variable a thing in nature as a lady's head-dress: within my own memory I have known it rise and fall above thirty degrees. About ten years ago it shot up to a very great height, insomuch that the female part of our species were much taller than the men. The women were of such enormous stature, that 'we appeared as grasshoppers before them': at present the whole sex is in a manner dwarfed and shrunk into a race of beauties that seems almost another species. I remember several ladies, who were once very near seven foot high, that at present want some inches of five: how they came to be thus curtailed I cannot learn.

SOURCE: Joseph Addision, *The Spectator*, No. 98, Friday, June 22, 1711.

iv. *Hair powder for the army*

The British Army, in the third George's reign, used 6,500 tons of flour for powdering [the hair] every year.

SOURCE: T. H. White, *The Age of Scandal*, Jonathan Cape, 1950, Ch. 2.

HENRIETTA MARIA (1609–1669), queen of Charles I.

i. *Henrietta takes Lady Strickland's silver for the King*

In February 1643 Henrietta Maria landed at Bridlington, Yorkshire with munitions and supplies for the king. Before she left on her march for York she quartered herself with a Parliamentarian family, the Stricklands of Boynton Hall. Sir William Strickland, a member of Parliament, was away, and Lady Strickland loyally did her best to entertain the queen, bringing out all the family silver.

Thanking Lady Strickland for her hospitality, she dropped her little bombshell.

'I am afraid I may be accused of ill appreciating the courtesy you have shown me,' she told her hostess. 'But unhappily the affairs of the King, thanks to the disaffection and evil conduct of those who should show themselves his most loyal defenders, have arrived at a point where he has need of money. Parliament having refused the subsidies necessary to sustain the honour of the Crown, it is incumbent to obtain it by other methods, and it is with real regret that I find myself compelled to take possession of the silver which I have seen during my stay here.'

Dumbfounded, Lady Strickland could only bow her submission, while the Queen hastened to explain that it was just a loan, which would soon be repaid, because she had no doubt of the early pacifying of the country. The silver would then be returned, or at least its value, and meanwhile she left a portrait of herself as much a pledge as a souvenir of her visit.

SOURCE: Janet Mackay, *Little Madam—a Biography of Henrietta Maria*, G. Bell & Sons, 1939, p. 219. *Note:* the portrait left by the Queen is still at Boynton Hall!

ii. *Henrietta Maria and the jawbone of an ass*

Lord Paget (1609–1678) was at first in sympathy with the Parliamentary cause, but joined the king's forces on the outbreak of war. He had 'a long lean face, not differing in length from that of an ass'.

Once, informing the Queen of the strength of his party, he had remarked:

'Madam, we are as strong as Samson.'

'My lord,' she had replied, 'I easily believe it, seeing you want not among you the jawbone of an ass.'

Thereafter at Court he was known familiarly as 'Samson'.

SOURCE: Hugh Ross Williamson, *John Hampden, A Life*, Hodder & Stoughton, 1933, p. 291.

iii. *A dispute at dinner*

Queen Henrietta incurred great unpopularity through dismissing Protestants from her service and retaining a number of French Catholics.

The king and queen dining together in the presence, Mr. Hacket (chaplain to the Lord Keeper Williams) being then to say grace, the confessor would have prevented him, but that Hacket shoved him away; whereupon the confessor went to the queen's side, and was about to say grace again, but that the king pulling the dishes unto him, and the carvers falling to their business, hindered. When dinner was done, the confessor thought, standing by the queen, to have been before Mr. Hacket, but Mr. Hacket again got the start. The confessor, nevertheless, begins his grace as loud as Mr. Hacket, with such confusion that the king in great passion instantly rose from the table and, taking the queen by the hand, retired into the bedchamber.

SOURCE: letter from Mr. Mead to Sir Martin Stuteville, October 1625, Brit. Museum, Sloane MSS.

HENRY I (1068–1135), King of England.

'From that day he was never seen to smile' (the loss of the *White Ship*)

As he was embarking at Barfleur [in 1120], according to Orderic Vitalis, a Norman called Thomas Fitz-Stephen came to him and, offering him a gold mark, said:

'My father served your family at sea all his life; it was on his ship that your father was borne to England when he went to fight against Harold. My lord king, grant me in fief the same office. I have for your royal service a vessel thoroughly equipped, known as the *White Ship*.'

The king answered:

'I have chosen the vessel on which I shall cross, but I willingly entrust to you my sons, William and Richard, and all their retinue.'

By order of the king nearly three hundred persons embarked on the *White Ship*. There were great barons, among them eighteen ladies of noble birth, daughters, sisters, nieces, or wives of kings and counts. All this brilliant youth prepared joyously for the voyage. They gave wine to the fifty oarsmen, and drove away with derision the priests who wished to bless the vessel.

Meanwhile, night fell, but the moon illumined the still surface of the waters. The young princes begged Thomas, the captain, to urge on the oarsmen that they might overtake the king's vessel which was already far ahead. The crew, excited by the wine, eagerly obeyed, and in order to take the shortest route, the captain coasted close by the Race of Catteville, which is bordered by rocks just below the surface of the water. The *White Ship* struck one of them violently, a gaping hole was made. A terrible cry arose from the whole crew; but the water gained. All became silent. Two men seized hold of the main-yard, Berold, a butcher of Rouen, and young Godfrey, son of Gilbert of the Eagle. They saw a man's head appearing in the water; it was Thomas, the pilot, who, after having plunged into the waves, came up again to the surface.

'What has become of the king's son?' he asked them.

'He has not reappeared, neither he nor his brother, nor any of the family,' answered the two shipwrecked men.

'Woe is me!' cried Thomas, and he sank once more into the sea. Young Godfrey of the Eagle could not stand the cold of that freezing night of December; he loosed his hold of the yard, and allowed himself to sink to the bottom, after having commended his companion to God. Berold, the butcher, the poorest of the shipwrecked company, who was picked up the next morning by some fishermen, alone remained to recount the disaster. . . .

It was from a child that King Henry first heard the terrible news. At the first words he fell to the ground as if thunderstruck, and from that day he was never seen to smile again.

SOURCE: Orderic Vitalis or Orderic Vital (1075–1143?), monk of St. Evroult, Normandy, author of *Historia Ecclesiastica*; the above account from Victor Duruy, *A Short History of France*, 1873, Everyman's Library edition, J. M. Dent & Son, 1917, Vol. 1, pp. 233–234.

HENRY II (1133–1189), King of England.

The King who never sat down

Although his legs are bruised and livid from hard riding, he never sits down except when on horseback or at meals.

SOURCE: Peter of Blois, *Epistolae*, edit. John Allen Giles, 1848. See also BECKET, THOMAS.

HENRY II (1519–1559), King of France.

'The Fatal Tournament'

A double marriage was to cement the peace [between France and Spain]; Philip II was to marry Elizabeth, daughter of the French king, and Emmanuel-Philibert was to marry the king's sister Marguerite. Brilliant fêtes were held before the departure of the princesses. The tournament was still popular, and Henry II showed much skill and grace in it. After many brilliant passages of arms and when the sports seemed to be ended he wished to have a final course against the captain of his guard, Count Montgomery. The two lances struck each other, but the count did not lower the lance he held in his hand quickly enough, and striking the king on the visor, his lance pierced it, the point entering Henry's eye and penetrating to his brain. The king fell mortally wounded. . . .

SOURCE: Victor Duruy, *A Short History of France*, 1873, Everyman's Library edition, J. M. Dent & Sons, 1917, Vol. 1, p. 506. Duruy's account does not perhaps make it clear that the King and Montgomery both splintered their lances by direct hits on the opponent's armour. The rules of the tournament obliged a knight immediately to lower his lance to avoid accident with the jagged end. This Montgomery neglected to do, and it was the splintered shaft that did the damage. Lances by this time were not made of solid wood, but of hollow construction, the object being not to hurl the opponent from the saddle, as in lustier days, but simply to score a hit.

HENRY V (1387–1422), King of England.

i. *Change of heart*

As soon as he was made King he was changed suddenly into another man, zealous for honesty, modesty and gravity; there being no sort of virtue that he was not anxious to display.

SOURCE: Thomas Walsingham (fl. 1380–1420), author of *Chronica Majora* (now lost), *Chronicon Angliae* and, probably, *Historia Anglicana*. The contemporary evidence for Henry V's wild youth is, however, very slight; and, e.g., the well-known story of the

Prince being committed to prison by Chief Justice Gascoigne (used by Shakespeare) is first mentioned in Sir Thomas Elyot's *Boke called the Governour*, 1521. For an examination of the evidence in State Papers, see Alex. Charles Ewald, *Stories from the State Papers*, 1881, pp. 12–29.

ii. *The ever-durable name of Agincourt*

He then asked Montjoye* to whom the victory belonged; to him or to the king of France? Montjoye replied that the victory was his, and could not be claimed by the king of France. The king then asked the name of the castle he saw near him: he was told it was called Azincourt.

'Well then,' added he, 'since all battles should bear the name of the fortress nearest to the spot where they were fought, this battle shall, from henceforth, bear the ever-durable name of Azincourt.'

SOURCE: *The Chronicles of Enguerrand de Monstrelet*, trans. Thomas Johnes.

iii. *'I would not have one more'*

'Sire,' said a friend, 'I would that we had ten thousand more good archers who would gladly be here with us to-day.'

'You speak as a fool!' cried Henry. 'By the God of heaven, on whose grace I lean, I would not have one more even if I could. This people is God's people. He has entrusted them to me to-day, and he can bring down the pride of these Frenchmen who boast of their numbers and their strength.'

SOURCE: Philip Lindsay, *Kings of Merry England . . .*, Ivor Nicholson & Watson, 1935, p. 506.

iv. *Henry V's thanksgiving after Agincourt*

When Henry the fifth had given that famous overthrow unto the French at Agincourt, he fell down upon his knees, and commanded his whole army to do the same, saying that verse in the Psalm:

'Non nobis Domine, non nobis, sed nomini tuo da gloriam—

* Chief herald to the King of France.

Not unto us, O Lord, not unto us, but unto thy name give the glory.'

SOURCE: William Camden, *Remains Concerning Britain*, 7th impression, 1674. Shakespeare puts the same words into the mouth of the King when Henry tells Exeter to proclaim it through the host as an offence punishable by death to boast of the victory or to take the praise from God, which is his only.

HENRY VI (1421–1471), King of England. Henry VI, the son of Henry V, began to reign at the age of nine months.

The King on his mother's knee

In the third year of this king's reign, when the war against France was still carried on with various success, the Protector and Council thought it necessary, in order to engage both Lords and Commons more zealously in their interests, to bring the infant king into the house; and accordingly, on the day of their meeting, he was carried through the city on a great horse to Westminster. Being come to the palace, he was thence conducted to the House of Lords, and sat on his mother's knee on the throne.

'It was a strange sight,' says Speed,* 'and the first time it was ever seen in England, an infant sitting in his mother's lap, and before it could tell what English meant, to exercise the place of sovereign direction in open Parliament.'

SOURCE: Thomas Byerley and Joseph Clinton Robinson, *The Percy Anecdotes*, 1820–1823.

HENRY VII (1457–1509), King of England.

'My attorney must speak with you'

The Statutes of Livery and Maintenance (1495 and 1504). The practice of granting distinctive uniforms or costumes to the servants of barons and great landowners grew to formidable proportions in the Middle Ages. These bodies of retainers, wearing the colours and devices of their lords, were equivalent to

* John Speed (1552?–1629), author of *History of Great Britaine*, 1611, etc.

private armies and often acted as though they were above the law. A number of attempts were made to break this practice, but it was left to Henry VII to bring in effective legislation. The famous Court of Star Chamber, which was later to be used for less worthy purposes, was set up by Henry to deal with offences against the new statutes.

'There remaineth to this day a report that the king was on a time entertained by the Earl of Oxford (that was his principal servant for both war and peace) nobly and sumptuously at his Castle at Henningham [Hedingham]. And, at the king's going away, the earl's servants stood, in a seemly manner, in their livery-coats, with cognizances, ranged on both sides, and made the king a lane. The king called the earl unto him and said:

'My lord, I have heard much of your hospitality, but I see that it is greater than the speech. These handsome gentlemen and yeomen which I see on both sides of me are sure your menial servants.'

The earl smiled, and said:

'It may please your grace, that were not for mine ease. They are most of them my retainers that are come to do me service at such a time as this, and chiefly to see your grace.'

The king started a little, and said:

'By my faith, my lord, I thank you for my good cheer, but I may not endure to have my laws broken in my sight. My attorney must speak with you.'

And it is part of the report that the earl compounded for no less than fifteen thousand marks.

SOURCE: Francis Bacon, *Historie of the Raigne of K. Henry VII*, 1622. See also BOSWORTH, BATTLE OF and MORTON, JOHN.

HENRY VIII (1491–1547), King of England.

i. *The Flemish mare*

The King found her [Anne of Cleeves (1515–1557), his fourth Queen] so different from her picture . . . that . . . he swore they had brought him a Flanders mare.

SOURCE: Smollett, *History of England*, vi, p. 68.

ii. *A Bishop's confession*

Bishop Stubbs did, indeed confess (while he was only a professor) that the portraits of those wives 'were, if not a justifica-
tion, at least a colourable occasion for understanding the
readiness with which he put them away.'

SOURCE: A. F. Pollard, *Henry VIII*, in *The Great Tudors*, edit.
Katherine Garvin, Ivor Nicholson & Watson, 1935, pp. 23–24.

iii. *Judgment from Sir Walter Ralegh*

. . . if all the pictures & patterns of a merciless Prince were
lost in the World, they might all again be painted to the life,
out of the story of this King.

SOURCE: Sir Walter Ralegh, *The Historie of the World*, 1614,
Preface.

iv. *Verse for the six wives*

> *Three Kates, two Nans, and one dear Jane I wedded;*
> *One Spanish, one Dutch, and four English wives;*
> *From two I was divorced, two I beheaded,*
> *One died in childbed, and one me survives.*

SOURCE: Thomas Fuller, *The English Worthies*, 1662.

See also ANNE BOLEYN; MORE, SIR THOMAS; and
WOLSEY, CARDINAL.

HENRY BENEDICT MARIA CLEMENT, CARDINAL YORK
(1725–1807); the Jacobite **HENRY IX,** second son of the
Chevalier de St. George, the Jacobite 'James III'.

The Cardinal's cur

His Eminence was an invalid, and under a strict regimen; but
as he still retained his taste for savoury meats, a contest usually
took place between him and his servants for the possession
of each rich dish which they formally set before him, and then
endeavoured to snatch away, while he, with greater eagerness,
strove to seize it in its transit.

Among the Cardinal's most favourite attendants was a miserable cur dog, which one day attached itself to His Eminence at the gate of St. Peter's, an occurrence to which he constantly referred, as a proof of his true royal blood—the cur being, as he supposed, a King Charles spaniel, and therefore endowed with an instinctive hereditary acquaintance with the House of Stuart.

SOURCE: based on Lord Cloncurry's *Personal Reminiscences*, 1846; John Timbs, *A Century of Anecdote, 1760–1860*.

HERBERT, EDWARD, first **BARON HERBERT OF CHERBURY** (1583–1648), historian, diplomat and philosopher.

i. *'It is pity he was married so young'*

About the year of our Lord 1600 I came to London. . . . Not long after this, curiosity rather than ambition brought me to Court; and as it was the manner of those times for all men to kneel down before the great Queen Elizabeth who then reigned, I was likewise upon my knees in the Presence Chamber when she passed by to the Chapel at Whitehall. As soon as she saw me she stopt, and swearing her usual oath demanded:

'Who is this?'

Every body here present looked upon me, but no man knew me, till Sir James Croft . . . finding the Queen stayed, returned back and told who I was, and that I had married Sir William Herbert of St. Gillian's daughter. The Queen hereupon looked attentively upon me, and swearing again her ordinary oath, said:

'It is pity he was married so young,' and thereupon gave her hand to kiss twice, both times gently clapping me on the cheek.

SOURCE: *The Life of Edward Lord Herbert of Cherbury written by Himself*, first pub., 1764; 1770 issue, p. 53.

ii. *A sign from heaven*

Herbert published his chief philosophical work, *De Veritate*, in 1624 (Paris) (1645, London).

Being thus doubtful in my Chamber, one fair day in the Summer, my casement being opened towards the South, the sun shining clear and no wind stirring, I took my book De Veritate in my hand, and kneeling on my knees devoutly said these words:

'O Thou Eternal God, Author of the Light which now shines upon me, and Giver of all inward illuminations, I do beseech Thee of thy infinite goodness to pardon a greater request than a sinner ought to make; I am not satisfied enough whether I shall publish this book De Veritate; if it be for thy Glory, I beseech thee give me some sign from Heaven; if not I shall suppress it.'

I had no sooner spoken these words, but a loud tho' yet gentle noise came from the heavens (for it was like nothing on earth) which did so comfort and cheer me, that I took my petition as granted, and that I had the sign I demanded, whereupon also I resolved to print my book. This (how strange soever it may seem) I protest before the Eternal God is true, neither am I any way superstitiously deceived herein, since I did not only clearly hear the noise, but in the serenest sky that ever I saw. . . .

SOURCE: ibid., pp. 171–172.

HIGHWAYMEN.

i. *The earl who would not surrender*

The fifth Earl of Berkeley, who died in 1810, had always declared that any one might without disgrace be overcome by superior numbers, but that he would never surrender to a single highwayman. As he was crossing Hounslow Heath one night, on his way from Berkeley Castle to London, his travelling carriage was stopped by a man on horseback, who put his head in the window and said:

'I believe you are Lord Berkeley?'

'I am.'

'I believe you have always boasted that you would never surrender to a single highwayman?'

'I have.'

'Well,' presenting a pistol, 'I am a single highwayman, and I say, "Your money or your life".'

'You cowardly dog,' said Lord Berkeley, 'do you think I can't see your confederate skulking behind you?'

The highwayman, who was really alone, looked hurriedly round, and Lord Berkeley shot him through the head.

SOURCE: George W. E. Russell, *Collections and Recollections*, Smith, Elder & Co., 1903, Ch. 1.

ii. *George II is robbed*

William IV was accustomed to relate how his great-grand-father George II, when walking alone in Kensington Gardens, was robbed by a single highwayman who climbed over the wall, and pleading his great distress, and with a manner of much deference, deprived the King of his purse, his watch, and his buckles.

SOURCE: W. E. H. Lecky; quoted T. H. White, *The Age of Scandal*, 1950, Ch. 9.

See also DUVAL, CLAUDE.

HOGG, QUINTIN (b. 1907), formerly Viscount Hailsham; renounced his peerage; offices have included those of Lord Privy Seal, Minister of Education, Minister for Science and Lord President of the Council.

The meaning of 'deplorable'

At the time of the introduction of the Commonwealth Immigrants Bill I allowed myself to become nettled when, having described the Bill as 'deplorable', Michael Ramsay, Archbishop of Canterbury, left the Chamber before waiting to hear the Government reply.

In reply to my note of rebuke, I received a courteous answer couched in terms of admirable Christian charity.

By calling the Bill 'deplorable', it seemed that the archbishop was not meaning to criticise it. He had merely wished to convey that the need for it was truly to be deplored.

At the time I seem to remember that I replied acidly that in that case His Grace would hardly complain if I said that he had made a deplorable speech.

SOURCE: Quintin Hogg, *Sunday Express*, April 2, 1967.

HOUSING PROBLEM (17th Century).

The 'obstenate and refractorie fellowe'

. . . we the Inhabitantes of the towne of Wivenhoe doe informe your worshippes of one Edward Mayer the elder of our towne, an obstenate and refracterie fellowe who will not live in Ranke and order amongst his neyghbours in a house, But will live in a boate drawn up on dry land in which he hath built a chimney. . . .

SOURCE: Essex Record Office; court action, Michaelmas, 1641.

HOWARD, CHARLES, second BARON HOWARD OF EFFINGHAM (1536–1624); held command against the Spanish Armada, 1588.

*The Admiral of osier**

His service in the eighty-eight is notoriously known, when, at the first news of the Spaniards' approach, he towed at a cable with his own hands to draw out the harbour-bound ships into the sea. I dare boldly say he drew more . . . by his presence and example, than any ten in the place. True it is, he was no deep seaman (not to be expected from one of his extraction), but had skill enough to know those who had more skill than himself, and to follow their instructions; and would not starve the

* i.e. willow, tough but amenable to persuasion.

R

queen's service by feeding his own sturdy wilfulness, but was ruled by the experienced in sea matters; the queen having a navy of oak, and an admiral of osier.

SOURCE: Thomas Fuller, *The Worthies of England*, 1662; 1952 edition, George Allen & Unwin, p. 549.

HUDSON, JEFFERY (1619–1682), dwarf; served as a captain of horse in the Civil War; captured by Barbary pirates and taken into slavery; killed a man in a duel, when his opponent derisively armed himself with a squirt.

'When the pie was opened. . . .'

His father . . . presented him at Burley-on-the-Hill to the Duchess of Buckingham, being then nine years of age and scarce a foot and a half in height, as I am informed by credible persons then and there present, and still alive. . . .

He was without any deformity, wholly proportionable. . . . It was not long before he was presented in a cold baked pie to King Charles and Queen Mary [i.e., Henrietta Maria] at an entertainment; and ever after lived (whilst the court lived) in great plenty therein.

SOURCE: Thomas Fuller, *The Worthies of England*, 1662. Hudson was 18 inches high till he was about thirty years of age, but afterwards reached 3 feet 6 inches or a little more.

HUNDRED YEARS WAR, THE. Various dates are given as the starting and finishing points of this prolonged period of warfare and squabbling between England and France. From Edward III's first expedition to the death of Sir John Talbot at Castillon (i.e. 1338–1453) is as reasonable a definition as any.

i. *The battle-prayer of La Hire, soldier of France*

La Hire was one of the staunchest supporters of Joan of Arc, half-brigand, half-knight, who is said to have renounced his mighty gift for swearing at the Maid's request; though, in order to allow him some scope for expressing his rage, she permitted him to swear by his stick.

[At the Siege of Montargis, 1427] Dunois and La Hire set out with 1600 men to attempt the forcing of an entry into the place. On the way La Hire met a priest and sought absolution from him.

'Confess first,' said the priest.

'I have not time, for I must fall upon the English. But I have done all that a man of war is wont to do.'

The chaplain gave him absolution such as it was. La Hire, content, fell on his knees by the roadside and uttered his prayer:

'God, I pray thee that to-day thou wilt do for La Hire that which thou wouldst have La Hire do for thee, if he were God and thou were La Hire.'

SOURCE: Victor Duruy, *A Short History of France*, 1863, Everyman edition, 1917, J. M. Dent & Sons, 1917, Vol. i, p. 360.

Another version given of La Hire's prayer is: 'I pray my God to do for La Hire what La Hire would do for Him, if he were Captain and La Hire was God.'

ii. *A noble lady shows her mettle*

The Earl of Montfort, who had claimed the dukedom of Brittany in defiance of the King of France, was captured at Nantes in 1341. His wife, sister of Lewis of Flanders, appealed to Edward III for help and he sent Sir Walter Manny with a considerable force, including 6000 archers. They were, however, delayed forty days by contrary winds. Meanwhile, the Countess showed what stuff she was made of at Hennebon, where she was besieged by Charles of Blois, whom the French king's council had decided was the rightful Duke of Brittany.

The virago Countess was herself armed *cap-à-pied* [head to foot], and rode about on a large strong courser from street to street, desiring and commanding all men to make good their defence. The very women and maidens she ordered to cut their garments shorter, and to carry stones and pots of quick-lime to the walls, to throw down upon the enemy.

And she herself, to set an example of hardiness to her sex, performed that day such an exploit as few ages can equal. . . . When she had thus set all hands to work, she mounted the highest tower to see how the Frenchmen were disposed without:

and there she saw how all the army was engaged at the asault, and had left the camp unguarded. Hereupon she descended, took again her courser, all armed as she had been, and, selecting 300 horsemen, went with them to another gate, which was not assaulted. Here she issued forth with all her company and, taking a course, dashed into the French camp, cutting down and setting fire to their tents and pavilions.

SOURCE: various chroniclers, including Froissart; this version from Joshua Barnes, *The History of that Most Victorious Monarch Edward III . . .* , 1688, p. 257.

iii. *A Scots knight seeks diversion*

Sir John Ashton performed the following feat at the siege of Noyon, in 1370.

At that time there was done an extraordinary feat of arms by a Scotch knight named Sir John Ashton, one of those men of arms of Scotland who had now entered King Edward's pay. This man left his rank with his spear in his hand, his page riding behind him, and went towards the barriers of Noyon, where he alighted, saying:
'Here, hold my horse, and stir not from hence.'
And so he came to the barriers. There were at that time [behind the barriers] Sir John de Roye and Sir Lancelot de Lorris, with ten or twelve more, who all wondered what this knight designed to do. He for his part, being close at the barriers, said unto them:
'Gentlemen, I come hither to visit you; and because I see you will not come forth of your barriers to me, I will come into you if I may, and prove my knighthood against you. Win me if you can.'
And with that he leap'd over the bars and began to lay about him like a lion, he at them, and they at him; so that he fought thus against them all for near the space of an hour, and hurt several of them.
And all the while those of the town beheld with much delight, from the walls and their garret windows, his great

activity, strength and courage; but they offered not to do him hurt, as they might very easily have done, if they had been minded to cast stones or darts at him. But the French knights charged them to the contrary, saying how they should let them alone to deal with him.

When matters had continued thus about an hour, the Scotch page came to the barriers with his master's horse in his hand, and said in his language:

'Sir, pray come away. It is high time for you to leave off now, for the army is marched off, out of the fight.'

The knight heard his man, and then gave two or three terrible strokes about him to clear the way, and so, armed as he was, he leap'd back again over the barriers, and mounted his horse, having not received any hurt; and, turning to the Frenchmen said:

'Adieu, Sirs! I thank you for my diversion.'

SOURCE: Ibid. p. 801.

iv. *The cattle that recognized the alarm bell*

The chaotic state of France at the time of Joan of Arc's revival of her country's fortunes is vividly described by a French historian.

In sooth, the estate of France was then most miserable. There appeared nothing but a horrible face, confusion, poverty, desolation, solitariness, and fear. . . . The least farms and hamlets were fortified by these robbers, English, Burgundians, and French, every one striving to do his worst; all men of war were well agreed to spoil the countryman and the merchant.

Even the cattle, accustomed to the alarm bell, the sign of the enemy's approach, would run home of themselves without any guide, by this accustomed misery.

SOURCE: De Serres; quoted Southey, *Joan of Arc* and Sir Edward Creasy, *The Fifteen Decisive Battles of the World*.

See also CRÉCY; EDWARD III; DU GUESCLIN, BERTRAND; and TALBOT, SIR JOHN.

INDIAN MUTINY, THE (1857–1858).

i. *'Touch not, taste not, handle not'*

> One of the main causes of the smouldering discontents in India being brought to a head was the issue to the native troops of, instead of the ordinary cartridge, the lubricated type, for the new Enfield rifle.

The cartridges served out to them, lubricated, as they thought, with the fat of the cow, the sacred animal of the Hindus, and of the pig, the unclean animal of the Mohammedans, were, at once, a cause and a sympton of the fast-spreading panic; for they furnished one more, and, as it seemed, a crowning proof of the blow which Government was insidiously preparing to strike at the most sacred feelings and institutions of both sections of the community. . . . What booted it that the obnoxious grease had been analysed and found to be harmless; that it was, henceforward, to be mixed by the Sepoys themselves from ingredients which they themselves should be at liberty to choose; that they were bidden to tear off, and no longer to bite off, the end of the cartridge—to touch, that is, and not to taste the unclean thing?

'Touch not, taste not, handle not,' was still the cry of the poor, panic-stricken Sepoy. . . . If they were no longer obliged to touch the greased cartridge with their hands, the very flour which they were eating had been mixed, as they believed, by their insidious enemies with the bone-dust of the same forbidden animals! They would henceforward be looked upon— in fact, they were already looked upon by their more fortunate comrades who had not been thought worthy of the honour of handling the Enfield rifle—as outcasts. . . .

What happened at Umballa . . . may be taken as a sample of that which was taking place elsewhere. There was at Umballa a detachment of the 36th Native Infantry, a regiment which formed part of the escort of General Anson, the Commander-in-Chief, who was, at that time, engaged on a tour of inspection. When he approached Umballa, on his way to Simla, the non-commissioned officers of the detachment went forth to greet their comrades. They were received with averted looks.

The *lotah* and the *hookah* were refused them; they were, in fact, treated as outcasts, and returned to their detachments ruined men.

SOURCE: H. Bosworth Smith, *Life of Lord Lawrence*, Nelson & Sons, pp. 267–269.

ii. *John Nicholson visits the outposts*

About this time a stranger of very striking appearance was remarked visiting all our picquets, examining everything, and making most searching enquiries about their strength and history. His attire gave no clue to his rank; it evidently never gave the owner a thought. Moreover, in those anxious times, everyone went as he pleased; perhaps no two officers were dressed alike. . . . He was a man cast in a giant mould, with massive chest and powerful limbs, and an expression ardent and commanding, with a dash of roughness; features of stern beauty, a long black beard, and deep sonorous voice. There was something of immense strength, talent, and resolution in his whole gait and manner, and a power of ruling men on high occasions that no-one could escape noticing at once.

SOURCE: *History of the Siege of Delhi*, by an Officer who served there; quoted H. Bosworth Smith, *Life of Lord Lawrence*, Nelson & Sons.

iii. *The fall of Nicholson, Delhi, 1857*

. . . the one street by which they could approach the Lahore gate was, like many streets in Eastern towns, so narrow that six men could hardly walk abreast along it. It had been barricaded by the watchful enemy. It was swept, from the other end, by a gun loaded with grape, and the windows and the flat roofs of the houses on either side of it bristled with riflemen. What wonder, if from death in such manifold and such insidious forms even the stoutest hearts shrunk? Nicholson saw how things stood, and, knowing that if his force hesitated they were lost, sprang to the front, and, waving his sword over his head, as if he were a simple captain, called aloud upon his men to follow him. Had he been serving in the ranks in the open field, his noble stature would have marked him out as a target for the enemy's sharpshooters, but now his commanding presence and gestures, as he strode forward alone between the muzzles of an unseen foe, made escape impossible. There was death in every window and on every house-top; and the 'brute bullet' which did the deed was but one of many which must have found its way to that noble heart before he could have crossed swords with the foe. He fell, mortally wounded, and with him, young as he was, and little known to fame as he had been, till the extremity of the peril brought him to the front and revealed him in his Titanic mould of heart and limb, there fell the man whom, perhaps, of all the heroes of the Mutiny—the Lawrence brothers alone excepted—India could, at that juncture, least afford to lose. He begged that he might be left lying on the ground till Delhi was ours. But this could not be, and he was borne off by his followers to his old quarters on the Ridge.

SOURCE: H. Bosworth Smith, *Life of Lord Lawrence*, Nelson & Sons, pp. 389–390.

HYDER ALI (d. 1782), Sultan of Mysore.

i. *The lad to be pitied*

In 1780, Hyder Ali invaded the Carnatic at the head of 100,000 men and ravaged the country. Among his successes was the heavy defeat of Baillie's forces, as a result of which about two hundred Europeans were imprisoned in Seringapatam. Among them was Captain, later General Sir David, Baird (1757–1829), who was not released for four years. Baird was of great stature, a grim, dour soldier, many times wounded in battle.

He is now best remembered by the famous remark made by his mother, when she heard in 1780 that Hyder had chained his prisoners together two by two:

'I pity the chiel [lad] that's chained to our Davie.'

SOURCE: C. R. L. Fletcher, *Historical Portraits 1700–1850*, Oxford, 1919.

ii. *The Prince with no eyebrows*

One of the circumstances which most excited the English Governor's astonishment was to see that Hyder had no eyebrows; nor, indeed, a single hair left on any part of his face. A man constantly attended near him, whose sole function and employment consisted in pulling out, with a pair of nippers, the first hair that made its appearance on the Sultan's countenance. Hyder, perceiving the surprise which this fact occasioned in Du Pré, said to him:

'I observe that you wonder at my having no eye-brows; as well as my attention to cause every hair that appears on my face to be immediately eradicated. The reason I will explain to you. I am the Nabob of Mysore, and it is an object of policy with me that my Subjects should see no face in my dominions resembling the countenance of their Sovereign.'

SOURCE: Sir N. William Wraxall, *Historical Memoirs of My Own Time*, 1815, Vol. II, pp. 383–384.

IRELAND.

i. *The Red Hand of Ulster*

The Red Hand appears in the officially registered arms of the Province of Ulster. It derived from the princes of Ulster, the O'Neills.

In an ancient expedition of some adventurers to Ireland, their leader declared that whoever first touched the shore should possess the territory which he reached. O'Neil, from whom descended the princes of Ulster, bent upon obtaining the reward, and seeing another boat likely to land, cut off his hand and threw it on the coast.

SOURCE: a common tradition; this version from John Timbs, *Ancestral Stories and Traditions of Great Families*, 1869, p. 171.
When James I created the rank of baronet 'in place between the degree of a Baron and the degree of a Knight', it cost the holders about £1000 each, the money being destined as a contribution to

the settlement of Ireland. The baronets so created were granted the Red Hand on their shields as an indication of their rank, and this is usually called the Red Hand of Ulster. Some Irish heralds, however, insist that it is not, in fact, the Ulster badge; because the Red Hand of Ulster is a right hand, and the one found on nearly every one of James's baronets is a left hand. Two of the Irish authorities, Sir Christopher and Adrian Lynch-Robinson, say despairingly, 'We give it up'. So, presumably, can everyone else.

ii. *The harp of Ireland and the royal arms of England*

The harp of Ireland first appeared on the Royal Arms in the reign of James I.

Of the harp of Ireland, the Earl of Northampton wittily remarked:

'The best reason that I can observe for the bearing thereof is that it resembles that country in being such an instrument that it requires more cost to keep it in tune than it is worth.'

SOURCE: C. Wilfrid Scott-Giles, *The Romance of Heraldry*, J. M. Dent & Sons, 1957 reprint, p. 177.

iii. *The Earl who was saved by an ape*

John FitzThomas, first Earl of Kildare (d. 1316), was an adherent of Edward I and served him in the Scottish wars.

There is a tradition connected with John FitzThomas which explains the origin of the crest. . . . While an infant, he was in the Castle of Woodstock, near Athy, co. Kildare, when an alarm of fire was raised; in the confusion that ensued the child was forgotten, and on the servants returning to search for him, the room in which he lay was found in ruins. Soon after a strange sound was heard on one of the towers, and on looking up, they saw an ape, which was usually kept chained, carefully holding the child in his arms. The earl afterwards, in gratitude for his preservation, adopted a monkey for his crest.

SOURCE: Sir Bernard Burke and Ashworth Burke, *A Genealogical and Heraldic History of the Peerage and Baronetage . . .* , 1930 edition, p. 1461. It is a fact that certain of John FitzThomas's descendants, including the Dukes of Leinster, have a chained ape as a crest, and similar apes as supporters to their shield of arms.

iv. *The Irish Rebellion of 1641, and the girl called Honour*

The rebellion of 1641 was headed by Sir Phelim O'Neill, who had been expelled from the Irish Parliament as a rebel. An appalling massacre of Protestants followed, some putting the figure at 300,000 murdered and expelled from their homes in two years. One of the 'prohibited' clergy was an Englishman named Brooke, who held a living near Kells, on the borders of Cavan County, but who was in London at the outbreak of the rebellion. He had married an Irish girl, who had remained at Kells and who was expecting a baby. One evening she received warning that the parsonage was to be sacked by a rebel called Black Mulmore, and she fled on foot, accompanied by a four-year-old daughter, in an effort to get to a friend's house. She was intercepted by a young rebel, who found out who she was.

He drew a naken skeane, or long dagger, from his belt . . . and the glitter of it in the cold moonlight made the blood bound from her heart.

'I must kill you,' he said, 'we are sworn to it—you must die, as well as the child by your side: come, say your last prayer and prepare for death.'

She looked at him steadily . . .and said:

'I have been praying to God, and *he* has told me that I am not to die by your hand. No, you dare not do it. God will not suffer you.'

Three times he brandished his skeane, and pointed it at her heart; and three times she lifted her hands and face to heaven, and said:

'No. God will not suffer you.'

Dashing his weapon on the grass, he cried:

'You are right, God will not suffer me. You are a brave woman . . . but come, you are in great danger here. Will you trust to my honour and let me guide you to a place of safety?'

'With all my heart,' she answered, 'I will trust to your honour.'

He took her lower down to a ford in the river, which she crossed on stepping-stones nearly dryshod, and . . . pointed out to her the road which led to her friend's house, and prepared to leave her, when she addressed him solemnly, and said:

'I cannot find language to express my joy at my escape, or

my grateful sense of the conduct of my generous enemy; but if God gives me the baby I am carrying . . . it shall surely be called *Honour,* in remembrance of your honourable conduct to a weak and desolate woman.'

SOURCE: Sir Bernard Burke, *The Rise of Great Families,* 1873, pp. 87–93. Burke says that the story comes from an old manuscript, that the baby was born and 'was in due time baptized *Honour,* and the name, as well as the story, has been handed down and repeated among Mrs. Brooke's female descendants, through six generations.'

v. *Precaution by a King of Arms*

Sir Bernard Burke, Ulster King of Arms for much of Victoria's reign, was posed a difficult problem in about 1860 by different branches of the O'Conor or O'Connor family who almost came to blows on the subject of whether there should be one 'n' or two in the name.

So angry with each other were the contending parties, that I deemed it advisable to receive them in separate apartments. I deemed it prudent to take example from the meeting of the rival chiefs of Desmond and Ormonde, who agreed on one occasion to shake hands, but took the precaution of doing so through an aperture of an oak door, each fearing to be poinarded by the other.

SOURCE: Sir Bernard Burke, *The Rise of Great Families,* 1873, p. 143.

vi. *The Minister who didn't understand Habeas Corpus*

Forster* really acted badly. . . . He did not understand the nature of the Habeas Corpus Act. I will give you an example of what I mean. There was a doctor in Dublin. He was Medical Officer to the Local Government Board. He afterwards became a member of Parliament. I think his name was Kenny. Forster put him in gaol under the Habeas Corpus Suspension Act, and he then dismissed him from his office under the Local Government Board. He never told me a word about it. Of course it

* Appointed Chief Secretary for Ireland by Gladstone, 1880.

was monstrous. He could put a man into gaol on suspicion, but he could not dismiss him from his post on suspicion. The first thing I heard of the matter was when an Irish member asked a question about it in the House of Commons. I was sitting next to Forster at the time. I turned round and said to him:

'Why, you can't do this. It is quite unwarrantable.'

He said:

'Well, I suppose you will get up and say so.' I said:

'Indeed I will,' and I did. Now that is an instance of how little Forster knew about the Habeas Corpus Act. In fact, Forster, like a good many Radicals, had no adequate conception of public liberty.

SOURCE: W. E. Gladstone, talking to Barry O'Brien, 1897; quoted Barry O'Brien, *The Life of Charles Stuart Parnell*, Nelson & Sons, 1910.

JACOBITES, THE. (Latin *Jacobus*=James.) The adherents of the exiled James II and his descendants.

i. *Take it either way*

The following verses can be taken to support the Stuarts or the Hanoverians, according to the way they are read. The two verses taken separately, or read downwards one after the other, support the Hanoverian regime; taken as one verse, reading right across the page, they declare for the Stuarts.

I love with all my heart	*The Tory party here*
The Hanoverian part	*Most hateful do appear;*
And for that settlement	*I ever have deny'd*
My conscience gives consent	*To be on James's side.*
Most righteous is the cause	*To fight for such a king*
To fight for George's laws	*Will England's ruin bring.*
It is my mind and heart	*In this opinion I*
Tho' none will take my part	*Resolve to live and die.*

SOURCE: British Museum, Lansdown MSS.; quoted Stephen Collet, *Relics of Literature*, 1823, p. 170.

ii. *A Jacobite Joan of Arc*

Another . . . celebrated heroine, Miss Jenny Cameron of Glendessery, likewise attended the prince in all his warlike exploits. This lady, finding her nephew, the laird, a minor and a youth of no capacity, as soon as she heard of the prince's arrival, set about raising the men herself, and on the summons being sent by Lochiel to her nephew, she set off to Charles's head-quarters, at the head of 250 well armed men.

She was dressed in a sea-green riding habit, with a scarlet lapell, trimmed with gold, her hair tied behind in loose buckles, with a velvet cap, and scarlet feather; she rode on a bay gelding decked with green furniture, which was fringed with gold; instead of a whip, she carried a naked sword in her hand, and in this equipage arrived at the camp.

A female officer was a very extraordinary sight, and it being reported to the young chevalier, he went out of the lines to meet this supply. Miss Jenny rode up to him without the least concern, and gave him a soldier-like salute, and addressed him in words to the following effect—That as her nephew was not able to attend the royal standard, she had raised his men, and brought them to his highness; that she believed them ready to hazard their lives in his cause, and though at present they were commanded by a woman, yet she hoped they had nothing womanish about them. . . .

'These men, sir, are yours, they have devoted themselves to your service; they bring you hearts as well as hands. I can follow them no further, but I shall pray for your success.'

SOURCE: James Hogg, *The Jacobite Relics of Scotland*, 2nd series, 1821, p. 351. 'Colonel Cameron' as she was affectionately called thereafter, continued with the army till she was taken prisoner at Falkirk Muir and confined in Edinburgh Castle.

iii. *A noteworthy courier*

After the Battle of Prestonpans, September 21, 1745, in which the government forces, commanded by Sir John Cope, were heavily defeated by Prince Charles Edward's Highlanders, Cope fled ignominiously.

Sir John Cope himself was among the fugitives, and it is said that he fled in headlong speed to Berwick, where Lord Mark Ker welcomed him with the observation that he believed he was the first general in Europe that had brought the first tidings of his own defeat.

SOURCE: Charles Knight, *Old England*.

iv. *A premature hatchet*

Two Jacobite noblemen executed after Culloden were Lord Kilmarnock (1704–1746) and Lord Balmerino (1688–1746). One observer at their trial was George Augustus Selwyn (1719–1791), wit and holder of a number of minor political posts. Another was a Mrs. Bethel, who is described as 'hatchet-faced'.

At the trial of Lord Kilmarnock and Balmerino, observing Mrs. Bethel . . . looking wistfully at the rebel lords, 'What a shame it is,' said Selwyn, 'to turn her face to the prisoners till they are condemned.'

SOURCE: John Timbs, *A Century of Anecdote, 1760–1860*.

v. *The closed gates*

Prince Charles Edward paid a visit to Traquair House, a mile south of Innesleithen, Peebleshire, in 1745. After he had gone down the avenue from the house and out through the great gates, Lord Traquair shut and locked them, and swore that they should never be opened again till a Stuart came back to the throne. The gates have remained shut ever since, and another entrance constructed to the house. Though this was made more than two hundred years ago, it is still referred to as the 'new' entrance.

vi. *The resourcefulness of Flora Macdonald*

After the defeat of Prince Charles Edward at Culloden (April 16, 1746), he was helped to escape by the resourcefulness of Flora Macdonald, a lady of South Uist, who dressed him as her maidservant and brought him to the Isle of Skye, whence he was taken to France. The following incident occurred after the landing in

Skye, while the Prince was being brought to Port Rei. He was dressed at that time in 'a linen or cotton gown, with purple twigs, thickly stamped, and a white apron', and was accompanied by Flora Macdonald, Mr. Macdonald of Kingsborough, Mrs. Macdonald and her maid, and the Prince's personal servant, O'Neil.

When they overtook the prince and Kingsborough, Mrs. Macdonald was very desirous of seeing the prince's face, which he as carefully avoided by looking away from her, but, however, she had several opportunities of observing it. In wading a rivulet, the prince lifted his petticoats so high that Neil M'Echan called to him for God's sake to take care, or else he would discover himself. The prince laughed heartily and thanked him for his kind concern.

Mrs. Macdonald's maid could not keep her eyes off the prince, and said to Flora:

'I think I ne'er saw sic an impudent-looking woman as Kingsborough is a-walking with. I dare say she is an Irishwoman, or a man in woman's claes.'

Miss Macdonald replied that she was an Irish-woman, for she knew her, and had seen her before.

'Bless me,' quoth the maid, 'what lang strides she takes, and how awkwardly she wurks her petticoats. I believe those Irishwomen could fecht [fight] as weel as the men.'

SOURCE: James Hogg, *The Jacobite Relics of Scotland*, 2nd series, 1821, pp. 361–362. Hogg says: 'This relation is taken from the journal of O'Neil, and the mouths of Kingsborough, his lady, and Miss Flora Macdonald.'

vii. *Prince Charles Edward, philosopher*

On being condoled with, after the defeat at Culloden and during the escape to Skye:

'The wretched to-day be happy tomorrow. All great men would be the better to feel a little of what I do.'

SOURCE: ibid., p. 359.

viii. *A Jacobite expresses his feelings*

Extract from the Journal of David Polhill of Chipstead, Kent. Polhill's mother was a grand-daughter of Oliver Cromwell, and he inherited from her a portrait of the Protector.

June, 1730. Paid £4.4.0 to Mr. Gouge, a Painter, tho' a papist yet a good man, for mending an original picture (half length) of Cromwell. The picture was defaced by some Tory who came to see my house when I was from home, by thrusting the ferule of a cane thro' the left eye.

N.B. my housekeeper was a Jacobite, then unknown to me.

SOURCE: Manuscript Journal in possession of editor.

ix. *Young Boswell turns his coat*

Dr. Johnson used to tell the following story of his biographer's early years, which Boswell has confessed to be literally true:

'In 1745, Boswell was a fine boy, wore a white cockade, and prayed for King James, till one of his uncles (General Cochran) gave him a shilling on condition that he would pray for King George, which he accordingly did.'

SOURCE: Robert Chambers, *A Biographical Dictionary of Eminent Scotsmen*, 1837, Vol. 1, p. 267. Boswell was five years old at the time.

JAMES I (JAMES VI OF SCOTLAND) (1566–1625), King of England.

i. *A preacher hits out at fashionable ladies*, 1607

On January 6, 1607, Robert Wilkinson preached before the King at Whitehall, on the occasion of the marriage of Lord Hay. The text was 'She is like a merchant's ship, she bringeth her food from afar' (Proverbs xxxi. 14).

But of all qualities, a woman must not have one quality of a ship, and that is too much rigging.

Oh what a wonder it is to see a ship under sail, with her tacklings and her masts, and her tops and her top gallants, with

S

her upper decks and her nether decks, and so bedeckt with her streamers, flags and ensignes and I know not what; yea, but a world of wonders it is to see a woman, created in God's image, so miscreate oft times, and deformed with her French, and her Spanish, and her foolish fashions, that he that made her, when he lookes upon her, shall hardly know her, with her plumes, her fannes, and a silken vizard, with a ruffe like a saile, yea a ruffe like a raine-bow, with a feather in her cap like a flag in her top, to tell (I thinke) which way the wind will blow.

SOURCE: Robert Wilkinson, *The Merchant Royall, A Sermon preached . . . at the nuptialls of the Right honorable the Lord Hay and his ladie,* 1607.

ii. *The union of the lions*

And if all the Historians since then have acknowledged the uniting of the Red Rose and the White, for the greatest happiness (Christian Religion excepted) that ever this Kingdom received from God, certainly the peace between the two Lions of gold and gules . . . doth by many degrees exceed the former.

SOURCE: Sir Walter Ralegh, *The Historie of the World,* 1614, Preface. The reference is to the union of the crowns of England and Scotland under James I, symbolized by the golden lions of England and the red (gules) lion of Scotland from thenceforth appearing in the Royal Arms.

iii. *A week-old Pope*

When King James I visited Sir Thomas Pope, knt., in Oxfordshire, his lady had lately brought him a daughter, and the babe was presented to the king, with a paper of verses in her hand; 'which', quoth Fuller, 'as they pleased the king, I hope they will please the reader'.

> *See this little mistress here*
> *Did never sit in Peter's chair,*
> *Or a triple crown did wear,*
> > *And yet she is a Pope.*

A female Pope, you'll say, a second Joan! *
No, sure, she is Pope Innocent, or none!

SOURCE: Thomas Fuller, *Worthies of England*, 1662; *The Percy Anecdotes*, 1820–1823.

iv. *King James takes a tumble into the river, January 1622*

The Parliament having been full ten days in suspense whether to hold or not, was, on Wednesday, clean dissolved by proclamation.

The same day his Majesty rode by coach to Theobalds to dinner, not intending . . . to return till towards Easter. After dinner, riding on horseback abroad, his horse stumbled and cast his Majesty into the New River, where the ice brake. He fell in, so that nothing but his boots were seen. Sir Richard Young was next, who alighted, went into the water and lifted him out. There came much water out of his mouth and body. His Majesty rode back to Theobalds, went into a warm bed, and, as we hear, is well, which God continue.

SOURCE: letter from Joseph Meade to Sir Martin Stuteville, Jan. 11, 1622. British Museum, Harleian MSS. Inc. in Henry Ellis, *Original Letters, Illustrative of English History*, 1st series, 1825, Vol. iii, pp. 116–117.

vi. *The Duke of Buckingham's barber has to swallow some plaster*

James I died on March 27, 1625.

The 27 March [1625] after, when I waited on my Lord at the back stairs I saw him, Buckingham, and the Sweet Prince, afterwards K. Charles, come forth of the bed-chamber, when he made Jo. Baker, who was his Grace's barber, eat a great piece of the plaster that he had applied to K. James for cure of the ague.

SOURCE: Sir Edward Nicholas, Secretary of State to Charles I and Charles II; *The Nicholas Papers*, edit. G. F. Warner, Camden Society, 1886, Vol. I, p. xiii.

* The reference is to the alleged election of a woman to the Pontificate in the middle of the 9th Century. The story was widely believed up till the time of the Reformation.

vi. *How to become a Court favourite*

> *Let any poor lad that is handsome and young,*
> *With parle vous France and a voice for a song,*
> *But get on a horse and seek out good James,*
> *He'll soon find the house, 'tis great near the Thames*
> *It was built by a priest, a butcher by calling,**
> *But neither priesthood nor trade could keep him from falling.*
> *As soon as you ken the pitiful loon,*
> *Fall down from your nag as if in a swoon;*
> *If he doth nothing more, he'll open his purse;*
> *If he likes you ('tis known he's a very good nurse)*
> *Your fortune is made, he'll dress you in satin,*
> *And if you're unlearn'd he'll teach you dog Latin.*

SOURCE: contemporary ballad; quoted W. R. Chetwood, *Ben Jonson*, 1756, and A. Charles Ewald, *Stories from the State Papers*, 1882. The ballad is directed against the rise of Robert Carr, Earl of Somerset, to the position of Court favourite. When he first came to Court he was thrown from his horse and broke a leg. James had him removed to Whitehall and sent his own physician to attend him. During his convalescence, the King tried to repair some of the gaps in Carr's education and, among other subjects, taught him some Latin.

vii. *Ralegh's widow pleads in vain*

I mun have it for Carr.

SOURCE: James I's reply to Lady Ralegh, when she pleaded that the manor of Sherborne and other property formerly held by Ralegh in Dorset should be restored to her children.

See also RALEGH, SIR WALTER.

JAMES II (1633–1701), King of England.

A horse's leg for a new bell

A large equestrian bronze statue of James II, formerly standing in Newcastle, was demolished by the mob and thrown into the river. The following entry appears in the Common Council Book:

* A reference to Cardinal Wolsey, reputedly the son of an Ipswich butcher.

'April 1, 1695. All-Saints' parish humbly request the metal of the statue, towards the repair of their bells.'

The parish of St. Andrew asked for a share of the spoils, and the Council's decision recorded:

'Ordered that All-Saints have the metal belonging to the horse of the said statue, except a leg thereof, which must go towards the casting of a new bell for St. Andrew's parish.'

SOURCE: William Hone, *The Every-day Book*, 1830, Vol. II.
See also SEYMOUR, CHARLES.

JAMES V (1512–1542), King of Scotland.

The King is rebuked by a poet

Sir David Lindsay, or Lyndsay (1490–1555) was a Scottish poet and herald. As a poet he was popular for his broad humour and his satirical attacks on abuses in Church and State.

Of the felicity and point with which he could exercise this dangerous gift [i.e. of satire] the following curious instance is related by Dr. Irving in his Life of the poet:

The king being one day surrounded by a numerous train of nobility and prelates, Lindsay approached him with due reverence, and began to prefer an humble petition that he would instal him in an office which was then vacant.

'I have,' said he, 'served your grace long, and look to be rewarded as others are; and now your master tailor, at the pleasure of God, is departed, wherefore I would desire of your Grace to bestow this little benefit upon me.'

The king replied that he was amazed at such a request from a man who could neither shape nor sew.

'Sir,' rejoined the poet, 'that makes no matter, for you have given bishoprics and benefices to many standing here about you, and yet they can neither teach nor preach. And why not I as well be your tailor, though I can neither shape nor sew?'

SOURCE: Robert Chambers, *A Biographical Dictionary of Eminent Scotsmen*, 1837, Vol. iii, p. 442.

JEFFERSON, THOMAS (1743–1826), third President of the United States (1801–1809); author of the Declaration of Independence.

When Thomas Jefferson dined alone

The first real tenant of the White House, and one who left his mark on it, was Thomas Jefferson, and it was characteristic of the late President Kennedy that when he gave his famous party for the American Nobel Prizemen in literature and science he should have said there was more talent and genius gathered in the White House that night than there had ever been except when Thomas Jefferson dined alone.

SOURCE: D. W. Brogan, *American Aspects*, Hamish Hamilton, 1964, p. 3, first pub. in *Encounter* (*The Presidency*).

JEFFREYS, JUDGE (GEORGE JEFFREYS, first **BARON JEFFREYS)** (1648–1689). The most notorious judge in English history; a clever and quick-witted lawyer, but a drunken and dissipated bully of great brutality. At one trial, of a Puritan, Jeffreys sang through his nose in imitation of Puritan prayers. After the Battle of Sedgemoor in 1685, he conducted the 'Bloody Assizes' in the West Country, as a result of which large numbers were put to death.

i. 'Judge Jeffreys' ground'

Young children sometimes play a game called 'Tom Tiddler's Ground'. One stands with his back to the rest, who have a safe home base. They then venture forth into the forbidden territory between their 'home' and the redoubtable 'Tom Tiddler', chanting the while:

'I'm on Tom Tiddler's ground, picking up gold and silver!'

Tom Tiddler suddenly whips round and tries to catch one of the trespassers before they can get back to base. If he is successful, the trapped one takes over as Tom Tiddler.

The interesting thing about all this is that, as late as the middle of the 19th Century (does it still happen?) children in the West Country playing this game, instead of Tom Tiddler's Ground, used to call it 'Judge Jeffreys' Ground'.

ii. *When Jeffreys met his match*

There are cases on record, however, which show that even this terrible cross-examiner sometimes met his match. . . . Occasionally the examiner was astonished and 'woke up' by finding that he had got as good as he had given. In one case a country fellow clad in a leather doublet was giving his evidence, and Mr. Jeffreys, who was counsel for the opposite party, found that his testimony was 'pressing home'. Accordingly when his turn to cross-examine came, he bawled forth:

'You fellow in the leather doublet, pray what have you for swearing?' [i.e. How much have you been paid to give false evidence?]

The man looked steadily at him, and, 'Truly, sir,' said he, 'if you have no more for lying than I have for swearing, you might wear a leather doublet as well as I.'

SOURCE: quoted John Timbs, *Abbeys, Castles and Ancient Halls of England and Wales* (revised Alexander Gunn), Frederick Warne, 1883.

iii. *Another rebuff*

After having been appointed a Recorder [Jeffreys was Recorder of London, 1678–1680] he had another rebuff. A wedding had taken place, and those to whom it appertained to pay for the music at the nuptials refused the money, on which an action was brought; and, as the musicians were proving their case, Jeffreys called out from the bench:

'You fiddler!'

This made the witness wroth. He called himself not a fiddler, but a 'musitioner'. Jeffreys asked what was the difference between a musitioner and a fiddler?

'As much, sir,' answered the man . . . 'as there is between a pair of bagpipes and a recorder.'

SOURCE: ibid.

JENKINS'S EAR, WAR OF (1739).

The ear has its day of importance

... it is nice to think that this rather attractive organ, with the delicate pink cartilaginous whorls of helix and antihelix, has had its day of importance. It was so important that they actually went to war about it. A sea-captain whose ear had been amputated by the Spaniards brought it back in a box, and displayed it before the House of Commons, amid scenes of 'the utmost public indignation'. They asked him what his feelings were when he found himself in the hands of such barbarians?

'I committed my soul to God,' he nobly replied, 'and my cause to my country.'

So England went to war with Spain in 1739, the War of Jenkins's Ear, and this is probably the only war on record which has taken its name from a part of the human body.

SOURCE: T. H. White, *The Age of Scandal*, Jonathan Cape, 1950, Ch. 15.

Robert Jenkins was master of the trading sloop *Rebecca*. Doubts were cast on his story, some asserting that he had lost his ear, not at the hands of the Spanish *guarda costa*, but in the pillory. True or not, and despite Walpole's opposition, the story served to fan the flame of public opinion to such an extent that war became inevitable.

JOAN OF ARC (JEANNE D'ARC) (1412–1431), French heroine of the Hundred Years War.

i. *Joan's Description of her Voices*

Joan's own words were recorded at her trial.

At the age of thirteen, a voice from God came near to help her in ruling herself, and that voice came to her about the hour of noon, in summer time, while she was in her father's garden. And she had fasted the day before. And she heard the voice on her right, in the direction of the church; and when she heard the voice she also saw a bright light. Afterwards, St. Michael and St. Margaret and St. Catherine appeared to her. They were always in a halo of glory; she could see that their heads were crowned with jewels; and she heard their voices, which were sweet and mild. . . . She heard them more frequently than she saw them; and the usual time when she heard them was when the church bells were sounding for prayer. . . . They told her that France would be saved, and that she was to save it.

SOURCE: *Procès de Jeanne d'Arc*, Vol. i, p. 52; quoted Sir Edward Creasy, *The Fifteen Decisive Battles of the World* (32nd edition, 1886), pp. 322–323.

ii. *Joan picks out the King*

A score of torches held by pages lit the sides of the chamber. Before these were ranged the knights and ladies, the latter clothed in the fantastically rich costume of that time, with high erections on their heads, from which floated long festoons of cloth, and glittering with the emblems of their families on their storied robes. The King, in order to test the divination of the Maid, had purposely clad himself in common garb, and had withdrawn himself behind his more brilliantly attired courtiers.

Ascending the flight of eighteen steps which led into the hall, and following Vendôme, Joan passed across the threshold of the hall, and, without a moment's hesitation, singling out the King at the end of the gallery, walked to within a few paces of him, and falling on her knees before him—'the length of a lance,' as one of the spectators recorded—said:

'God give you good life, noble King!' ('*Dieu vous donne bonne vie, gentil Roi.*')

'But,' said Charles, 'I am not the King. This,' pointing to one of his courtiers, 'is the King'.

Joan, however, was not to be hoodwinked, and, finding that in spite of his subterfuges he was known, Charles acknowledged his identity. . . .

SOURCE: based on Jean Pasquerel and other witnesses; Lord Ronald Gower, *Joan of Arc*, John C. Nimmo, 1893.

JOHN (1167?–1216), King of England.

i. *The man who held the King's head*

King John gave several lands, at Kepperton and Atterton, in Kent, to Solomon Attefeld, to be held by this singular service—that as often as the king should be pleased to cross the sea, the said Solomon, or his heirs, should be obliged to go with him, *to hold his majesty's head*, if there should be occasion for it, 'that is if he should be sea-sick'; and it appears, by the record in the Tower, that this same office of head-holding was actually performed in the reign of Edward I.

SOURCE: Stephen Collet, *Relics of Literature*, 1823, p. 152.
For other curious tenures, see TENURES.

ii. *The King called 'Lackland'*

Forasmuch as when he came to die he possessed none of his land in peace, he is called Lackland.

> It seems, however, that the nickname 'Lackland' or 'Sansterre' was given him jokingly by his father, Henry II, because he was the youngest son and had not received any great fiefs as his brothers had done. (*Dictionary of English History*, etc.)

JOHNSON, DOCTOR SAMUEL (1709–1784), lexicographer and writer.

The conversation and eccentricities of Doctor Johnson

i. Next day, Sunday, July 31, I told him I had been that morning at a meeting of the people called Quakers, where I had heard a woman preach.

Johnson: 'Sir, a woman's preaching is like a dog walking on his hind legs. It is not done well; but you are surprised to find it done at all.'

ii. In the year 1763, a young bookseller ... waited on him with a subscription to his 'Shakespeare'; and, observing that the Doctor made no entry in any book of the subscriber's name, ventured diffidently to ask whether he would please to have the gentleman's address, that it might be properly inserted in the printed list of subscribers.

'I shall print no list of subscribers,' said Johnson, with great abruptness: but, almost immediately recollecting himself, added, very complacently:

'Sir, I have two very cogent reasons for not printing any list of subscribers—one that I have lost all the names, the other that I have spent all the money.

iii. 'I have, all my life long, been lying till noon; yet I tell all young men, and tell them with great sincerity, that nobody who does not rise early will ever do any good.'

iv. Johnson, for sport perhaps, or from the spirit of contradiction, eagerly maintained that Derrick had merit as a writer. Mr. Morgann argued with him directly, in vain. At length he had recourse to this device.

'Pray, sir,' said he, 'do you reckon Derrick or Smart the best poet?'

Johnson at once felt himself roused; and answered:

'Sir, there is no settling the point of precedency between a louse and a flea.'

v. Johnson having argued for some time with a pertinacious gentleman, his opponent, who had talked in a very puzzling manner, happened to say:

'I don't understand you, Sir'; upon which Johnson observed:

'Sir, I have found you an argument; but I am not obliged to find you an understanding.'

vi. Talking to himself was, indeed, one of his singularities ever since I knew him. I was certain that he was frequently uttering pious ejaculations; for fragments of the Lord's Prayer have been distinctly overheard. . . .

He had another particularity, of which none of his friends ever ventured to ask an explanation. It appeared to me some superstitious habit, which he had contracted early, and from which he had never called upon his reason to disentangle him. This was his anxious care to go out or in at a door or passage, by a certain number of steps from a certain point, or at least so as that either his right or his left foot (I am not certain which) should constantly make the first actual movement when he came close to the door or passage. This I conjecture: for I have, upon innumerable occasions, observed him suddenly stop, and then seem to count his steps with a deep earnestness; and when he had neglected or gone wrong in this sort of magical movement, I have seen him go back again, put himself in a proper posture to begin the ceremony, and having gone through it, break from his abstraction, walk briskly on, and join his companion....

While talking or even musing as he sat in his chair, he commonly held his head to one side towards his right shoulder, and shook it in a tremulous manner, moving his body backwards and forwards, and rubbing his left knee in the same direction, with the palm of his hand. In the intervals of articulating he made various sounds with his mouth; sometimes as if ruminating, or what is called chewing the cud; sometimes giving a half whistle, sometimes making his tongue play backwards from the roof of his mouth, as if clucking like a hen, and sometimes protruding it against his upper gums in front, as if pronouncing quickly under his breath, *too, too, too*; all this accompanied with a thoughtful look, but more frequently with a smile.

vii. His brown suit of clothes looked very rusty: he had on a little old shrivelled unpowdered wig, which was too small for his head; his shirt-neck and knees of his breeches were loose; his black worsted stockings ill drawn up; and he had a pair of unbuckled shoes by way of slippers. But all these slovenly peculiarities were forgotten the moment that he began to talk.

SOURCE: James Boswell, *The Life of Samuel Johnson*, 1791, and *Journal of a Tour to the Hebrides*, 1786.

JOHNSON, THOMAS (d. 1644), apothecary, herbalist and royalist; published the first local catalogue of plants issued in England, and an enlarged edition of the most famous 'Herbal' in the English language, John Gerard's *Herball, or Generall Historie of Plants* (1597).

i. *Epitaph for an apothecary*

Thomas Johnson, born near Hull in Yorkshire, was an Apothecary in London and the best Herbalist of his age. . . . He was of great modesty, as being more learned and valiant than he pretended to be; for at the siege of Basingstoke in Hampshire he lost his life on the Royal side, 1644.

SOURCE: 17th Century manuscript note in editor's copy of Johnson's edition of Gerard.

ii. *The first banana in England*

Thomas Johnson . . . had a shop on Snow Hill [London]. It was in this shop on Snow Hill that the banana was first exhibited in England. Johnson received the bunch of fruit from Dr. Argent, who got it from Bermuda. . . . Johnson hung the bunch up in his shop until it ripened. He says:

'Some have judged it the forbidden fruit: other-some the grapes brought to Moses out of the Holy Land.'

SOURCE: Hon. Alicia Amherst, *A History of Gardening in England*, Bernard Quaritch, 1896 (2nd edition), p. 172.

JONAH, A MODERN.

The ordeal of James Bartley

The most amazing story you will find in the whole literature of travel is that a man has been actually swallowed by a whale and lived to tell the tale. In 1891 the American whaler *Star of the East* was off the Falkland Islands when, in the excitement and confusion of a catch, a seaman named James Bartley went overboard and was given up for lost. The whale was killed, brought alongside and stripped of its blubber. Next day the stomach was searched for the valuable amerbris which is often found in unpleasant surroundings of this nature. The men noticed that something alive seemed to be stirring in the folds and creases, and when they investigated they found the doubled-up and unconscious figure of Bartley.

He was delirious for a fortnight, but when he recovered sufficiently to tell his story he said that when he went overboard he seemed to enter a warm moving passage. Presently he found himself in the whale's stomach, where the heat was terrific but where a certain amount of air reached him.

Bartley recovered completely from his terrible ordeal, except for the fact that his skin became a fixed bleached white.

SOURCE: *Strange Reading*, George Newnes (n.d.).

JOSEPH II (1741–1790), Emperor of Germany and of the Holy Roman Empire; described as 'a sort of philosopher-king, than whom few have more narrowly missed greatness'.

The pleasure of blowing the bellows

During the Emperor's voyage in Italy, one of the wheels of his coach broke down on the road. With much difficulty he reached a poor village. On his arrival there, his Majesty got out at the door of a blacksmith, and desired him to repair the damaged wheel without delay.

'That I would very willingly,' replied the smith, 'but, it being holiday, all my men are at church; my very apprentice who blows the bellows is not at home.'

'An excellent method then presents of warming one's self,' replied the Emperor, still preserving the incognito; and the great Joseph set about blowing the bellows while the blacksmith forged the iron. The wheel being repaired, six *sols* were demanded for the job; but the Emperor, instead of them, put into his hand six ducats. The blacksmith, on seeing them, returned them to the traveller, saying:

'Sir, you have undoubtedly made a mistake, owing to the

darkness; instead of six *sols*, you have given me six pieces of gold, which nobody in this village can change.'

'Change them where you can,' replied the Emperor. 'The over-plus is for the pleasure of blowing the bellows.'

His Majesty then continued his journey, without waiting for an answer.

SOURCE: Mr. Addison (pseud.), *Interesting Anecdotes, Memoirs . . . ,* etc., 1794.

JOURNEY, A RECORD (17th Century).

A summer day's journey, 1619

Despite a lack of modern means of transport, early travellers sometimes put up a surprising performance. In 1619, a citizen of Andover, Hampshire, covered nearly 150 miles by land and nearly 50 miles by sea in only 17 hours.

Saturday, the 17th day of July, 1619, Bernard Calvert, of Andover, about three o'clock in the morning, took a horse at St. George's Church in Southwark, and came to Dover about seven the same morning; where a barge with eight oars, formerly sent from London thither, attended his sudden coming. He instantly took barge, and went to Calais, and in the same barge returned back to Dover about three o'clock of the same day: where, as well there as in divers other places, he had laid sundry swift horses, besides guides. He rode back from Dover to St. George's Church, Southwark, the same evening, a little after eight o'clock, fresh and lusty.

SOURCE: quoted *The Percy Anecdotes,* 1820–1823 from one of the later and enlarged editions of John Stowe (1525?–1605), the antiquary and chronicler of London.

See also CAREY, SIR ROBERT.

JULIUS CAESAR (102?–44 B.C.).

i. *'I came, I saw, I conquered'*

Veni, vidi, vici.

SOURCE: Suetonius, *Divus Julius*, 37.2; according to Plutarch written in a letter from Caesar announcing the successful end of the Pontic campaign.

ii. *Caesar in Gaul, 58 B.C.*

Caesar, then Consul, had been nominated governor of the province of Narbonne, with a special commission to check the inroads of the Suevi, under Ariovistus, and the Helvetii from Switzerland.

Having finished this first undertaking [against the Helvetii] he found himself opposed to Ariovistus. He suggested an interview.

'If I have need of Caesar,' answered Ariovistus, 'I will go to him; if he has need of me, let him come to me.'

The proconsul resorted to threats.

'No one,' said the barbarian, 'has yet attacked me without repenting. When Caesar so desires, we will measure our strength against each other, and he will learn what manner of warriors are those who for fourteen years have not slept beneath a roof.'

SOURCE: Victor Duruy, *A Short History of France*, 1873, Everyman's Library edition, J. M. Dent & Sons, 1917, Vol. I, p. 51.

Ariovistus was defeated in the subsequent battle and retired wounded across the River Saône.

iii. *The elephant on the public money*

When Caesar was one of the masters of the Roman mint, he placed the figure of an elephant upon the reverse of the public money; the word Caesar signifying an elephant in the Punic language. This was artificially contrived by Caesar, because it was not lawful for a private man to stamp his own figure upon the coin of the commonwealth.

SOURCE: Joseph Addison, *The Spectator*, No. 59, May 8, 1711.

iv. *Caesar refuses his horse*

He gained . . . a strong post for his troops against the Tigurini in their passage over the River Arar . . . ; and when he had drawn them up, his horse was brought him. Upon which he said:

'When I have won the battle I shall want my horse for the pursuit; at present let us march as we are against the enemy.'

SOURCE: Plutarch's *Lives*, trans. J. and W. Langhorne, 1821.

v. *The landing in Britain*

Our troops . . . were still hesitating, largely because of the depth of the sea, when the standard-bearer of the Tenth legion, with a prayer to the gods for a happy outcome for his legion, shouted:

'Jump down, men, unless you want the enemy to get your standard. You will not find me failing in my duty to my country or my leader.'

This he yelled at the top of his voice, and then springing off the boat began to bear the eagle forward against the enemy. Our troops, with mutual words of encouragement not to commit a terrible wrong, all jumped down into the sea. Their fellows in the next boats saw what they were doing, followed suit and came to grips with the enemy.

SOURCE: Caesar, *Gallic War*, IV, 23; translation by B. K. Workman in *They Saw it Happen in Classical Times*, Basil Blackwell, 1964, p. 102.

vi. *The murder of Caesar*

. . . his friends were alarmed at certain rumours and tried to stop him going to the Senate-house, as did his doctors, for he was suffering from one of his occasional dizzy spells. His wife, Calpurnia, especially, who was frightened by some visions in her dreams, clung to him and said she would not let him go out that day. But Brutus, one of the conspirators who was then thought of as a firm friend, came up and said:

'What is this, Caesar? Are you a man to pay attention to a

T

woman's dreams and the idle gossip of stupid men, and to insult the Senate by not going out, although it has honoured you and has been specially summoned by you? But listen to me, cast aside the forebodings of all these people, and come. The Senate has been in session waiting for you since early this morning.'

This swayed Caesar and he left. . . . The Senate rose in respect for his position when they saw him entering. Those who were to have part in the plot stood near him. Right next to him went Tillius Cimber, whose brother had been exiled by Caesar. Under pretext of a humble request on behalf of this brother, Cimber approached and grasped the mantle of his toga. . . . This was the moment for the men to set to work. All quickly unsheathed their daggers and rushed at him. First Servilius Casca struck him with the point of the blade on the left shoulder a little above the collar-bone. He had been aiming for that, but in the excitement he missed. Caesar rose to defend himself, and in the uproar Casca shouted out in Greek to his brother. The latter heard him and drove his sword into the ribs. After a moment, Cassius made a slash at his face, and Decimus Brutus pierced him in the side. . . . They were just like men doing battle against him. Under the mass of wounds, he fell at the foot of Pompey's statue. Everyone wanted to seem to have had some part in the murder, and there was not one of them who failed to strike his body as it lay there, until, wounded thirty-five times, he breathed his last.

SOURCE: Nicolaus Damascenus, in *Historici Graeci Minores*; trans. by B. K. Workman in *They Saw it Happen in Classical Times*, Basil Blackwell, 1964, pp. 112–114.

vii. *And you Brutus?*

Some say he opposed the rest, and continued struggling and crying out, till he perceived the sword of Brutus; then he drew his robe over his face and yielded to his fate.

SOURCE: Plutarch's *Lives*, trans. J. and W. Langhorne, 1821.

KEPLER, JOHANN (1571–1630), German astronomer and originator of Kepler's Laws.

i. *The man in the little black tent*

He hath a little black Tent which he can suddenly set up where he will in a Field; and it is convertible (like a wind-mill) to all quarters at pleasure; capable of not much more than one man, as I conceive, and perhaps at no great ease; exactly close and dark—save at one hole, about an inch and a half in the diameter, to which he applies a long perspective Trunk, with the convex glass fitted to the said hole, and the concave taken out at the other end. . . .

SOURCE: Sir Henry Wotton, ambassador to the King of Bohemia.
Thomas Carlyle, commenting on Wotton's description, said:

ii. *An ingenious person*

An ingenious person, truly, if ever there was one among Adam's posterity. Just turned fifty, and ill-off for cash. This glimpse of him, in his little black tent with perspective glasses, while the Thirty Years' War blazes out, is welcome as a date.

SOURCE: *Frederick the Great*, Book III, Chapter XIV.

KING'S CHAMPION, THE, or **CHAMPION OF ENGLAND.**
This office is thought to have been instituted by William I. The best-known holders of it have been the family of Dymoke, who have held it by hereditary right since the reign of Richard II. The Champion's most spectacular duty was to ride into Westminster Hall during the coronation banquet, armed cap-à-pie, and challenge to combat anyone who was bold enough to dispute the title of the new king or queen.

The champion refuses a challenge

A ludicrous circumstance occurred at the coronation of King William and Mary. Charles Dymock, Esq., who then exercised the right of being champion, cast his gauntlet on the pavement in the usual form, and the challenge was proclaimed, when an old woman, who had entered the hall on crutches, immediately took it up, and quitted the spot with extraordinary agility, leaving her crutches behind her, and a female glove, with a challenge in it to meet the champion the next day, in Hyde Park. Accordingly, the old woman, or, as is generally supposed, a good swordsman in that disguise, attended at the hour and place named in the challenge; but the champion did not make his appearance, nor does it appear whether any measures were taken to discover who had passed so disloyal a joke.

SOURCE: *The Manual of Rank and Nobility*, 1832, p. 431.

KITCHENER, HORATIO HERBERT, first **EARL KIT-CHENER** (1850–1916), field marshal; Secretary of State for War, 1914.

What would have made Kitchener happy

He distrusted most people, and such as might have come to like him were repelled by his aloofness. . . . And how he hated what he called the 'club-frequenting politicians'! Once, when he was in a bitter mood, I asked him if anything could make him really happy.

'Yes,' he said with surprising promptness. 'First secure a full sitting of the House of Commons, then bar and bolt all the exits and entrances to it except one; next place me with half a dozen men and a couple of machine guns at that one, and finally set fire to the building. I think I could promise you a smile of satisfaction at the end of the entertainment.'

SOURCE: (anon.) *The Whispering Gallery, being Leaves from a Diplomat's Diary*, John Lane, 1926, pp. 15–16.

KNOX, CAPTAIN ROBERT (1640?–1720), traveller and writer; captured and held prisoner in Ceylon for nineteen years, 1660–1679; wrote first account of Ceylon in the English language.

Knox finds a Bible

It chanced, as I was fishing, an old man passed by; and, seeing me, asked of my boy, 'if I could read in a book?' He answered 'Yes.'

'The reason I ask,' said the old man, 'is because I have one I got when the Portuguese lost Colombo; and if your master please to buy it, I will sell it him.'

Which when I heard of, I bade my boy go to his house with him, which was not far off, and bring it to me to see it; making no great account of the matter, supposing it might be some Portuguese book.

The boy having formerly served the English, knew the book; and as soon as he had got it in his hand, came running with it, calling out to me 'It is a Bible.'

It startled me to hear him mention the name of a 'Bible': for I neither had one, nor scarcely could ever think to see one. Upon which, I flung down my angle [fishing tackle], and went to meet him. The first place the book opened in, after I took it in my hand, was the sixteenth chapter of the Acts, and the first place my eye pitched on, was the 30th and 31st verses, where the gaoler asked St. Paul 'What must I do to be saved? And he answered saying, 'Believe in the Lord Jesus Christ, and thou shalt be saved and thine house.'

The sight of this book so rejoiced me, and affrighted me together; that I cannot say which passion was greater, the Joy for that I had got sight of a Bible, or the Fear that I had not enough to buy it, having then but one pagoda [a gold or silver coin] in the world: which I would willingly have given for it, but my boy dissuaded me from giving so much, alleging my necessity for money in many other ways, and undertaking to procure the book for a far meaner price; provided I would seem to slight it in the sight of the old man. This counsel after I considered, I approved of, my urgent necessities earnestly craving, and my ability being but very small to relieve the same: and however, I thought, I could give my piece of gold at the last cast, if other means should fail. . . .

Upon the sight of it I left off fishing; God having brought to me a fish that I longed for: and now how to get it and enjoy the same, all the powers of my soul were employed. I gave God hearty thanks that He had brought it so near me, and most earnestly prayed that He would bestow it on me. Now it being well towards evening, and not having the where withal to buy it about me, I departed home; telling the old man that in the morning I would send my boy to buy it of him.

All that night I could take no rest for thinking on it, fearing lest I might be disappointed of it. In the morning, as soon as it was day, I sent the boy with a knit cap he had made for me to buy the book, praying in my heart for good success: which it pleased God to grant. For that cap purchased it, and the boy brought it to me to my great joy; which did not a little comfort me in all my afflictions.

SOURCE: *Nineteen Years' Captivity in the Kingdom of Conde Uda in the Highlands of Ceylon, sustained by Captain Robert Knox . . . together with his Singular Deliverance from that Strange and Pagan Land*, 1681; reproduced in Edward Arber, *An English Garner*, Vol. I, 1887.

LATIMER, HUGH (1485?–1555), Bishop of Worcester; burnt at the stake, at Oxford, October 16, 1555, with Bishop Ridley.

i. *'Be of good comfort, Master Ridley'*

Then they brought a faggot, kindled with fire, and laid the same down at Dr. Ridley's feet. To whom Master Latimer spake in this manner:

'Be of good comfort, Master Ridley, and play the man. We shall this day light such a candle, by God's grace, in England, as I trust shall never be put out.

SOURCE: John Foxe, *The Actes and Monuments of the Church*, 1563, popularly known as *The Book of Martyrs*, Rev. John Cumming's edition, Chatto & Windus, 1875, Vol. iii, p. 492.

ii. *Latimer knows fear*

'I am sometimes so fearful that I would creep into a mouse-hole.'

SOURCE: *Certen godly, learned, and comforting conferences betwene the two Reverende fathers and holye Martyrs of Christe, D. Nicolas Rydley . . . and M. Hughe Latymer . . . during the tyme of theyre emprisonmentes*, 1556.

See also RIDLEY, NICHOLAS.

LAUD, WILLIAM (1573–1645).

Jenny Geddes's stool

On July 23, 1637, an attempt was made to introduce Archbishop Laud's service book, as part of his process of restoring the Church to its medieval authority and power.

On the day mentioned, being Sunday, the service-book was, by an imperious command from the king, to be read in every parish-church in Scotland. Before the day arrived, the symptoms of popular opposition appeared almost everywhere so ominous, that few of the clergy were prepared to obey the order.

In the principal church of Edinburgh, the chancel of the old cathedral of St. Giles, which contained the seats of the judges, magistrates, and other authorities, the liturgy was formally introduced under the auspices of the bishop, dean, and other clergy. Here, if anywhere, it might have been expected that the royal will would have been implicitly carried out. And so it would, perhaps, if there had been only a congregation of official dignitaries. But the body of the church was . . . filled by a body of the common sort of people, including a large proportion of citizens' wives and their maid-servants—Christians of vast zeal, and comparatively safe by their sex and their obscurity.

There were no pews in those days; each godly dame sat on her own chair or clasp-stool, brought to church on purpose. When the dean, Mr. James Hannay, opened the service-book and began to read the prayers, this multitude was struck with a horror which defied all control. They raised their voices in discordant clamours and abusive language, denouncing the dean as of the progeny of the devil . . . and calling out that it was rank popery they were bringing in. A strenuous female (Jenny Geddes) threw her stool at the dean's head, and whole sackfuls of small clasp-Bibles followed. The bishop from the pulpit endeavoured to calm the people, but in vain. A similar 'ticket of remembrance' to that aimed at the dean was levelled at him, but fell short. . . . The magistrates from their gallery made efforts to quell the disturbance—all in vain; and they were obliged to clear out the multitude by main force, before the reading of the liturgy could be proceeded with.

SOURCE: *The Book of Days* (edit. R. Chambers), 1865, Vol. I, pp. 108–109.

Whether 'Jenny Geddes' was the real name of the woman who threw the first stool has been seriously questioned. Some have maintained that it was a man in disguise; though one commentator on this theory has observed that, in that case, the stool would have hit the bishop.

LAWRENCE, JOHN, first **BARON LAWRENCE** (1811–1879), Governor-General of India.

A school exploit

We had a rough enough life of it at school; our bedrooms were so cold that the water used to freeze in the basins, and the doctor used to remark that it was no wonder that we were all in such good health, for every room had a draught in it. This was true enough. The window-frames of our bedroom were of stone, and an iron bar across the centre was supposed to prevent ingress or egress. Lawrence managed to loosen it so that it could be taken out and replaced without attracting observation, and when the nights were hot he would creep through it in his nightshirt and, reaching the ground by the help of a pear-tree which grew against the wall, would go and bathe in the neighbouring stream.

We were fast friends, and in the kindness of his heart he would have done anything for me. I was very fond of bird-nesting. A swallow had built its nest at the top of our chimney, and I expressed a wish to get at it.

'I'll get the eggs for you,' said John, and went straight to the chimney, and began to climb up inside. It soon became too narrow for his burly frame.

'Never mind, I'll get them yet,' he said, and at once went to the window. I and my brother followed him through it, and, climbing a wall twelve feet high, which came out from one end of the house and formed one side of the court, pushed him up from its summit as far as we could reach towards the roof. He was in his nightshirt, with bare feet and legs; but, availing himself of any coign of vantage that he could find, he actually managed to climb up the wall of the house by himself.

When he reached the roof, he crawled up the coping stones at the side on his knees, and then began to make his way along the ridge towards the chimney; but the pain by this time became too great for human endurance: 'Hang it all,' he cried, 'I can't go on!' and he had to give up.

SOURCE: His school-friend Wellington Cooper; quoted H. Bosworth Smith, *Life of Lord Lawrence*, Nelson & Sons, n.d.

LEÓN, FRAY LUÍS DE (1527–1591), Spanish monk and lyric poet.

'*As I was saying when I was interrupted* . . . '
Como deciamos ayer
As we were saying yesterday . . .

SOURCE: Fray Luís de León, in the lecture hall of the University of Salamanca, December 30, 1576, after he had returned from an imprisonment of nearly five years by the Spanish Inquisition.

LEONARDO DA VINCI (1452–1519), Italian painter, sculptor, poet, inventor and engineer. It is one of the mysteries of his career that, though he called war 'a bestial folly', he became military engineer to one of the greatest scoundrels of his time, Cesare Borgia.

i. *Commission from a Borgia*
To all our lieutenants, governors, captains, *condottieri* [leaders of mercenaries] officers, soldiers and subjects who may read this letter, we order and command: to our very excellent and very dear architect and engineer general, Leonardo da Vinci, bearer of this letter, entrusted by our commission to examine the places and fortresses of our states, so that according to their needs and his advice, we may see to their maintenance, they

will give free passage, without subjecting him to any public tax whatsoever, either for himself or those with him, receive him with kindness and allow him to measure and examine whatever he wishes. To this end, provide him with men when he requires and give him every help and favour when he demands. It is our wish that in all works to be executed within our states, all engineers should confer with him and conform with his opinion.

SOURCE: document signed by Cesare Borgia and his secretary Agapito in the archives of Milan; quoted Anny Latour, *The Borgias* (trans. Neil Mann), Elek Books, 1963, pp. 112–113.

ii. *Leonardo the strong man*

He possessed so great a degree of physical strength that he was capable of restraining the most impetuous violence, and was able to bend one of those iron rings used for the knockers of doors, or a horse-shoe, as if it were lead.

SOURCE: Giorgio Vasari, *Lives of the Most Eminent Painters, Sculptors and Architects*, trans. Mrs. Jonathan Foster, 1851.

LEPANTO, BATTLE OF (October 7, 1571); the great Mediterranean galley battle in which the Christian fleets, under Don John of Austria defeated the Turkish fleet under Ali Pasha, and secured the release of 15,000 Christian galley slaves. The battle is the subject of a brilliant poem by G. K. Chesterton.

Cervantes refuses to remain in bed

In the *Marquesa* galley, in the division of Doria, was lying in his bed sick of a fever a young man twenty-four years of age. . . . When this young man heard that a battle was imminent he rose from his bed and demanded of his captain, Francisco San Pedro, that he should be placed in the post of the greatest danger. The captain, and others, his friends, counselled him to remain in his bed.

'Señores,' replied the young man, 'what should be said of Miguel de Cervantes should he take this advice? On every occasion up to this day on which his enemies have offered battle to his Majesty I have served like a good soldier; and to-day I intend to do so in spite of this sickness and fever.'

He was given command of twelve soldiers in a shallop, and all day was to be seen where the combat raged most fiercely. He received two wounds in the chest and another which cost him the loss of his left hand. To those to whom he proudly displayed them in after-years he was accustomed to say:

'Wounds in the face or the chest are like stars which guide one through honour to the skies.'

Of him the chronicler says:

'He continued the rest of his life with honourable memory of this wonderful occurrence, and, although he lost the use of his left hand, it added to the glory of his right.'

SOURCE: Commander E. Hamilton Currey, *Sea Wolves of the Mediterranean*, Thomas Nelson & Sons, pp. 355–356.

The young Spaniard was the writer who was later to give the world one of the greatest characters in literature—Don Quixote de la Mancha.

LINCOLN, ABRAHAM (1809–1865), 16th President of the United States.

i. *Lincoln's farewell to his law partner*

Then he gathered up some books and papers, talked for a moment or so, and the two men walked downstairs together. At the bottom Lincoln glanced up at the battered law shingle.*

'Let it hang there undisturbed,' he asked, lowering his voice. 'Give our clients to understand that the election of a President makes no change in the firm of Lincoln and Herndon. If I live

---

* The sign outside the firm's premises.

I'm coming back sometime, and then we'll go right on practising law as if nothing had ever happened.'

SOURCE: David Donald, *Lincoln's Herndon*, p. 147.

ii. *Not Apollo, but not Caliban*

This orator and lawyer has been caricatured. He is not Apollo but he is not Caliban. He was made where the material for strong men is plenty. . . .

SOURCE: Diary of Gideon Welles, later Secretary of the Navy in Lincoln's cabinet.

iii. *Lincoln's judgment on a book*

(Quoted by G. W. Russell as an instance of the 'perilous art' of putting things 'carried to a high perfection'.)

People who like this sort of thing will find this the sort of thing they like.

SOURCE: G. W. E. Russell, *Collections and Recollections*, 1903, Ch. 30.

iv. *Lincoln forgets the order*

Abraham Lincoln was probably our most resourceful public man. One joke he liked to tell on himself was about the time he was a captain during the Black Hawk Indian War. One day part of his company was marching across a field, and Lincoln saw ahead of them the gate through which they must pass.

'I could not for the life of me remember the proper word of command for getting my company endwise,' he said. 'Finally, as we came near, I shouted: "This company is dismissed for two minutes, when it will fall in again on the other side of the gate".'

SOURCE: Frances Cavanah and Lloyd E. Smith, *I am an American*, Whitman Publishing Co., Racine, Wisconsin, 1940, p. 122.

See also AMERICAN CIVIL WAR.

LIVINGSTONE, DAVID (1813–1873). Missionary and explorer. Discovered Lake Ngami and Zambesi river. In 1866, led expedition into interior to search for source of the Nile. After sighting Lake Tanganyika on April 1, 1867, pushed on and was lost to the outside world till July 1871, when H. M. Stanley, a journalist sent out by J. Gordon Bennett, proprietor of the *New York Herald*, had his historic meeting with him.

i. *Livingstone's early studies*

His parents were poor, and, at the age of ten he was put to work in the factory as a piecer. . . . After serving a number of years as a piecer, he was promoted to be a spinner. Greatly to his mother's delight, the first half-crown he ever earned was laid by him in her lap. Livingstone has told us that, with a part of his first week's wages he purchased Ruddiman's *Rudiments of Latin*, and pursued the study of that language with unabated ardour for many years afterwards at an evening class which had opened between the hours of eight and ten.

'The dictionary part of my labours was followed up till twelve o'clock, or later, if my mother did not interfere by jumping up and snatching the book out of my hands. I had to be back in the factory by six in the morning, and continue my work, with intervals for breakfast and dinner, till eight o'clock at night. I read in this way many of the classical authors, and knew Virgil and Horace better at sixteen than I do now.'

In his reading, he tells us that he devoured all the books that came into his hands but novels, and that his plan was to place the book on a portion of the spinning-jenny, so that he could catch sentence after sentence as he passed at his work. . . . The utmost interval that Livingstone could have for reading at one time was less than a minute.

SOURCE: William Garden Blaikie, *The Life of David Livingstone*, 1880; a small but valuable biography, written at the request of Livingstone's family and containing a good deal of material unknown till then. Quotations are from the 6th edition, 1910.

ii. *Livingstone has a busy day*

Told by Rev. Joseph Moore, afterwards a missionary in Tahiti, who trained with Livingstone as a student, after they had been accepted by the London Missionary Society, and had been sent to Ongar, in Essex, to serve a probationary period there with the Rev. Richard Cecil.

One foggy November morning, at about three o'clock, he set out from Ongar to walk to London to see a relative of his father's. It was about twenty-seven miles to the house he sought. After spending a few hours with his relation, he set out to return on foot to Ongar. Just out of London, near Edmonton, a lady had been thrown out of a gig. She lay stunned on the road. Livingstone immediately went to her, helped to carry her into a house close by, and having examined her and found no bones broken, and recommending a doctor to be called, he resumed his weary tramp.

Weary and footsore, when he reached Stanford Rivers he missed his way, and finding after some time that he was wrong, he felt so dead-beat that he was inclined to lie down and sleep; but finding a directing post he climbed it, and by the light of the stars deciphered enough to know his whereabouts. About twelve that Saturday night he reached Ongar, white as as sheet, and so tired he could hardly utter a word. I gave him a basin of bread and milk, and I am not exaggerating when I say I put him to bed. He fell at once asleep, and did not awake till noon had passed on Sunday.

SOURCE: Blaikie, op. cit., pp. 20–21. In London, Livingstone spent much of the day going from shop to shop on business for his eldest brother, so that, in all, he probably walked well over 60 miles that November Saturday. On the way to London, he fell into a ditch in the darkness and plastered himself with mud.

iii. *Livingstone forgets his sermon* (also related by Rev. Joseph Moore)

One part of our duties was to prepare sermons, which were submitted to Mr. Cecil, and, when corrected, were committed to memory, and then repeated to our village congregations. Livingstone prepared one, and one Sunday the minister of Stanford Rivers . . . having fallen sick after the morning service, Livingstone was sent for to preach in the evening. He took his text, read it out very deliberately, and then—then—his sermon had fled! . . . He abruptly said:

'Friends, I have forgotten all that I had to say,' and, hurrying out of the pulpit, he left the chapel.

SOURCE: ibid., p. 22.

iv. *Stanley's meeting with Livingstone*

'As I advanced towards him,' says Mr. Stanley, 'I noticed he was pale, looked wearied, had a grey beard, wore a bluish cap with a faded gold band round it, had on a red-sleeved waistcoat and a pair of grey tweed trousers. I would have run to him, only I was a coward in the presence of such a mob,—would have embraced him, only he being an Englishman, I did not know how he would receive me; so I did what cowardice and false pride suggested was the best thing—walked deliberately to him, took off my hat and said:

'Dr. Livingstone, I presume?'

'Yes,' said he, with a kind smile, lifting his cap slightly.

I replace my hat on my head, and he puts on his cap, and we both grasp hands, and I then say aloud:

'I thank God, Doctor, I have been permitted to see you.'

He answered:

'I feel thankful that I am here to welcome you.'

SOURCE: ibid., pp. 353–354. Stanley, of course, recorded the meeting in *How I Found Livingstone*, 1872, Ch. 11.

Confirmation of two of the above stories comes from Mrs. Anne Gilbert (Anne Taylor, the poetess) whose father at one time held the living at Stanford Rivers. She writes:

The Cecils were now at Ongar, Mr. Cecil having taken a pastorate there. Several missionary students were then under his care for preliminary training, and among them David Livingstone, who showed the future explorer by walking . . . to London on a straight line by compass over hedge and ditch. Livingstone was sent one Sunday afternoon to officiate on an emergency at the small chapel at Stanford Rivers, when his performance astonished the congregation. He gave out his text, and then, after a pause, descended the pulpit stairs, took up his hat, walked straight out of the chapel, and sped back to Ongar.

SOURCE: *Autobiography . . . of Mrs. Gilbert* (edit. Josiah Gilbert), 5th edition, 1888, p. 386.

LOCOMOTIVE, THE AMERICAN, 1846.

'Look out for the locomotive'

The train calls at stations in the wood, where the wild impossibility of anybody having the smallest reason to get out, is only to be equalled by the apparently desperate hopelessnsss of there being anybody to get in. It rushes across the turnpike road where there is no gate, no policeman, no signal: nothing but a rough wooden arch, on which is painted:

'WHEN THE BELL RINGS, LOOK OUT FOR THE LOCOMOTIVE.'

SOURCE: Charles Dickens, *American Notes*, 1842.

LONDON IN THE 18th CENTURY.

'What has become of all the Englishmen?'

John West, father of Benjamin West, historical painter and President of the Royal Academy, emigrated to America in about 1714, and did not see London again for half a century.

Mr. West told me that, on asking his father how he was struck with the appearance of London after his long absence, he replied:

'The streets and houses look very much as they did; but can thee tell me what has become of all the Englishmen? When I left England, the men were a portly, comely race, with broad skirts and large flowing wigs; rather slow in their movements, and grave and dignified in their deportment: but now they are docked and cropped, and skipping about in scanty clothes like so many monkeys.'

The impression made on the old man shows how greatly French fashions and manners had gained ground in England during the half century he had passed in America.

SOURCE: Charles Robert Leslie, R.A., *Autobiographical Recollections*, 1860, Vol. I, pp. 61–62.

LORDS OF THE ISLES, THE. The title claimed in the 14th and 15th Centuries by the Macdonalds or M'Donalds of Isla, involving the overlordship of the Hebridean Isles. The title was annexed to the Crown in the reign of Henry VIII.

'Wherever Macdonald sits . . .'

For many years . . . they were distinguished for a pride of spirit which seemed to disdain comparison with any state short of royalty itself. One of the lords, Macdonald, happening to be in Ireland, was invited to an entertainment given by the Lord Lieutenant. He chanced to be among the last in coming in, and sat himself down at the foot of the table near the door. The Lord Lieutenant asked him to sit beside him. Macdonald, who spoke little English, asked:
'What says the carle [man]?'
'He bids you move to the head of the table.'
'Tell the carle that wherever Macdonald sits, *that* is the head of the table.'

SOURCE: Thomas Byerley and Joseph Clinton Robertson, *The Percy Anecdotes*, 1820–1823.

LOUIS IX (ST. LOUIS) (1226–1270), King of France. Canonized for his devotion as a Crusader. He led two Crusades, was captured by the Saracens, and died beneath the walls of Tunis with a great part of his army. He was a great and pious king, but his expeditions brought little but disaster to France and Palestine. Among his lesser troubles was a very trying Queen Mother, Blanche, who carried out a relentless persecution of her daughter-in-law, Queen Margaret.

U

A 13th Century mother-in-law

The unkindness that the Queen Blanche showed to the Queen Margaret was such that she would not suffer, in so far as she could help it, that her son should be in his wife's company, except at night when he went to sleep with her.

The palace where the king and his queen most liked to dwell was at Pontoise, because there the king's chamber was above and the queen's chamber below; and they had so arranged matters between them that they held their converse in a turning staircase that went from the one chamber to the other; and they had further arranged that when the ushers saw the Queen Blanche coming to her son's chamber, they struck the door with their rods, and the king would come running into his chamber so that his mother might find him there; and the ushers of Queen Margaret's chamber did the same when Queen Blanche went thither, so that she might find Queen Margaret there.

SOURCE: Joinville, *Chronicle of the Crusade of St. Lewis,* trans. Sir Frank Marzials, Everyman edition, J. M. Dent & Sons, 1908, p. 288.

LOUIS XI (1423–1483), King of France.

The army of thistles

An incident during the internecine wars in France, when the King was in Paris while the rebel princes—The League of Public Good—were advancing on the city.

This prodigious cannonading made both sides believe some great design was in agitation: and, to be sure, we sent out our scouts, and the weather being cloudy and duskish, those who got nearest the town discovered a party of horse upon the patrol, and beyond them (as they fancied) they perceived a great number of lances standing upright, which they imagined to be the king's battalions drawn up in the field, and all the people of Paris with them. . . .

And being come up to us, Duke John said:

'Well, gentlemen, we are now where we desired to be; the

king, and all his army (as our scouts inform us), are drawn out
of Paris, and marching to engage us; so let us each behave with
courage and good will, and as they march out, we will march
in. . . .'

By this time our scouts, perceiving the enemy were weak,
began to assume a little more courage, ventured something
nearer the town, but still found the battalions in the same place
and posture in which they had left them, which put them into
a new quandary. However, they stole up to them as near as they
could, but could make nothing of them; till at length the day
cleared, and they discovered them to be tall thistles.

SOURCE: *Memoirs of Philip de Commines, Lord of Argenton*, edit.,
Andrew Scoble, Bohn's French Memoirs, 1855, Vol. i, pp. 64–65.

LOUIS XIV (1638–1715), King of France; called the 'Sun King'
from the splendour of his court at Versailles, and his pre-eminence
in Europe during a reign of 72 years. It is said that the King had
such a hatred of Paris, his capital, that in the last 28 years of his
reign, he visited it only 8 times, and for nearly 50 years never
spent a night there.

i. *Cardinal Mazarin's prophecy*

'You do not know him. He will set out a little late, but he will
travel further than any. He has in him the makings of four
kings and one honest man.'

SOURCE: Victor Duruy's *History of France*.

ii. *At the beginning of his reign,* he said:

'Our subjects are our true wealth. If God gives me grace to do
all that I have in mind, I hope to bring the happiness of my
reign to such a height that . . . no-one, however wretched he
may be, shall not be assured of his daily bread, either through
his own toil or through the ordinary and regulated assistance
of the state.'

iii. *Towards the end of his reign*, the Marquis de Vauban wrote:

'Almost a tenth of the population is reduced to beggary; of the other nine-tenths, five cannot aid the tenth, being in a similar position; three tenths are ill-at-ease; the remaining tenth, containing not more than 100,000 families, has only 10,000 who are comfortably off.'

SOURCE: Victor Duruy, *History of France*, trans. L. Cecil Jane and Lucy Menzies, Everyman edition, J. M. Dent & Sons, 1917, pp. 134, 135 and 195.

iv. *'Dinna let him fa' in'*

A Mr. Stirling, who was Minister of Barony Church, Glasgow during the War which this and other Countries maintained against the insatiable Ambition of Louis XIV, in that part of his Prayer which related to public affairs, used to beseech the Lord that he would take the haughty Tyrant of France & shake him over the mouth of Hell; 'but, good Lord,' added the worthy Man, 'dinna let him fa' in.'

SOURCE: Manuscript note-books (1773–1830) of Richard Hickman; Editor's collection.

v. *The King's time-table*

Those who had been granted the exceptional honour of private audiences were expected to arrive always a few minutes before the appointed time. To one Minister, who appeared exactly as the clock was striking, the King remarked in cold displeasure:
'I almost had to wait.'

It was said that a Frenchman who 'knew his court' would, even if he were stranded in the Gobi desert, tell you exactly what the King was doing at 3.30 on that Tuesday afternoon.

SOURCE: Harold Nicolson, *Monarchy*, Weidenfeld & Nicolson, 1962, p. 220.

vi. *Le Pour*

One of the most absurd details of etiquette concerned what they called *le pour*. The Master of the Household would at Marly write in chalk upon the door panels the names of the occupants of the several bedrooms. In general he merely wrote the name of the person thus billetted; but if he added the word *pour* before the name, then a very high distinction had been accorded. The Princess des Ursins, on visiting Marly, and finding that on her door panel the Master of the Household had written '*pour Mme des Ursins*', instead of just '*Princesse des Ursins*', actually fainted with joy and had to be given salts. Such was the ecstasy conveyed by a single preposition scribbled in chalk upon a bedroom door.

SOURCE: ibid., p. 225.

vii. *Final word from Mme de Maintenon*

'What torture it is to have to amuse a man who is unamusable.'

LOUIS PHILIPPE (1773–1850), King of the French. Abdicated February 24, 1848, and died in exile in England in August 1850.

The abdication scene

The King and some members of his family were at luncheon, when the Duc de Montpensier came hurriedly into the room crying out:

'Sire, the army has thrown in its lot with the Reds. You must abdicate immediately.'

The old man turned up the tablecloth and proceeded to write his abdication, while Montpensier kept thumping the table, saying:

'Hurry, Sire!'

The King finished his proclamation and, handing it to his son, remarked:

'Even to abdicate takes a little time.'

SOURCE: Charles George Barrington, *Recollections of Lord Palmerston*, History To-day, March 1961, pp. 184–185.

LUTHER, MARTIN (1483–1546), leader of the Reformation.

i. '*I can do no other*'

Here I stand. I can do no other.

SOURCE: speech to Diet of Worms, April 18, 1521. The second five words appear on his monument at Worms.

ii. '*By works of love . . .*'

. . . by works of love, love grows and a man becomes a better man, whereas by pardons he does not become a better man but only more free from penalties.

SOURCE: one of Luther's Ninety-Five Theses; trans. Bertram Lee Woolf, *Reformation Writings*, Lutterworth Press, 1937, p. 23.

LYTTLETON, WILLIAM HENRY, first Baron (1724–1808). Governor of South Carolina, 1755–1762, ambassador to Portugal, Commissioner of the Treasury, etc.

An indelicate conversation

Lord Lyttleton, the Statesman, was a very absent man, of formal manners, who never laughed. In conversation he would frequently forget propriety in regard to the subject of it before the company he happened to be in. At Lady Hervey's, one evening when Lady Bute and her daughter, afterwards Lady Macartney, were present, he began to relate a conversation which he that day had with Mr. Wildman, on the subject of bees, & proceeded to describe the *generation* of bees, with many particulars, which put the ladies into some confusion.

At another time, Lord Orford met him at Lady Hervey's, when, with a tea cup in his hand, he advanced towards the table &, returning back, talking solemnly and moving backwards, before he reached his chair he crossed his legs & sat down, not on his chair but on the floor. The wig went one way and the tea-cup another, while His Lordship, with unmoved gravity continuing his conversation, recovered himself.

SOURCE: *The Farington Diary*, edit. James Greig, Vol. 1, 1793–1802, Hutchinson & Co. First published in the *Morning Post*, beginning Jan. 23, 1922.

LYTTON, EDWARD GEORGE BULWER (1803–1873), novelist. Author of 'The Last Days of Pompeii', 'The Last of the Barons' etc.

Industry of a crusader's wife

The children of Lord Lytton organised a charade. The scene displayed a Crusader knight returning from the wars. At his gate he was welcomed by his wife to whom he recounted his triumphs and the number of heathen he had slain. His wife, pointing to a row of dolls of various sizes, replied with pride, 'And I, too, my lord, have not been idle.'

SOURCE: G. W. E. Russell, *Collections and Recollections*, Ch. 31.

MACAULAY, THOMAS BABINGTON, first **BARON MACAULAY** (1800–1859), historian.

Verdict by a nephew

... Uncle Tom—not quite a gentleman.

SOURCE: dying words of George Otto Trevelyan, historian, nephew of Macaulay; confirmed by G. M. Trevelyan; letter in *History To-day*.

MACBETH (d. 1057). King of Scotland. Commander of the forces of King Duncan, whom he murdered. The well-known encounter with the witches in Shakespeare's 'Macbeth' is a good example of the way Shakespeare used the chronicler Holinshed as a source-book.

i. *Encounter with witches*

Shortly after happened a strange and uncouth wonder, which afterward was the cause of much trouble in the realm of

Scotland as ye shall after hear. It fortuned that as Macbeth and Banquo journeyed toward Fores, where the king as then lay, they went sporting by the way together without other company, save only themselves, passing through the woods and fields, when suddenly . . . there met them three in a strange and ferly [fearsome or wonderful] apparel, resembling creatures of an elder world, whom when they attentively beheld, wondering much at the sight, the first of them spake and said:

'All hail! Macbeth, Thane of Glamis' (for he had lately entered into that dignity and office by the death of his brother Synel). The second of them said:

'Hail! Macbeth, Thane of Cawdor.'

But the third said:

'All hail! Macbeth, that hereafter shall be king of Scotland.'

SOURCE: Raphael Holinshed, *The Historie of Scotlande*, 1577, p. 243.

ii. *Birnham Wood marches against Dunsinane Castle*

'A certain witch whom he had in great trust' told Macbeth that he should not be vanquished till the 'wood of Bernane came to the Castell of Dunsinnane'. Macbeth was besieged in the castle of Dunsinane by Malcolm Canmore, later Malcolm III of Scotland (d. 1093).

Malcolm following hastily after Macbeth, came the night before the battle unto Byrnan wood, and when his army had rested a while there to refresh them he commanded every man to get a bough of some tree or other of that wood in his hand, as big as he might bear, and to march forth therewith in such wise that on the next morrow they might come closely and without sight in this manner within view of his enemies.

On the morrow, when Macbeth beheld them coming in this sort, he first marvelled what the matter meant, but in the end remembered himself that the prophecy which he had heard long before that time, of the coming of Byrnane Wood to Dunsinnane Castle, was likely to be now fulfilled.

SOURCE: ibid., p. 251.

MANNING, HENRY EDWARD (1808–1892), Cardinal.

i. *A Cardinal's knowledge of London*

A well-known publicist, who perhaps thinks of himself rather more highly that he ought to think, once ventured to tell the Cardinal that he knew nothing about the subject of a painful agitation which pervaded London in the summer of 1865.

'I have been hearing confessions in London for thirty years, and I fancy more people have confided their secrets to me than to you . . .', was the Cardinal's reply.

SOURCE: George W. E. Russell, *Collections and Recollections*, Smith Elder and Co., 1903, Ch. IV.

ii. *Receiving orders*

His sense of humour was peculiarly keen, and though it was habitually kept under control, it was sometimes used to point a moral with admirable effect.

'What are you going to do in life?' he asked a rather flippant undergraduate at Oxford.

'Oh, I'm going to take Holy Orders,' was the airy reply.

'Take care you get them, my son.'

SOURCE: ibid.

MARCUS AURELIUS (121–180), Roman Emperor and philosopher.

i. *Infinite boredom*

His wisdom was absolute, which is another way of saying that his *ennui* was without limit.

SOURCE: Ernest Renan (1823–1892).

ii. *The purpose of life*

I exist to do some work.

SOURCE: Marcus Aurelius, *Meditations*.

iii. *A citizen of the world*

My nature is civic and rational; my city, my country, is Rome; but as a man, I am a citizen of the world.

SOURCE: Marcus Aurelius, *Meditations*.

MARIA CRISTINA OF NAPLES (1806–1878), Regent of Spain, 1833–1840, mother of Isabella II.

. . . *'so often in fiction, so rarely in real life'*

One blazing summer afternoon, the Queen's carriage left Madrid, surrounded, as usual, by her escort. The officer in command rode by the side of the royal conveyance. When they were half-way there [to La Granja, San Ildefonso, built by Philip V], my grandmother's nose began to bleed. It bled so profusely that she had soon used up all her own handkerchiefs and those of her lady-in-waiting. In this extremity, they were forced to apply to the young officer, who instantly bent from his horse and offered his handkerchief to the Queen. A few minutes later Cristina recovered, and stretching her tiny white hand out of the window, she smilingly returned the handkerchief to its owner. With old-world chivalry, Muñoz raised it to his lips. That kiss on the dusty highway sealed the fate of the Queen and the officer.

When the royal cavalcade reached its destination, Her Majesty summoned the captain who had made so bold a gesture. My grandmother's severity and the rectitude of her conduct were known to all, and it was feared that Muñoz would be disgraced. But these fears proved to be unfounded; Cristina was still in her twenties, she was a beautiful and emotional Italian—and she had never been in love. Muñoz was handsome and gallant. The story ended like those artless love tales that we find so often in fiction and so rarely in real life. The Queen married the captain.

But the marriage of the Regent to an officer of her bodyguard would have involved Spain in a tangle of dangerous complications; it was therefore solemnised in secret, and a secret it remained for many years, although the happy couple had nine children. Cristina had to make unbelievable sacrifices to conceal the fact that she was a wife and a mother. Muñoz was made Duke of Rianzares; he and his children lived far from the Court, and the lovers longed for the day when the Regent's daughter Isabella would ascend the throne. Maria Cristina had to carry on the duties of the State, and conform to the etiquette of the Court. When her youngest child was but a few hours old, she was obliged to dress and drive to the Cortes to read the opening speech. She fainted, and although this was attributed to a passing indisposition, it gave rise to Court gossip and to endless rumours.

SOURCE: the Infanta Eulalia, *Memoirs*; quoted in Sir Charles Petrie, *The Spanish Royal House*, Geoffrey Bles, 1958, pp. 165–166.

MARINERS OF ENGLAND, THE.

i. *Cosmopolitan crews*

Of 633 officers and men accounted for on board H.M.S. *Victory* on October 17th 1805, the last muster before Trafalgar, 71 were foreigners, drawn from every quarter of the globe. They included:

Dutchmen	7	Swedes	6	Bengal	1		
Americans	22	North Germans	2	Madras	1		
Danes	2	Prussians	1	Italians	4		
Frenchmen	3	West Indians	9	Maltese	4		
Russian	1	Swiss	2	Portuguese	2		
Norwegians	3	African	1				

SOURCE: figures from Edward Fraser, *Champions of the Fleet*, John Lane, 1908, pp. 229–230. Before 1794, British merchantmen trading overseas were allowed to enter up to 75% foreigners as crew; after that date, by an Act of Parliament 'for the encouragement of British seamen', the proportion was limited to 25%. The merchant fleet was a recognised source of supply for H. M. ships, and most of the foreigners in *Victory's* crew as shown above were taken from merchant ships by means of impress warrants.

ii. *A diversity of occupations*

Another indication of the wide-spread activities of the press-gang, and of the type of untrained material that was brought to such a surprising pitch of efficiency in the French wars, is the range of previous occupations followed by the crew of a man-o'-war. The following is the list for the *Elizabeth*, a 74-gun ship with a company of 395. Of these only 177 were seamen or came from callings directly or indirectly associated with the sea. The rest were made up of:

Labourers	108	Dry-salter	1	Brickmaker	1
Joiners	5	Farmers	7	Soldier	1
Tailors	6	Coppersmith	1	Stonecutter	1
Weavers	5	Servants	4	Sawyers	2
Coopers	5	Gardeners	3	Painters	7
Blacksmiths	6	Curriers	2	Corn-factor	1
Whitesmiths	3	Mattress-maker	1	Stay-maker	1
Slaters	1	Tobacco-manufacturer	1	Glassmaker	1
Umbrella maker	1	Fustian cutter	1	Hatters	2
Butcher	1	Cotton manu-facturer	1	Wiremaker	1
Shoemakers	10	Clockmaker	1	Potter	1
Poulterer	1	Watchmaker	1	Miller	1
Stocking-makers	2	Waiters	2	Mason	1
				Miner	1
				Chimney sweep	1

SOURCE: figures from Edward Fraser, *Champions of the Fleet*, John Lane, 1908.

MARLBOROUGH, JOHN CHURCHILL, first DUKE OF (1650–1722), soldier; commander-in-chief of allied armies in War of Spanish Succession.

i. *The forty pieces*

Inconsistent as the Duke of Marlborough's character may appear to you, yet it may be accounted for if you gauge his actions by his reigning passion, which was the love of money. . . .

He was calm in the heat of battle; and when he was so near being taken prisoner (in his first campaign) in Flanders, he was quite unmoved. It is true that he was like to lose his life in the one and his liberty in the other; but there was none of his money at stake in either. This mean passion of that great man operated very strongly in him in the very beginning of his life, and continued to the very end of it. One day as he was looking over some papers in his scrutoir [writing desk] with Lord Cadogan, he opened one of the little drawers, took out a green purse, and turned some broad pieces out of it. After viewing them for some time with a satisfaction that appeared very visibly on his face:

'Cadogan,' said he, 'observe these pieces well! They deserve to be observed; there are just forty of them: 'tis the very first sum I ever got in my life, and I have kept it always unbroken from that time to this day.'

SOURCE: Alexander Pope, in Joseph Spence's *Anecdotes*.

ii. *The fare home*

He was playing there [at Bath] with Dean Jones at piquet, for sixpence a game; they played a good while, and the Duke left off when winner of one game. Some time after, he desired the Dean to pay him his sixpence; the Dean said he had no silver; the Duke asked him for it over and over, and at last desired that he would change a guinea to pay it him, because he should want it to pay the chair that carried him home.

The Dean, after so much pressing, did at last get change, paid the Duke his sixpence; observed him a little after leave the room, and declares that (after all the bustle that had been made for his sixpence) the Duke actually walked home to save the expense a chair would have put him to.

SOURCE: ibid. For his great victories of Blenheim, Ramillies, Malplaquet and Oudenarde, Marlborough was given the estate of Woodstock and a perpetual pension of £4,000 a year. The second incident quoted by Pope is supposed to refer to the close of his career, when his health and mind were impaired.

iii. *The Point of Honour*

Marlborough once answered Godolphin, who expostulated with him for exposing his life so freely on the field of battle, by saying that he did not lead cavalry charges out of mere vainglory, but because he should think himself unworthy of the kindness which his army had always shown him if he did not share its perils.

SOURCE: David Hannay, *Ships and Men*, William Blackwood, 1910, p. 265.

iv. *Record of a commander*

There are few successful commanders on whom Fame has shone so unwillingly as upon John Churchill, Duke of Marlborough, Prince of the Holy Roman Empire—victor of Blenheim, Ramillies, Oudenarde, and Malplaquet—captor of Liege, Bonn, Limburg, Landau, Ghent, Bruges, Antwerp, Oudenarde, Ostend, Menin, Denderminde, Ath, Lille, Tourney, Mons, Douay, Aire, Bethune, and Bouchain; who never fought a battle that he did not win, and never besieged a place that he did not take.

SOURCE: Sir Edward Creasy, *The Fifteen Decisive Battles of the World*, 1851

See also BLENHEIM; RAMILLIES; MARLBOROUGH, SARAH, DUCHESS OF.

MARLBOROUGH, SARAH, DUCHESS OF (1660–1744), wife of John Churchill, Duke of Marlborough. Confidante of Queen Anne and exercised dominating influence over her till her disgrace in 1710. In her correspondence with the Queen ('Mrs. Morley'), used the name 'Mrs. Freeman'. She was a woman of great ability marred by an unpredictable temper which did not improve with age.

i. *The Duchess's temper*

One of her Grace's principal charms was a prodigious abundance of fine hair; one day, at her toilet, in anger to her heroic lord, she cut off her commanding tresses, and flung them in his face.

SOURCE: John Timbs, *A Century of Anecdote, 1760–1860.*

ii. 'Mrs. Morley and Mrs Freeman'

She [Queen Anne] grew uneasy to be treated by me with the form and ceremony due to her rank; nor could she hear from me the sound of words which implied in them distance and superiority. It was this turn of mind that made her one day propose to me, that whenever I should happen to be absent from her, we might in all our letters write ourselves by feigned names, such as would import nothing of distinction of rank between us. *Morley* and *Freeman* were the names her fancy hit upon; and she left me to choose by which of them I would be called. My frank, open temper, naturally led me to pitch upon Freeman, and so the princess took the other; and from this time Mrs. Morley and Mrs. Freeman began to converse as equals, made so by affection and friendship.

SOURCE: Sarah, Duchess of Marlborough, *An Account of the Conduct of the Dowager Duchess of Marlborough,* 1742.

MARTIN OF TOURS, ST. (336?–401?).

i. Martin the soldier

He became a cavalry officer, and was ranked in a patrol-service which involved the confidence of his superiors. His means would have allowed him to have two soldier-servants, but he was content with one, whom he treated not as a slave, but as a friend and brother. Even as a soldier his one aim was to assist the toilers, to aid the wretched, to clothe the naked, to feed the poor; of his pay he only retained sufficient for his daily maintenance. . . .

It was in his eighteenth year that the incident occurred with which Christian art has identified his name, and which practically decided his future destiny. He was in winter quarters at Amiens, and the winter was one of intense severity, during which Martin had freely given of his goods to feed the poor.

One day in January 354 he was passing through the gate of the city when he saw a poor man half-naked in the bitter cold. Martin was unable to give him alms, for he had already parted with all his money. But he was warmly clad. On his head was the gilded iron helmet with its red plume, and over his short tunic the ample sagum or military cloak . . . was fastened by a brooch and flowed over his shoulders. He did not hesitate. Drawing his short sword, he cut the mantle into two halves, gave half to the shivering sufferer, and was content to wrap the disfigured fragment round his own person.

SOURCE: F. W. Farrar, *Lives of the Fathers*, Adam and Charles Black, 1907, Vol. I, pp. 629–630. The main authority for the life of St. Martin is Sulpicius Severus.

ii. *Martin dines with the Emperor and Empress*

When first invited to his [Maximus's] table, he had replied with singular boldness:

'I cannot sit at the table of one who has robbed one Emperor [Gratian] of his life, and another [Valentinian II] of his throne.'

. . . But the pleas of the Emperor in his own defence had some weight, and at last Martin consented to dine with him. He was placed in a seat of conspicuous honour, while his attendant chaplain was seated between the brother and uncle of the Emperor. During the feast a great goblet was brought to the Emperor, and before tasting it he ordered it to be handed to Martin, hoping to receive it again from his hand. But when Martin had tasted it he handed it, not to the Emperor, but to his own chaplain, as though a priest were a person of higher rank than even a crowned head.

The Empress, a devout woman, obtained her husband's leave to entertain him alone. She prepared the banquet with her own hands, waited on him herself, sat at his feet, mingled and handed to him his wine, and at the end of the feast gathered all the crumbs and fragments and made her own meal of them.

SOURCE: ibid., pp. 652–653.

MARY I (1516–1558), Queen of England.

i. 'I am a-weary of mine office'

After the death of Henry VIII, the Privy Council tried to place severe restrictions on Mary, requiring her to give up the Roman Catholic religion, imprisoning her officers, and putting in one of their own nominees as comptroller of her household.

In no way intimidated, her parting thrust was a complaint that, since they had robbed her of her own comptroller, she had been forced to do her own accounts:

'Have I learned how many loaves of bread be made of a bushel of wheat? I wis [know] my father and mother never brought me up to brewing and baking; and, to be plain with you, I am a-weary of mine office!'

SOURCE: M. St. Clare Byrne, *Mary I*, in *The Great Tudors*, edit. Katharine Garvin, Ivor Nicholson & Watson, 1935, p. 191.

ii. *The way she wished to be married*

Her marriage ring was a rownd hoope of gould without anye stone, which was her desire, for she said she would be married as maydens were in the olde tyme, and so she was.

SOURCE: letter from John Elder to Lord Robert Stuart, 1554. Mary married Philip II of Spain on July 25, 1554.

iii. *The loss of Calais*

During her reign, Calais, 'the sole vestige of the English conquests in France', was captured by the Duke of Guise, largely through the lackadaisical attitude of the English government, which had left the town ill-equipped to withstand siege or attack. Calais first came into English hands in 1347.

When I am dead and opened, you shall find 'Calais' lying in my heart.

SOURCE: Mary's reaction to the news as reported by Raphael Holinshed, *Chronicles*, iii, 1160.

x

iv. *The mystery of Timothy Malt*

In 1555, there were widespread reports that Queen Mary was about to give birth to a child. These were apparently confirmed by the Queen's physicians and orders were given for prayers in church for her safe delivery. In June, about Whitsuntide, the news was circulated that a fair and strong prince had actually been born, and there were wide-spread celebrations, processions, gun-salutes, etc. What the truth of it was may never be fully known; but the following incident is attested to by John Foxe, later Canon of Salisbury.

One thing of mine own hearing and seeing I cannot pass over unwitnessed. There came to me, whom I did both hear and see, one Isabel Malt, a woman dwelling in Aldersgate Street in Horn Alley, not far from the house where this present book *The Actes and Monuments of the Church* was printed, who before witnesses made this declaration unto us: that she, being delivered of a man-child upon Whit Sunday in the morning, which was the eleventh day of June, anno 1555, there came to her the Lord North [Edward North, 1st baron—a Privy Councillor], and another lord to her unknown, dwelling then about Old Fish Street, demanding of her if she would part with her child, and would swear that she never knew nor had any such child; which, if she would, her son (they said) should be well provided for, she should take no care for it; with many fair offers, if she would part with the child . . . but she in no wise would let go her son, who at the writing hereof being alive, and called Timothy Malt, was of the age of thirteen years and upward.

Thus much, I say, I heard of the woman herself. What credit is to be given to her relation, I deal not withal, but leave it to the liberty of the readers to believe it they that list.

SOURCE: John Foxe, *The Actes and Monuments of the Church*, popularly known as *The Book of Martyrs*; Rev. John Cummin's edition, Chatto and Windus, 1875, Vol. iii, p. 187.

v. *John Heywood comes to Court*

Heywood was a singer and player on the virginals at Henry VIII's court and also came to high favour with Mary I.

He, being asked of the said Queen Mary, what wind blew him to Court, answered her:

'Two; especially the one in hope that I might see your Majesty.'

'We thank you for that,' said Queen Mary, 'but I pray you, what is the other?'

'That your Grace might see me.'

SOURCE: William Camden, *Remains Concerning Britain*, 7th impression, 1674.

See also PHILIP II.

MARY QUEEN OF SCOTS (1542-1587). Sent to France, 1548, contracted for marriage to the dauphin, later Francis II; educated with French royal children and married in 1558; laid claim to throne of England; on death of Francis II, returned to Scotland, 1561.

The Queen of Scots's farewell to France

Forced by the death of her husband to abandon the land of her adoption in order to return to her savage Scotland, she wept long at leaving France, where 'misfortune had left her and good fortune had taken her by the hand'.

Supported on the poop of her galley, her eyes full of tears fixed on the horizon, she remained, says Brantôme, for five hours in that attitude, repeating incessantly:

'Adieu, France! Adieu, France!'

When night came she caused a hammock to be stretched in the same place and lay there, refusing all food. At daybreak she could still see a point on the horizon, and cried:

'Adieu, dear France. I shall never see you more.'

SOURCE: based on Pierre de Bourdeilles, Seigneur de Brantôme, *Mémoires*; Victor Duruy, *A Short History of France*, 1873, Everyman's Library edition, J. M. Dent & Sons, 1917, Vol. 2, p. 9.

MATILDA (MAUD), (1080–1118), Queen of Henry I of England.

The Queen's charity

Among her good works, she built a leper hospital at St. Giles-in-the-fields, London, a priory at Aldgate, and a bridge over the River Lea, Stratford.

Queen Maud, wife of Henry the first of England, and daughter to Malcolm Canmore, King of Scotland, was so devoutly religious that she would go to Church barefoot, and always exercise herself in works of charity; insomuch that when David, her brother, came out of Scotland to visit her, he found her in her privy chamber with a towel about her middle, washing, wiping, and kissing poor people's feet, which he, disliking, said:

'Verily, if the King your husband knew this, you should never kiss his lips.'

She replied:

'The feet of the King of Heaven are to be preferred before the lips of a King on earth.'

SOURCE: William of Malmesbury and Matthew Paris; William Camden, *Remains Concerning Britain*, 7th impression, 1674.

MATILDA, OR MAUD (1102–1167), Empress. Daughter of Henry I of England, wife of Henry V of Germany, king and Emperor, and mother of Henry II of England.

'Henry's daughter, wife and mother'

Here lies Henry's daughter, wife and mother. Great by birth, greater by marriage, but greatest by motherhood.

SOURCE: epitaph in the Abbey of Bec.

MAZARIN, JULES, CARDINAL (1602–1661). The pupil of Richlieu and chief minister to Louis XIV. 'A great diplomat, he was not a great minister.' According to one estimate, at the end of his life there was a public debt of 430,000,000 francs, while he had amassed a personal fortune of 100,000,000.

i. *The wealth of the Cardinal*

On one occasion, one of the king's lesser ministers said:
'Sire, there is no money in your coffers, but M. le Cardinal can lend you some.'

SOURCE: Victor Duruy's *History of France.*

ii. *The character of the Cardinal*

He had a great, farseeing, and inventive mind, a straightforward and true judgment; his character was supple rather than weak, less firm than persevering; his motto was 'Time is on my side'.

He acted not according to his likes and dislikes, but by calculation. Ambition had mastered his sense of personal honour; he cared not what was said, provided that he gained his end, but he aided his judgment by that which the world had pronounced.

Before giving his confidence to a man he used to ask, 'Is he happy?' This question was not the result of some blind belief in fate; for him, to be happy meant the possession of a spirit which prepared and a character which could master fortune.

SOURCE: ibid. (quoted), Everyman's Library edition, J. M. Dent & Sons, 1917, Vol. II, p. 114.

MELBOURNE, WILLIAM LAMB, second VISCOUNT (1779–1848). Prime minister and statesman.

i. *'Can't you let it alone?'*

When I say 'indolent', I do not mean that he would sit doing nothing, but that he would not attend to business which bored him. . . . He was an easy going man whose character came within his own favourite expression:
'Can't you let it alone?'
. . . About the Reform Bill time, a deputation came to him at the Home Office (he was then Secretary of State for that Department) to urge that a procession should be allowed to march to

the Houses of Parliament to present a monster petition. He pointed out that this would be against the law and could not be permitted, on which the Deputation replied that, if force was used to stop the procession, it was to be feared that a riot might ensue.

Lord Melbourne expressed his regret, but added:

'It is well, gentlemen, that you should know that, should there be rioting, the troops have orders to fire not upon the people, but upon you personally.'

No procession took place.

SOURCE: Charles George Barrington, 'Political Recollections', *History To-day*, August, 1961, p. 575; from the MS. in the possession of Lord Lambton.

ii. *Melbourne's swearing checked*

Men and women of the highest fashion swore like troopers; the Princes of the Blood, who carried down into the middle of the nineteenth century the courtly habits of their youth, setting the example. . . . The Duke of Wellington's 'Twopenny damn' has become proverbial; and Sydney Smith neatly rebuked a similar propensity in Lord Melbourne by saying:

'Let us assume everybody and everyone to be damned and come to the point.'

SOURCE: George W. E. Russell, *Collections and Recollections*, Smith, Elder & Co., 1903, Ch. VIII.

MERRIE ENGLAND. It is sometimes thought that 'Merrie England' is a phrase used only by misguided modern romantics.

i. *Anglia plena jocis*

The first writer to do so, Henry of Huntingdon, had done so before 1150, writing in Latin of *Anglia plena jocis*. It is characteristically in the fourteenth century that the phrase is first used in English, by the anonymous author of the northern poem *Cursor Mundi*, who probably wrote early in the century.

SOURCE: Derek Brewer, *Chaucer in His Time*, Nelson and Sons, 1963, p. 3.

ii. 'A land full of mirth . . .'

England is a strong land and a sturdy, and the plenteousest corner of the world; so ruch a land that scarcely it needeth help of any land, and every other land needeth help of England. England is full of mirth and of game, and men oft-times able to mirth and game; free men of heart and tongue, but the heart is more better and more free than the tongue.

SOURCE: Bartholomew Anglicus, *De Proprietatibus Rerum*, 1470; English trans. by John Trevisa, *c.* 1495; modernized version quoted ibid., p. 4.

MICHELANGELO (1475–1564), Florentine painter, sculptor and architect.

i. *Michelangelo gets his nose flattened*

Now talking of his adventures, he [Piero Torrigiani] fell to speaking of Michel Agnolo Buonarotti, led to this by a drawing I had made from a cartoon of that most divine master . . . . Torrigiani . . . holding my drawing in his hand, spoke thus:

'Buonarotti and I, when we were lads, used to go to the church of the Carmine to study in the chapel of Masaccio. Now Buonarroti had a habit of teasing all the rest of us who were drawing there; and one day in particular he was annoying me, and I was more vexed than usual; so I stretched out my hand and dealt him such a blow on the nose that I felt the bone and the cartilage yield under my fist as if they had been made of crisp wafer. And so he'll go with my mark on him to his dying day.'

SOURCE: *Memoirs of Benevenuto Cellini*, trans. Anne Macdonell, Everyman's Library, J. M. Dent & Sons, 1907, pp. 17–19.

ii. *Michelangelo re-uses the spoilt block of stone*

Michelangelo's most famous work is his gigantic statue of David, hewed when he was only 26 from a block of marble which had been spoilt by another sculptor and discarded.

Unluckily one Simone da Fiesole had begun a giant, cutting between the legs and mauling it so badly that the wardens of S. Maria del Fiore had abandoned it without wishing to have it finished, and it had rested so for many years. Michelagnolo examined it afresh, and decided that it could be hewn into something new . . . and he decided to ask the wardens . . . for it. They gave it to him. . . . Accordingly Michelagnolo made a wax model of a youthful David holding the sling to show that the city should be boldly defended and righteously governed, following David's example. . . . The marble had been hacked and spoiled by Simone, so that he could not do all he wished with it, though he left some of Simone's work at the end of the marble, which may still be seen. This revival of a dead thing was a veritable miracle.

SOURCE: Giorgio Vasari, *Lives of the Painters*, etc., Everyman's Library edition, J. M. Dent & Sons, Vol. 4.

iii. *The sculptor performs some sleight of hand*

After the statue of David had been erected and still stood in its scaffolding, Piero Soderini, one of the city's chief officials, came to see it and said he thought the nose too large.

Piero Soderini came to see it, and expressed great pleasure to Michelagnolo who was retouching it, though he said he thought the nose was too large. Michelagnolo, seeing the gonfaloniere below and knowing he could not see properly, mounted the scaffolding and taking his chisel dexterously let a little marble dust fall on to the gonfaloniere, without, however, actually altering his work. Looking down, he said:

'Look now.'

'I like it better,' said the gonfaloniere, 'you have given it life.'

SOURCE: ibid.

MILNES, RICHARD MONKTON, first **BARON HOUGHTON**
(1809–1885), traveller, literary figure and member of Parliament; supported penny banks and mechanics' institutes. Nicknamed 'The Cool of the Evening', 'London Assurance' and 'In-I-go Jones'.

i. *'The Cool of the Evening'*

The assured ease of young Milnes's social manner, even among complete strangers, so unlike the morbid self-repression and proud humility of the typical Englishman, won for him the nick-name of 'The Cool of the Evening'.

SOURCE: George W. E. Russell, *Collections and Recollections*, Smith, Elder & Co., 1903, Ch. V.

ii. *Milnes resents his nick-names*

One very hot evening in summer, Lady Holland and a large party of friends were suffering from the stifling atmosphere, and a general dulness had crept over the company. Then Milnes was seen to enter.

'Ah! here comes the cool of the evening,' cried Sydney Smith, and immediately everybody grew brighter. [Milnes resented this and other nick-names, and Sydney Smith wrote to him: 'The names of "Cool of the evening", "London Assurance", and "In-I-go Jones", are, I give you my word, not mine.']

SOURCE: T. Wemyss Reid, *Life of Lord Houghton*, 1890; *Oxford Dictionary of Quotations*.

MONARCHY, THE ENGLISH.

The 1100-year-old institution

This century [the 20th] has witnessed the disappearance of five Emperors, eight Kings, and fifteen minor dynasties. The British monarchy, being sufficiently elastic to stand the strains and stresses of successive upheavals, has survived them all. It remains the most ancient institution in the country. Our Law Courts are eight hundred years old: our Parliament seven hundred years old; but our monarchy, as a political institution, is eleven hundred years old. Queen Elizabeth traces her descent from Egbert who was proclaimed Bretwalda in A.D. 829. Apart from the eleven years' interlude of Cromwell's Republic the descendants of Egbert have reigned in England ever since.

SOURCE: Harold Nicolson, *Monarchy*, Weidenfeld and Nicolson, 1962, p. 305.

MONTROSE, JAMES GRAHAM, MARQUIS OF (1612–1650), covenanter and royalist; hanged at Edinburgh.

Montrose's insufficiency of limbs

When the Marquis of Montrose was condemned by his judges to have his limbs nailed to the gates of four cities, the brave soldier said that he was 'sorry he had not limbs sufficient to be nailed to all the gates of the cities in Europe, as monuments of his loyalty'.

SOURCE: Isaac D'Israeli, *Curiosities of Literature*, 1881 edition, Vol. III, p. 419. Montrose scratched a verse, embodying much the same sentiments, on the window of his prison, the night before his execution.

MORE, SIR THOMAS (1478–1535). The first layman to hold the office of Lord Chancellor of England. He was a scholar, a good coversationalist, a devoted family man, a faithful servant of his king, but, as he said himself, 'God's first'. He was executed for high treason, his 'treason' consisting of refusing to take the oath which recognized the supremacy of the king, rather than the Pope, in church matters; and also declining to acknowledge that the Princess Elizabeth was legitimate.

i. *The Chancellor sings the service*

He used, when he was Lord Chancellor, upon every Sunday, when he was at home, to sit in the quire [choir] in his surplice, and sing the service: and being one day espied in that attire by the Duke of Norfolk, the Duke began to chafe, crying:

'Fie! Fie! my Lord, the Lord Chancellor of England, a parish priest, and a paltry singing man! You dishonour the King, you dishonour the King.'

'No, my Lord,' quoth Sir Thomas, 'it is no shame for the King if his servant serve his Sovereign and Saviour, who is the King of Kings.'

SOURCE: William Camden, *Remains Concerning Britain*, 7th impression, 1674, p. 300.

ii. 'Madam, my lord is gone'

During the time of his chancellorship of England, he used to send his Gentleman-Usher to his wife's pew, after Divine Service was done, to tell her that he was gone; but the next Sunday after he gave up his chancellorship of England, he came himself to her pew, and used the usual words of his Gentleman-Usher:

'Madam, my Lord is gone.'

SOURCE: ibid., pp. 300–301.

iii. More's re-action to a domestic disaster

On one occasion, while he was with the King at Woodstock, More heard that part of his house at Chelsea and all his barns full of corn had been destroyed by fire.

Therefore I pray you to be of good cheer, and take all the household with you to church, and there thank God: both for that he hath given us and for that He hath taken from us, and for that He hath left us; which if it please Him, He can increase when He will. And if it please Him to leave us yet less, at His pleasure be it.

I pray you make some good ensearch what my poor neighbours have lost, and bid them take no thought therefore: for and I should not leave myself a spoon, there shall no poor neighbour of mine, bear no loss by any chance happened in my house.

SOURCE: letter to Mistress Alice, his wife; *The Workes of Sir Thomas More, Knyght, sometyme Lorde Chancellour of England* . . . , 1557. Included in Edward Arber, *An English Garner*, 1887.

iv. A long day to pay

When he was Lord Chancellor, he decreed a gentleman to pay a sum of money to a poor widow, whom he had wronged; to whom the gentleman said:

'Then I hope your lordship will grant me a long day to pay it.'

'I will grant your motion,' said the Chancellor. 'Monday next is St. Barnabas's Day, which is the longest day in the year; pay

it to the widow that day, or I will commit you to the Fleet.'
[i.e., the Fleet Prison, used mainly for debtors].

SOURCE: Mr. Addison (pseudonym), *Interesting Anecdotes, Memoirs, etc.* . . . London, 1794.

v. *More thanks God for being a fool*

On one occasion, it is said, the Cardinal [Wolsey], with much complacency, laid before him the draught of a measure which he was about to carry into execution, and requested his sentiments freely on every part of it. More, having attentively considered it, began, with his usual sincerity, to point out some things to be suppressed, others to be amended, others to be added; till, at length, Wolsey, unable to suppress his mortification and wrath, asked him if he was not ashamed to prove himself a fool, by objecting to what all the other wise men of the council had approved?

'Thanks be to God,' replied More gravely, 'that the king's majesty hath but one fool in his right honourable council!'

SOURCE: Thomas More (his great-grandson) *The Life and Death of Sir Thomas More, Lord High Chancellor of England*, Paris, 1626, London, 1726; quoted John Macdiarmid, *Lives of British Statesmen*, 1820, Vol. I, pp. 55–56.

vi. *'I have no cause to be proud'*

The king having one day paid him an unexpected visit to dinner, and having afterwards walked with him for an hour in the garden, with his arm round his neck, Mr. Roper, son-in-law to More, took occasion, after Henry was gone, to congratulate him on his rare good fortune, in being treated by the king with a degree of familiarity never experienced by any other subject.

'I thank our Lord,' replied More, 'I find his Grace my very good lord indeed; and I believe he doth as singularly favour me as any subject in this realm. However, son Roper, I may tell thee, I have no cause to be proud thereof; for if my head would win him a castle in France, it would not fail to be struck off.'

SOURCE: William Roper, *Life of Sir Thomas More*, Paris, 1626; quoted John Macdiarmid, *Lives of British Statesmen*, 1820, Vol. I, pp. 66–67.

vii. *More's concern for justice to all men*

'. . . for this one thing I assure you, that if the parties will call for justice at my hands, then, though it were my father, whom I love so dearly, stood on one side, and the devil stood on the other, his cause being just, the devil of me should have his due.'

SOURCE: ibid., p. 85.

viii. *More returns a gift*

A lady, in whose favour he had made a decree in Chancery against a nobleman of rank, having, as a token of her gratitude, presented him with a pair of gloves, and in them forty pounds in angels [i.e., gold coins worth about 10/– each] as a new year's gift, More took the gloves, but, pouring out the money, and returning it, said with a smile:

'Since it would be contrary to good manners to refuse a new year's gift from a lady, I am content to take your gloves, but, as for the lining, I utterly refuse it.'

SOURCE: ibid., pp. 121–122.

ix. *More's three wishes*

So at a time, walking with me along the Thames's side at Chelsea, in talking of other things he said unto me:

'Now would to our Lord, son Roper, upon condition that three things were well established in Christendom, I were put in a sack, and here presently cast into the Thames.'

'What great things be those, Sir,' quoth I, 'that should move you so to wish?' . . .

'In faith, son, they be these,' said he. 'The first is, that where the most part of Christian princes be at mortal war, they were all at an universal peace. The second, that where the Church of Christ is at this present sore afflicted with many errors and heresies, it were settled in a perfect uniformity of religion. The third, that where the king's matter of his marriage [i.e. to Catherine of Arragon, whom Henry wished to divorce] is now come in question, it were to the glory of God and quietness of all parties brought to a good conclusion.'

SOURCE: William Roper's *Life*; quoted *The Great Tudors*, Ivor Nicholson and Watson, 1935, pp. 105–106.

x. *The end of the man 'of the greatest virtue this kingdom ever produced'*

Perceiving that the scaffold was weakly erected, he said, in his usual tone, to the attending officer:

'I pray thee, friend, see me safe up, and for my coming down, let me shift for myself.'

Observing the executioner pale and trembling, he said to him:

'Pluck up thy spirits, man, and be not afraid to do thy office. My neck is very short. See, therefore, that thou do not mar thy credit by cutting awry.'

Having spent a short time in devotion, he took the napkin with which his eyes were to be bound, and calmly performed that office for himself; then, laying his head on the block, he bade the executioner stay till he removed his beard:

'For it,' said he, 'has committed no treason.'

SOURCE: Roper's *Life*; John Macdiarmid, *Lives of British Statesmen*, 1820, pp. 147–148. Addison said of More's end: 'That innocent mirth, which had been so conspicuous in his life, did not forsake him to the last. He maintained the same cheerfulness of heart upon the scaffold which he used to show at his table; and, laying his head on the block, gave instances of that good humour with which he had always entertained his friends, in the most ordinary occurrences.'

xi. *An epigram on More*

It was said that, owing to More's industry as Chancellor, all the outstanding cases in the Court of Chancery were cleared up. This prompted the verse:

> *When More some years had Chancellor been,*
> *No more suits did remain.*
> *The same shall never more be seen,*
> *Till More be there again.*

SOURCE: quoted *A Book of Days* (edit. R. Chambers), 1864, Vol. I, p. 67. Thomas Fuller, *The English Worthies*, 1662.

MORTON, JOHN (1420?–1500), Archbishop and Cardinal; Lord Chancellor to Henry VIII and a great provider of money for the King by means of 'Morton's Fork', the two-pronged device for extracting contributions from both the extravagant and the niggardly.

'Morton's fork'

He was a great instrument in advancing a voluntary contribution to the king through the land; persuading prodigals to part with their money, because they did spend it most, and the covetous, because they might spare it best; so making both extremes to meet in one medium, to supply the king's necessities.

SOURCE: Thomas Fuller, *The Worthies of England,* 1662; 1952 edition, George Allen & Unwin, p. 149.

MOSS TROOPERS. The marauders who infested the English-Scottish borders, particularly in the 16th and 17th Centuries.

The infrequent attenders at church

They are called moss troopers because dwelling in the mosses, and riding in troops together. They dwell in the bounds or meeting of two kingdoms, but obey the laws of neither. They come to church as seldom as the twenty-ninth of February comes into the calendar.

SOURCE: Thomas Fuller, *The Worthies of England,* 1662.

MUHAMMAD, MAHOMET, or MOHAMMED (570?–632), founder of the Muhammaden religion.

i. *The Prophet gathers his disciples, 622*

The little dry water-course of Aqaba, some three to four miles east of Mecca in the mountains, had been chosen as the rendezvous. The time was an hour before midnight. The Prophet arrived on foot, accompanied by his uncle Abbas. . . . Then the men of Yathrib began to arrive, in twos and threes to avoid observation. Seventy-three men grouped themselves in the dark valley, lit only by the silvery radiance of the Arabian moon.

'We stole along as softly as sandgrouse to our meeting with God's messenger,' one of them subsequently reported.

After addressing the gathering, the Prophet invited the men to swear allegiance, thereby undertaking to receive and to protect him in Yathrib. Al Baraa ibn Maroor, a chief of Yathrib, was the first to swear, and was followed by his seventy-two comrades, filing past Muhammad in the darkness, each one in turn striking his hand against his.

'I am of you and you are of me,' cried the Apostle at the end of the swearing. 'I will war against them that war against you, and I will be at peace with those who are at peace with you.'

Twelve leaders were then chosen, possibly in imitation of the twelve apostles of Christ. . . . Then the Muslims silently dispersed, in two and threes as they had come. . . . Seventy Arab tribesmen in a dry water-course in far Arabia had changed the history of the world.

SOURCE: Sir John Bagot Glubb, *The Great Arab Conquests*, Hodder and Stoughton, 1963, pp. 51–52.

NAMES, A GALAXY OF (1619 A.D.).

'Persons of very great renown and quality'?

> Maximilian King of Poseland.
> Henry Prince of Godmanchester.
> George Duke of Sommersham.
> William Marquess of Stukely.
> Edmund Earl of Hartford.
> Richard Baron of Bythorn.
> Stephen Pope of Newton.
> Stephen Cardinal of Kimbolton.
> Humphrey Bishop of Bugden.
> Robert Lord of Wasely.
> Robert Knight of Winwick.
> William Abbott of Stukely.

Robert Baron of Saint Neots.
William Dean of Old Weston.
John Archdeacon of Paxton.
Peter Esquire of Easton.
Edward Fryar of Ellington.
Henry Monk of Stukely.
George Gentleman of Spaldech.
George Priest of Graffan.
Richard Deacon of Catworth.
Thomas Yeoman of Barham.

SOURCE: Rev. James Brome, *Travels*. These are, in fact, not a list of illustrious names, but those of a jury at Huntingdon in 1619. Brome says:

It is not thought improper to add now a copy of a Jury taken before Judge Dodrige, at the Assizes holden at Huntingdon, 1619 . . . which is the more remarkable because the surnames of some inhabitants of this county, annexed to the town or villages to which they belonged seem to make them at the first sight, persons of very great renown and quality.

NAPOLEON I (1769–1821), Emperor of the French.

i. *The First Consul makes an extempore speech*

We were received in the magnificent rooms of the Tuileries, in great state; the stairs and ante-rooms being lined by men of the *corps d'élite*, in their splendid uniforms, and baldricks of buff leather, edged with silver. Upon our introduction, refreshments were offered, and a circle was formed, as at a private *entrée*. Napoleon entered freely into conversation with Lord Holland and myself. . . . While we were conversing, three knocks were heard at the door, and a deputation from the Conservative Senate presented itself, as if unexpectedly, and was admitted. The leader of the deputation addressed the First Consul, in a set oration, tendering him the Consulate for life, to which he responded in an *extempore* speech, which, nevertheless, he read from a paper concealed in the crown of his hat.

SOURCE: Lord Cloncurry, *Personal Reminiscences*, 1849.

Y

ii. *The sentry who nearly bayoneted Napoleon*

It was in 1809, after the victory of Ebersberg, that I was posted at the entrance of a half-destroyed building, in which the Emperor had taken up his quarters. My orders were not to allow anybody to pass unless accompanied by an officer of the staff. In the evening a person wearing a grey overcoat came towards my post and wanted to pass. I lowered my bayonet, and called out:

'Nobody passes here.' Those were the words I used, and I never added 'even if you were the little corporal himself,' as has been wrongly imputed to me since, because I did not know I had the Emperor before me. The person came on without seeming to notice what I said; and I then brought my bayonet to the charge, and called out:

'If thou takest another step, I will run my bayonet into thy stomach.'

The noise brought out the whole of the staff, the Emperor returned to his quarters, and I was carried off to the guard-house.

'You are lost, my boy,' said my comrades; 'you have committed an assault on the Emperor!'

'Stop a bit,' I said; 'what of my orders? I shall explain all that to the court-martial.'

The Emperor sent to fetch me, and when I came into his presence, he said:

'Grenadier, thou mayest put a red riband in thy button-hole; I give thee the cross!'

'Thanks, my Emperor,' I answered; 'but there is no shop in this country where I can buy the riband.'

'Well,' replied the Emperor with a smile, 'take a piece from a woman's red petticoat; that will answer the purpose just as well!'

SOURCE: account by the Grenadier Coluche; quoted John Timbs, *A Century of Anecdote, 1760–1860*.

iii. *Napoleon snubs Marshal Soult*

We heard that Soult, on remonstrating upon the uselessness of charging our squares with cavalry, had been severely reprimanded, and had undergone the biting and sarcastic remark from the Emperor:

'Vous croyez Wellington un grand homme, Général, parce qu'il vous a battu.'

(You think Wellington a great man, General, because he has beaten you.)

SOURCE: *The Reminiscences and Recollections of Captain Gronow*, 1892; abridged edition by John Raymond, Bodley Head, 1964, p. 153.

See also AUSTERLITZ, WATERLOO and NAPOLEONIC WARS.

NAPOLEON III (1808–1873), Emperor of the French.

i. *The 'briefest and the justest' repartee*

One of the best repartees ever made, because the briefest and the justest, was made by 'the gorgeous Lady Blessington' to Napoleon III. When Prince Louis Napoleon was living in impecunious exile in London he had been a constant guest at Lady Blessington's hospitable and brilliant but Bohemian house. And she, when visiting Paris after the *coup d'état* naturally expected to receive at the Tuileries some return for the boundless hospitalities of Gore House. Weeks passed, no invitation arrived, and the Imperial Court took no notice of Lady Blessington's presence. At length she encountered the Emperor at a great reception. As he passed through the bowing and curtsying crowd, the Emperor caught sight of his former hostess.

'Ah, Lady Blessington! Are you staying in Paris long?'

'Are you, Sire?'

SOURCE: George W. E. Russell, *Collections and Recollections*, Smith, Elder & Co., 1903, Ch. XIX.

ii. *Bismarck's estimate of the Emperor*

It was not until the following winter, during which the King had again approached me, that he asked me once at dinner, straight across the table, my opinion concerning Louis Napoleon; his tone was ironical. I replied:

'It is my impression that the Emperor Napoleon is a discreet and amiable man, but that he is not so clever as the world esteems him. The world places to his account everything that happens, and, if it rains in eastern Asia at an unseasonable moment, chooses to attribute it to some malevolent machination of the Emperor.'

SOURCE: Otto, Prince von Bismark, *Reflections and Reminiscences*, 1898; Tauchnitz edition (trans. A. J. Butler), 1899, Vol. I, p. 196.

NAPOLEONIC WARS, THE.

i. *Fortitude during an amputation*

An English soldier belonging to, if I recollect rightly, the 1st. Royal Dragoons, evidently an old weather-beaten warfarer, while undergoing the amputation of an arm below the elbow, held the injured limb with the other hand without betraying the slightest emotion, save occasionally helping out his pain by spirting forth the proceeds of a large plug of tobacco, which he chewed most unmercifully while under the operation.

Near to him was a Frenchman, bellowing lustily, while a surgeon was probing for a ball near the shoulder. This seemed to annoy the Englishman more than anything else, and so much so that, as soon as his arm was amputated, he struck the Frenchman a smart blow across the breech with the severed limb, holding it at the hand-wrist, saying:

'Here, take that, and stuff it down your throat, and stop your damned bellowing!'

SOURCE: Edward Costello, *The Adventures of a Soldier.*

ii. *Quarrel in the Basque Roads,* * *1809*

In 1809 the French ships were being blockaded by the Channel Fleet under Lord Gambier. Plans were afoot to destroy the French shipping off Isle d'Aix, and the officers serving under

* 'Road' or 'roads' in the nautical sense means a place where ships may ride at anchor some distance from the shore.

Gambier were much incensed when a junior officer, Lord Cochrane (afterwards the Earl of Dundonald) was sent by the Admiralty to take charge of the operation. They found their spokesman in Admiral Eliab Harvey, one of the heroes of Trafalgar. Having publicly insulted Gambier on the quarter-deck, Harvey followed Cochrane into Captain Neale's cabin and continued his diatribe there.

'Well,' said Admiral Harvey, 'this is not the first time I have been lightly treated, and that my services have not been attended to in the way they deserved; because I am no canting methodist, no hypocrite, no psalm-singer, and do not cheat old women out of their estates by hypocrisy and canting! I have volunteered to perform the service you came on, and should have been happy to see you on any other occasion; but am very sorry to have a junior officer placed over my head.'

'You must not blame me for that,' replied I: 'but permit me to remark that you are using very strong expressions relative to the commander-in-chief.'

'I can assure you, Lord Cochrane,' replied Admiral Harvey, 'That I have spoken to Lord Gambier with the same degree of prudence as I have now done to you in the presence of Captain Sir H. Neale.'

'Well, admiral,' replied I, 'considering that I have been an unwilling listener to what you really did say to his lordship, I can only remark that you have a strange notion of prudence.'

SOURCE: Thomas, 10th Earl of Dundonald, *The Autobiography of a Seaman*, 1861, pp. 223–224.

Admiral Harvey was court-martialled on May 2, 1809 and dismissed the service. He was restored the next year, but was never given another ship.

iii. *A Ship of the line rescues a small boy on Christmas Eve*

The 98-gun H.M.S. *Téméraire* had reached Cawsand Bay in 1809, after a cruise in the Baltic.

We were obliged to wait for a fair wind, to sail up the harbour and to get into dock; when we encountered, on the 24th. of December, a most tremendous gale of wind. By eight at night it blew a perfect hurricane. We had then three feet [of] water in our lower decks, and two in the middle: it had entered through the hawse-holes, and through the bow-ports also. The sea kept rolling in so fast that we expected every moment either to go to the bottom, or to be driven on shore. All hands were at the pump: every exertion was made to save our ship and our lives.

In the midst of all this distress, we beheld a small boat driven towards us, with the sails torn into tatters and flying at the mast-head. As it came nearer, we could distinguish the cries of a boy singing out for help. Notwithstanding our own sad condition, we felt much for this poor creature, and still more because we could give him no aid, for the sea ran mountains high; so that, to us, it seemed as if no boat could live on it.

The cries continued, which our humane captain, (and there never was a more feeling man) could scarcely bear to hear, when he said if any of our crew chose to volunteer to try to save him, they might. We were none of us backward to do so; and at length, the boat being lowered with eight sailors, off she went.

It was some time before they could reach the little boat, the waves tossing it over and over, and the boy clinging to it. At last he was removed into our boat from his own, which it was not possible for them to take in tow; and before they had parted five yards from it, they saw it go to the bottom. The sea was so strong against them, and the waves rose to such a height, that the boat could not again come near the ship. We on board were then obliged to let go the life-buoy astern; and they getting hold of that, we at last saw them safe on board.

When the captain inquired of the boy how he came into the boat, and by what means she had got adrift, he replied that his father and himself had been coming from North-corner in Dock, and had reached Cawsand Bay, when his father left him alone in the boat, whilst he went on shore to get something to drink: that, being cold and tired, he laid himself down, and, drawing the sail over him, fell asleep. The surf running high on the beach, took the boat off, and he never awoke till he was tossing up and down a hundred yards from the beach. Then he put up his sail, and tried to get back again; but the gale blowing hard against him, it was soon shivered to pieces, and his oars had gone over-board. The waves had carried him past three other ships, which did not seem to have it in their power to render him any assistance. . . . The captain ordered him dry clothes, and every care to be taken of him.

During all this time we were working hard at the pumps; and it was not before five the next morning that the storm abated and we were again in safety. This was Christmas day; and that morning, which was one of rejoicing to the whole Christian world, was doubly so to us; for, by the mercy of a gracious Providence, our own lives had been wonderfully preserved, and we had been permitted, under Him, to save that of a fellow-creature also.

In the meantime, the distressed mother of the boy had gone on board (regardless of the storm) the three ships mentioned by him. They had all seen him pass; but, unable themselves to give him any help, they did not suppose he could have it from others, and told her that both he and his boat must have gone to the bottom. The poor broken-hearted mother had ventured her own life to learn something of her child, and returned again to her miserable home.

The Temeraire lay so far out at sea, so much beyond the other ships, that there seemed no hope of his having reached it: yet her boat was once more put out to sea; and when she got to us, she beheld her son in safety, standing on deck by the captain. She did not speak one word, but fell, as we thought, dead at his feet; and, when she did recover from her fit, who can ever forget her tears, and her thanksgivings to the preservers of her child?

After she had had some refreshment, she departed from the ship, and her son with her. We had then no money; but we promised that, when we were paid off, we would give the boy a present. We did not forget it; but, collecting the sum of eight pounds, five shillings and sixpence, we bought him a new boat, and christened it the Temeraire Johnson.

SOURCE: *A Journal of Voyages and Travels by the late Thomas Rees, Serjeant of Marines*, London, 1822, pp. 23–27.

NAUNTON, SIR ROBERT (1563–1635), Secretary of State.

'Two hundred were better than one'

One Mr. Wiemark, a wealthy man . . . hearing the news that day of the beheading of Sir Walter Ralegh, 'His head,' said he, 'would do very well on the shoulders of Sir Robert Naunton, secretary of state.'

These words were complained of, and Wiemark summoned to the privy council, where he pleaded for himself that he intended no disrespect to Mr. Secretary, whose known worth was above all detraction; only he spake in reference to an old proverb, 'Two heads are better than one.' And so for the present he was dismissed. Not long after, when rich men were called on for a contribution to Saint Paul's, Wiemark at the council-table subscribed a hundred pounds, but Mr. Secretary told him two hundred were better than one; which, betwixt fear and charity, Wiemark was fain to subscribe.

SOURCE: Thomas Fuller, *The English Worthies*, 1662; 1952 edition, George Allen & Unwin, p. 537.

NAVAL MUTINIES, 1797. In April and May, 1797, there were serious naval mutinies at Spithead and the Nore. The first was a well-conducted, responsible affair, approximating to a sit-down strike, chiefly for increased and regular pay. The seamen were prepared to call the strike off immediately should the French need dealing with. The other was a more vicious and far less justified affair, since the men's grievances had largely been dealt with after Spithead. The seamen soon became sickened by the excesses and came back to their allegiance, leaving the ringleaders to face the music.

The harm done by Sunday schools

December 20, 1797 [when Joseph Farington was taking breakfast with Admiral Sir Alan Gardner, who had had a rope shaken over his head during the mutiny]: Sir Alan said a great change had taken place in the Navy. The sailors were no longer the same sort of men as formerly. He thinks the Sunday Schools have done much harm, by giving education disproportionate to situation.

SOURCE: *The Farington Diary*, edit. James Greig, Vol. 1, 1793–1802, Hutchinson & Co. First published in the *Morning Post*, beginning Jan. 23, 1922.

NELSON, HORATIO, VISCOUNT NELSON (1758–1805), Admiral.

Nelson's way with midshipmen

The following extract from a letter written by Lady Hughes, who took a passage to the West Indies on board the *Boreas* frigate, when commanded by Lord Nelson, will show the manner in which the young men in that ship were trained and gradually inured to hardihood and enterprise, by their parental commander.

'It may reasonably be supposed, that among the number of thirty, there must have been timid souls as well as bold. The timid he never rebuked; but always wished to show them he desired nothing that he would not instantly do himself. And I have known him say:

"Well, sir, I am going a race to the mast head, and I beg I may meet you there."

No denial could be given to such a request. . . .'

SOURCE: Thomas Byerley and Joseph Clinton Robertson, *The Percy Anecdotes*, 1820–1823.

See also COPENHAGEN AND TRAFALGAR, BATTLES OF.

NERO (37–68), Roman Emperor.

i. *The public performer*

To acquire the fame of a charioteer, and to figure in the race with a curricle and four horses, had been long the passion of

Nero. He had besides another frivolous talent: he could play on the harp, and sing to his own performance. With this pitiable ambition he had often been the minstrel of convivial parties. . . . The rage of Nero for these amusements was not to be controlled. Seneca and Burrhus endeavoured to prevent the ridicule, to which a prince might expose himself by exhibiting his talents to the multitude. By their directions, a wide space, in the vale at the foot of the Vatican, was enclosed for the use of the emperor, that he might there manage the reins, and practise all his skill, without being a spectacle for the public eye. But his love of fame was not to be confined within those narrow bounds. He invited the multitude. . . .

The general corruption encouraged Nero to throw off all restraint. He mounted the stage, and became a public performer for the amusement of the people. With his harp in his hand, he entered the scene; he tuned the chords with a graceful air, and with delicate flourishes gave a prelude to his art.

SOURCE: Tacitus, *Annals* (trans. Arthur Murphy), J. M. Dent & Sons (Everyman's Library), 1908, Book IXV, IXV–XV.

ii. *While Rome burnt*

A dreadful calamity followed in a short time after, by some ascribed to chance, and by others to the execrable wickedness of Nero. . . . It is, however, certain, that of all the disasters that ever befell the city of Rome from the rage of fire, this was the worst, the most violent, and destructive. . . . A report prevailed that, while the city was in a blaze, Nero went to his own theatre, and there, mounting the stage, sung the destruction of Troy, as a happy allusion to the present misfortune.

SOURCE: ibid., Book IV, XXXVIII–XXXIX. Another Roman historian, Suetonius, states that Nero saw the fire from a tower on top of the house of Maecenas, and was so thrilled with the sight that he went to his theatre, put on his scenic costume and sang of the destruction of Troy.

NEWTON, SIR ISAAC (1642–1727), mathematician and natural philosopher.

i. *The absent-minded scholar*

At some seldom times when he designed to dine in hall, would turn to the left hand and go out into the street, when making a stop when he found his mistake, would hastily turn back, and then sometimes instead of going into hall, return to his chamber again.

SOURCE: Humphrey Newton, 1728, letter to John Conduit, Master of the Mint.

ii. *His weakness at ordinary sums*

Sir Isaac Newton, though so deep in Algebra and Fluxions [the differential calculus] could not readily make up a common account; and, when he was Master of the Mint, used to get somebody to make up his accounts for him.

SOURCE: Alexander Pope, Joseph Spence's *Anecdotes*.
   One is reminded of a famous Chancellor of the Exchequer who suffered similarly. See CHURCHILL, RANDOLPH.

iii. *His modesty*

Sir Isaac Newton, a little before he died, said: 'I don't know what I may seem to the world, but, as to myself, I seem to have been only like a little boy playing on the sea-shore, and diverting myself in now and then finding a smoother pebble or a prettier shell than ordinary, whilst the great ocean of truth lay all undiscovered before me.'

SOURCE: the Chevalier Ramsay (Andrew Michael Ramsay, tutor to Prince Charles Edward); Spence's *Anecdotes*. Sir David Brewster, *Memoirs of Newton*, 1828.

iv. *The apple story*

It was Voltaire who gave the apple story currency in its present shape. His nephew's record was:
   'In the same year [1665], at his mother's garden in Lincoln-

shire, when musing in a garden it came into his thought that the same power of gravity which made an apple fall from the tree to the ground was not limited to a certain distance.'

He saw that there was a remarkable power or principle which caused all bodies to descend towards the centre of the earth, and that this unseen power operated at the top of the highest mountains and at the bottom of the deepest mines. When the true cause, the law of gravitation, dawned upon his mind, Newton was so much agitated as to be unable to work out the problem.

SOURCE: Chambers's *Cyclopaedia of English Literature*, new edition, 1902, W. & R. Chambers, p. 23.

It is curious to trace the manner in which this apple-story has been told by different writers, and the different opinions formed concerning it. Pemberton, who received from Newton himself the history of his first ideas of gravitation, does not mention the apple, but speaks simply of the idea having occurred to the philosopher 'as he sat alone in a garden'. Voltaire says:

'One day, in the year 1666, Newton went into the country, and seeing fruit fall from a tree (as his niece, Madame Conduit, has informed me), entered into a profound train of thought as to the causes which could lead to such a drawing-together or attraction.'

SOURCE: *The Book of Days* (edition R. Chambers), 1864, Vol. II, p. 757.

NICHOLAS I (1796–1835), Emperor of Russia.

i. *The September Sovereign*

An impoverished landowner once petitioned him to grant free education to his son. The man, having spent his whole life among woods and fields, had no idea how to begin such a petition but, having heard of the Tsar being called 'August sovereign', he decided that, as he was writing in the autumn, he must begin by 'September Sovereign'.

Nicholas's marginal comment ran:

'Have the boy admitted into the Artillery School, otherwise he may become as much a fool as his father is.'

SOURCE: E. L. Almedingen, *The Romanovs*, The Bodley Head, 1966, p. 237.

ii. *The Tsar puts a comma in the wrong place*

In 1833, a Polish rebel was arrested after two years spent in hiding. The man's wife petitioned the Emperor for clemency. He marked the letter with three terse words:

'Pardon impossible, execute' (*Prostit nielzid, kaznít*), and misplaced the comma. When the Minister of Justice drew his attention to it, Nicholas stared at the paper and sighed.

'Yes, I meant the man to be hanged. But the mistake is mine and I must abide by it. Let him go free.'

SOURCE: ibid.

NICHOLAS II (1868–1918), Tsar of Russia; assassinated by revolutionaries, with all his family.

i. *'Lovely weather'*

Meanwhile, the Tsar, who in the past resented his wife's admonitions to stand firm when he had been in the mood to compromise, ignored her telegram. In her plight, surrounded with her sick children by hostile Red troops, she had telegraphed: 'Concessions are necessary'. But he now took a strong line and refused out of hand all concessions. He telegraphed that he was well, missed their nightly game of dominoes, and was returning to Petrograd, adding: 'Lovely weather'.

He travelled home, having ordered General Russky to march on the capital and quell the Revolution. But Russky's Army joined in with the revolutionaries, and the Tsar's white-and-gold train was turned off to Pskov. Whereupon the Emperor telegraphed to the President of the Duma, Rodzianko:

'Will now make the necessary concessions.' And the pot-bellied man telegraphed in return: 'Too late.'

SOURCE: William Gerhardi (who witnessed the beginnings of the Russian revolution), *When the Tsar's Hour Struck*, Sunday Telegraph, March 12, 1967.

ii. *Two salutes*

The symbols of the change-over of power are exactly reflected in the gestures of his [Nicholas II's] Chief-of-Staff succeeding him as Supreme Commander-in-Chief, General Alekseiev. When the Tsar's face at the train window slowly passed by, the General stood on the platform stretched to almost quivering attention with all the zeal he could put into an awesome, parting, dynastic salute. But when the last coach containing representatives of the Revolution went noisily by, the lone warlord whipped off his cap and bowed low to the people.

SOURCE: ibid.

NICK-NAMES.

i. *Creevey's nick-names*

There are no great names in his [Thomas Creevey's*] vocabulary—only nicknames: George III is 'old Nobs', the Regent 'Prinney', Wellington 'the Beau', Lord John Russell 'Pie and Thimble', Brougham, with whom he was on very friendly terms, is sometimes 'Bruffam', sometimes 'Beelzebub', and sometimes 'Old Wickedshifts'; and Lord Durham, who once remarked that one could 'jog along on £40,000 a year', is 'King Jog'.

SOURCE: Lytton Strachey; quoted T. H. White, *The Age of Scandal*, Jonathan Cape, 1950, Ch. 1.

* Author of *The Creevey Papers*.

ii. '*Est-il permis?*'

Thomas Pelham Holles [the Duke of Newcastle, 1693–1768, Secretary of State, etc.] was a buffoon . . . who lost half an hour every morning when he got up and chased it for the rest of the day—who was nicknamed Permis because he always said, 'Est-il permis?' before he addressed a remark to the King.

SOURCE: T. H. White, *The Age of Scandal*, Jonathan Cape, 1950, Ch. 10.

NIGHTINGALE, FLORENCE (1820–1910), nursing pioneer and reformer; 'The Lady with the Lamp'.

i. *The men who kissed her shadow*

What a comfort it was to see her pass. She would speak to one, and nod and smile to as many more; but she could not do it to all you know. We lay there by the hundreds; but we could kiss her shadow as it fell and lay our heads on the pillow again content.

SOURCE: one of her patients in the Crimea; quoted Cecil Woodham-Smith, *Florence Nightingale*, Constable, 1950, p. 207.

ii. *The honoured Lady in Chief*

The magic of her power over men was felt in the room . . . where operations took place. There perhaps the maimed soldier if not yet resigned to his fate, might be craving death rather than meet the knife of the surgeon, but when such a one looked and saw the honoured Lady in Chief was patiently standing beside him—and with lips closely set and hands folded—decreeing herself to go through the pain of witnessing pain, he used to fall into the mood of obeying her silent command and—finding support in her presence—bring himself to submit and to endure.

SOURCE: A. W. Kinglake, *The Invasion of the Crimea*, 1863–1887; quoted ibid.

NOBLEMAN'S HOUSEHOLD, A (*c.* 1660).

Lord Aston's quart glasses

Dear Phil,

When you were here I intended to have given you some relation of the very grand manner of my lord grandfather's living at Standon, being there is scarce anybody but myself left that remembers it, but it went out of my mind again. . . .

My lord's table was daily served with twenty dishes at a course, three courses the year about; and I remember it was brought up by twenty of his men, who, as they came up the great stairs and in the dining-room, affected to stamp louder than needed, which made a great noise like a clap of thunder every course that was brought up. My lord had every day four servants that waited behind his own chair, his gentleman, his house-steward, his chief park-keeper, and a footman to fetch to them what my lord called for; who was very curious in his wine, but Frontiniac was his favourite: but he first drank a whole quart at one draft, either of malt drink or wine and water, being advised to it by his physician as a remedy for the stone and gravel, which he was sometimes troubled with; insomuch that upon all the roads where he travelled, either into Staffordshire, or to us in Surrey, all the inns where he used to lodge kept a glass that held a quart, called 'My Lord Aston's Glass'. I saw one of them at the 'Altar Stone' at Banbury not many years ago.

SOURCE: letter from Sir Edward Southcote to his son Philip; transcribed from the manuscript in the Priory of the Annunciation, Woodchester, by Father John Morris in *The Troubles of Our Catholic Forefathers*, 1872, Vol. 1, pp. 400 and 402.

NORSEMEN, THE.

Three Norse sayings:

No man is so good but there is a flaw in him, nor so bad as to be good for nothing.

A ship for speed; a shield for shelter; a sword for stroke; a maid for marriage.

A man should not step a foot beyond his weapons, for he can never tell where, on his path without, he may need his spear.

SOURCE: Vigfusson and Powell, *Corpus Poeticum Boreale*; quoted Keatinge and Frazer, *A History of England for Schools*, 1919, p. 166.

NORTH, FREDERICK (usually known as **LORD NORTH**), second **EARL OF GUILFORD** (1732–1792), statesman; at various times a Privy Councillor, Chancellor of the Exchequer and Prime Minister. His most critical period of office was during the War of American Independence.

i. *Lord North removes the Treasurer of the Navy's wig*

In Parliament, the deficiency of Lord North's sight was productive to him of many inconveniences. For, even at a distance of a few feet, he saw very imperfectly; and, across the House, he was unable to distinguish persons with any degree of accuracy. In speaking, walking, and every motion, it is not enough to say that he wanted grace: he was to the last degree awkward.

It can hardly obtain belief that, in a full House of Commons, he took off on the point of his sword the wig of Mr. Welbore Ellis, and carried it a considerable way across the floor, without ever suspecting or perceiving it. The fact happened in this manner.

Mr. Ellis, who was then Treasurer of the Navy, and well advanced towards his seventieth year, always sat at the lowest corner of the Treasury Bench, a few feet removed from Lord North. The latter having occasion to go down the House, previously laid his hand on his sword, holding the chase of the scabbard forward, nearly in a horizontal direction. Mr. Ellis, stooping at the same instant that the First Minister rose, the point of the scabbard came exactly in contact with the Treasurer of the Navy's wig, which it completely took off and bore away.

The accident, however ludicrous, was completely unseen by Lord North, who received the first intimation of it from the involuntary bursts of laughter that it occasioned in every quarter

z

of the House. Mr. Ellis, however, without altering a muscle of his countenance, and preserving the utmost gravity in the midst of the general convulsion, having received back his wig, readjusted it to his head, and waited patiently till the House had recovered from the effect of so extraordinary, as well as ridiculous, occurrence.

SOURCE: Sir N. William Wraxall, *Historical Memoirs of My Own Life*, 1815, Vol. i, pp. 480–481.

ii. *Snores in unison*

(a) In addition to his defect of sight, Lord North was subject likewise to a constitutional somnolency, which neither the animated declamations of Fox, nor the pathetic invocations of Burke, nor the hoarse menaces of Barré, could always prevent.

(b) Selwyn held several Government appointments. . . . In Parliament, he often amused the House, during a long debate, by snoring in unison with the First Minister, Lord North.

SOURCE: (a) Sir N. William Wraxall, *Historical Memoirs of My Own Life*, 1815; (b) John Timbs, *A Century of Anecdote, 1760–1860*.

O'CONNELL, DANIEL (1775–1847), Irish politician and agitator, called 'The Liberator'; worker for Catholic emancipation; killed one man in a duel and tried to arrange one with Peel.

How to deal with O'Connell

The only way to deal with such a man as O'Connell is to hang him up and erect a statue to him under the gallows.

SOURCE: Rev. Sydney Smith; quoted H. Pearson, *The Smith of Smiths*, 1934, p. 272.

PAGE, WALTER H. (1855–1918), American Ambassador to the Court of St. James during the First World War.

An American Ambassador on England

I asked him why he thought England had touched and passed the zenith of its power. . . .

'You will have mothered and fathered the better part of the universe,' he replied; 'what more do you want? . . . it's my firm and certain conviction that long before another century is out England *as* England will be a back number. But she'll have peopled the greatest countries in the world, and the nation that takes her place will call her "Mother". '

SOURCE: (anon.) *The Whispering Gallery—Leaves from a Diplomat's Diary*, John Lane, 1926, pp. 243–244.

PALMERSTON, (LORD TEMPLE, HENRY JOHN, third VISCOUNT) (1784–1865), statesman.

i. *Their fill of fighting*

I had a book in my hand by Erckmann-Chatrian called *Le Conscrit*. Lord P. inquired what I was reading and I replied that in it was an account of the battle of Waterloo.

'Well,' said he, 'how does the author account for the loss of the battle?'

I told him that it was put down to the French troops not having had their breakfast in the morning.

'At all events,' was his comment, 'if they did not get their food in the morning, they had a belly-full before night.'

SOURCE: Charles George Barrington, 'Recollections of Lord Palmerston', *History To-day*, March 1961, p. 185; from the manuscript in the possession of Lord Lambton, M.P.

ii. *The statesman who earned his wages*

That Lord Palmerston was popular is not surprising; perhaps the knowledge that he got through an amazing amount of work useful to the country had something to do with it. An omnibus driver, who worked in Piccadilly, as he passed along would point out to the passengers Lord P's grey head, which could be plainly seen at the window where he wrote at his standing-up desk, and say:

' 'E earns 'is wages; I never come by without seeing 'im 'ard at it.'

SOURCE: ibid., p. 186.

iii. *English, or not at all*

One thing Lord Palmerston always got angry at, and that was at the introduction of an adopted French phrase in a despatch. I once saw a pencil note in his handwriting on the back of a despatch from some one, to this effect:

'Damn the fellow, tell him to write English or not at all.'

SOURCE: Sir Edmund Hornby, *An Autobiography*, Constable & Co., 1929, p. 186.

iv. *Palmerston indulges in anti-climax*

His style was not only devoid of ornament and rhetorical device, but it was slip-shod and untidy in the last degree. He ... seemed actually to revel in an anti-climax.

'I think the hon. member's proposal an outrageous violation of constitutional propriety, a daring departure from traditional policy, and, in short, a great mistake.'

SOURCE: George W. E. Russell, *Collections and Recollections*, Smith, Elder & Co., 1903, Ch. XII.

PANAMA CANAL, THE. The first project for a canal linking the Atlantic and Pacific Oceans, dates from 1550–1551. After many schemes and failures, Theodore Roosevelt, in 1906, decided to have the construction done under direct government control and in 1907 Colonel George Washington Goethals was appointed chief engineer, with complete control in the canal zone.

i. *Colonel Goethals sits in judgment*

The most remarkable part of Colonel Goethals' routine is his Sunday Court of Low, Middle, and High Justice. Even as the Caliphs of Bagdad sat in the city gate to hear the plaints of their people, so, in his very modern setting—principally maps and blue prints—the Colonel holds session every Sunday morning. ...

I had the good fortune to be admitted one Sunday morning to the audience chamber.

The first callers were a negro couple from Jamaica. They had a difference of opinion as to the ownership of thirty-five dollars which the wife had earned by washing. Colonel Goethas listened gravely until the fact was established that she had earned it, then ordered the man to return it. He started to protest something about a husband's property rights under English law.

'All right,' the Colonel said, decisively. 'Say the word, and I'll deport you. You can get all the English law you want in Jamaica.' The husband decided to pay and stay. . . .

A man came in who had just been thrown out of the service for brutality to the men under him. This action was the result of an investigation before a special committee. The man sought reinstatement. The Colonel read over the papers in the case, and when he spoke his language was vigorous:

'If you have any new evidence, I will instruct the committee to reopen your case. But as long as this report stands against you, you will get no mercy from this office. If the men had broken your head with a crowbar, I would have stood for them. We don't need slave-drivers on this job.'

SOURCE: Albert Edwards, *Panama: The Canal, the Country and the People*, New York, 1912.

ii. *Money for the mosquito battle*

The Chief Sanitary officer was W. C. Gorgas, one of whose great contributions to the achievement was the stamping out of yellow fever by wiping out the mosquito which carried it.

They tell a story about Gorgas in Cuba, and people who know him say that it sounds true.

In the early days there were men who made light of the mosquito work. Gorgas went to one of his superiors for some money to carry on his campaign.

'Is it worth while to spend all this money to save the lives of a few niggers?' the Commandant protested.

'That's not the point, General,' Gorgas shot back at him. 'We're spending it to save *your* life. And that's worth while.' He got the money.

SOURCE: ibid.

PARNELL, CHARLES STEWART (1846–1891), political leader and agitator.

i. *Parnell on the window-sill*

He got a great reception in Limerick. He spoke from Cruise's Hotel, and insisted on standing right out on the window sill, while a couple of people inside the room held him by the coat tail.

SOURCE: Mr. Russell, a Dublin journalist; quoted R. Barry O'Brien, *The Life of Charles Stewart Parnell*, Nelson & Sons, 1910.

ii. *Unsappable independence*

I saw Parnell for the last time towards the end of the summer at Euston Station. He was starting on his weekly visit to Ireland. . . . He arrived about ten minutes before the train started. Having despatched the business in his quiet ready way . . . he said, quietly and leisurely:

'I should like to know what you think will be the result of the General Election?' I answered:

'I should think that you will come back with about five followers, and I should not be surprised if you come back absolutely alone.'

'Well,' he answered impassively, 'if I do come back absolutely alone, one thing is certain, I shall then represent a party whose independence will not be sapped.'

SOURCE: R. Barry O'Brien, *The Life of Charles Stewart Parnell*, Nelson & Sons, 1910.

iii. *Gladstone's belated discovery*

. . . I did not discover anything remarkable in Mr. Parnell until much later than I ought to have discovered it.

SOURCE: W. E. Gladstone, talking to Barry O'Brien, 1897.

PAXTON, SIR JOSEPH (1801–1865), gardener; from humble origins, became superintendent of the gardens at Chatsworth and the intimate friend of his employer, the Duke of Devonshire; designed the Crystal Palace to house the Industrial Exhibition of 1850.

A good morning's work

Paxton had just been appointed (a young and untried man), as gardener at Chatsworth, having previously been on the staff of the Horticultural Society's Garden at Chiswick.

I left London by the Comet coach for Chesterfield, and arrived at Chatsworth at half-past four o'clock in the morning of the 9th of May, 1826. As no person was to be seen at that early hour I got over the greenhouse gate by the old covered way, explored the pleasure-grounds, and looked round the outside of the house. I then went down to the kitchen garden, scaled the outside wall and saw the whole of the place, set the men to work there at six o'clock; then returned to Chatsworth, and got Thomas Weldon to play me the waterworks, and afterwards went to breakfast with poor dear Mrs. Gregory and her niece: the latter fell in love with me, and I with her, and thus completed my first morning's work at Chatsworth before nine o'clock.

SOURCE: Paxton's own account, given to the Duke of Devonshire; *Notes and Queries*, 3rd Series VII, June 24, 1865.

PEEL, SIR ROBERT (1788–1850). Prime Minister and statesman. Built up the party which became known as the Conservative Party, the name being used in 1831. Its strength may be judged from the fact that at one time Peel had seven past or future prime ministers and five future viceroys of India with him.

i. *Peel makes a joke*

It has been said of him that he never made a joke; this is not so; he certainly made one, and here it is. He happened to be at a dinner where the late George Tomline's name was mentioned. George Tomline was the son of Bishop Pretyman, who had been Mr. Pitt's tutor; and at his death a large fortune came to his son.

'Ah!' said one of the party, 'I wonder what Bishop would say if he could look up and see how young Tomline is making his money fly.'

'Sir,' remarked Sir Robert, 'I perceive that you do not say look *down*.'

SOURCE: Charles George Barrington, 'Political Recollections', *History To-day*, August, 1961, p. 575; from the manuscript in the possession of Lord Lambton, M.P.

ii. *Sir Robert tries the three-card trick*

A few years before his death, Sir Robert, with one or two friends, happened to be going to Alexandra Park to witness a balloon ascent, or something of the sort . . . when, making his way to the grounds, he found himself in close proximity to a man who was doing the three-card trick. Drawing himself up, as he used to do, he said to his companions:

'I thought this old swindle was extinct; however' (with a wink), 'as we have come across it, I shall expose the rascal.'

He at once proceeded to push himself to the front of the little crowd which stood around the illicit operator, but as soon as he got there his expression softened, and, relenting, he whispered:

'The poor man is but a sad bungler; he cannot do the trick at all.'

Soon, however, Sir Robert yielded to the blandishments of the sharper whilst his friends were present (and no money was on), proving completely successful in spotting the court card, which he did almost every time.

The rest of the party, having applauded his skill, said they would walk slowly on to the Palace, which they did; but, finding after some time that no Sir Robert appeared, someone went back to look for him, and, to his great astonishment, discovered the missing Baronet still in close proximity to the card-sharper, but now in a furious rage, all his money being lost.

'I ought to convict you,' he was saying. 'I am a magistrate, and you, sir (this in his grandest manner, his hat fiercely cocked, and one hand in a Napoleonic pose just inside his coat) you sir, are a rogue, a thief, and a vagabond!'

The fact was that Sir Robert, finding he could so easily select the right card when there had been no money on, had not been able to resist taking advantage of what he thought was a good thing, though . . . it was in reality an excessively bad one.

SOURCE: *Reminiscences of Lady Dorothy Nevill* (edit. Ralph Nevill), Thomas Nelson & Sons, 1906.

PELLEW, SIR EDWARD, first **VISCOUNT EXMOUTH** (1757–1833), Admiral; a famous frigate captain who earned high promotion for gallantry and had a great reputation with his crews.

i. *Pellew at school*

The Reverend Richard Polwhele, who was at school with him, writes in his reminiscences with a sort of gloomy relish:

'Pellew was one of the most daring of Conan's boys. I confess I rather stood in awe of him, though, with his high spirit he had a very kind heart. Pellew would never suffer the weak to be trampled upon, but would fight their battles. But I think he once thrashed me.'

SOURCE: Rev. Richard Polwhele, *Recollections*.

ii. *Pellew disappears from a carriage*

On the afternoon of 16th January, 1796, a fierce gale was blowing and the *Dutton*, a large transport ship filled with troops for the West Indies, was forced into Plymouth Sound for shelter. But the violence of the wind drove her right under the Citadel, her masts crashed in a tangle of twisted and broken rigging, and the seas were soon battering the helpless ship to pieces. The captain and senior officers were ashore, the crew were panic-striken, and the young officers left on board lost all control of the situation. Some of the soldiers broke open the spirit room and tried to drown their terror in rum.

Sir Edward Pellew was also on shore. He had hired a carriage and was driving with his wife to dine with Doctor Hawker, a local clergyman. As the carriage stopped outside the Doctor's house, he came down the steps to greet them, and spoke to Lady Pellew through the nearer window. Had she heard, he asked, of the ship in distress under the Citadel.

There was a quick movement from the other side of the coach and the slam of a door. Pellew had disappeared, leaving his wife to cope as best she could, and was well down the road towards the beach. Soon he was with the anxious onlookers, a giant of a man, bellowing through a speaking trumpet, trying to organise help for the doomed ship. He was heard to offer five guineas to any man who would let himself be hauled aboard the *Dutton* to convey to the men on board his orders for their safety. But no-one accepted the challenge. In the end, it was Pellew himself who was drawn aboard, still in his frock-coat, with his sword at his side.

He arrived at the height of the disorder and confusion ... apparently unperturbed by the imminent disaster, rallying the crew to their duty and bringing back some semblance of dis-cipline to the helpless Indiaman. Hawsers were got ashore and, with their aid, every man got safely ashore before the ship finally broke up.

SOURCE: Grant Uden, *Collector's Case-Book*, Constable Young Books, 1963, p. 80.

iii. *The wrong brother*

Villeneuve's surrender after Trafalgar.

'To whom,' asked Admiral Villeneuve, in good English, 'have I the honour of surrendering?'

'To the Captain Pellew of the *Conqueror*.'

'I am glad to have struck to the fortunate Sir Edward Pellew.'

'It is his brother,* sir,' said Captain Atcherley.

'His brother! What! are there two of them? Hélas!'

SOURCE: Edward Fraser, *The Enemy at Trafalgar*, Hodder and Stoughton, 1906, p. 141.

* Israel Pellew, later admiral and knighted, Edward's brother.

PENN, WILLIAM (1644–1718), Quaker; founder of Pennsylvania.

His Majesty takes off his hat

A rebuke . . . was given by Charles the Second to William Penn, when the sturdy Quaker kept on his hat on being presented to him.

'Friend Penn,' said the king, 'it is the custom of this court for only one person to be covered at a time;' and then his majesty took off his own hat.

SOURCE: *The Percy Anecdotes*, 1820–1823.

PHILIP II (1527–1598), King of Spain and husband of Mary I of England.

i. '*It would have been better to have used the sand*'

Philip's cold eyes explored the increasing evidence of English intrigues, insults, injuries and, most infuriating of all, the impudent, friendly and specious letters of the English Queen; but they never changed expression, nor could ever shut in sleep, so his exhausted secretary believed, as his own blinked helplessly at two in the morning over a letter that the King had just written and handed to him. Jerking himself awake, the wretched man snatched at the ink-stand in mistake for the sand-castor, and poured the ink all over the carefully-composed interminable screed. Even then the King's eyes only bulged a little more, but did not flicker; his flat comment fell heavy as lead:

'It would have been better to have used the sand.'

SOURCE: Margaret Irwin, *That Great Lucifer*, Chatto and Windus, 1960, p. 45.

ii. *The Princess who would not change her shift*

Isabella, daughter of Philip II and wife of the Archduke Albert, vowed not to change her linen till Ostend was taken; this siege, unluckily for her comfort, lasted three years; and the supposed colour of the archduchess's linen gave rise to a fashionable colour . . . called . . . Isabella; a kind of whitish-yellow-dingy.

SOURCE: Isaac D'Israeli, *Curiosities of Literature*, 1881 edition, Vol. 1, p. 217. The incident is also ascribed to Isabelle of Austria in connection with the siege of Granada. But the use of 'isabelle' to describe a colour is certain. It was sometimes applied to horses of a dun-yellow colour.

iii. *Philip gets an unexpected reception when he comes courting*

The following incident occurred when Philip II came to England in 1554 to marry Mary I. It is a surprising example of England's insistence on recognition of her sovereignty of the seas.

In the year 1554, in Queen Mary's reign, Lord William Howard was sent with a fleet of twenty-eight sail to escort Philip of Spain up the Channel. Prince Philip was accompanied by 160 of his own ships: and the Spanish Admiral came along proudly with the Spanish flag flying at the main topmast-head. He was probably surprised to find himself greeted with a good round shot by Lord William Howard, who flatly refused to give the Prince any other welcome till the Spanish colours were hauled down.

SOURCE: *The Story of the Sea* (edited 'Q'), Cassell & Co., 1898, p. 126; among the eye-witnesses was the Spanish general Sciriago, who related it to Sir William Monson (1569–1643), Monson himself was the centre of a later incident.

See SOVEREIGNTY OF THE SEAS. See also MARY I.

PHILIP IV (1270–1314), King of France. Called 'the Fair'. His reign was ruthless and unsavoury, marked by financial chicanery, bloodshed—as in the destruction of the Order of the Knights Templar—and his quarrel with the aged Pope Boniface VIII.

A letter and a reply

(1) Pope Boniface to Philip IV, December 1301.

Fear God and keep his commandments. We would have thee to

know that thou art subject to us. The collation [i.e., the gift of church livings and offices] of benefices and prebends in no wise pertaineth to thee. If you hast the charge of any that be vacant reserve their fruits for them that shall succeed thereto; and if thou hast made any collation, such collation we decree to be null and void, and in so far as it have actually proceeded, we revoke the same. And those who think otherwise we esteem to be heretics.

(2) Philip IV to Pope Boniface.
Philip, by the grace of God King of the Franks, to Boniface, pretended Chief Pontiff, wisheth little or no health.

Thy supreme fatuity must know that in temporal matters we are subject to none; that the collation of churches and prebends pertains to us by royal prerogative; that we make their fruits our own, that the collations hitherto are made valid for the future and in perpetuity, and that we will defend the possession of them right manfully against all comers. And those who think otherwise we esteem to be demented.

SOURCE: quoted L. Ragg, *Dante and his Italy*; and Hedley Hope-Nicholson, *The Mindes Delight*, Cayme Press, 1928, p. 8.

PHILIP V (1683–1746), King of Spain. Philip V was a grandson of Louis XIV, a hunchback, amiable, obstinate, pious, and dominated by his wife, Elizabeth Farnese, who was a crack shot, hunted in man's attire, and was known to appear on the field of battle, pistols at the saddle.

The King gets ready to be off
Philip could hardly be described as a wit, but he occasionally gave evidence of a sense of humour which he may well have inherited from his ancestor, Henry of Navarre. On one occasion when relations with France were particularly strained, the government issued an order giving French subjects a choice between naturalisation and expulsion from the country. Shortly afterwards, the Queen went into her husband's apartments to find his boxes and portmanteaux open and his wardrobes empty. In astonishment she asked what all this meant.

'Why,' replied the King, 'have not all Frenchmen been ordered to leave Spain? . . . I am French, and so I am getting ready to be off.'

The order was, needless to say, immediately rescinded.

SOURCE: Sir Charles Petrie, *The Spanish Royal House*, Geoffrey Bles, 1958, p. 65.

PHILIP, H.R.H. PRINCE, DUKE OF EDINBURGH (b. 1921).

Cricket at the races

He has been known to go to Ascot with a transistor wireless concealed in his top hat so that he can listen to the cricket commentaries.

SOURCE: Christopher Hibbert, *The Court at Windsor*, Longmans, 1964, p. 298.

PITT, WILLIAM, first EARL OF CHATHAM (1708–1778), statesman and orator; a great war minister, planning the expeditions, and choosing the commanders, which led to some of the greatest victories of the Seven Years War.

i. *England gives birth to a man*

Il faut avouer que l'Angleterre a été longtemps en travail, et qu'elle a beaucoup soufferte pour produire M. Pitt; mais enfin elle est accouchée d'un homme.

It must be confessed that England has been in labour for a long time, and that she has suffered greatly in order to produce Mr. Pitt; but at last she has given birth to a man.

SOURCE: Frederick the Great, King of Prussia (1712–1786).

ii. *The Englishman's home*

The poorest man may in his cottage bid defiance to all the forces of the Crown. It may be frail—its roof may shake—the wind may blow through it—the storm may enter—the rain may enter—but the King of England cannot enter—all his force dares not cross the threshold of the ruined tenement!

SOURCE: Lord Brougham, *Historical Sketches of Statesmen in the time of George III*, 1839–1843, 1st series.

PITT, WILLIAM (1759–1806), statesman, second son of William Pitt, Earl of Chatham; Prime Minister at the age of 24; called the 'Great Commoner'.

i. *Fox assesses the new member*

These distinguished orators and rivals, notwithstanding their political hostility, entertained the utmost respect for each other's talents. After the close of the first session in which Mr. Pitt appeared in Parliament, a friend of Mr. Fox saying 'Mr. Pitt, I think promises to be one of the first speakers ever heard in the House of Commons,' he instantly replied:

'He is so already.'

SOURCE: *The Percy Anecdotes*.

ii. *Pitt lends his longest horse*

A curious correspondence once arose between Mr. Pitt and Mr. Dundas.* When the latter applied to Pitt for the loan of a horse 'the length of Highgate', Pitt wrote back to say that he was afraid he had not a horse in his possession quite as long as Mr. Dundas had mentioned, but he had sent the longest he had.

SOURCE: John Timbs, *A Century of Anecdote, 1760–1860*.

iii. *Pitt replies to two Members at the same time*

Mr. Fox having made an able speech, Mr. Erskine followed him with one of the very same import. Mr. Pitt rose to answer them: he announced his intention to reply to both; 'but,' said he, 'I shall make no mention of the honourable gentleman who

---

* Henry Dundas, first Viscount Melville.

spoke last: he did no more than regularly repeat what was said by the member who preceded him, and regularly weaken all he repeated.'

SOURCE: John Timbs, *A Century of Anecdote, 1760–1860*, Frederick Warne & Co.

iv. *A welcome from the King*

George III had a sincere liking and regard for Pitt. . . . When Pitt resumed office in 1804, he congratulated the King on looking much better than he did when Pitt last saw him in the spring of 1801.

'That is not to be wondered at,' said the King. 'I was then on the point of parting with an old friend; I am now about to regain one.'

SOURCE: John Timbs, *A Century of Anecdote, 1760–1860*, Frederick Warne & Co.

v. *'Billy Pitt's Pictures'*

'Pitt's Pictures', or 'Billy Pitt's Pictures', was the name popularly given to the blocked up windows that followed on Pitt's introduction of a window tax in 1784 and 1797. Filling them in reduced the number of taxable windows. Numbers of them can still be seen about the countryside.

vi. *The last words in public*

'England has saved herself by her exertions, and will, I trust, save Europe by her example.'

SOURCE: William Pitt, speech at the Guildhall, 1805.

See also STANHOPE, LADY HESTER.

PLAGUE, THE (1665).

King Charles II's Medicine for the Plague

Take a little handful of Herb grace, as much of Sage, the like quantity of Elder leaves, as much of red bramble leaves, stamp them together, and strain them through a fair linnen cloth, with a quart of white-wine, and a quantity of white Ginger, and mingle all together; after the first day you shall be safe four and twenty dayes: after the ninth day a whole year by the grace of God, and if it fortune that one be strucken with the Plague before he hath drunk the Medicine, then take the aforesaid with a spoonful of Scabiosa, and a spoonful of Bettony-water, and a quantity of fine Treacle, and put them together, and cause the Patient to drink it, and it will put out all venome, and if it fortune that the botch appear, take the leaves of red Brambles, Elder leaves, and Mustard-seeds, stamp them together, and make a plaister thereof, and lay it to the sore, and it will draw out all the venome, and the person shall be whole by the grace of God.

SOURCE: *The Queens Closet Opened, Incomparable Secrets in Physick, Chyrugery. . . . Which were presented the Queen by the most experienced Persons of the Times . . . etc.*, 1679 edition, pp. 28–29.

PLAGUE, 1897. The Aga Khan (1877–1957) was Imam of the Ismaili Muslims. In the First World War he influenced the Muslim world in support of the Allies; headed the Indian delegation to the Round Table Conferences, 1930–1931, in preparation for Indian self-government; and was President of the League of Nations in 1937.

The young Prince shows the way

During the previous year [1896] there had been sinister rumours that an epidemic of bubonic plague was sedulously and remorselessly spreading westwards across Asia. There had been a bad outbreak in Hong Kong; sporadically it appeared in towns and cities farther and farther west. When in the late summer of 1897 it hit Bombay there was a natural and general tendency to discredit its seriousness; but within a brief time we were all compelled to face the fact that it was indeed an epidemic of disastrous proportions. . . . The medical authorities in Bombay were overwhelmed by the magnitude, and (as it seemed) the complexity of the catastrophe that had descended

AA

on the city. Cure they had none, and the only preventative that
they could offer was along lines of timid general hygiene,
vaguely admirable but unsuited to the problem with which they
had to deal. Open up, they said, let fresh air and light into the
little huts, the hovels and the shanties in which hundreds of
thousands of the industrial and agricultural proletariat in
Bombay Presidency lived; and when you have let in fresh air,
sprinkle as much strong and strong-smelling disinfectant as you
can. These precautions were not only ineffective; they ran
directly counter to deep-rooted habits in the Indian masses. Had
they obviously worked, they might have been forgiven, but as
they obviously did not, and the death-roll mounted day by day,
it was inevitable that there was a growing feeling of resent-
ment. . . .

Now it happened that the Government of Bombay had at
their disposal a brilliant scientist and research worker, Professor
Haffkine, a Russian Jew, who had come to work on problems
connected with cholera by mass inoculation and had had in his
sphere considerable success. He was a determined and energetic
man. He was convinced that inoculation offered a method of
combating bubonic plague. He pressed his views on official
quarters in Bombay without a great deal of success. Controversy seethed around him; but he had little chance to put his
views into practice. Meanwhile people were dying like flies—
among them many of my own followers.

I knew that something must be done, and I knew that I must
take the initiative. . . . The impact of the plague among my own
people was alarming. It was in my power to set an example. I
had myself publicly inoculated, and I took care to see that the
news of what I had done was spread as far as possible as quickly
as possible. My followers could see for themselves that I, their
Imam, having in full view of many witnesses submitted myself
to this mysterious and dreaded process, had not thereby
suffered. . . .

I was twenty years old. I ranged myself (with Haffkine, of
course) against orthodox medical opinion of the time—among
Europeans no less than among Asiatics. And if the doctors were
opposed to the idea of inoculation, what of the views of ordi-

nary people, in my own household and entourage, and in the public at large. Ordinary people were extremely frightened. Looking back across more than half a century, may I not be justified in feeling that the young man that I was showed a certain amount of courage and resolution?

At any rate it worked. . . . Deliberately I put my leadership to the test. It survived and vindicated itself in a new and perhaps dramatic fashion. My followers allowed themselves to be inoculated, not in a few isolated instances but as a group. Within a short time statistics were firmly on my side; the death-rate from plague was demonstrably far, far lower among Ismailis than in any other section of the community. . . .

A man's first battle in life is always important.

SOURCE: *The Memoirs of Aga Khan*, Cassell & Co., 1954, pp. 36–39.

PRESS GANG, THE.

The pressed man who became an Admiral

Campbell* was the son of the minister of Kirkbean, in Kirkcudbrightshire, who . . . had a large family and a small income. The boy was little more than a child when he was obliged to shift for himself and was bound apprentice to the master of a coasting vessel. He was growing a big lad when one day—it must have been about 1736 or 1737—the coaster was boarded by a party from a ship of war in want of men, who, according to the exigences of the time, pressed every soul on board except the master and his apprentice. The mate, who had a wife and family at home, wept bitterly; so much so that Campbell begged the impress officer to let the mate go, and take him instead.

'Aye, my lad, that I will,' was the answer; 'I would much rather have a boy of spirit than a blubbering man. Come along.'

SOURCE: *The Story of the Sea* (edited 'Q'), Cassell & Co., 1898, p. 143.

* Admiral John Campbell (1720?–1790), who sailed round the world with Anson, commanded the *Royal George* at Quiberon Bay (1759) and became Governor of Newfoundland.

PRESTONPANS, BATTLE OF (September 21, 1745). Fought at a village nine miles east of Edinburgh between Prince Charles Edward's forces and the royal army under Sir John Cope. Cope was ignominiously routed.

A ballad and a challenge

After the battle a popular ballad was written by a Lothian farmer named Skirving. It consisted of about fifteen verses, two of which ran:

> And Major Bowle, that worthy soul,
> Was brought down to the ground, man;
> His horse being shot, it was his lot
> For to get mony a wound, man.
> Lieutenant Smith, of Irish birth,
> Frae whom he call'd for aid, man,
> But full of dread, lap [leapt] o'er his head,
> And wadna be gainsaid, man.
>
> He hade sic haste, sae spurr'd his beast,
> 'Twas little there he saw, man;
> To Berwick rade [rode] and falsely said
> The Scots were rebels a', man.
> But let that end, for weel 'tis kend
> His use and wont's to lie, man.
> The Teague* is naught; he never faught
> When he had room to flee, man.

After the publication of this song this gentleman [Lieut. Smith] came to Haddington, and sent a challenge to the author to meet him there, and answer for the unworthy manner in which he had noticed him in his song.

'Gang awa back,' said the honest farmer to the bearer of the challenge, 'and tell Mr. Smith that I havena leisure to come to Haddington; but tell him to come here, and I'll tak a look o' him, an' if I think I'm fit to fecht [fight] him, I'll fecht him; and if no', I'll do as he did—*I'll run awa.*'

SOURCE: James Hogg, *The Jacobite Relics of Scotland*, Second Series, 1821, p. 337.

* A contemptuous term for an Irishman.

PRINTING, INVENTION OF.

The magician of Mayence

When Fust [or Faust, Johann, d. 1466] had ... printed off a considerable number of copies of the Bible to imitate those which were commonly sold as manuscripts, he undertook the sale of them at Paris. It was his interest to conceal this discovery, and to pass off his printed copies for manuscripts. But, enabled to sell his Bibles at sixty crowns, while the other scribes demanded five hundred, this raised universal astonishment; and still more when he produced copies as fast as they were wanted, and even lowered his price. The uniformity of the copies increased the wonder. Informations were given to the magistrates against him as a magician; and in searching his lodgings a great number of copies were found. The red ink, and Fust's red ink is peculiarly brilliant, which embellished his copies, was said to be his blood; and it was solemnly adjudged that he was in league with the Infernals. Fust at length was obliged, to save himself from a bonfire, to reveal his art to the Parliament of Paris, who discharged him from all prosecution. . . .

SOURCE: Isaac D'Israeli, *Curiosities of Literature*, 1881 edition, Vol. 1, pp. 75-76.

PRONUNCIATION, CHANGES IN.

i. *Changes in fashion*

It is curious how fashion changes pronunciation. In my youth everybody said 'Lunnon', not 'London'. Fox said 'Lunnon' to the last. . . . The now fashionable pronunciation of several words is to me at least very offensive: cóntemplate is bad enough; but 'bálcony' makes me sick.

SOURCE: Samuel Rogers (1763-1855).

ii. There was an old Lady Robert Seymour, who lived in Portland Place, and died there in 1855, in her ninety-first year. Probably she is my most direct link with the past, for she carried down to the time of the Crimean War the habits and phraseology of Queen Charlotte's early Court. 'Goold' of course she said for gold, and 'yaller' for yellow, and 'laylock' for lilac. She laid stress on the second syllable of 'balcony'. She called her maid her ' 'ooman'; instead of sleeping at a place, she 'lay' there, and when she consulted the doctor she spoke of having 'used the "potticary" '.

SOURCE: George W. E. Russell, *Collections and Recollections*, Smith, Elder & Co., 1903.

iii. *Caleb Bingham tries to correct the pronunciation of New England*

The following list shows not so much how pronunciation has changed as the extraordinary kinship between English country dialects, now being rapidly eradicated, and the speech of New England in the 18th Century.

IMPROPRIETIES in PRONUNCIATION

common among the people of New-England*

Afraid	not	Afeard
afterwards		arterwards
chimney		chimbly
cucumber		cowcumber
eternity		etarnity
however		howzever
handkerchief		handkercher
ours		ourn
rheumatism		rheumatiz
potatoes		taters
nervous		narvous
this		this-ere

SOURCE: Appendix to Caleb Bingham's *The Child's Companion*, an 18th Century American text-book.

* Only a few examples have been quoted from the list supplied by Bingham.

PRYNNE, WILLIAM (1600–1669), puritan writer of pamphlets. In 1634, Prynne, for a supposed attack on Charles I and Queen Henrietta Maria in *Histriomastix*, a book directed against stage-plays, was sentenced by the Court of Star Chamber to be imprisoned, to be fined £5000 and to lose his ears in the pillory. In fact, his ears were 'cropped', only a part of them being removed.

On June 14, 1637, Prynne was again before Star Chamber, this time for a series of attacks on Archbishop Laud and the Bishops, written during his confinement in the Tower of London.

i. *Ears or no ears?*

'I had thought Mr. Prynne had no ears; but methinks he hath ears.'

SOURCE: Chief Justice Sir John Finch, at the opening of Prynne's second trial, upon seeing the remainder of his ears. We are told:

... the usher of the court was commanded to turn up his hair and shew his ears; upon the sight whereof the Lords were displeased they had been formerly no more cut off, and cast some disgraceful remarks of him. To which Mr. Prynne replied:

'My Lords, there is never a one of your Honours but would be sorry to have your ears as mine are.'

SOURCE: *Harleian Miscellany*. Prynne was again fined £5000, to lose what was left of his ears, to suffer life imprisonment and to have the letters 'S.L.' (for 'Seditious Libeller', though Prynne said it was 'Stigmata Laudis') burnt in both cheeks. He was released in 1640 and proved himself equally cantankerous in his own party. At the Restoration in 1660, he turned out to be a King's man and was made Keeper of Records in the Tower.

ii. *The refocillation* of Prynne*

He wore a long quilt cap which came two or three inches over his eyes, which served him as an umbrella to defend his eyes against the light. About every three hours his man was to bring him a roll and a pot of ale to refocillate his wasted spirits.

SOURCE: John Aubrey, *Brief Lives*.

* *refocillare* = to revive by warmth.

QUAKERS, THE. The name was first applied in derision, in about 1650, to the members of the Society of Friends, founded by George Fox (1624–1691).

i. *The origin of the name*

Justice Bennet, of Derby, was the first to call us Quakers, because I bade him quake and tremble at the word of the Lord.

SOURCE: George Fox, *Journal*, 1694.

ii. *The Quaker and the sword*

Mr. Dillwyn's son told me that this father, in his younger days, was in a stage coach with a party of military officers. One of them, a pert, effeminate, young dandy, undertook to quiz the plain Quaker, and after some indifferent jokes, asked him at an inn where they stopped, to hold his sword for a minute, supposing he would consider it an abomination to touch it. Mr. Dillwyn, however, eyeing the young man from head to foot said:

'As I believe from thy appearance it has never shed human blood, and is not in the least likely to do so, I have not the smallest objection.'

SOURCE: Charles Robert Leslie, R.A., *Autobiographical Recollections*, 1860, Vol. I, p. 79.

QUEEN'S (or **KING'S**) **MESSENGERS.** The élite Corps of Foreign Service Messengers employed under the Foreign Office to carry confidential despatches to and from the Sovereign's representatives abroad. Their badge, the Silver Greyhound, has been associated with them for some three centuries, though its origins are not certain.

i. *The silver greyhound*

The story goes that the Silver Greyhound first appeared when the throne was occupied by the House of Lancaster. John Beaufort, Duke of Beaufort and Somerset, a descendant of John of Gaunt, had as his crest or cognizance 'a greyhound courant argent'. He recommended the institution of State Messengers, more popularly known as King's Messengers. When the Royal Arms was conferred upon them as their badge, the Duke obtained the King's permission to append his crest therefrom. . . .

Another attractive tale connects the greyhound with . . . Charles II. In exile in Holland, Prince Charles frequently employed secret agents to carry messages to and from his supporters in England. They were difficult times and some means had to be devised whereby his emissaries could establish their *bona fides* when they met each other during their clandestine trips. Charles happened to have in his possession a silver dish with a lid, on which were four greyhounds courant. Breaking off the silver greyhounds, he gave them to his couriers to be shown whenever they were called upon to identify themselves. On his Restoration he decreed that the silver greyhound, worn with the Garter ribbon, should become his Messengers' badge. One of the original greyhounds is supposed to be still in existence, but the truth is that there are no authentic records of a greyhound badge before the days of William and Mary.

SOURCE: Colonel Michael O'Brien-Twohig, *Diplomatic Courier*, Elek Books, 1960, pp. 211–212.

ii. *A mistake at the Embassy*

Right up to the early part of the present century, the badge was much more than a decoration. The traveller who could display one at the right moment was not only recognized as being a King's or Queen's Messenger; he could also count on assistance and co-operation—fresh horses, alternative conveyances, special sea transport, and on one occasion, I believe, the stoppage of a mail train at some remote village station.

In these days the badge works no such miracles. Worn at official gatherings when protocol demands decorations, the silver greyhound emblem is purely ornamental. That its real signficance is not always appreciated is illustrated in an amusing anecdote told me by a colleague. He was wearing the badge with his war miniatures at an Embassy function one evening, and was asked by one of the staff if he was the President of the Greyhound Racing Association.

SOURCE: Colonel Michael O'Brien-Twohig, op. cit., pp. 212–213.

QUIBERON BAY, BATTLE OF (November 20, 1759).

The smuggler who sighted the French

On another occasion Paulet* happened to be sneaking across with a cargo of Brandy when he sighted the French fleet, which, under Conflans, had stolen out of Brest. This was on the 14th of November, 1759. There had been a good deal of rough weather previously, and Conflans thought that Hawke, who was watching him with the British fleet, was still sheltering at Torbay. As it happened, Hawke had left Torbay, and reached his station just as Paulet, who loved his country better than his cargo, sailed into sight, steered boldly for the Admiral's ship, and reported that the French had slipped out to the southward, and were steering east.

'If you are telling me the truth,' said Hawke, 'I will make your fortune; if you have lied to me, I will hang you at the yard-arm.'

The fleet weighed instantly, soon sighted the French, and overtook them in Quiberon Bay. The Admiral now ordered Paulet back into his little vessel; but the smuggler begged leave to remain and have a share in the fight. This was granted, and Paulet fought like a Briton; and when the fight was over and the great victory won, Hawke sent him home with letters of commendation in his pocket and money in his purse that enabled him to buy a public-house in London and spend the rest of his days in ease.

SOURCE: *The Story of the Sea* (edited 'Q'), Cassell & Co., 1898, p. 634.

* Harry Paulet (d.1804), a famous Hampshire smuggler. Paulet also claimed to have brought news to England which led to Wolfe's expedition to Quebec in 1759. Confirmatory evidence is difficult to find, though the above story is countenanced by some prominent naval historians.

QUO WARRANTO, INQUEST OF (1278–1279): enquiry set on foot by Edward I into the private jurisdictions and franchises exercised by the barons.

The warrant of Earl Warenne

Shortly afterwards the king disturbed some of the nobles of the realm by wishing to know, through his justices, on what warrant they held their lands; and if they had no good warrant to show, he immediately seized their estates. Among the others Earl Warenne was summoned before the king's justices, and was asked by what warrant he held. He thereupon produced in court an ancient rusty sword and said:

'See, sirs, see, here is my warrant. For my ancestors came across with William the Norman, and conquered their lands with the sword, and with the sword shall I defend them against whosoever wishes to take them from me.'

SOURCE: Walter of Hemingford, or Hemingburgh (fl. 1300), *Chronicon*, edit. E. H. S. Hamilton, 1848; inc. in M. W. Keatinge and N. L. Frazer, *A History of England for Schools*, A. & C. Black, 1919, p. 255.

RALEGH,* SIR WALTER (1552?–1618), military and naval commander, adventurer and author.

i. *Sir Walter boxes his son's ears for discourtesy*

Sir Walter, being strangely surprised and put out of his countenance at so great a table, gives his son a damned blow over the face. His son, as rude as he was, would not strike his father, but strikes over the face the gentleman that sat next to him and said:

'Box about [i.e. pass the blow round the table] 'twill come to my father anon.'

SOURCE: John Aubrey, *Brief Lives*.

*This spelling is the one generally used by Ralegh himself, though he was not consistent. The family wrote it in more than 70 different forms.

ii. *The learning of Ralegh*

It has been computed that six hundred and sixty authors are cited by him in his *History*, and there exists a letter to [Sir Robert] Cotton asking for the loan of thirteen books, none of which is included amongst the works of the six hundred and sixty authors quoted.

SOURCE: *The Cambridge History of English Literature*, 1932 edition, Vol. IV, p. 60.

iii. *The writing on the window*

To put the queen in remembrance, he wrote in a window obvious to her eye:
Fain would I climb, yet fear I to fall.
Which her majesty, either espying or being shown, underwrote this answer:
If thy heart fail thee, climb not at all.

SOURCE: *The Life of the Valiant and Learned Sir Walter Raleigh, Knight . . .* 1677. The story is also given by Thomas Fuller, *The Worthies of England*, 1662.

iv. *Who is the best warrier?*

If therefore it be demanded whether the Macedonian or the Roman were the best warrior, I will answer, 'The Englishman'.

SOURCE: Sir Walter Ralegh, *Historie of the World*.

v. *The new plush cloak*

This captain Ralegh, coming out of Ireland to the English court in good habit (his clothes being then a considerable part of his estate) found the queen walking, till meeting with a plashy place, she seemed to scruple going thereon. Presently Ralegh cast and spread his new plush cloak on the ground, whereon the queen trod gently, rewarding him afterwards with many suits, for his so free and seasonable tender of so fair a footcloth.

SOURCE: Thomas Fuller, *The Worthies of England*, 1662; 1952 edition, George Allen & Unwin, p. 133.

vi. *The last word*

In November, 1603, Ralegh was tried by a Special Commission for high treason, on a charge of conspiring against James I. The Court sat at Winchester because the plague was raging in London.

Now the business seemed to be at an end.

Sir Walter Ralegh: Mr. Attorney, have you done?

Attorney-General: Yes, if you have no more to say.

Sir Walter Ralegh: If you have done, then I have somewhat more to say.

Attorney-General: Nay, I will have the last word for the King.

Sir Walter Ralegh: Nay, I will have the last word for my life.

SOURCE: quoted in David Jardine, *Criminal Trials*, London, 1832, Vol. 1, p. 443. Jardine's account is compiled from several different reports, the most important of which is among the Harleian MSS. (No. 39).

vii. *The pride of Ralegh*

Ralegh at times earned himself great unpopularity for his pride and arrogance (John Aubrey tells us his chief fault was that 'he was damnable proud'), but during his trial public sympathy swung towards him and he became something of a popular hero.

'Never was a man so hated and so popular in so short a time.'

SOURCE: the diplomatist Sir Dudley Carleton (1573–1632), who was present at the trial and who reported another spectator as saying:

... that whereas when he saw Ralegh first he was so moved with the common hatred that he would have gone a hundred miles to see him hanged, he would, ere he parted, have gone a thousand to have saved his life.'

viii. *Ralegh on the best policy towards invaders*

'Surely I hold that the best way is to keep our enemies from treading upon our ground: wherein, if we fail, then must we seek to make him wish that he had stayed at his own home.'

SOURCE: Sir Walter Ralegh, *Historie of the World*, p. 799.

ix. *Ralegh is extinguished by his Servant*

There is a well-known tradition that Sir Walter Raleigh first began to smoke it [i.e. tobacco] privately in his study, and that the servant coming in with his tankard of ale and nutmeg, as he was intent upon his book, seeing the smoke issuing from his mouth, threw all the liquor in his face by way of extinguishing the fire, and running downstairs, alarmed the family with piercing cries that his master, before they could get up, would be burnt to ashes.

SOURCE: Patrick Fraser Tytler, *Life of Sir Walter Raleigh*, 1833; based on William Oldys's *Life of Raleigh*, 1736.

x. *Ralegh performs an experiment and wins a wager*

On another occasion it is said that Raleigh, conversing with his royal mistress upon the singular properties of this new and extraordinary herb, assured her that he had so well experienced the nature of it that he could tell her the exact weight of the smoke in any quantity proposed to be consumed.

Her majesty immediately fixed her thoughts upon the most impracticable part of the experiment, that of bounding the smoke in a balance . . . and laying a wager that he could not solve the doubt.

Upon this Raleigh selected the quantity agreed on, and having thoroughly smoked it, set himself to weighing—but it was of the ashes; and, in conclusion, demonstrating to the queen the difference between the weight of the ashes and the original weight of the tobacco, her majesty did not deny that this must be the weight of what was evaporated in smoke.

Upon this Elizabeth, paying down the money, remarked that she had heard of many labourers in the fire who had turned their gold into smoke, but that Raleigh was certainly the first who had turned his smoke into gold.

SOURCE: William Oldys's *Life of Raleigh*, prefixing his edition of Ralegh's *Historie of the World*, 1736.

xi. *Ralegh is sure of a place*

The eve of execution.

As he went from Westminster to the Gatehouse, he espied Sir Hugh Beeston in the throng and calling to him prayed he would see him die tomorrow. Sir Hugh to make sure work got a letter from Secretary Lake to the Sheriff to see him placed conveniently, and meeting them as they came near the scaffold delivered his letter; but the Sheriff by mishap had left his spectacles at home and put the letter in his pocket.

In the meantime, Sir Hugh being thrust by, Sir Walter bade him farewell and said:

'I know not what shift *you* will make, but *I* am sure to have a place.'

SOURCE: John Chamberlain in a letter to Dudley Carleton, October 31, 1618.

xii. *'So the heart be straight'*

The execution of Ralegh, October 29, 1618.

Then, a proclamation being made that all men should depart the scaffold, he prepared himself for death, giving away his hat, his cap, with some money, to such as he knew that stood near him. And then, taking his leave of the Lords, Knights, Gentlemen, and others of his acquaintance, and amongst the rest taking his leave of my Lord of Arundel, he thanked him for his company, and entreated him to desire the King that no scandalous writing, to defame him, might be published after his death; saying further unto him:

'I will now take my leave; for I have a long journey to go, and an assured hope to be quickly there.'

And then putting off his doublet and gown, desired the executioner to show him the axe; which, not being suddenly granted unto him, he said:

'I prithee let me see it. Dost thou think I am afraid of it?'

So, it being given unto him, he poised it in his hand, and felt along the edge of it with his thumb, to see if it was keen; and, smiling, spake unto Mr. Sheriff, saying:

'This is a sharp medicine, but it will cure all diseases.'

And then he kneeled down to prayer, and entreated the people to pray for him. After that, he called for the executioner, who, kneeling down and asking for his forgiveness, he laid both his hands upon his shoulders, and he said he heartily forgave him. And there being some dispute that his face should be towards the east, he made answer and said:

'So the heart be straight, it is no matter which way the head lieth.'

As he was laying his head on the block, the executioner would have blindfolded him; upon which he rebuked him, saying:

'Think you I fear the shadow of the axe, when I fear not the axe itself?'

SOURCE: David Jardine, *Criminal Trials*, 1832, Vol. i, pp. 508–509; incorporating a contemporary account.

See also JAMES I.

RAMILLIES, BATTLE OF (May 23, 1706).

Fault in a great captain

... the Duke of Marlborough ... fulfilled that day all the parts of a great captain, except in that he exposed his person as the meanest soldier.

SOURCE: Colonel Cranstoun, the *Portland Papers*; quoted Sir William Churchill, *Marlborough*, 1947.

RATS.

Report from His Majesty's Rat-Catcher

It is most likely that, when the Norway Rats first laid siege to this kingdom, they landed in or near the city of London, from the shipping in the river; but, there finding a greater number of the Black tribe than they were able to engage, were forced to disperse themselves into the different counties, where they have had great success in killing and destroying their antagonists the Black Rats. I have travelled, pursuing my employment, 25 years through the following counties, viz., Berkshire (where I was born), Wiltshire, Hampshire, Surrey, Sussex, Oxfordshire, Buckinghamshire, Northamptonshire, Hertfordshire, Bedfordshire, Essex, Suffolk, Norfolk, Middlesex and Kent (where I now reside), in all which counties I never found the Black Rat, except in Bucks and Middlesex; and in Bucks only some few of them at High Wycomb, about ten years ago. But, what is singular, within the city of London there are very few of the Norway rats to be found, but almost everywhere the Black Rats. Hence I am of opinion, that the Norway Rats have destroyed the Black Rats in almost all the above-mentioned counties, but that within the city of London the Black Rats may be said still to be masters; and, having withstood their enemies and prolonged the siege for so many years, they may be likely to hold it another century. . . .

SOURCE: Thomas Swaine, Ratcatcher to his Majesty's Royal Navy, etc., *The Universal Directory for Taking alive, or Destroying, Rats and Mice*, 1788, pp. 19–23.

Ship-borne rats are considered as being one of the chief agencies for the introduction and spread of such pestilences as the Black Death of 1348–1349 and 1361–1362. Some evidence of the prevalence of rats on board ship may be gathered from the small book quoted above, a rare little volume by a professional ratcatcher, who manufactured 'Swaine's Paste', a compound of white arsenic, lump sugar and wheatmeal.

He gives 'for the better satisfaction of the Reader in regard to the efficacy of the above Paste' a list of the rats he has destroyed on H.M. ships of war. The list includes:

Victory:	*171*
Achilles:	*704*
Diligente:	*665, 104 and 141*
Prince of Wales:	*1,015*
Duke:	*415 and 2,475.*

REFORM BILL, GREAT (1832). Passed to secure a more even distribution of Parliamentary seats, abolish the old 'rotten' boroughs and establish a ten-pound household franchise in all boroughs. It was forced through after fifteen months of political agitation in the teeth of violent opposition from, among other quarters, the House of Lords.

Mrs. Partington's mop

'The attempt of the Lords to stop the progress of reform reminds me very forcibly of the great storm off Sidmouth, and of the conduct of the excellent Mrs. Partington on that occasion. In the winter of 1824, there set in a great flood upon that town; the tide rose to an incredible height, the waves rushed in upon the houses, and everything was threatened with destruction. In the midst of this sublime and terrible storm, Dame Partington, who lived upon the beach, was seen at the door of her house, with mop and pattens, trundling her mop, squeezing out the sea-water, and vigorously pushing away the Atlantic ocean. The Atlantic was roused; Mrs. Partington's spirit was up; but I need not tell you that the contest was unequal. The Atlantic beat Mrs. Partington.'

SOURCE: Rev. Sydney Smith, in a speech at Taunton on the Lord's rejection of the Reform Bill in October, 1831.

Sydney Smith also declared on one occasion, gently ridiculing those who expected Parliamentary reform to be the answer to all evils:

All young ladies expect that as soon as this bill is carried they will be instantly married; schoolboys believe that gerunds and supines will be abolished, and that currant tarts must ultimately come down in price.

REFORMATION, THE.

Four changes in 20 years

It is observed in England, that in the space of twenty years the English changed oftener their religion than all Christendom had for 150 years; for they made four mutations from 1540 to 1560. King Henry VIII abolished the pope's supremacy, suppressed abbeys, but retained the bulk of the popish religion; his son, king Edward, brings in the protestant religion; queen Mary throws it out; but queen Elizabeth brings it in again.

SOURCE: Diary of Lord Fountainhall (1646–1722) in the Advocates' Library, Edinburgh. Part of the diary, called *Chronological Notes of Scottish Affairs from 1680 till 1701*, was published by Sir Walter Scott in 1822; and the full diary by the Bannatyne Club, 1840.

REGALIA, THE ROYAL. These possessions form one of the most valuable collections, historically and intrinsically, in England. Most of the items were ruthlessly destroyed during the Commonwealth and had to be replaced, from the old designs, following the Restoration.

i. *The Destruction of the Regalia*

Henry or Harry Marten (1602–1680), one of the men who signed Charles's death warrant, and who bore a personal grudge against the King for having called him 'an ugly rascal' and a 'whoremaster', obtained the keys of the great chest holding the ancient royal regalia, some of it used since the coronation of Edward the Confessor, and tossed it all out. One of those present was George Wither (1588–1667), the poet, who should have known better, but was persuaded to parade in the royal robes.

'Wither being crowned and royally arrayed, had first marched about the room with a stately mien and afterwards, with a thousand apish and ridiculous actions, exposed these sacred ornaments to contempt and laughter.'

SOURCE: Anthony Wood, *Athenae Oxoniensis* 1691–1692.

ii. *The Sword of Murphy*

Curtana, the Sword of Mercy, or Edward the Confessor's Sword, is one of the swords always carried at the coronation of English monarchs. Its end is blunted as a symbol of mercy. The original sword is first mentioned by name in a document relating to the coronation of Eleanor, wife of Henry II, in 1236.

At the coronation of Richard III in 1483, Curtana was carried by Henry, fourth Earl of Northumberland; 470 years later, his descendant, Hugh, tenth Duke of Northumberland, bore the sword at the coronation of Queen Elizabeth II, June 2, 1953. Just before, an Irish visitor to the Duke's home asked him what his responsibilities were to be at the ceremony. Recounting the conversation, the Duke said:

'I said I was carrying Curtana. He asked "Whatever is that?" I said "It's the Sword of Mercy". He was overjoyed because he thought I said "The Sword of Murphy".'

SOURCE: Eye-witness.

iii. *The Crown's Baubles*

In January, 1886, when Parliament was opened during Lord Salisbury's administration, Queen Victoria decided to perform the ceremony herself, for the first time for many years and also, as it turned out, for the last time. I had the honour of carrying the Crown on that occasion.

In company with Lord Salisbury, who carried the Sword of State, I went to a room in the House of Lords; and there we found Lord Winchester, whose family are hereditary bearers of the Cap of Maintenance, sitting in his robes by the fire. The Crown, the Sword of State, and the Cap of Maintenance were conveyed from the Tower, as was customary, in a four-wheeled cab under the guard of a sergeant and guardsman of the Foot Guards; and Sir Spencer Ponsonby Fane brought them to the waiting room. He delivered the Sword of State to Lord Salisbury, and handed the Crown to me, whispering as he did so:

'Now, take care you don't drop it!'—for I believe that, some years before, a noble Duke *had* dropped it and then put his foot on it. The Crown rested on a cushion, suspended by a ribbon from my neck; and I must confess that by the time the ceremony was over I had had quite enough of it, for my hands were almost numbed by the tight gloves I was wearing and the slippery edge of the cushion.

When Sir Spencer handed the Cap of Maintenance to its bearer, he said:

'And here is your bauble, my Lord.'

Lord Winchester immediately flamed up. . . .

'What the —— do you mean by calling the Cap of Maintenance a bauble? I would have you know, Sir, that my family
sets great store by the privilege of carrying it; and I will not
have it called a bauble.'

Sir Spencer did not reply, but as he passed me he whispered,
'What an old ruffian!' and Lord Salisbury added:

'I fear the noble Lord has got a little out of his depth.'

It was explained to me afterwards that the lesser objects in the
regalia, the Cap of Maintenance among them, are technically
and correctly known as 'the baubles of the Crown'; so Sir
Spencer Ponsonby-Fane was right.

SOURCE: The Duke of Portland, *Men, Women and Things*, Faber
and Faber, 1937, p. 113.

RESOLUTE, VOYAGE OF THE (1854–1855).

A thousand miles without a crew

Perhaps the most remarkable voyage on record was that of the
arctic exploring-ship *Resolute*. Abandoned by her officers and
crew to anticipated destruction, she, as if instinct with life, made
a voyage of a thousand miles *alone*, back to regions of civilisation
—as if in indignant protest against her abandonment.

In 1852, Sir Edward Belcher, with the ships *Assistance*,
Pioneer, *Resolute*, *Intrepid*, and *North Star*, left England to search
for Sir John Franklin, and his companions. . . . On the 15th. of
May, 1854, at his [Belcher's] express command, but sorely
against their will, Captain Kellett and Commander M'Clintock
finally abandoned the *Resolute* and *Intrepid*, locked in ice off the
shores of Melville Island. On the 24th. of August, in the same
year, again at the express command of Belcher, Commander
Sherard Osborn abandoned the *Pioneer*, while Belcher himself
abandoned the *Assistance*. . . . The officers and crews of no less
than five abandoned ships reached England before the close of
the year.

It was one of these five deserted ships which, we may almost say, came to life again many months afterwards, to the astonishment of every one conversant with the arctic region. Late in the year 1855, Captain Buddington, in the American whaler *George Henry*, was sailing about in Davis's Strait, when, on the 17th of September, about forty miles from Cape Mercy, he descried a ship presenting unusual appearances; no signals were put out or answered; and, when he approached, no crew were visible.

It was the *Resolute*, as sound and hearty as ever, with the exception of a little water which had got into the hold, and the spoiling of some of the perishable articles inside. Any one with a map of the arctic regions before him will see what a lengthened voyage the good old ship must have made from Melville Island, through Barrow Straits, Lancaster Sound, and Baffin's Bay, during the period of 474 days which intervened between her abandonment and her recovery. The probable track is marked in a map attached to Mr. M'Dougall's *Eventful Voyage of the Resolute*.

SOURCE: *The Book of Days* (edit. R. Chambers), 1864, Vol. II, p. 768. The *Resolute* was brought back to the United States, completely restored, as a result of a resolution in Congress, and presented to Queen Victoria for further service. 'With such care had the repairs and re-equipment been performed, that not only the ship's stores—even to flags—been replaced, but the officers' libraries, pictures, musical-boxes, etc., had been preserved, and with excellent taste had all been restored to the original positions.' It is regrettable that the Admiralty, in a fit of short-sighted economy, rapidly allowed the *Resolute* to deteriorate, and it never saw active service again.

RICHARD I, called **RICHARD CŒUR DE LION** (1157–1199) king of England. 'A bad son, a bad husband, and a bad king, but a gallant and splendid soldier.'

i. *Richard's life is spared by William Marshal*

Before his accession to the throne, Richard rebelled against his father Henry II and nearly lost his life at the hands of Henry IV's great servant, William Marshal.

Richard spurred forward triumphantly, thinking that at last Henry was at his mercy. William [Marshal] lifted his spear, and when he saw that hero of innumerable tournaments barring his way, Richard cried in sudden terror:

'God's feet, Marshal, don't kill me! I have no hauberk.

'Kill you?' answered William coldly. 'No. I leave that to the devil.' And he lowered his spear. . . .

SOURCE: Philip Lindsay, *Kings of Merry England from Eadward the Confessor to Richard the Third*, Ivor Nicholson & Watson, 1935, p. 198. Marshall remained faithful to Henry II to the end. To Richard's credit, on his accession he forgave his former opponent for the salutary lesson and continued him in high office; so did King John, though Marshal took up arms against him on Richard's behalf.

ii. *King Richard refuses to turn his back*

When it was signified unto King Richard the First, son to . . . King Henry, sitting at supper in his Palace at Westminster . . . that the French King besieged his town of Vernoil [Verneuil] in Normandy, he, in greatness of courage protested in these words:

'I will never turn my back till I have confronted the French.'

For performance of which his princely word, he caused the wall in his palace at Westminster to be broken down directly towards the south, posted to the coast, and immediately into Normandy, where the very report of his sudden arrival so terrified the French that they raised the siege and retired themselves.

SOURCE: William Camden, *Remains Concerning Britain*, 7th impression, 1674.

iii. *Richard glimpses the Holy City*

Richard came within striking distance of Jerusalem twice during the Third Crusade; in January, 1192, after the fall of Acre and the Battle of Arsuf, and, six months later, in the hills above Emmaus, when he actually caught sight of the distant walls and towers.

While they were speaking . . . one of his knights cried: 'Sire, sire, come so far hither, and I will show you Jerusalem!'

And when the king heard this he threw his coat-armour [i.e., probably, his shield] before his eyes, all in tears, and said to our Saviour:

'Fair Lord God, I pray Thee suffer me not to see Thy Holy City, since I cannot deliver it from the hands of Thine enemies!'

SOURCE: Jean, Sire de Joinville, *Memoirs of the Crusades*, completed October, 1309; trans. Frank T. Marzials, Everyman edition, J. M. Dent and Sons, 1908, p. 275.

iv. *The potency of Richard's name*

So soon as Acre was taken, King Philip returned to France, for which he was greatly blamed; but King Richard remained in the Holy Land, and did there such mighty deeds that the Saracens stood in great fear of him; so much so, as it is written in the book of the Holy Land, that when the Saracen children cried, their mothers called out:

'Whisht! here is King Richard!', in order to keep them quiet.

And when the horses of the Saracens and Bedouins started at a tree or bush, their masters said to the horses:

'Do you think that is King Richard?'

SOURCE: Jean, Sire de Joinville, cit., op. p. 155.

v. *The minstrel Blondel*

After leaving the Holy Land in October, 1192, Richard was taken prisoner by his old rival Leopold of Austria, while the King was trying to travel through Germany in disguise. Richard was imprisoned at Durrenstein (Styria). Within about fifty years the story was current that his minstrel Blondel, determined to find his master, wandered through Europe till he heard of a closely guarded prisoner in a nearby castle; that the minstrel secured employment there and waited his chance to learn the identity of the mysterious captive. His opportunity came when:

. . . he went out one day on the Easter festival alone in a garden which was by the tower, and looked about him and bethought himself that haply he might see the prisoner. As he was in this mind, the king looked through a loophole and saw

Blondel. And he thought how he could make himself known to him, and he remembered a song which they had made between them and which no one knew except the two of them. So he began to sing the first phrase loud and clear, for he sang very well; and when Blondel heard him, he knew for certain that this was his lord. So he had the greatest joy at heart he ever had at any time. Forthwith he left the garden and went to the chamber where he slept and took his viol and began to play, and while playing rejoiced for his lord whom he had found.

SOURCE: *Récits d'un menestral de Reims*, c.1260; Robert Birley, *The Undergrowth of History*, Historical Association, 1955, p. 22.
See also SALADIN.

RICHARD III (1452–1485). In his short reign of two years, Richard was served by a number of unpopular advisers, three of them being Sir Richard Ratcliffe, the lawyer Sir William Catesby and Lord Lovell. Their names are immortalized in a political rhyme for which the author was executed.

i. *Passport to execution*

> The cat, the rat, and Lovel our dog,
> Rule all England under a hog.

One of the badges of Richard III was the wild boar, hence the 'hog'. Lord Lovell's badge was a dog.

ii. *A hasty alteration of inn-signs*

During the sovereignty of Richard, the White Boar . . . was a common sign . . . but at his death, the landlords took down their White Boars, and where any one omitted it, the fickle public pulled it down for him; and to this day, we often behold the sign of the Black Boar, and the Blue Boar, but never the white.

SOURCE: W. Hutton, *The Battle of Bosworth Field, between Richard the Third and Henry Earl of Richmond* . . . , Birmingham, 1788, p. 145.

iii. *A coincidence*

'two similar incidents . . . to which history cannot add a third.'

Henry Stafford, second Duke of Buckingham, was responsible for the crowning of Richard III, acting as Great Chamberlain at the coronation. Three months later he was executed by the king he had crowned.

Sir William Stanley, after the Battle of Bosworth, set the crown on Henry VII's head. He was later beheaded by the king, for complicity in Perkin Warbeck's rebellion.

iv. *The Last Plantagenet*

In the parish registers of Eastwell, Kent, is recorded, in December 1550, the death of an old bricklayer named Richard Plantagenet.

At a short distance [i.e., from Eastwell House] in a retired situation, shaded by trees, is a plain building . . . said to occupy the very spot where the humble cottage formerly stood, erected by Richard Plantagenet, natural son of Richard III . . . the truth of his history is not doubted. The battle of Bosworth field took place on the 22d of August, 1485, when, upon the defeat of Richard III, his son fled to London, and subsequently tendered his services as a bricklayer at Eastwell park, where he continued nearly sixty years. Near the cottage there was a fine spring of pure water, which is yet to be seen, retaining the name of Plantagenet's Well.

SOURCE: W. H. Ireland, *New and Complete History of Kent*, 1829, Vol. ii, p. 426. It is said that the credit for having discovered the identity of the last of the Plantagenets goes to Sir Thomas Moyle, Speaker of the House of Commons in Elizabeth's reign, who rebuilt Eastwell House and who noticed one of the workmen, called Richard, who would sometimes go apart and read a book, a rare accomplishment among labourers. According to this account, Sir Thomas had the small cottage specially built for the old man and ordered his steward to provide for him.

Anciently, when any person of noble family was interred at Eastwell, it was the custom to affix a special mark against the name of the deceased in the register of burials. The fact is a significant one, that this aristocratic symbol is prefixed to the name of Richard Plantagenet.

SOURCE: John Heneage Jesse, *Memoirs of Richard III*, 1862.

v. *Where is Plantagenet?*

What race in Europe surpassed in royal position, personal achievement, or romantic adventure, our Plantagenets, equally wise as valiant, no less renowned in the cabinet than in the field? Yet, as late as 1637, the great-grandson of Margaret Plantagenet, herself daughter and heir of George, Duke of Clarence, was following the cobbler craft at Newport, in Shropshire. Among the lineal descendants of Edmund Woodstock, Earl of Kent, son of Edward the First, entitled to quarter the royal arms, occur a butcher and a toll-gatherer, the first a Mr. Joseph Smart, of Hales Own (Salop), the latter Mr. G. Wymot, keeper of the turnpike-gate, Cooper's Bank, Dudley.

SOURCE: Sir Bernard Burke, *Vicissitudes of Families*

RIDDLES.

i. *Demaundes joyous*

In days when entertainment was neither so easily come by, nor as diverse, as in more modern times, the riddle or conundrum was popular. An amusing collection, itself an abridgement of an earlier work, was published in 1511 by Wynkyn de Worde, successor to Caxton, with the title *Demaundes joyous*, meaning light-hearted questions. Here are six examples, the answers being given below:

  i. What bare the best burden that ever was borne?
  ii. How many calves' tails would it take to reach from the earth to the sky?
  iii. What is the distance from the surface of the sea to the deepest part thereof?
  iv. How may a man discern a cow in a flock of sheep?
  v. What is it that never freezeth?
  vi. Who killed the fourth part of all the people in the world?

Answers: i. The ass that carried Our Lady, when she fled with

Our Lord into Egypt; ii. No more than one if it be long enough; iii. Only a stone's throw; iv. By his eyesight; v. Boiling water; vi. Cain, when he killed Abel.

ii. *Who is the father?*

The riddle of Cleobulus

There is a father with twice six sons; these sons have thirty daughters a-piece, party-coloured, having one cheek white and the other black, who never see each other's face, nor live above twenty-four hours.

SOURCE: Cleobulus, one of seven sages of Greece (6th Century B.C.). It will perhaps serve as a clue to say that, by modern reckoning, there are sometimes thirty-one daughters.

iii. *A circumnavigatory problem*

Three men went on a journey, in which, though their heads travelled 12 yards farther than their feet, all returned alive, with their heads on.

SOURCE: *The Monitor's Instructor*, Wilmington, Delaware, 1804; quoted Clifton Johnson, *Old-Time Schools and School-Books*, Macmillan Company, 1904.

The solution given is that 'If any person should travel round the globe, the space travelled by his head will exceed that his feet travelled' by about 12 yards.

RIDLEY, NICHOLAS (1500?–1555), successively Bishop of Rochester and of London; burnt at the stake, at Oxford, October 16, 1555, with Bishop Latimer.

i. *The wonderful loud voice*

And so, the fire being given unto them, when Dr. Ridley saw the fire flaming up towards him he cried with a wonderful loud voice:

'In manus tuas, Domine, commendo spiritum meum:

Domine recipe spiritum meum.' And after, repeated this latter part often in English:

'Lord, Lord, receive my spirit'; Master Latimer crying as vehemently on the other side:

'O Father of heaven, receive my soul!'; who received the flame as it were embracing of it. After that he had stroked his face with his hands, and as it were bathed them a little in the fire, he soon died (as it appeareth) with very little pain or none.

SOURCE: John Foxe, *The Actes and Monuments of the Church*, 1563, popularly known as *The Book of Martyrs*; Rev. John Cumming's edition, Chatto and Windus, 1875, Vol. iii, p. 492.

See also LATIMER, HUGH.

ii. *The white-livered knight*

'For surely, except the Lord assist me with his gracious aid in the time of his service, I know I shall play but the part of a white-livered knight.'

SOURCE: *Certen godly, learned, and comforting conferences betwene the two Reverende fathers and holye Martyrs of Christe, D. Nicolas Rydley . . . and M. Hughe Latymer . . . during the tyme of theyre emprisonmentes*, 1556.

iii. *Help me to buckle on this gear a little better*

In Tyndale, where I was born, not far from the Scottish borders, I have known my countrymen watch day and night in their harness . . . especially when they had any privy warning of the coming of the Scots. And so doing, although at every such bickering some of them spent their lives, yet by such means, like pretty men, they defended their country. And those that so died, I think that before God they died in a good quarrel. . . . I pray you, help me to buckle on this gear a little better; for ye know the deepness of Satan, being an old soldier.

SOURCE: Ridley to Latimer, ibid.; quoted William Haller, *Foxe's Book of Martyrs and the Elect Nation*, Jonathan Cape, 1963, pp. 35–36.

ROCROY, BATTLE OF (May 19, 1643). The battle in which the Spanish infantry, supreme for a century and a half, were smashed by the brilliant 22-year old French commander the Prince de Condé (the 'Great Condé'). The Spanish general was the octogenarian Count de Fuentes (1560–1643), helpless with age and gout.

The chair on the battle-field

There is something inexpressibly pathetic in the figure of the old Count of Fuentes, seated on his chair in the middle of the fast diminishing square of his choicest troops, for the gout would not permit him even to stand, calmly and patiently awaiting inevitable death, as the defending ranks became thinner and thinner, without the thought of surrender, without the power even of striking a blow in self-defence, the type of his country and of his country's greatness, which was passing away with the shouts of victory which hailed the young conquerer of Rocroy.

SOURCE: H. O. Wakeman, *The Ascendancy of France*, pp. 119–120.

ROOSEVELT, FRANKLIN DELANO (1882–1945), 31st President of the United States.

Roosevelt died suddenly on April 12, 1945, while sitting for his portrait. The exchange below is between reporters and members of the President's staff.

Last words of a President

'Who was with him when he was stricken?'

'Madame Shoumatoff was working on her portrait of him.'

'Did he have any warning of the attack, or know it was coming?'

'Madame Shoumatoff says he had reminded her that "we have just fifteen minutes" .'

Those were the last words he spoke. It had been exactly fifteen minutes after those words that he collapsed.

SOURCE: Grace Tully, *F.D.R. My Boss*, Charles Scribner's Sons, 1949.

ROOSEVELT, THEODORE (1858–1919), 26th President of the United States.

i. *The President who could not spell*

Of course there are flaws. Roosevelt was a very bad speller indeed; it took him a long time to learn how to spell the name of Grover Cleveland, who was not merely President of the United States but, for a time, his official chief.

SOURCE: D. W. Brogan, *American Aspects*, Hamish Hamilton, 1964, p. 79; first published in *The Times Literary Supplement*.

ii. *Protection for a Jew-baiter*

At one point in his career, Roosevelt was Police Commissioner of New York. An anti-Semitic preacher from Berlin asked for police protection during one of his attacks on the Jews.

The proper thing to do was to make him ridiculous. Accordingly I sent a detail of police under a Jewish sergeant, and the Jew-baiter made his harangue under the active protection of some forty police, every one of them a Jew.

SOURCE: Theodore Roosevelt, *Autobiography*.

ROYAL GEORGE, LOSS OF THE (August 29, 1782). This famous ship went down at Spithead, with the loss of Admiral Richard Kempenfelt and many hundreds of her crew, when she had been heeled over to have her under-water timbers examined.

i. *A poet talks nonsense*

The tragedy sent a thrill of horror throughout the land, and before very long Cowper's solemn monody, *Toll for the Brave*, was tugging at men's heartstrings and inducing all the charitable to contribute generously to a fund for the widows and children. But what would the world have said if it had been generally known that the simple-minded poet was talking nonsense, and screening by means of his immortal poem the wrongs of a service which else would have cried to heaven for vengeance? 'A land breeze shook the shrouds,' he wrote of the ship which at Quiberon had defied the tempest throes! 'A land breeze shook the shrouds; and she was overset'!

The court-martial which sat at Portsmouth examined all the survivors, and found themselves at variance with the poet when he said that the *Royal George* was perfectly sound in her timbers and 'sprang no fatal leak'. They agreed unanimously that she had been so long neglected that decay had eaten deep into her vitals, and that, on the day of the fatality, the under-water parts of the *Royal George* had literally dropped from under her. In a word, Kempenfelt and his gallant fellows were the victims of that corrupt administration which had lately also forfeited North America.

SOURCE: Geoffrey Callender, *The Naval Side of British History*, Christophers, 1924, p. 177.

ii. *The pocket-sized midshipman*

Captain Crispo (Lieutenant Durham's signal midshipman) was on the quarter deck at the moment of the accident, and escaped by swimming. He was very young and so small in stature, that when about to be examined before the court martial, which sat to enquire into the circumstances of this lamentable event, one of the gallant members of the court lifted him up on the table and said.

'Now, my lad, you can be seen; speak up and boldly, for from this moment you are an adopted son of the British Navy.'

At the end of twenty-eight years from the day of its date, John Crispo was promoted to the rank of post-captain. Lately, speaking of the exertions of Colonel Pashley,* Captain Crispo said, with some earnestness:

'I wish he may fish up my chest, for there are twenty-two guineas and two half-guineas in it.'

SOURCE: *A Narrative of the Loss of the Royal George*, Portsea, 1845.

* The officer in charge of the demolition and removal of the wreck, 1839–1843.

RUSKIN—versus—WHISTLER. A *cause célèbre* of the 19th
Century was the libel suit brought against John Ruskin (1819–
1900), the great writer, critic and artist, by James McNeill
Whistler (1834–1903), the painter, because of Ruskin's con-
demnation of some of his pictures, particularly 'The Falling
Rocket', a Nocturne in Black and Gold, for which Whistler asked
two hundred guineas.

i. *Ruskin's opinion*

For Mr. Whistler's own sake, no less than for the protection of
the purchaser, Sir Coutts Lindsay ought not to have admitted
works into the gallery in which the ill-educated conceit of the
artist so nearly approached the aspect of wilful imposture. I
have seen, and heard, much of cockney impudence before
now; but never expected to hear a coxcomb ask two hundred
guineas for flinging a pot of paint in the public's face.

SOURCE: Fors Clavigera, July, 1877.

ii. *I ask it for the knowledge of a life-time*

Part of the cross-examination of Whistler by the Attorney-
General.

'Now, Mr. Whistler. Can you tell me how long it took you to
knock off that nocturne?'

'I beg your pardon?' (*Laughter.*)

'Oh! I am afraid that I am using a term that applies rather
perhaps to my own work. I should have said, How long did it
take you to paint that picture?'

'Oh, no! permit me, I am too greatly flattered to think that
you apply, to work of mine, any term that you are in the habit
of using with reference to your own. Let us say then how long
did I take to—"knock off", I think that is it—to knock off that
nocturne; well, as well as I remember, about a day.'

'Only a day?'

'Well, I won't be quite positive; I may have still put a few
more touches to it the next day if the painting were not dry. I
had better say, then, that I was two days at work on it.'

CC

'Oh, two days! The labour of two days, then, is that for which you ask two hundred guineas?'

'No; I ask it for the knowledge of a lifetime.' (*Applause*).

SOURCE: apart from contemporary press accounts, etc., the most amusing record of the dispute is Whistler's *The Gentle Art of Making Enemies*, William Heinemann, 1890. Whistler won his case, but was awarded the derisory damages of one farthing.

RUSSELL, LORD JOHN (1792–1878). Introduced Reform Bill of 1832; held many high offices, including that of Prime Minister.

An autocratic Liberal

Lord John Russell always irritated me; he had a knack of standing up with his back to the fire-place and not asking me to sit down. . . . He generally began with a phrase implying that something had been done wrong. 'Well, I understand you have done so-and-so', or 'said so-and-so', and then get huffy at the only answer that could be given, viz.,

'I was not aware of it,' because it apparently forced him into an explanation. Once he turned on me and said:

'Have you?' and on my saying as curtly 'No', did not speak for two or three minutes, looking as black as thunder.

As I had been sent for a distance of over a thousand miles without being told what for, I was determined to wait, till Doomsday if necessary, before speaking. At last he gave tongue about some outrageous story he had been told, and I replied that if he had for one moment believed me capable of such conduct he ought at once to have dismissed me and not simply have sent for me. . . .

On his asking for particulars so that he might form an opinion, I refused to give any, on the ground that a Minister of the Crown had no right to catechise a Judge on a decision given in his Court from which an appeal lay to a Superior Court. Upon this he told me I took high ground and that I forgot I only held office 'during pleasure.'

I replied I was quite aware of it, and if he thought my conduct justified him he had better then and there dismiss me.

All this struck me as slightly autocratic in so eminent a Liberal and Reformer. However, he climbed down a little and stopped paring his nails.

SOURCE: Sir Edmund Hornby, *An Autobiography*, Constable & Co., 1929, pp. 186–187. Hornby was a Consular Judge in Turkey, China and Japan, in the hey-day of Victorian England.

RUTHERFORD, ERNEST, BARON (1871–1937), physicist.

i. *The man on the crest of the wave*

'You're always at the crest of the wave,' someone said to Rutherford.

'Well, after all, I made the wave, didn't I?' said Rutherford.

SOURCE: C. P. Snow, *Variety of Men*, Macmillan, 1967.

ii. *Two tall stories*

Worldly success? He loved every minute of it: flattery, titles, the company of the high official world. He said in a speech:

'As I was standing in the drawing-room at Trinity, a *clergyman* came in. And I said to him: "I'm Lord Rutherford." And he said to me: "I'm the Archbishop of York." And I don't suppose either of us believed the other.'

SOURCE: ibid.

iii. *A dog's life for the Archbishop*

He hated the faintest suspicion of being patronised, even when he was a world figure. Archbishop Lang was once tactless enough to suggest that he supposed a famous scientist had no time for reading. Rutherford immediately felt that he was being regarded as an ignorant roughneck. He produced a formidable list of his last month's reading. Then half-innocently, half-malevolently:

'And what do you manage to read, your Grace?'

'I am afraid,' said the Archbishop, somewhat out of his depth, 'that a man in my position really doesn't have the leisure. . . .'

'Ah, yes, your Grace,' said Rutherford in triumph, 'it must be a dog's life! It must be a dog's life!'

SOURCE: C. P. Snow, op. cit.

ST. FRANCIS OF ASSISI (1182–1226).

St. Francis rescues the doves

As he journeyed once to Siena he met a lad carrying some turtle doves which he had caught, and which he was intending to sell.

'O good young man,' he said to him at once, 'these are innocent birds which are compared in Holy Scripture to chaste and faithful souls. I pray you not to give them over to those who will kill them, but give them to me.'

The young man assented, and when they were given to him, St. Francis placed them in his bosom saying:

'O my little sisters, the turtle doves, so simple, innocent and chaste, why did you let yourselves be taken? Now I will save you from death and make nests for you that you may bring up your young and multiply according to the commandment of our Creator.'

And the saint kept his word and gave a home to the little strangers, who, laying their eggs and bringing up their young, dwelt with the brethren, and refused to leave them until St. Francis gave them his benediction and bade them depart.

SOURCE: W. J. Knox Little, *St. Francis of Assisi* (Lectures delivered in the Lady Chapel of Worcester Cathedral, 1896), Isbister & Co., 1897, p. 234.

ST. VINCENT, JOHN JERVIS, EARL OF (1735–1823), Admiral of the Fleet; defeated Spanish fleet off Cape St. Vincent, February 14, 1797.

i. *Only the air is left*

'I don't say the French can't come; I only say they can't come by sea.'

SOURCE: speech in the House of Lords.

ii. *St. Vincent leaps from the quarter-deck*

One of this great officer's strongest qualities was his keen understanding of the importance of working on the imagination of men and their feelings of awe and reverence. During the mutiny of 1797, when he was in command of the Mediterranean fleet, he set himself resolutely to make authority dignified and conspicuous. Every morning he held a solemn parade of the Marines, when 'God save the King' was played, arms presented, and all hats off at the time. The Earl himself was always there in full uniform.

'Though,' says his biographer, 'it was not required of other officers, yet it was noticed that his lordship invariably appeared in full-dress uniform; and as a general warning to all, was remarked the very violent displeasure which he one day manifested, springing from the quarter-deck upon a seaman, a captain of a top,* whose head his lordship spied in the distance for an instant covered while the National anthem sounded.'

SOURCE: David Hannay, *Ships and Men*, William Blackwood, 1910, pp. 273–274. The admiral's biographer was Jedediah Stephens Tucker, who wrote *Memoirs of Admiral the Right Hon. the Earl of St. Vincent*, 1844.

iii. *The future Admiral makes his own breeches*

St. Vincent went to sea at the age of 13.

My father had a very large family, with limited means. He gave me twenty pounds at starting, and that was all he ever gave me. After I had been a considerable time at the station [Jamaica] I drew for twenty more, but the bill came back protested. I was mortified at this rebuke and made a promise, which I have ever kept, that I would never draw another bill, without a certainty of its being paid.

I immediately changed my mode of living, quitted my mess, lived alone, and took up the ship's allowance, which I found to be quite sufficient; washed and mended my own clothes, made a pair of trousers out of the ticking of my bed, and, having by

---

* The captain of a top was the leader of the prime seamen who worked the mast—fore, main or mizzen—above the lower yards.

these means saved as much money as would redeem my honour, I took up my bill; and from that time to this . . . I have taken care to keep within my means.

SOURCE: quoted *A Book of Days* (edit. R. Chambers), 1864, Vol. I, p. 80. The *Memoirs of Admiral the Right Hon. the Earl of St. Vincent* were written by Jedediah Tucker, 1844.

iv. *The Admiral finds the Order of the Bath*

He always wore the Star of the Order of the Bath; and to a child who one day asked what it was, and where he had found it, he replied:

'I found it upon the sea; and if you become a sailor, and search diligently, perhaps you will find just such another.'

SOURCE: Jedediah Tucker, *Memoirs of Admiral the Right Hon. the Earl of St. Vincent*, 1844.

v. *The first 'V'-Day*

The famous 'V' for Victory Day which marked the end of World War II in 1945, was not the first. At one time, the letter was always associated with Admiral Sir John Jervis (afterwards Earl St. Vincent) and the battle of Cape St. Vincent—fought on February 14th, 1797—in which Jervis's fleet of 15 sail heavily defeated a Spanish fleet 27 strong. It was the battle in which Nelson, at considerable risk to his career, showed his greatness and his ability to take a split-second decision by breaking the centuries-old rule of the fleet and left the battle-line in the middle of the action in order to fling himself into a critical gap. Nelson, then only a captain, was commanding *Captain*. Jervis was in *Victory*.

'It was known at that time as the "V" battle—fought on St. Valentine's Day, off Cape St. Vincent; flag-ship, Victory.'

SOURCE: letter to *Daily Telegraph* from Captain Caspar Swinley, R.N., October 27th, 1966.

SALADIN (SALAH AD-DIN YUSUF) (1137–1193), Sultan; the most famous and most chivalrous of the Saracen leaders in the Crusades.

His help to Richard I in the battle, Jaffa, 1192

There were only fifty-four knights fit for battle and only fifteen horses, and about two thousand infantrymen. Behind a low palisade of tent-pegs, designed to disconcert the enemy horses, Richard set his men in pairs, their shields fixed as a fence in front of them and their long spears planted in the ground at an angle. . . . Between each pair an archer was stationed. The Moslem cavalry charged in seven waves of a thousand men each. But they could not pierce the wall of steel. . . . Then, when the enemy horses seemed to be tiring, Richard passed his bowmen through to the front line and discharged all his arrows into the oncoming host. The volley checked the enemy. The archers passed back again behind the spearmen, who charged with Richard on horseback at their head. Saladin was lost in angry admiration at the sight. When Richard's horse fell under him, he gallantly sent a groom through the midst of the turmoil with two fresh horses as a gift to the brave King.

SOURCE: Sir Steven Runciman, *A History of the Crusades,* C.U.P., 1954.

On another occasion, when Richard Cœur-de-Lion was tossing with fever in his tent, Saladin sent him pears, peaches, and snow from Mount Ascalon to cool him.

SANCTUARY, RIGHT OF. The right of sanctuary for criminals and hunted men existed from very early times until the 18th Century, though sanctuaries were legally suppressed at the end of James I's reign.

Sometimes the sanctuary was the church itself, sometimes it extended over a defined area, with the church at its centre. At Hexham, in Northumberland, concentric circles were marked out; and the nearer the fugitives were to the centre, the greater the penalty for violating the sanctuary and taking them.

Numbers of churches had their frith or frid stools [peace chairs], which spelt safety for the hunted one if they could be reached.

The cathedral at Durham still has its great sanctuary knocker, which the criminal knocked to gain admission. Some sanctuaries were reckoned safer places than others, since greater penalties were imposed for breaking them. Beverley, in Yorkshire, was one of the most highly regarded sanctuaries in England.

i. *The seat of quiet*

If any one, moved by a spirit of madness, ventured with diabolical boldness to seize one in the stone chair near the altar which the English call *fridstol*, that is a chair of quiet or peace, or at the shrine of the holy relics, back of the altar, no compensation will be determined for such a glaring sacrilege, no amount of money will serve as an atonement.

SOURCE: *The Priory of Hexham*, Surtees Society, 1864–1865.

Near the seat of peace at Hexham was an ugly stone figure, with a long buttoned coat and a tall staff, with three coils round his ankles.

... It was intended to represent an officer of justice, with his staff and plume, his feet bare and manacled, to show that within the bounds of sanctuary he dared not move towards his design and that there his authority availed him not.

SOURCE: A. B. Write, *Essay towards the history of Hexham*, 1823.

The numbers of people seeking sanctuary were often considerable. The Durham registers from 1464–1524, in which were entered the details of those claiming sanctuary, shows 283 people, guilty of, among other crimes, 195 murders and killings. In the Westminster sanctuary in 1532 there were 50 fugitives, including a priest wanted for murder, ten others for various killings, eighteen for debt and most of the rest for robbery. One refugee had been there twenty years.

ii. *An Archbishop violates sanctuary*

Hubert Walter (d. 1205) was Justiciar and Archbishop of Canterbury.

A certain lawyer named William FitzOsbert had led an agitation of the poorer citizens against the alleged malpractices of the aldermen who assessed the tallage. The only immediate result had been a formal petition to the King; but suspicions of a general rising of the poor led the Justiciar to order the ringleader's arrest. FitzOsbert took sanctuary at Bow Church. The Justiciar's officers had then dislodged their quarry by setting fire to the church, and had finally dragged off the half-dead agitator to summary trial and execution. The King's congratulations to Hubert Walter had apparently closed the episode when an unexpected sequel in 1198 cost the Justiciar his office. The monks of Canterbury, to whom Bow Church belonged, reported to Rome the sacrilege committed by the Justiciar's orders, with the result that, on the demand of Innocent III, the Archbishop was removed from his secular office.

SOURCE: A. Gordon Smith, *A Short History of Medieval England*, Burnes Oates and Washbourne, 1925, p. 155.

iii. *Another punishment*

In 1313 Bishop Richard gave this order concerning Nicholas le Porter, who had helped take from a church in Newcastle some fugitives who had sought sanctuary. These had later been executed. The instruction was issued to the priest of St. Nicholas of Durham.

We order that on Monday, Tuesday, and Wednesday of the Whitsun-week just coming, he shall receive the whip from your hands publicly, before the chief door of your church, in his shirt, bare-headed, and barefoot. He shall there proclaim in English the reason for his penance and shall admit his fault; and when he has been whipped the said Nicholas will go to the cathedral church of Durham, bareheaded, bare-foot, and dressed as above, he will walk in front and you will follow him and you will whip him in the same manner before the door of the cathedral these three days, and he will repeat there the confession of his sin.

SOURCE: *Registrum Palatinum Dunelmense*, edit. Sir. T. D. Hardy, 1875.
NOTE: Most of the above information on Sanctuary has been taken from J. J. Jusserand, *English Wayfaring Life in the Middle Ages*, first published 1889; revised and enlarged edition, 1929, Ernest Benn, Part I, Ch. III.

SANDWICH, JOHN MONTAGU, fourth **EARL OF** (1718–1792):
first lord of the Admiralty. Though he had earlier, with Anson's
help, uncovered many abuses and instituted stringent reforms, in
the end he himself used his high office for extensive bribery and
political jobbery, with the result that the outbreak of war in 1778
found the navy virtually bankrupt. At his best he was an able
administrator, as his brief to petitioners and civil servants shows:

i. *Recipe for petitioners*

'If any man will draw up his case, and put his name at the foot
of the first page, I will give him an immediate reply. Where he
compels me to turn over the sheet, he must wait my leisure.'

SOURCE: Sir N. William Wraxall, *Historical Memoirs of My Own
Time*, 1815, Vol. 1, p. 519.

ii. *The man who walked both sides of the street at once*

He was by no means a handsome man; when seen in the street,
he had an awkward, careless gait. Two gentlemen observing
him, one remarked:

'I think it is Lord Sandwich coming'; which the other thought
to be a mistake. 'Nay,' said the first gentleman, 'I am sure it is
Lord Sandwich, for, if you observe, he is walking down both
sides of the street at once.'

But Lord Sandwich used to tell a better story of himself:

'When I was at Paris,' he said, 'I had a dancing master;
the man was very civil, and on my taking leave of him, I
offered my service in London. "Then," said the man, bowing,
"I would take it as a particular favour, if your lordship would
never tell any one of whom you learned to dance." '

SOURCE: John Timbs, *A Century of Anecdote, 1760–1860*. Sandwich
received the unenviable nickname of 'Jeremy Twitcher', a
treacherous highwayman in Gay's *Beggar's Opera*, after the Earl
had played a despicable part in the prosecution of John Wilkes,
his former friend and colleague. He himself gave his name to two
things—the Sandwich Islands (Hawaii Archipelago), discovered
by Cook in 1778; and the slice of meat, or other food, between
two pieces of bread. This method of sustenance was called for by
the Earl during his long sessions at the gaming-tables. There is,

regrettably, little chance of authenticity in the remark ascribed
to an onlooker—'What's that you're eating, my dear fellah—a
tram?', unless tram was being used in its old meaning of a beam
or shaft.

SARDIS, CAPTURE OF (498).

Remember the Athenians

Now when it was told to King Darius that Sardis had been
taken and burnt by the Athenians and Ionians, he took small
heed of the Ionians, well knowing who they were, and that their
revolt would soon be put down: but he asked who, and what
manner of men, the Athenians were. And when he had been
told, he called for his bow; and, having taken it, and placed an
arrow on the string, he let the arrow fly towards heaven; and as
he shot it into the air, he said:

'O supreme God! grant me that I may avenge myself on the
Athenians.'

And when he had said this, he appointed one of his servants
to say to him every day as he sat at meat:

'Sire, remember the Athenians.'

SOURCE: Herodotus; quoted Sir Edward Creasy, *The Fifteen
Decisive Battles of the World*, 1851, Ch. I.

SAVONAROLA, GIROLAMO (1452–1498), Italian monk and
reformer, whose conflict with Pope Alexander VI led to his arrest,
torture and execution.

The alteration of the gallows

On this day [29th] of May, 1498, they decided to put him to
death and to burn him alive; at last, in the evening they built
a wooden platform which covered all the steps of the Seigniory
from the lion right to the middle of the square. And a great
gallows was erected here, a number of feet high, and a great
scaffold round the gallows; across the gallows was fixed a piece
of wood which gave it the form of a cross; seeing this men said:

'They want to crucify him.'

When this murmur about the cross was heard, the wood was sawn until it no longer resembled a cross.

SOURCE: Luca Landucci, *Diario fiorentino dal 1450 al 1516*; quoted Anny Latour, *The Borgias* (trans. Neil Mann), Elek Books, 1963, p. 79.

SCOTT, ROBERT FALCON (1868–1912), Antarctic explorer; reached Pole in January, 1912, shortly after Amundsen; lost on return journey with all his party.

Message to the public

Had we lived, I should have had a tale to tell of the hardihood, endurance, and courage of my companions which would have stirred the heart of every Englishman. These rough notes and our dead bodies must tell the tale.

SOURCE: Robert Falcon Scott (1868–1912), *Message to the Public*; found, with diaries, specimens, etc., by search party eight months later.

SELKIRK, ALEXANDER (1676–1721), sailor and privateer; marooned on Juan Fernandez, 1704–1709; rescued by privateer Captain Woodes Rogers, who introduced Selkirk to Richard Steele. It was either Steele's account of Selkirk's adventures in *The Englishman* of December 2, 1713, or one of the editions of Woodes Rogers's published journal of his voyage, that caught Daniel Defoe's attention and led to his best-known book, *The Life and Surprising Adventures of Robinson Crusoe of York, Mariner . . .* 1719.

i. *Selkirk out-runs the goats*

When his powder failed, he took them [the goats] by speed of foot; for his way of living, and continual exercise of walking and running, cleared him of all gross humours, so that he ran with wonderful swiftness through the woods, and up the rocks and hills, as we perceived, when we employed him to catch goats for us. We had a bull-dog, which we sent with several of our nimblest runners, to help him in catching goats; but he distanced and tired both the dog and the men, catched the goats, and brought them to us on his back.

SOURCE: *Providence Displayed: or a very surprising Account of one Mr. Alexander Selkirk . . .*, 1712. A tract in the Harleian Miscellany based almost verbatim on Woodes Rogers's *A Cruising Voyage Round the World*, 1712.

ii. *Selkirk dances*

He was at first pestered with cats and rats, that had bred in great numbers from some of each species, which had got a-shore from the ships that put in there to wood and water. The rats gnawed his feet and clothes, while asleep; which obliged him to cherish the cats with his goats-flesh; by which many of them became so tame, that they would lie about him in hundreds, and soon delivered him from the rats. He likewise tamed some kids; and, to divert himself, would now and then sing and dance with his cats.

SOURCE: ibid.

SEYMOUR, CHARLES, sixth **DUKE OF SOMERSET** (1662–1748). Under James II, second peer of the realm, Colonel of the Queen Consort's Dragoons and Lord of the King's Bedchamber; but dismissed from office for refusing to escort the Papal Nuncio d'Adda, when James wished to receive him in great state at Windsor.

'*While I obey the law I fear nothing*'

The King . . . added to his defiance of Church and Parliament by inviting the Pope to send an ambassador to his Court and planning to receive him in great state. . . . He [Somerset] rebelled against his last imposition and refused to carry the Sword of State in the Papist ceremonies.

'I thought, my Lord,' said King James, 'that I was doing you a great honour in appointing you to escort the minister of the first of all crowned heads.'

'Sir,' said the Duke, 'I am advised that I cannot obey Your Majesty without breaking the law.'

'I would have you fear me as well as the law,' answered the King. 'Do you know that I am above the law?'

The young Duke answered, 'Your Majesty may be above the law, but I am not; and while I obey the law I fear nothing.'

SOURCE: Gilbert Burnet, Bishop of Salisbury; this version from Hector Bolitho, *The Galloping Third*, John Murray, 1963.

SHACKLETON, SIR ERNEST HENRY (1874–1922), explorer; led trans-Antarctic expedition, 1914 and, when the *Endurance* was crushed in the ice, made epic voyage of 800 miles in small boat to South Georgia.

i. *The three strangers*

Everybody at Stromness knew Shackleton well, and we were very sorry he is lost in ice with all hands. But we do not know three terrible-looking bearded men who walk into the office off the mountainside that morning. Manager say:

'Who the *hell* are you,' and terrible bearded man in the centre of the three say very quietly:

'My name is Shackleton.'

Me, I turn away and weep. I think manager weep, too.

SOURCE: Mansell, who was present when Shackleton and his two companions walked into the manager's office at the end of their incredible journey. The last thirty-six hours had been spent crossing the snow-fields and mountains of South Georgia. R. B. Robertson, *Of Whales and Men*, 1956; quoted Margaret and James Fisher, *Shackleton*, Barrie, 1957.

ii. *The fourth member of the party*

When I look back on those days, I have no doubt that Providence guided us, not only across those snow-fields, but across the storm-white sea that separated Elephant Island from our landing-place in South Georgia. I know that during that long and racking march of thirty-six hours over the unnamed mountains and glaciers of South Georgia it seemed to me often that we were four, not three. I said nothing to my companions on the point, but afterwards Worsely said to me:

'Boss, I had a curious feeling on the march that there was another person with us.'

SOURCE: Sir Ernest Shackleton, *South*, Heinemann, 1919.

SHAFTESBURY, ANTHONY ASHLEY COOPER, seventh **EARL OF** (1801–1885), philanthropist; worked for reform of lunacy laws and for improvements in the lot of factory workers, chimney-sweeps, miners, etc.; an advocate of 'ragged schools' and of more enlightened treatment of juvenile delinquents.

i. *The welfare of mankind*

At the age of twenty-seven he wrote in his diary: 'On my soul, I believe that I desire the welfare of mankind.'

At eighty-four he exclaimed in view of his approaching end: 'I cannot bear to leave the world with all the misery in it.'

SOURCE: George W. E. Russell, *Collections and Recollections*, Smith, Elder & Co., 1903, Ch. III.

ii. *The Lord helps those . . .*

'Poor dear children!' he exclaimed to the superintendent of a ragged school, after hearing from some of the children their tale of cold and hunger. 'What can we do for them?'

'My God shall supply all their need,' replied the superintendent with easy faith.

'Yes,' said Lord Shaftesbury, 'He will, but they must have some food directly.'

He drove home, and instantly sent two churns of soup, enough to feed four hundred.

SOURCE: ibid.

SHAKESPEARE, WILLIAM (1564–1616), playwright and poet.

Biography in sixty words

I have heard that Mr. Shakespear was a natural wit, without any art at all; he frequented the plays all his younger time, but in his elder days lived at Stratford, and supplied the stage with two plays every year, and for it, had an allowance so large that he spent at the rate of £1000 a year, as I have heard.

SOURCE: MS. diary, begun 42 years after Shakespeare's death by Doctor John Ward of Stratford-on-Avon. The diary was sold for £10,500 in London, in 1928, to an American dealer.

SHERIDAN, RICHARD BRINSLEY (1751–1816). Sheridan (familiarly known as 'Sherry'), as well as a front-rank dramatist, with 'The Rivals', 'The School for Scandal' and 'The Critic' among his achievements, held a number of high government offices, including those of secretary to the Treasury and treasurer of the Navy in the 'Ministry of all the Talents'. He was among the finest parliamentary orators of his day and one of the wittiest and most companionable of men.

Among his quips were:

i. 'The Right Honourable gentleman is indebted to his memory for his jests, and to his imagination for his facts.'

ii. 'It contained a great deal both of what was new and what was true, but unfortunately what was new was not true, and what was true was not new.'

iii. *The Member he would not name*

On one occasion, he accused a member of the Government of corrupting members to obtain their votes for Pitt's East India Bill, having in mind John Robinson, secretary to the Treasury, 1770–1782. There was an angry uproar in the House and many cries of 'Who is it? Name him! Name him!'

'Sir,' said Sheridan to the Speaker, 'I shall not name the person. It is an unpleasant and invidious thing to do, and therefore I shall not name him. But don't suppose, Sir, that I abstain because there is any difficulty in naming him. I could do that, Sir, as soon as you could say Jack Robinson.'

iv. *'My Lords, I have done'*

Sheridan's greatest effort in Parliament was a unique display of oratory on February 7, 1787, in a speech against Warren Hastings, which Burke called 'the most astonishing effort of eloquence, argument and wit united, of which there is any record'; Fox declared all he had ever heard or read 'when compared with it, dwindles into nothing and vanishes like vapour before the sun'; and Pitt that 'it surpassed all the eloquence of ancient and modern times, and possessed everything that genius or art could furnish to agitate and control the human mind'. After speaking for nearly six hours, Sheridan fell back exhausted into the arms of Burke, with the words:

'My Lords, I have done.'

SHREWSBURY, BATTLE OF (July 23, 1403). Fought between Henry IV and the northern rebels under Henry Percy (Hotspur) and his uncle, the Earl of Worcester. Hotspur hoped to join up with Glendower, but was intercepted by the King.

i. *Hotspur leaves his sword behind*

When he knew that rebellion had truly broken out, Henry called for levies and started immediately in pursuit. Hotspur rode south with his Cheshire reinforcements, trying to meet Glendower, and after about a forty-five mile march from Lichfield he came to Shrewsbury on July 21; the banner of Henry was on the walls and it did not flutter down to the trumpetings of the rebels. The gates remained closed and wearily Hotspur had to lead his men three miles towards Whitchurch until he reached a small hill by the roadside. He drew up his men in a field known as Hayteley with a stretch of thick peas before them, and with mushy ground and scattered ponds below the slope on which he waited.

Henry was riding fast, he came to Shrewsbury, then hurried on, desiring combat. Early on the morning of the 21st he drew his army into three battles, giving the van to the Earl of Stafford, himself taking the centre, and Prince Henry the rear. Watching the enemy move into place, Hotspur called for his sword, and it could not be found. It was his favourite weapon used in all his battles, and it seems that it had been left behind at the village of Berwick where he had slept the night before. Hotspur blanched when he was told, he cried:

'We have ploughed our last furrow, for a wizard in mine own country prophesied that I should die at Berwick!'

SOURCE: Philip Lindsay, *Kings of Merry England from Eadward the Confessor to Richard the Third*, Ivor Nicholson & Watson, 1935, p. 481.

ii. *The end of Hotspur*

Hotspur and the Earl of Douglas . . . would 'fight neither with small nor great, but only with the King'. Followed by thirty men they hacked a path through the medley of bodies until they reached the royal standard itself and ripped it from its staff. Douglas, using a mace, smashed his way along; Henry he could not find, he killed only 'the appearance of the King', but not the King himself. Then suddenly Hotspur died, was struck down by an unknown hand; he was killed 'and no man wist of whom'. His troops missed his great presence, they failed to see his . . . sword flashing above the swords of lesser men, they cried, seeking to hear his answer, 'Henry Percy—King! Henry Percy—King!' and the King of England ran before them and with his own voice answered, 'Henry Percy dead! Henry Percy dead!'

SOURCE: ibid., p. 480.

SIDDONS, SARAH (1755–1831), the greatest actress of her time; among her most celebrated rôles was that of Lady Macbeth, during one performance of which the following incident occurred.

i. *A pint of beer for Lady Macbeth*

Once during her engagement, the evening being hot, Mrs. Siddons was tempted by a torturing thirst to avail herself of the only relief to be obtained at the moment. Her dresser, therefore, despatched a boy in great haste to 'fetch a pint of beer for Mrs. Siddons.'

Meanwhile the play proceeded, and on the boy's return with the frothed pitcher, he looked about for the person who had sent him on his errand, and not seeing her, enquired:

'Where is Mrs. Siddons?'

The scene-shifter whom he questioned, pointing his finger to the stage, where she was performing the sleeping-scene of *Lady Macbeth*, replied:

'There she is.'

To the horror of the performers, the boy promptly walked on to the stage close up to Mrs. Siddons. . . . Her distress may be imagined; she waved the boy away in her grand manner several times without effect. At last the people behind the scenes, by dint of beckoning, stamping, etc., succeeded in getting him off with the beer, while the audience were in an uproar of laughter, which the dignity of the actress was unable to quell for several minutes.

SOURCE: *Life of Charles Mathews*, 1839.

ii. *The endless nose*

'Dammit, madam, there is no end to your nose.'

SOURCE: Thomas Gainborough, while painting Sarah Siddons's portrait.

SIDNEY, SIR PHILIP (1554–1586), soldier, courtier and man of letters.

i. *Advice to a brother*

I would, by the way, your Worship would learn a better hand. You write worse than I and I write evil enough. Once again, have a care of your diet; and consequently of your complexion. . . .

SOURCE: from a letter to his brother Robert, October 18, 1580. It finished 'Lord! how I have babbled!' Robert was about seventeen at the time.

ii. *News of Drake*

Now, Sir, for news; I refer myself to this bearer. He can tell how idly we look on our neighbour's fires: and nothing is happened notable at home; save only Drake's return. Of which yet, I know not the secret points: but about the world he hath been, and rich he is returned.

SOURCE: ibid.

iii. *The song that moved Sidney's heart*

Certainely I must confesse mine owne barbarousnesse; I never heard the old Song of Percie & Douglas: that I found not my heart moved more than with a Trumpet.

SOURCE: Sir Philip Sidney, *The Defence of Poesie*, 1621 edition, p. 516. Sidney is referring to the popular ballad about the small-scale fight on the Scottish border, at Otterburn, 1388, when James, Earl of Douglas was killed and Henry Percy (Hotspur) taken prisoner. The ballad of Chevy Chase, based on the Otterburn foray, very much distorts the facts, e.g., in having Hotspur killed along with Douglas.

Sidney's essay also contains the famous lines about the function of the poet:

. . . and with a tale forsooth he commeth to you, with a tale, which holdeth children from play, and old men from the Chimdey corner.

iv. '*Thy necessity is yet greater than mine*'

Zutphen (September 22, 1586), the battle in which Sir Philip Sidney received his fatal wound, was, in fact, only a skirmish outside the town, which was held by a Spanish garrison, and Sidney was largely responsible for his own death by an act of quixotry or bravado. The English threw themselves against a heavily defended food-train bringing provisions to the beleaguered town. Sir William Pelham, marshal of the forces, rode into the attack without his leg-armour and Sidney, not to be outdone, discarded his. He was struck by a musket ball three inches above the left knee and lingered another sixteen days, bearing considerable suffering with great fortitude. It was while he was being carried back to the English camp that the following immortal incident occurred.

In which sad progress, passing along by the rest of the army, where his uncle the general was, and being thirsty with excess of bleeding, he called for drink, which was presently brought him; but as he was putting the bottle to his mouth he saw a poor soldier carried along who had eaten his last at the same feast, ghastly casting up his eyes at the bottle; which Sir Philip, perceiving, took it from his head before he drank, and delivered it to the poor man with these words:—

'Thy necessity is yet greater than mine.'

And when he had pledged this poor soldier, he was presently carried to Arnhem.

SOURCE: Sir Fulke Greville, *Life of Sir Philip Sidney* (1652); Percy Addleshaw, *Sir Philip Sidney*, Methuen & Co., 1909, pp. 231–232. It is perhaps worthy of note that, according to C. Henry Warren, Sidney was 'the only Elizabethan of noble rank to die in battle'.

SILHOUETTE, ETIENNE DE (1709–1767), French minister of finance.

The origin of the silhouette

Silhouette found the French treasury exhausted and devised extreme measures to secure economies. His name survives in the word *silhouette*, a cheap form of portrait, being merely a black outline without any attempt at colour or detail.

SOURCE: see etymological dictionaries, etc.

SIND (SCINDE), ANNEXATION OF (1843). Sind was the country, ruled over by three independent amirs, in the lower valley and delta of the Indus.

i. *A very humane piece of rascality*

Intrigues deceived Napier into provoking a war which ended with the annexation of Sind by Ellenborough in 1843. Sir Charles Napier himself remarked of these proceedings:

'We have no right to seize Sind, yet we shall do so, and a very advantageous, useful, and humane piece of rascality it will be.'

SOURCE: Low and Pulling, *Dictionary of English History* (revised and enlarged Hearnshaw, Chew and Beales), 1928.

ii. *'Peccavi'*

After the victory at Hyderabad (Feb. 17, 1843), General Sir Charles Napier sent a despatch consisting of the Latin word *Peccavi* (I have sinned [Sind]).

SMITH, CAPTAIN JOHN (1580–1631), soldier and colonizer of Virginia.

i. *Smith and Pocohontas*

If ingratitude be a deadly poison to all honest virtues, I must be guilty of that crime if I should omit any means to be thankful. So it is that some ten years ago being in Virginia, and taken prisoner by the power of Powhatan their chief King, I received from this great savage exceeding great courtesy, especially from his son Nantaquaus, the most manliest, comeliest, boldest spirit I ever saw in a savage, and his sister Pocohontas, the King's most dear and well-beloved daughter, being but a child of twelve or thirteen years of age, whose compassionate, pitiful heart, of my desperate estate, gave me much cause to respect her: I being the first Christian this proud King and his grim attendants ever saw: and thus enthralled in their barbarous power, I cannot say I felt the least occasion of want that was in the power of those my mortal foes to prevent, notwithstanding all their threats. After some six weeks fatting amongst those savage courtiers, at the minute of my execution, she hazarded the beating out of her own brains to save mine; and not only that, but so prevailed with her father, that I was safely conducted to Jamestown.

SOURCE: Captain John Smith, *Generall Historie of Virginia*, 1624.

ii. *Fuller has his doubts*

Yet have we two witnesses to attest them [i.e., his exploits], the prose and the pictures, both in his own book [see Source above]; and it soundeth much to the diminution of his deeds, that he alone is the herald to publish and proclaim them.

Two captains being at dinner, one of them fell into a large relation of his own achievements, concluding his discourse with this question to his fellow:

'And pray, sir,' said he, 'what service have you done?' To whom he answered:

'Other men can tell that.'

SOURCE: Thomas Fuller, *The Worthies of England*, 1662; 1952 edition, George Allen & Unwin, pp. 75–76.

SMITH, SYDNEY REV. (1771–1845), wit and conversationalist; canon of St. Paul's.

i. The Smiths never had any arms, but have always sealed their letters with their thumbs. (Answer to a county historian who had enquired for the coat-of-arms of the Smith family.)

ii. I have, alas, only one illusion left, and that is the Archbishop of Canterbury.

iii. I never read a book before reviewing it; it prejudices a man so.

iv. I am just going to pray for you at St. Paul's, but with no very lively hope of success.

SOURCE: various, inc. Lady Holland, *Memoir*, 1855; H. Pearson, *The Smith of Smiths*, 1934, etc.

SMUGGLING.

i. *The parson lights the smugglers*

It was full six in the evening of an autumn day when a traveller arrived where the road ran along by a sandy beach just above

high-water mark. The stranger, who was a native of some
inland town and utterly unacquainted with Cornwall and its
ways, had reached the brink of the tide just as a 'landing' was
coming off. It was a scene not only to instruct a townsman, but
to dazzle and surprise. At sea, just beyond the billows, lay the
vessel, well moored with anchors at stem and stern. Between the
ship and the shore, boats, laden to the gunwhale, passed to and
fro. Crowds assembled on the beach to help the cargo ashore.
. . . Horrified at what he saw, the stranger lost all self-command,
and, oblivious of personal danger, he began to shout:

'What a horrible sight! Have you no shame? Is there no
magistrate at hand? Cannot any Justice of the Peace be found
in this fearful country?'

'No; thanks be to God,' answered a hoarse, gruff voice.
'None within eight miles.'

'Well, then,' screamed the stranger, 'is there no clergyman
hereabout? Does no minister of the parish live among you, on
this coast?'

'Aye! to be sure, there is,' said the same deep voice.

'Well, how far off does he live? Where is he?'

'That's he, sir, yonder, with the lanthorn.'

And, sure enough, there he stood on a rock, and poured, with
pastoral diligence, the 'light of other days' on a busy congregation.

SOURCE: Rev. Robert Stephen Hawker (1803–1875), vicar of
Morwenstowe, Cornwall; poet and Cornish historian. Quoted
The Story of the Sea (edited 'Q') Cassell & Co., 1898, pp. 618–619.

ii. *The 'King of Prussia'*

In the latter half of the last century [the 18th] there lived a
man by Porth Leah, in Mount's Bay, who was called John
Carter, but who was more usually known as the 'King of
Prussia'. From him Porth Leah took the name of Prussia
Cove, which it bears to this day. He cut harbours there and a
road, turned the caves into smuggling cellars, and even rigged
up a small battery, with which he boldly opened fire on a
Revenue cutter.

On one occasion, while he was away from home, the Excise officers from Penzance came around in their boats and found a cargo which had lately arrived from France. This they seized and carried off to Penzance, where they secured it in the Custom House store. In due course, John Carter returned to the cove and heard the news. What was he to do? As he explained to his comrades, he had agreed to deliver that cargo to his customers by a certain day, and his reputation as an honest man was at stake. He must keep his word.

That night, a number of armed men broke into the stores at Penzance, and the 'King of Prussia' took his own again and marched back to the cove. Next morning, the officers found that the place had been broken open. They examined the stores, and, having found what particular things were missing, they said to one another that John Carter had been there, and they knew it, because he was an honest man, who would not take anything that did not belong to him.

SOURCE: ibid., pp. 620–621.

iii. *Napoleon approves of English smugglers*

They did great mischief to your Government; they took from France annually forty or fifty millions of silk and brandy. . . . I ordered Gravelines to be prepared for their reception, where they had a little camp for their accommodation. At one time there were upwards of five hundred of them in Dunkirk. I had every information I wanted through them. They brought over newspapers and dispatches from the spies that we had in London. They took over spies from France, landed and kept them in their houses for some days, then dispersed them over the country, and brought them back when wanted. They came over in boats not broader than this bath. It was really astonishing to see them passing your 74-gun ships in defiance.

SOURCE: Barry O'Meara, *Napoleon in Exile*. O'Meara was surgeon to Napoleon on St. Helena.

iv. *The movable apple-tree at Overmoyne*

Thomas Hardy tells the story of a riding officer's pursuit of a cargo of brandy brought up from Lulworth Cove to Nether-Mynton (i.e., Overmoyne, a village on the Dorchester-Wareham Road). After a long search, the officer's attention becomes concentrated on an apple-tree standing in an orchard.

The excisemen, having re-entered the orchard, acted as if they were positive that here lay hidden the rest of the tubs, which they were determined to find before nightfall. They spread themselves out round the field, and advancing on all fours as before, went anew round every apple-tree in the enclosure. The young tree in the middle again led them to pause, and at length the whole company gathered there in a way which signified that a second chain of reasoning had led to the same results as the first.

When they had examined the sod hereabouts for some minutes, one of the men rose, ran to a disused porch of the church, where tools were kept, and returned with the sexton's pickaxe and shovel, with which they set to work.

The grass was so green and uninjured that it was difficult to believe that it had been disturbed. The smugglers . . . saw, to their chagrin, the officers stand two on each side of the tree, and, stopping and applying their hands to the soil, they bodily lifted the tree and the turf around it. The apple-tree now showed itself to be growing in a shallow box, with handles for lifting it at each of the four sides. Under the site of the tree a square hole was revealed, and an exciseman went and looked down. . . .

[The contraband brandy was taken out and the skilfully-hidden cellar smashed in.]

But the hole, which had in its time held so much contraband merchandise, was never completely filled up, either then or afterwards, a depression in the ground marking the spot to this day.

SOURCE: Thomas Hardy, *Wessex Tales*, 1888.

v. *The respectable trade of smuggling*

Their [the revenue men's] main difficulty was that smuggling was considered almost respectable: nearly everyone was in it—rich and poor—in some way or other. People got tea from the smuggler very much as we now get it from the grocer. And how respectable the *trade* of smuggler was can be judged from this advertisement taken from an 18th-Century newspaper, *The Ipswich Journal*. . . .

'Richard Chaplin, Sudbourn, Suffolk, near Orford, begs leave to acquaint his friends and the public in general, that he has, some time back, declined the branch of Smuggling, and returns thanks for all their past favours.

'Also, To be SOLD on Monday, August 8th, 1785, at the dwelling house of Samuel Bathers, Sudbourn, the property of Richard Chaplin aforesaid, A very useful CART, fit for a maltster, ashman, or a smuggler—it will carry 80 half-ankers or tubs; one small ditto that will carry 40 tubs; also two very good wooden Saddles, three Pads, Straps, Bridles, Girth, Horse-cloth, Corn-bin, a very good Vault, and many articles that are very useful to a Smuggler.'

SOURCE: George Ewart Evans, *Ask the Fellows Who Cut the Hay*, Faber and Faber, second edition, 1962, pp. 186–187.

SOCRATES (470?–399 B.C.), Athenian philosopher.

The philosopher who stood still for 24 hours

Once a problem occurred to him early in the morning, and he stood there thinking it over. When the answer would not come, he did not give up, but stayed searching for it. Midday came and men pointed out in amazement and astonishment to each other that Socrates had been standing wrapped in thought since daybreak. When evening finally arrived and they had had their dinner, some of the Ionians spread some blankets outside to sleep on (it was summer then), while keeping half an eye open to see if he would stand there all night. Stand there he did till dawn came and the sun rose. Then after a prayer to the sun he moved away at last.

SOURCE: Plato, *Symposium*, 219e; trans. B. K. Workman, *They Saw it Happen in Classical Times*, Basil Blackwell, 1964, p. 28.

SOUTH SEA BUBBLE (1720). The name given to the financial crisis which followed on the South Sea Company, which was formed in 1711, taking over the National Debt. In the frenzied speculation which occurred, many fraudulent companies sprang up, proposing absurd schemes which still managed to find investors. Thousands were ruined in every section of the population.

i. *An act of faith*

One of the schemes was 'A company for carrying on an undertaking of great advantage, but nobody to know what it is': each subscriber, for £2 deposit, to be entitled to £100 per annum share. Of this precious scheme 1000 shares were taken in six hours, and the deposit paid.

SOURCE: *A Book of Days* (edit. R. Chambers), 1864, Vol. I.

ii. *A number of large jackasses*

As a memento of the folly of the age, we insert the names of a few of these projects, on every one of which money was actually subscribed.

'Wrecks to be fished for on the Irish coast.'
'To make salt water fresh.'
'For improving the breed of horses.'
'For making of oil from poppies.'
'For transmuting quicksilver into malleable and fine metal.'
'For fattening of hogs.'
'For a wheel for a perpetual motion.'
'For importing a number of large jackasses from Spain, in order to propogate a larger kind of mules in England.'

SOURCE: quoted, with others, in *The Percy Anecdotes*, 1820–1823.

SOVEREIGNTY OF THE SEAS.

i. *King John rules the waves*

'If the governor or commander of the king's navie in his expeditions shall meet any ship whatsoever by sea, either laden or empty, that shall refuse to strike their sails at the command of the king's governor or admiral, or his lieutenant, but make resistance against them which belong to his fleet; that then they are to bee reputed enemies if they may be taken, yea, and their ships and goods confiscated.'

SOURCE: King John's enunciation of English sovereignty of the seas; John Selden, *Mare Clausum*, 1635.

ii. *Admiral Sir William Monson makes the Dutch Admiral strike his flag*

About the year 1604. . . . Sir William Monson was cruising up and down with his fleet with instructions to assert and convince foreigners of that supremacy which the Royal House of Stewart had just inherited from the Royal House of Tudor. In July, 1605, he put into Calais, and found there six Dutch ships newly arrived to join the Dutch squadron. . . . One of these was the Admiral's ship. On Sir William's approach this Dutch admiral dipped his flag thrice. Sir William sent him a message to take it in altogether. The Dutchman refused, asserting that he had struck his colours thrice, and that was acknowledgment enough. Sir William assured him that it was not, and added that if he did not promptly salute as he was told, the British Admiral would at once weigh anchor, fall down to him, and settle the question with powder and shot:

'For,' as he put it, 'rather than I would suffer his flag to be worn in view of so many nations as were to behold it, I resolve to bury myself in the sea.'

The Dutch Admiral, however, was convinced at last. He took down his flag, fired a gun for the rest of the fleet to follow him, and stood off to sea in a huff.

'And thus,' Sir William winds up very drily, 'I lost my guest the next day at dinner as he had promised.'

SOURCE: *The Story of the Sea* (edited 'Q'), Cassell & Co., 1898, p. 126.

iii. *Another Dutchman refuses to 'take off his hat'*

The 17th Century method of saluting was not a simple flag dipping, but the much more laborious business of lowering topsails.

The fishing quarrel raged hotly through the first half of the seventeenth century: and up to the year 1674 we had a deal of trouble in forcing the Dutch to pull off their hats to us. In 1652 Commodore Young fell in with a Dutch man-of-war that refused to salute. He sent a boat and requested the captain to take off his hat.

'If I do,' answered the Dutchman, 'the States* have promised to take off my head.'

(A fight ensued, in which the Dutch ship was beaten.)

SOURCE: ibid., p. 132.

SPENSER, EDMUND (1552?–1599), poet: author of *The Faerie Queene*, dedicated to Queen Elizabeth—'the only great poem that had been written in England since Chaucer died'.

'*Turn that fellow out of the house*'

When Spenser had finished his famous poem . . . he carried it to the Earl of Southampton, the great patron of the poets of those days. The manuscript being sent up to the Earl, he read a few pages, and then ordered his servant to give the writer £20. Reading on, he cried in a rapture:

'Carry that man another £20.'

Proceeding still, he said:

'Give him £20 more.' But at length, he lost all patience, and said:

---

* The Dutch United Provinces.

'Go turn that fellow out of the house, for if I read on I shall be ruined.'

SOURCE: Mr. Addison, *Interesting Anecdotes, Memoirs* . . . etc., 1794.

SPUR MONEY.

Perquisites for the choristers

By the 17th Century it had become a recognised practice in a number of cathedrals and churches for 'spur-money' to be demanded from anyone entering the building in spurs. It had, in fact, become one of the cherished perquisites of the choristers or minor church officials.

As early as the reign of Henry VII an item of 4s. appears in the privy purse expenses as having been paid 'to the children for the king's spurs'.

Sometimes the fine could be avoided; e.g., a notice of 1622, issued by the Dean of the Chapel Royal, stated:

If any knight, or other person entitled to wear spurs, enter the chapel in that guise, he shall pay to the quiristers the accustomed fine; but if he command the youngest quirester to repeat his gamut,* and he fail in the so doing, the said knight or other shall not pay the fine.

STAGE-COACH, TRAVEL BY.

i. *An early 19th Century description*

Crammed full of passengers—three fat, fusty old men—a young mother and sick child—a cross old maid—a poll-parrot—a bag of red herrings—double-barrelled gun (which you are afraid is loaded)—and a snarling lap-dog, in addition to yourself—awaking out of a sound nap, with the cramp in one leg, and the

* 'To repeat his gamut' probably meant to recite the notes of the diatonic scale.

other in a lady's band-box . . . getting out in the dark, at the half-way house, in the hurry stepping into the return coach, and finding yourself next morning at the very spot you had started from the evening before—not a breathe of air— asthmatic old man, and child with the measles—windows closed in consequence—pretend sleep, and pinch the child—mistake— pinch the dog and get bit . . . pay the coachman, and drop a piece of gold in the straw—not to be found—fell through a crevice—coachman says, 'he'll find it'—can't—get out yourself —gone—picked up by the 'ostler—No time for 'blowing-up' —coach off for next stage—lose your money—get in—lose your seat—stuck in the middle—get laughed at—lose your temper. . . .

SOURCE: William Hone, *The Table Book*, 1838.

ii. *Travel on the Brighton Road*

There were in 1811 twenty-eight coaches on the road, and eleven years later no less than sixty, thirty going each way; on October 25, 1833, the coaches took down four hundred and eighty passengers.

Many amateur coachmen took the reins, some more or less regularly for a period. The Marquis of Worcester frequently drove the 'Beaufort', and the Hon. Frederick Jerningham 'tooted' the day-mail; while the prince of amateur whips, Sir St. Vincent Cotton, had his own coach, the 'Age', with splendid horses and magnificent fittings, even the horse-cloths being edged with broad silver lace. The Cambridgeshire baronet . . . was as particular about the half-crown 'tip' as his professional brethren; and there is told an amusing story that when two old ladies objected to handing him the coin, protesting that they had known his mother, and he ought to be ashamed of asking for a fee, he retorted that if his mamma or his great grandmamma had ever patronised his coach, he should most assuredly have expected the usual 'tip' from them.

SOURCE: Lewis Melville, *Brighton: its History, its Follies, and its Fashions*, Chapman & Hall, 1909, pp. 122–123.

STANHOPE, CHARLES, third **EARL STANHOPE** (1753–1816), politician, inventor and scientist. Known as 'Citizen Stanhope' and 'Minority of One' because of his Parliamentary motions against any interference in the internal affairs of France when she was in the throes of revolution. A medal, with the motto 'The minority of one, 1795' was struck in his honour. Took out patents for steam vessels, invented printing appliances, etc.

A lesson for the Chancellor

'On another occasion I shall teach the noble and learned lord law, and I have this day taught the bench of bishops religion.'

SOURCE: remark to the Lord Chancellor, May 18, 1789, when Stanhope strove to introduce to the Lords a bill to relieve members of the Church of England from various penalties and disabilities.

STANHOPE, LADY HESTER LUCY (1776–1839), eccentric; niece of, and housekeeper (1803–1806) to, William Pitt; left England for the Levant, 1810, and settled on Mount Lebanon for the rest of her life, maintaining an oriental household despotism.

i. *The lady who could cheat the devil*

'I let her do as she pleases; for if she were resolved to cheat the devil she could do it.'

SOURCE: William Pitt. Hester Stanhope, retelling the story, added: 'And so I could'.

ii. *The broken spoon*

She corresponded with Pitt's friends, including Canning and Mulgrave, to whom she once retorted *à propos* of an unfortunate remark upon a broken spoon at the table:

'Have you not yet discovered that Mr. Pitt sometimes uses very slight and weak instruments to effect his ends?'

SOURCE: Thomas Seccombe, *Dictionary of National Biography*, 1898.

EE

iii. *The two-hour lectures*

I have known her lie for two hours at a time with a pipe in her mouth (from which the sparks fell and burned the counterpane into innumerable holes) when she was in a lecturing humour, and go on in one unbroken discourse, like a parson in his pulpit.

SOURCE: Charles Lewis Meryon, her physician and biographer; author of *Memoirs of Lady Hester Stanhope*, 1845, and *Travels of Lady Hester Stanhope*, 1846.

STEAM, COMING OF.

A prophecy

Steam will prove a universal peacemaker. The natives of all counties will cease to regard each other as enemies. Man will meet Man as his brother. War will cease. Similar reflections to these will naturally suggest themselves to the visitors while lounging on the Pier.

SOURCE: *Guide to Folkestone of the 1850's;* quoted Edith Oliver, *Country Moods and Tenses*, Batsford, 1941, p. 47.

STEPHEN (1097?–1154), King of England.

'It was said that Christ and his saints slept'

When the traitors perceived that he was a mild man, and a soft and a good, and that he did not enforce justice, they did all wonder. They had done homage to him and sworn oaths, but they no faith kept; all became forsworn, and broke their allegiance, for every rich man built his castles, and defended them against him, and they filled the land full of castles. They greatly oppressed the wretched people by making them work at these castles, and when the castles were finished they filled them with devils and evil men. Then they took those whom they suspected to have any goods, by night and by day, seizing both men and women, and they put them in prison for their gold and silver, and tortured them with pains unspeakable, for never were there any martyrs tormented as these were. They hung some up by their feet, and smoked them with foul smoke; some by their thumbs, or by the head, and they hung burning things on their feet. They put a knotted string about their heads, and twisted it till it went into the brain. They put them into dungeons wherein were adders and snakes and toads, and thus wore them out. Some they put into a crucet house—that is, into a chest that was short and narrow, and not deep—and they put sharp stones in it, and crushed the man so that they broke all his limbs. . . . Many thousands they exhausted with hunger. I cannot and I may not tell you of all the wounds and all the tortures that they inflicted upon the wretched men of this land; and this state of things lasted the nineteen years that Stephen was king, and ever grew worse and worse . . . it was said openly that Christ and his saints slept.

SOURCE: *Anglo-Saxon Chronicle*, trans. Rev. J. A. Giles, 1881.

STOWE, HARRIET BEECHER (1812–1896), American writer; author of *Uncle Tom's Cabin*.

i. *Lincoln meets Mrs. Stowe*

'So this is the little lady who made this big war?'

SOURCE: Abraham Lincoln to Mrs. Harriet Beecher Stowe, at the White House during the Civil War. Mrs. Stowe's propaganda novel *Uncle Tom's Cabin* had an immense influence on public opinion and brought the whole system of slavery into the open as never before.

ii. *The audience rises*

Many in the North wondered whether Lincoln would, in fact, issue the final Proclamation of Emancipation due on January 1, 1863. Mrs. Stowe . . . went to the great meeting held in the Boston Music Hall to wait for the news that the proclamation had finally been issued. The telegram came and the hall burst into cheers. Then news came that Harriet Beecher Stowe was in the hall, and the whole audience rose, crying out, 'Mrs. Stowe! Mrs. Stowe!' She went to the front of the balcony and looked down on a sea of faces cheering the woman, who, as she thought, had by the direct inspiration of God helped to remove the great national sin and helped her to justify the justice as well as the goodness of God. For her they were the same thing.

SOURCE: D. W. Brogan, *Uncle Tom's Message: the Book of War and Freedom*, in *The Times Literary Supplement*.

STRATFORD DE REDCLIFFE, LORD (1786–1880). Called 'The Great Elchi', or ambassador *par excellence*. Held many important diplomatic appointments.

How to deal with an ultimatum

I think it was a little before the Treaty of Adrianople, but I will not be quite certain, when the Russian army had advanced in force as near Constantinople as that town, and had sent in peremptory and humiliating terms to the Porte [i.e., the Ottoman Empire, or, more specifically, the centre of government] as the price of their not marching on to the capital, that Lord Stratford heard from a courier who had just come from Vienna with dispatches and had managed to get through the Russian camp, that the army was being decimated by fever and altogether in a bad way.

Lord Stratford rang his bell for old Baptiste, his man, telling him to bring food and wine for the courier, a native: when this was done he locked the man in his room and getting on his horse rode straight to the Porte. This august body was tearfully considering the Russian ultimatum.

'Give it to me,' said the Great Elchee, and he tore it up and flung the pieces down on the floor. The Ministers were thunderstruck.

'Gracious heaven, what are we to do? The Russians are at our gates, we have nothing left but to give in.'

'Give in—nonsense—write that "unless the Russian army evacuate Adrianople within one week, and continue their march to the Pruth continuously, the Turkish army with march on Adrianople". '

The poor Turks thought that madness must have seized the British Ambassador and asked him what England would do if the Russians instead of retiring advanced.

'I pledge the honour of England that if you stand firm and follow *instantly* my advice you will be supported by the whole force of Britain.'

Such was the energy of the man who had never promised what he could not perform that . . . a dispatch was then and there written and sent. . . . The effect was as Lord Stratford anticipated: the Russian army, worn out by disease, was unequal to the task of carrying out its threats, and rapidly began a homeward-bound march.

SOURCE: Sir Edmund Hornby, *An Autobiography*, Constable & Co., 1929, pp. 72–73.

SUNDAY OBSERVANCE. One of the great struggles of the 19th Century, continuing to our own day, was that for securing modification of the official attitude towards Sunday observance. It was an issue always certain to arouse fierce controversy. One occasion for an exhibition of feeling on the issue was when the Government was being pressed, in the 1890's, to allow the Sunday opening of museums and art galleries. Objections were partly on religious, partly on economic, grounds. The Trades Union Congress, in 1885, voted against Sunday opening by 67 to 51, but had changed its mind in favour by 1887. By 1895, over eighty clergymen were preaching in favour of Sunday opening of national museums and galleries, their numbers including several Bishops.

i. *The plesiosaurus and the politicians*

John Burns of Battersea had much to say about the sad sights of the streets on a Sunday afternoon. He asked any opponent of the motion to question any police constable as a policeman first, as a citizen second, as a father third, and he would answer that it would be a godsend to the police if the boys and girls could go for recreation to some museum on a Sunday afternoon.

He especially invited any opponent of the measure to visit the Natural History Museum and examine the Plesiosaurus in the glass case there, and mark the evolution of the type of politicians opposing Sunday opening, and avoid him in future as an awful example.

SOURCE: A. C. R. Carter, *Let Me Tell You*, Hutchinson & Co., 1940, p. 263. The national museums were first opened on Easter Sunday, 1896.

ii. *An Archbishop speaks up for liquor*

On another, slightly earlier, controversial issue, the famous Dr. William Connor Magee, Bishop of Peterborough and, later, Archbishop of York, said:

'I declare . . . that I should say it would be better that England should be free than that England should be compulsorily sober.'

SOURCE: *Lords' Debate on the Intoxicating Liquor Bill*, May 2, 1872.

SWIFT, JONATHAN (1667–1745), satirist and Dean of St. Patrick's, Dublin.

Half-a-crown for the guests

Dr. Swift had an odd, blunt way, that is mistaken by strangers for ill-nature. 'Tis so odd that there is no describing it but by facts. I'll tell you one that just comes into my head. One evening Gay [John Gay, poet and dramatist] went to see him: you know how intimately we were all acquainted. On our coming in:

'Hey-day, gentlemen,' says the doctor, 'what's the meaning of this visit? How come you to leave all the great lords that you are so fond of, to come hither to see a poor dean?'

'Because we would rather see you than any of them.'

'Ay, any one that did not know you as well as I do might believe you. But since you are come, I must get some supper for you, I suppose?'

'No, doctor, we have supped already.'

'Supped already! that's impossible: why 'tis not eight o'clock yet.'

'Indeed we have.'

'That's very strange: but if you had not supped, I must have got something for you. Let me see, what should I have had? A couple of lobsters? Ay, that would have done very well—two shillings; tarts—a shilling. But you will drink a glass of wine with me, though you supped so much before your usual time, only to spare my pocket?'

'No; we had rather talk with you than drink with you.'

'But if you had supped with me, as in all reason you ought to have done, you must have drank with me. A bottle of wine —two shillings. Two and two is four, and one is five: just two-and-sixpence apiece. There, Pope, there's half-a-crown for you; and there's another for you, sir: for I won't save anything by you, I am determined.'

This was all said and done with his usual seriousness on such occasions; and in spite of everything we could say to the contrary, he actually obliged us to take the money.

SOURCE: Alexander Pope, in Joseph Spence's *Anecdotes*.

TALBOT, SIR JOHN, first **EARL OF SHREWSBURY** (1388?–1453), soldier; a famous commander in the Hundred Years War.

'The dogge Talbot' puts the children to sleep

Sir John Talbot, first Earl of Shrewsbury (1388?–1453) was one of the greatest soldiers of his age, owing much of his reputation to his dash and courage. The talbot was a large hound used for hunting, and this is still the badge of the Talbot (Shrewsbury) family.

It is said that when the peasant mothers of Normandy wanted to hush fractious children to sleep, they would say:

'Sh-h-h! the dogge Talbot is near!'

This is well in keeping with the practice of hard-pressed mothers through the centuries, enemy commanders frequently being called on to scare children into obedience by the mere mention of their names.

King Richard remained in the Holy Land, there did such mighty deeds that the Saracens stood in great fear of him; so much so . . . that when the Saracen children cried, their mothers called out:

'Whisht! here is King Richard!'

(Joinville's *Memoirs of the Crusades*).

In the 17th Century, royalist mothers threatened:

'Crummle (Cromwell) will get you!'

Along the south coast, during the Napoleonic Wars, 'Boney' did good service as a husher-to-sleep.

In our own day, things have degenerated a little. Harassed (and foolish) mothers have been heard to threaten their offspring not with captains and Kings, but with 'the bogey-man' or 'the policeman'.

TAYLOR, JOHN (1580–1653), waterman, innkeeper, poet, author and traveller; known as the 'water poet'; made a number of journeys, many of which resulted in a book with a curious title; was nearly drowned on one occasion trying to cross from London to Queenborough in a boat made of brown paper; at one time pressed into the navy and served at the siege of Cadiz.

Trials of an author

In some places, I was suspected for a Projector [i.e. someone with a fanciful scheme requiring financing]; or one that had devised some trick to bring the Carriers under some new taxation; and sometimes I was held to have been a Man-taker, a Sergeant, or Bailiff to arrest or attach men's goods or beasts. Indeed, I was scarce taken for an honest man amongst the most of them. All which suppositions I was enforced oftentimes to wash away with two or three jugs of beer, at most of the Inns I came to.

SOURCE: John Taylor, introduction to *The Carriers' Cosmography: or a Brief Relation of the Inns, Ordinaries, Hostelries . . . where the Carriers, Waggons, Foot-posts and Higglers do usually come from any parts, towns, shires and countries of the Kingdoms of England. Principality of Wales: as from the Kingdoms of Scotland and Ireland . . .*, 1637.

This is only about one third of the full title, a speciality of Taylor's being long-winded and highly eccentric title-pages. Other examples are:

The Liar: Or, A contradiction to those who in the titles of their Bookes affirmed them to be true, when they were false; although mine are all true, yet I terme them lyes. (1641)

Roger the Canterburian, that cannot say Grace for his Meat with a low-crown'd Hat before his Face, Or the Character of a Prelaticall Man affecting great Heightes. (1642)

What Will you have? A Calf with a White Face; or a Relation of his Travailes from England into Ireland, Scotland, Poland, Holland, Amsterdam, and other places, and is now newly arrived in the Citie of London, where he meanes to abide. (1649)

TENURES. Many strange payments and services were rendered in the Middle Ages in return for holding property from King or overlord. Some had a practical basis, some came about as a courtly formality, some by way of a jest. A curious example of the first type will be found under JOHN, King of England. Others are:

i. *The rose and the snowball*

A farm at Brook-house, in Langsett, in the parish of Peniston, and county of York, paid yearly to Godfrey Bosville, Esq. or his representative, a snow-ball at Midsummer, and a red rose at Christmas.

However extraordinary this tenure may appear, yet there is little doubt that it was very possible to perform the service, as snow is frequently found in caverns or hollows upon the high mountains in the neighbourhood of Peniston, in the month of June. The red rose at Christmas was probably one preserved until that time of the year: but . . . it is probable that the snow and the red rose were redeemable by a pecuniary payment fixed at the will of the lord.

SOURCE: Stephen Collet, *Relics of Literature*, 1823, p. 153.

ii. *Pie in the sky—mediaeval version*

Blount records a curious tenure by which, if the King crossed Shrivenham Bridge, a neighbouring landowner brought to him two white capons, saying:

'Behold, my lord, these two white capons which you shall have another time, but not now.' This is one of those strange jocular tenures whose origin is as tantalisingly held from us as were the capons from the King.

SOURCE: F. L. Salzman, *More Medieval Byways*, Methuen, 1926, p. 145.

iii. *The penny and the cart-whip*

Another curious service was the obligation of William de Valoignes, in the event of the King coming to his Kentish manor of Mappiscombe and going to hear Mass, to provide his royal guest with a penny for the offertory. Still more curious was the custom by which on Palm Sunday the representative of the lord of the manor of Broughton came to Castor Church with a new cart-whip, which he cracked three times in the church porch; he then took his seat in the manor pew, but came out at the beginning of the second lesson and knelt in front of the reading-desk, holding over the parson's head a purse, containing thirty silver pennies, tied on the end of the whip-lash.

SOURCE: ibid., pp. 154–155. Among the many other examples that could be cited, Ela, Countess of Warwick, had to carve for Edward I on Christmas Day for her manor of Hook Norton; the tenant of Lympstone, Dartmoor, had to produce three arrows, feathered of peacocks and stuck into an oaten loaf worth half a farthing, when the King came to hunt on Dartmoor; and the men of Hame, Surrey, paid to the men of Kingston three clove gilli-flowers at the King's coronation.

THEMISTOCLES (514?–449? B.C.), Athenian general and statesman.

The real ruler of Greece

His son being master of his mother . . . he said, laughing: 'This child is greater than any man in Greece; for the Athenians command the Greeks, I command the Athenians, his mother commands me, and he commands his mother.'

SOURCE: Plutarch's *Lives*, trans. J. and W. Langhorne, 1821.

TIPPOO SULTAN (1753–1799), ruler of Mysore.

Tippoo Sultan's Throne

Tippoo Sultan, son of Hyder Ali, after years of battle and intrigue against the British, was killed in 1799. Seringapatam was captured and the Mohammedan kingdom of Mysore wiped out. Among the booty was the sultan's throne.

The sultan's throne, being too unwieldy to be carried, had been broken up; it was a howdah upon a tyger, covered with sheet gold; the ascent to it was by silver steps gilt, having silver nails, and all the other fastenings of the same metal. The canopy was alike superb, and decorated with a costly fringe of fine pearls, all round it; the eyes and teeth of the tyger were of glass. . . .

Other advices from Seringapatam, dated the 27th. of May, mention that, in breaking up the throne . . . the sheet of gold with which it was covered was found to weigh 40,000 pagodas*; the silver work about it, the supporters of the canopy, and the fringe of pearls which went round it, were valued at 10,000 pagodas more. Every inch of the howdah contained an Arabic sentence, chiefly from the Koran, superbly stamped, being raised and polished in the most beautiful manner. A gold figure of a bird, covered over with the most precious stones, was screwed to the roof of the canopy; its beak is a large emerald, its eyes carbuncles, the breast covered with diamonds, and the wings, which are expanded as if hovering, completely lined with diamonds; on the back are many large jewels, well and fancifully disposed; the tail, which resembles a peacock's, is also studded in the same manner—the whole so arranged as to imitate the plumage, and so closely set that the gold is scarcely visible.

SOURCE: *An Impartial History of the War* . . . (anon.), Manchester, 1811.

* Gold or silver coin of varying sizes and values; e.g., the Madras gold pagoda was worth about three and a half rupees.

TITHES. The payment of a tenth part, usually from stock and produce raised on the land. At first voluntary, and then made compulsory, the practice in Europe dates from at least the 5th Century. Theoretically, laymen could not claim tithes, but after the dissolution of the monasteries and the redistribution of land during the Reformation, many tithes came into non-ecclesiastical hands. In 1836, one quarter of the net annual value of tithes (about £4,000,000) was in the possession of laymen. In the 19th Century, legislation made it possible for money rents to be paid instead of produce.

i. '*The tenth child, too*'

Last haymaking season [the author was writing in the early 1930s] an old Wiltshire labourer, who was still hard at work at eighty-four, beguiled the dinner-hour by telling stories which he had heard when a boy from an old man with whom he had worked. This man had explained to him how at harvest-time it had been his duty to carry round green boughs and lay one on every tenth stook [of corn], which was thus set apart for the parson. The farmer first carried his own sheaves, then the rector's waggon would follow and pick up all his, carrying them off to the tithe barn. This old labourer had several stories about tithing, always at the expense of the parson.

A certain very mean and grasping rector called on one of his parishioners, a poor widow with a large family, having heard that her sow had farrowed and intending to claim the tenth pig of the litter. For some time she argued the point, but he was firm and was not to be put to shame. At last she said:

'Well zur, if you do have the tenth pig then you do take the tenth child too, for I've got eleven o' they!'

SOURCE: T. Hennell, *Change in the Farm*, C.U.P., 1943 (first edition 1934), pp. 118–119.

ii. '*The bees is yourn and the hive's mine*'

The same parson had an argument with another of his parishioners on the subject of bees, claiming the tenth swarm of the season. In the end the bee-keeper entered his study one day

with a skep in his hand, turned it upside down and shook out all
the bees, exclaiming:

'Here you be sir, the bees is yourn and the hive's mine!'

He made good his retreat before the rector could collect his
wits, let alone the bees.

SOURCE: T. Hennell, op. cit., p. 119.

TRAFALGAR, BATTLE OF (October 21, 1805); fought off Cape
Trafalgar, between the Combined Fleet of France and Spain
(33 ships) under Vice-Admiral Villeneuve and Admiral Gravina,
and the British Fleet (27 ships) under Vice-Admiral Nelson and
Vice-Admiral Collingwood.

i. *Sam's letter*

'Honoured Father,

This comes to tell you I am alive and hearty except three
fingers; but that's not much, it might have been my head. I
told brother Tom I should like to see a greadly battle, and I
have seen one, and we have peppered the Combined rarely; and
for the matter of that, they fought us pretty tightish for French
and Spanish. . . . But to tell you the truth of it, when the game
began, I wished myself at Warnborough with my plough again;
but when they had given us one duster, and I found myself snug
and tight, I . . . set to in good earnest, and thought no more
about being killed than if I were at Murrell Green Fair, and I
was presently as busy and as black as a collier. How my fingers
got knocked overboard I don't know, but off they are, and I
never missed them till I wanted them.'

SOURCE: A letter signed 'Sam', a seaman on the *Royal Sovereign*;
quoted in many books, including Edward Fraser, *The Sailors
Whom Nelson Led*, Methuen & Co., 1913, pp. 258–259.

ii. *Rotherham's cocked hat*

Captain Rotherham [of the *Royal Sovereign*] had on his gold-
laced cocked hat (rather a remarkable one) and gold epaulets.
He was asked why he exposed himself so much to the enemy's

sharp-shooters in that conspicuous dress. With the same spirit that animated the bosom of his heroic chief, he replied:

'I have always fought in a cocked hat, and I always will.'

SOURCE: Archibald Duncan, *The Life of the Right Honourable Horatio Lord Viscount Nelson of the White* . . ., 1806, p. 308.

iii. *The Immortal Signal*

His lordship came to me on the poop and at about a quarter to noon said:

'I wish to say to the Fleet, ENGLAND CONFIDES THAT EVERY MAN WILL DO HIS DUTY'; and he added:

'You must be quick, for I have one more to make, which is for Close Action.'

I replied:

'If your lordship will permit me to substitute *expects* for *confides*, the signal will soon be completed, because the word "expects" is in the vocabulary, and "confides" must be spelt.'

His lordship replied, in haste, and with seeming satisfaction:

'That will do, Pasco, make it immediately!'

When it had been answered by a few ships in the Van, he ordered me to make the signal for Close Action and to *keep it up*: accordingly, I hoisted No. 16 at the top-gallant mast-head, and there it remained until shot away.

SOURCE: account by Lieutenant Pasco, quoted Oliver Warner, *Trafalgar*, B. T. Batsford Ltd., 1959, p. 82.

iv. *A midshipman records the signal*

Monday, 21 October. At daylight saw the Enemies fleet in the S. E. quarter, consisting of 33 Sail of the line, 4 Frigates and 2 Sloops. Cleared ship for Action and made sail, studding sails fore and aft, standing for the Enemies fleet. At ½ past 11 the Victory made the Telegraph Signal, England expects every man to do his duty.

SOURCE: Midshipman John Eastman, log on board H.M.S. *Téméraire* (manuscript); author's collection.

v. *Nelson refuses to change ship*

Captain Blackwood, of the busy *Euryalus* frigate, had used every argument to get his beloved commander-in-chief away from the point of extreme danger at the head of the weather line. He reasoned, quite properly, that the fight could be directed in greater safety from one of the frigates. Nelson had declined the suggestion. Now Blackwood tried another line. Could not Nelson at least let another ship lead the weather line? The obvious choice was the *Téméraire*, straining at the leash and riding light, since she had been at sea for many weeks and had used up much of her heavy stores. Nelson, reluctantly, yielded to this importunity, and Blackwood's heart filled with relief as Eliab Harvey received the message to take the lead and endeavour to break the enemy's line about the 14th. ship from the van. Eagerly, the *Téméraire* crept ahead, her head level with Victory's stern windows, with the mizzen mast, with the quarter deck. . . . There was a sudden commotion on *Victory*, and Nelson was at the ship's side, his slightly nasal Norfolk voice bellowing sharply across the narrow space of water:

'Captain Harvey, I'll thank you to keep your station, which is astern of *Victory*!'

. . . *Téméraire* dropped slowly back again, and remained almost nudging the flagship as silently, obdurately, she crept on.

SOURCE: Grant Uden, *The Fighting Téméraire*, Basil Blackwell, 1961, pp. 31–32. A well-authenticated incident when the ships were moving into battle, and referred to by Captain Eliab Harvey himself, in a letter to his wife immediately after the action: 'but Lord Nelson had sent to me and given me leave to lead and break through the enemy's line about the 14th ship from the van; but afterwards made the signal referred to above'.

vi. *Commander Dillon stands on the table*

I happened to enter the . . . Club about 11 o'clock one day, when one of the Committee came in with the English newspapers containing the account of Nelson's victory over the Combined Fleets of France and Spain. Lord Yarmouth, Co. Abercromby and several other of my friends seized hold of me as if by one accord, and, lifting me on the table, desired me to read in a loud voice the official report of that splendid victory. The most perfect silence having been secured, I communicated the details of Collingwood's letter to the Admiralty.

When I had finished it, three hearty spontaneous cheers were given by at least one hundred members present, and those who were not near the table closed up and requested me to read the account a second time, which I readily agreed to do.

I was then requested by Lord Yarmouth to explain the manner in which the battle was fought, as they did not understand the nautical description of the disposal of the two Fleets. I did so by placing a parcel of books that were lying on the table in the position of the adverse Fleets.

SOURCE: Vice-Admiral Sir William Henry Dillon, *A Narrative of My Professional Adventures* (edit. Professor Michael Lewis), Navy Records Society, Vol. XCVII.

vii. *The 'bus driver and the 'General Memorandum'*

This famous memorandum, written by Nelson himself and spread over eight pages, giving the detailed instructions which led to the victory at Trafalgar, disappeared for a hundred years, and was eventually sent to Sotheby's sale-rooms in 1906 by a London 'bus driver. It fetched £3600, and eventually found its way to the British Museum. The newspapers could not find out who the seller was till a 'bus conductor told the Medical Officer of Health for Putney:

'It seems as our Will was driving one day, and a gent on the front seat, affable-like, asks Will if he had ever been to Merton Abbey, where Nelson used to live.

"Nelson," says Will, "I know something about him."

"What?" says the gent.

"Well, it is like this," says Will. "My father was an old sailor man, and, when he gave up the sea, was an admiral's man. The old admiral liked him, and gave him an old desk with some letters in it, and one I know bears on Trafalgar."

'Presently the gent says, "If you show me that and I like it I will give you £10 and a suit of clothes for it."

'Will said he would see. But he axed another gent the next day about it, and he said. "You send it to Sotheby's." And Will has got a nice little pile now.'

'Is he not going to retire?' asked the medical man.

'No fear, he means to drive his 'bus still.'

SOURCE: A. C. R. Carter, *Let Me Tell You*, Hutchinson & Co., 1940, p. 93. William Jackson, the 'bus driver who owned one of the most precious documents in British history, and one which affected the fate of nations, used to drive a Tilling's 'bus between Clapham Junction and Raynes Park.

The last finished letter—there was an unfinished one found in Nelson's cabin after Trafalgar—written by Nelson to Lady Hamilton, was less fortunate than the memorandum. Lady Llangattock paid £1030 for it in 1904 and, leaving soon after for her country house in Monmouth, told her butler to hide the letter in the tissue paper in one of her bonnets, in a hat-box. A maid in Monmouth, not having been warned about the hidden treasure, unpacked Lady Llangattock's luggage and set fire to all the packing in the garden.

TROY, WOODEN HORSE OF.

A 19th Century parallel

The story of the Trojan horse is more nearly within possibility than we should readily suppose. In 1848, during the rebellion of the North Italians against the Austrians, eight or nine young men, for whom the authorities were hunting, hid themselves inside Donatello's wooden horse in the Salone at Padua and lay there for five days, being fed through the trap door on the back of the horse with the connivance of the custode of the Salone. No doubt they were let out for a time at night. When pursuit had become less hot, their friends smuggled them away. One of those who had been shut up was still living in 1898 and, on the occasion of the jubilee festivities, was carried round the town in triumph.

SOURCE: *The Note-Books of Samuel Butler* (edit. H. Festing Jones), A. C. Fifield, 1912.

FF

TWENTIETH CENTURY—THE PASSING OF AN AGE

i. *The end of civilization in England*

Well, we have lived to see the end of civilization in England. I was once a gentleman myself. When I was an undergraduate at Cambridge, the Master of a College was a fabulous being, who lived in a Lodge of breath-taking beauty and incalculable antiquity, tended by housemaids, footmen, and a butler. There he consumed vintage port, wrote abstruse treatises if the spirit moved him, and lived the life of an impressive, cultivated gentleman. Such posts were among the few and noble rewards rightly offered to scholarship by the civilization which then existed.

When I last stayed in Cambridge, I lunched with two Masters of colleges. Both of them had to help with the washing-up after luncheon.

SOURCE: T. H. White, *The Age of Scandal*, Jonathan Cape, 1950, Ch. 1.

ii. *When there was no boot polish.*

Hand-made black boots and shoes sixty years ago were all of untreated, unpolished, dull calf known as blacking leather. To-day it's almost unheard of, it's far too much trouble; the leather is already polished when it leaves the factories.

When I was a boy there was no such thing as boot polish. You'd go to the grocer's, the general stores, a cobbler, or a shoe shop, and ask for a ha'penny cake of Day and Martin's blacking. It used to be done up in a piece of blue, grease-proof paper. You'd put it in a saucer, pour a little vinegar over it, mix it into a paste, brush it on the boots and work it or bone it into the leather, preferably with the bone from the front leg of a deer.

SOURCE: Ernest King, *The Green Baize Door*, William Kimber, 1963, p. 18.

iii. *Reaching the heights*

Prior to 1914 when men servants were ten a penny, no one would employ you unless you were five foot ten or six foot tall.

For the Royal Household you would never be considered. I was five feet seven-and-a-half-inches. A former Lord Mount Edgcumbe, perhaps the last peer to 'britch' his footmen in white breeches and stockings, had turned me down on account of my height. He didn't think I could control the footmen.

SOURCE: ibid., p. 119.

iv. *Polishing the plate*

That first morning in my job, fifty and more years ago, Edgar, the footman, said to me: 'Come along, my boy, now I'll show you how to clean plate. . .'.

I went with him to the strong-room on the ground floor and next door to the pantry, where the daily plate was kept. Cutlery, cruets, silver entrée dishes, serving dishes, salvers, sauce boats, soup tureens, tea pots and kettles, and some two dozen silver plates were taken out and laid on a strip of felt. . . .

'Now,' said Edgar, the footman, 'the rouge.'

'Rouge,' I repeated. 'That's what the ladies put on their faces sometimes, isn't it?'

'Not this isn't,' he said. 'Watch.'

It proved to be a very soft, red powder, mixed in a saucer with ammonia. I then did as he did, dipped my fingers in the paste and began to rub it over the silver.

'Harder,' he said.

'But it hurts,' I said. 'It'll blister.'

'That's right,' he said. 'It's better when they burst.'

. . . The blisters burst and you kept on despite the pain and you developed a pair of plate hands that never blistered again. . . . I tried to train Princess Elizabeth's—the Queen's—footmen at Windlesham Moor to this routine. They didn't like it and I could hardly blame them. It was 1948 not 1908.

SOURCE: ibid., p. 16.

v. *Morning and Evening prayers*

What, I suppose, to-day would not be found the length and breadth of the land, required our daily attendance—Morning and Evening Prayers. Sunday was rigidly observed. At Youlston Park—Major Hamlyn Chichester's house—footmen had to wear their livery to church, the coachman his top boots and cape, even the chauffeur . . . a mechanic who knew nothing of domestic service, had to put on his driving coat, his breeches, peaked cap and big leather gauntlet gloves. The women wore dark costumes and black bonnets. Those of them off for the afternoon and evening would carry hat-boxes and leave them with the lodge-keeper's wife; her little hall would be piled high with them. Then after Morning Service off would come the girls' bonnets, on went their ordinary hats and they would set out to walk or cycle four miles into town or to their homes. At ten that night they would have to be back in their black dresses, aprons and caps, the footmen in their livery for Evening Prayers [in the house].

SOURCE: Ernest King, op. cit., pp. 21.

TYLER'S REBELLION, WAT (June 13–14, 1381).

i. *John Ball, priest, poses a famous riddle, 1381*

The riddle served as the text to the sermon which Ball preached to Wat Tyler's rebels at Blackheath.

> *When Adam delved and Eve span,*
> *Who was then the gentleman?*

SOURCE: Ball was probably quoting from verses written earlier by Richard Rolle of Hampole (1290?–1349), hermit and religious writer. One of his poems included the lines:

> *When Adam dalfe and Eve spane . . .*
> *Whare was than the pride of man?*

Religious Pieces in Prose and Verse, vii, Early English Text Society, No. 26.

ii. *Wat Tyler's revenge*

Wat, when in servitude, had been beaten by his master, Richard Lyons, a great merchant of wines, and a sheriff of London. This chastisement, working on an evil disposition,

appears never to have been forgiven; and when this Radical
[Wat Tyler] assumed his short-lived dominion, he had his old
master beheaded, and his head carried before him on the point
of a spear.

SOURCE: based on Richard Grafton's *Chronicle*; Isaac D'Israeli,
  Curiosities of Literature, 1881 edition, Vol. III, p. 470 (footnote).

iii. *The end of Wat Tyler*

'Truly,' replied the mayor, who found himself supported by the
king, 'does it become such a stinking rascal as thou art to use
such speech in the presence of the king. . . ? I will not live a
day, if thou pay not for it.'

Upon this, he drew a kind of scymitar he wore, and struck
Tyler such a blow on the head and felled him to his horse's feet.
When he was down, he was surrounded on all sides, so that his
men could not see him; and one of the king's squires, called
John Standwich, immediately leaped from his horse, and,
drawing a handsome sword which he bore, thrust it into his
belly, and thus killed him.

His men, advancing, saw their leader dead, when they cried
out:

'They have killed our captain: let us march to them, and
slay the whole.'

On these words, they drew up in a sort of battle-array, each
man having his bent bow before him.

The king certainly hazarded much by this action, but it
turned out fortunate; for, when Tyler was on the ground, he
left his attendants, ordering not one to follow him. He rode up
to these rebellious fellows, who were advancing to revenge their
leader's death, and said to them:

'Gentlemen, what are you about? You shall have no other
captain but me: I am your king: remain peaceable.'

When the greater part of them heard these words, they were
quite ashamed, and those inclined to peace began to slip away.

SOURCE: Sir John Froissart, *Chronicles of England, France, Spain,
  and the Adjoining Countries*, Thomas Johnes's trans., 1808, Vol.
  V. pp. 360–361.

Accounts of the incident vary somewhat, and it may well be that Froissart, who presented a copy of his *Chronicles* to Richard II, exaggerated the King's contribution out of deference to his royal patron.

iv. *The King watches from his turret*

During this time the King, being in a turret of the great Tower of London, saw the manor of the Savoy and Clerkenwell and the houses of Simon Hosteler by Newgate and the place of John de Butterwyk in flames, and he called all the lords about him into a room and asked their advice as to what should be done in such a crisis. None of them could or would suggest anything; whereupon the young King said he would order the Mayor of the city to command the sheriffs and aldermen to have cried in their wards that everyone between the ages of fifteen and sixty, on pain of life and limb, should be on the morrow at Mile End and meet him there at seven of the bell.

SOURCE: *The Anonimalle Chronicle*, edit. V. H. Galbraith, University of Manchester Historical Series, XLV, 1927, pp. 141–143.

UNION JACK, THE.

The Complexities of the Union Flag

The national flag has been known by various names, including the Union Flag, the King's Colours, the Union Banner and— the one now commonly adopted—the Union Jack. The term occurs fairly early though its origin is not clear. It may well come from the defensive coat of mail or leather, known as a 'jaque' or 'jack', on which badges or coats-of-arms were worn. The first Union Flag, combining the crosses of St. George and St. Andrew (for Scotland) appeared in 1606, just after the accession of James I. The cross of St. Patrick (for Ireland) was incorporated in 1800. There have been many arguments from the three countries involved about the dimensions and disposition of the respective crosses.

Yielding to howls of indignation from the Scotch at the befouling of their saltire by placing a heathen Irish one over it they [i.e. the heralds] gave equality to both Celtic peoples by the production of an ingenious composition, the official blazon of which, in its unintelligible complexity, is a serious rival to the best efforts of an income-tax official in one of his more lucid moments.

SOURCE: Sir Christopher and Adrian Lynch-Robinson, *Intelligible Heraldry*, Macdonald, 1948, p. 101.

VERNON, EDWARD (1684–1757), Admiral. Nicknamed 'Old Grog' in the service.

The Navy receives its first 'grog'

Until the time of Admiral Vernon, the British sailors had their allowance of brandy and rum served out to them unmixed with water. This plan was found to be attended with inconvenience on some occasions; and the admiral, therefore, ordered in the fleet he commanded, the spirit should be mixed with water before it was given to the men.

This innovation, at first, gave great offence to the sailors, and rendered the commander very unpopular. The admiral, at that time, wore a grogram coat, and was nicknamed 'Old Grog'. This name was afterwards given to the mixed liquor he compelled them to take; and it has since universally obtained the name of 'grog'.

SOURCE: Thomas Byerley and Joseph Clinton Robertson, *The Percy Anecdotes*, 1820–1823.

VICTORIA (1819–1901), Queen of Great Britain and Empress of India.

i. *The young Queen forgets to be stately*

At twelve o'clock the same day, she presided at a Council with as much ease as if she had been doing it all her life; after which she received the archbishops and bishops to whom she said nothing, but showed an extreme dignity and gracefulness of manner. This ceremony finished and the duties of the day at an end, she retired with slow stateliness; but forgetful that the door through which she had passed had glass panels which allowed her departure to be seen, she had no sooner left the Chamber than she scampered light-heartedly away like a child released from school.

SOURCE: Lord Albemarle, describing the young Queen's first Privy Council meeting.

ii. *The Queen as a dancer*

I remembered that it had been said, two years before, that the Queen . . . could scarcely walk, although I knew, from good authority, that she had danced out a pair of shoes at one of her own balls, and when the company thought she had retired for the evening, she reappeared with a new pair.

SOURCE: Charles Robert Leslie, R.A., *Autobiographical Recollections*, 1860, Vol. I, p. 172. Leslie was commenting on the rumours that circulated in London about the Royal household, e.g., that the three-month-old Princess Royal (Victoria Adelaide, b. 1840) whom he had just painted, had been born blind.

iii. *Sarah Bernhardt fails to portray the home life of the Queen*

As Cleopatra, Sarah Bernhardt stabbed the slave who bore to her the tidings of Mark Antony's defeat at Actium; she stormed, raved, wrecked some of the scenery in her frenzy and finally, as the curtain fell, dropped in a shuddering, convulsive heap.

As the applause died, a middle-aged British matron was heard to say to her neighbour:

'How different, how very different from the home life of our own dear Queen.'

SOURCE: Irvin S. Cobb, *A Laugh a Day*.

iv. *The Queen at Table*

Queen Victoria ate quickly, and etiquette demanded that when she had finished a course, the plates of all the guests were whipped away, too, whether they were ready or not. On one occasion Lord Hartington was much enjoying a dish of mutton and green peas.

The Queen could dispose of peas with marvellous skill and dexterity, and had got into conversation with Lord Hartington, thus delaying his own operations. They got on very well together. Though Lord Hartington, like Peel and the Duke of Wellington, had neither small talk nor manners, yet he seemed to me less shy with the Queen than with his neighbours. This may be accounted for, perhaps, by their both being absolutely natural and their both being in no sort of doubt about their positions.

Well, anyhow, in the full current of their conversation the mutton was taken away from him. He stopped in the middle of a sentence in time to arrest the scarlet-clad marauder:

'Here, bring that back!'

SOURCE: Lord Ribblesdale, *Impressions and Memoirs*, 1927.

v. *The guest who smoked up the chimney*

It was also well known that there must be no smoking in any room she might enter. Nor were her secretaries allowed to smoke when handling papers she might have to touch ... and visitors to Windsor waited until the Queen went to bed and they could go along to the billiard-room, the only place where smoking was tolerated. Once Count Hatzfeldt, who could not be bothered to make the long journey to the billiard-room, yet 'could not live without a cigar', was reduced to lying on his bedroom floor and blowing the smoke up the chimney.

SOURCE: Sir Frederick Ponsonby, *Sidelights on Queen Victoria* and Baron von Eckardstein, *Ten Years at the Court of St. James's*; Christopher Hibbert, *The Court at Windsor*, Longmans, 1964, p. 224.

vi. *The knight who did not kneel to Queen Victoria*

In due course I [the Aga Khan] was summoned to an audience with Her Majesty at Windsor Castle. She received me with the utmost courtesy and affability.... The Queen, enfolded in voluminous black wraps and shawls, was seated on a big sofa. Was she tall or short, was she stout or not? I could not tell; her posture and her wraps made assessments of that kind quite impossible. I kissed the hand which she held out to me.... She had an odd accent, a mixture of Scotch and German.... She also had the

German conversational trick of interjecting 'so'—pronounced 'tzo'—frequently into her remarks.

I was knighted by the Queen at this meeting but she observed that, since I was a prince myself and the descendant of many kings, she would not ask me to kneel, or to receive the accolade and the touch of the sword upon my shoulder, but she would simply hand the order to me.

SOURCE: *The Memoirs of the Aga Khan*, Cassell & Co., 1954.

vii. *Anne and the Diamond Jubilee, 1897*

On this great occasion [the Diamond Jubilee, 1897], processions were formed on a more numerous and even larger scale than those of 1887, and the Queen attended a service held on the steps of St. Paul's Cathedral. In arranging for Her Majesty's carriage and attendant horsemen, it was found that the statue of Queen Anne not only seriously blocked the way, but obstructed the view of the vast crowd of people in front of the Cathedral. It was proposed that I should suggest to Her Majesty that Queen Anne's statue should be temporarily moved; but this proposal met with little favour, for the Queen replied:

'What a ridiculous idea! Move Queen Anne? Most certainly not! Why, it might some day be suggested that *my* statue should be moved, which I should much dislike!'

SOURCE: The Duke of Portland, *Men, Woman and Things*, Faber and Faber, 1937, pp. 119–120.

See also ALBERT, PRINCE.

VOLTAIRE, FRANCOIS MARIE AROUET DE (1694–1778), poet, philosopher and playwright.

A mistake on both sides

Voltaire having paid some high compliments to the celebrated Haller [Albrecht von Haller, Swiss physiologist], was told that Haller was not in the habit of speaking so favourably of him.

'Ah!' said Voltaire, with an air of philosophic indulgence, 'I dare say we are both of us very much mistaken.'

SOURCE: Francis, Lord Jeffrey in the *Edinburgh Review*; quoted R. Chambers, *A Book of Days*, 1864.

WAGERS. A fondness for making wagers has always been a frailty of the human race, their nature tending to vary with the interests and social conditions of the time. This is a selection from the 18th and early 19th Centuries.

i. On the 23rd of September, 1751, a man ran, driving a coach-wheel, from the Bishop's-head in the Old Bailey, to the eleventh mile stone at Barnet, and back again, in three hours and fifty-one minutes, having four hours to do it in, for a wager of £50.

SOURCE: *Gentleman's Magazine.*

ii. October 2, 1751, a man, for a wager of twenty guineas, walked from Shoreditch Church to the twenty mile stone, near Ware, and back again, in seven hours.

SOURCE: ibid.

iii. About the middle of this month, a most desperate pitched battle, for five guineas, was fought at Newbury, between a tinker, of the name of Symester, celebrated for agility, and a jolly miller, named Harrison, equally noted for strength, both inhabitants of that town. The contest lasted an hour and twenty minutes, in which there were sixty severe rounds. Although the man of metal was assisted the whole time of action by his wife's affectionate attention with a bottle of rum and water, which at intervals she sent to him by his daughter, a damsel about seven years of age, and had also fought fifty pitched battles, and shewed much science, yet the athletic limbs and long wind of the miller at last prevailed.

SOURCE: *Sporting Magazine*, 1807.

iv. On Thursday, the 16th of April, Abraham Wood, the noted Lancashire pedestrian, ran forty miles over Newmarket Heath in four hours and fifty-six minutes, being four minutes within the time allowed. The stake is said to have been 500 guineas, and considerable bets were depending . . . he ran the first eight miles in forty-eight minutes, and the first twenty miles in two hours and seven minutes.

He is a remarkably fine, tall, well-made man. He ran without shoes or stockings, and had only a pair of flannel drawers and a jacket upon him, and at no time appeared fatigued or over-come by this most extraordinary exertion. When he had com-pleted half the distance, he jumped into a post-chaise, and took the refreshment of a glass of wine and a crust of bread or of biscuit. There were numerous riders who found it difficult to keep their horse up with him—he is supposed to have sprung nearly two yards every step; the wind was so very high as to occasion him considerable inconvenience. His arms kept nearly equal motion with his legs; the spot chosen was the four mile course, which he ran round ten times.

Captain Barclay, the celebrated pedestrian, has matched himself against Wood for 300 guineas, who shall go the greatest distance in twenty-four hours, Wood giving him twenty miles.

SOURCE: *Sporting Magazine*, 1807.

v. The extraordinary match between Capt. Barclay and the celebrated Wood, of Lancashire, which has long agitated the sporting circles, was finally settled at Brighton during the late races, which, from its extraordinary nature, caused betting to an immense amount. The parties are to undergo the prodigious fatigue of going on foot four-and-twenty successive hours!—an exertion hitherto unknown in the annals of pedestrian feats; and it is supposed, they will complete the distance of 130 miles in that time. It takes place at Newmarket on the 12th of October next, for 500 guineas a side, and it is expected to attract nearly as much company as the celebrated horse-race between Hambletonian and Diamond in the year 1799.

Although Wood gives Capt. Barclay twenty miles, he is still the favourite, from his astonishing speed, having lately gone with apparent ease, forty miles in four hours and fifty-seven minutes.

Capt. Barclay, who is in training at East Dean, under Gully and Ward, alternately takes physic and bathes every other morning; and after the lavings of old Neptune his appetite is so keen that two or three pounds of beef steaks are necessarily provided for his breakfast. The Captain, it is said, can now run seven miles an hour, for twelve successive hours. Wood, therefore, to beat his antagonist, calculating on the distance he is to give him, must maintain his speed at the rate of nine miles an hour.

SOURCE: ibid.

vi. This match . . . attracted together the greatest concourse of persons ever seen at Newmarket in the memory of the oldest inhabitant. Carriages of every description were innumerable, from the barouche in four to a dicky cart, and the horsemen and pedestrians exceed all accurate estimation of numbers.

The place chosen for the performance of this extraordinary exertion, was a single measured mile, on the left-hand side of the first mile of the turnpike road, leading from Newmarket to London, towards the Ditch, which mile was roped in, and the competitors both ran on the same ground.

They started precisely at eight o'clock on Monday morning (October 18th); when, after going forty miles, Wood resigned the contest, which has created considerable surprise and murmuring among the *cognoscenti*. The following is an accurate account of the race.

WOOD		BARCLAY	
Hours	Miles	Hours	Miles
1	8	1	6
2	7	2	6
3	7	3	6
4	6½	4	6
5	6	5	6
6	5½	6	6

The above is the number of hours the pedestrians performed

out of twenty-four hours. Wood made play at starting, and, as it will be seen above, went eight miles in an hour. . . . He performed twenty miles in two hours and forty-one minutes, and, in coming in the twenty-two miles in three hours, he had got off four miles of the twenty he had given the Captain, and they both came in together. Wood at one period tried running without his shoes but got his feet so cut that he resumed them. Eventually he gave up, having gone forty miles in six hours and twenty minutes.

Captain Barclay pursued a steady course of six miles an hour, without varying a minute. He stopped and took some warm fowl after having gone eighteen miles, and he stopped again after having gone the other eighteen miles; and it was whilst he was taking other refreshments that Wood resigned the contest. . . .

Captain Barclay is the lineal descendant of the celebrated author of 'The Apology for the Quakers.' Robert Barclay (1648–1690).

SOURCE: *Sporting Magazine,* 1807.

vii. The grand match of Cricket for 1,000 guineas a side, between two select elevens, made by Lord F. Beauclerc and T. Mellish, Esq. was decided in favour of the latter, on Wednesday, in Lord's Ground, by one innings and 37 runs.

SOURCE: ibid.

viii. The latter end of last month a match, twenty hops for 10 guineas, took place at Loughborough, Leicestershire, between James Shipley, of Nottingham, and a person named Moore, of Leicester; it was very closely contested. . . . The match, however, was won by Shipley. On measuring the distance, it appeared Shipley had hopped 75 yards 9 or 10 inches, and Moore something more than 75 yards.

SOURCE: ibid.

ix. Captain Bennet, of the Loyal Ongar Hundred Volunteers, engaged to trundle a hoop from Whitechapel Church to Ongar, in Essex, in three hours and a half, a distance of twenty-two miles for a wager of one hundred guineas.

He started on Saturday morning, Nov. 21, precisely at six o'clock, with the wind very much in his favour, and the odds two to one against him. Notwithstanding the early hour, the singularity of the match brought together a numerous assemblage. The hoop used by Captain B. on the occasion was heavier than those trundled by boys in general, and was selected by him conformably to the terms of the wager. The first ten miles Captain B. performed in one hour and twenty minutes, which changed the odds considerably in his favour. We did not hear in what time he performed the whole of the distance; but there is no doubt that he accomplished it considerably within the given time, as the Ongar coachman met him only five miles and a half from Ongar, when he had a full hour in hand.

SOURCE: ibid.

x. The sack race, between the coachman, who is 77 years of age, and the countryman, for twenty guineas a side, took place at half past ten o'clock, on Friday morning, the 11th inst. in Hyde Park. The ground was measured, 110 yards from Grosvenor-gate; and a numerous assemblage of spectators arranged themselves in a double line on either side. As soon as the two men had been sacked up to their necks, the odds were seven to four on the coachman at starting, but when they had proceeded ten yards, the coachman fell down, when the odds changed in favour of the countryman, who ran the 110 yards in forty-six seconds and a half. Several ladies who were passing in their carriages, were much diverted with the sport.

SOURCE: ibid.

xi. Captain George Dundas [at the Cape of Good Hope, c. 1800] was known to be passionately fond of tripe. Some of his friends wagered that he 'and one other' could consume sixteen pounds of it at one sitting. A time and place were appointed, and the officers gathered to watch as Dundas sat down at a table and was presently confronted with the monstrous pile of tripe prepared, we are told, in every sort of shape.

He attacked it vigorously, amidst encouraging cheers, but, after two or three pounds had disappeared, laid down his knife and fork. Those who had wagered the thing could not be done were jubilant and prepared to claim their money. But at that moment there was a strange grunting and shuffling outside, and one of Dundas's friends appeared leading a large bear. On being taken to the table, the bear finished up the tripe in very quick time and Dundas and his supporters triumphantly claimed the victory, on the ground that he 'and one other', as specified, had demolished the whole amount.

There were loud protests and a small committee of office solemnly considered the representations of both parties. At length they announced, amidst applause, that the terms of the wager had been properly fulfilled.

SOURCE: Grant Uden *Collector's Casebook*, Constable Young Books, 1963.

xii. [In 1812, at the York Assizes, the Rev. B. Gilbert brought an action against Sir Mark Sykes for failure to fulfil the terms of a wager.]

At a dinner party in his own house [Sir Mark Sykes] in the course of a conversation on the hazard to which the life of Bonaparte was exposed, had offered, on receiving a hundred guineas, to pay a guinea a day as long as Napoleon should remain alive. Mr. Gilbert suddenly closed with the proposal, sent the hundred guineas to the baronet, and the latter continued to pay the clergyman a guinea a day for nearly three years. At last he declined to pay any longer, and an action was brought to enforce the fulfilment of the obligation. . . .

It was contended by the defendant's counsel that he had been surprised into the bet by the clergyman's hasty acceptance of it, and also that the transaction was an illegal one, seeing that Mr. Gilbert, having a beneficial interest in the life of Bonaparte, might, in the event of invasion, be tempted to use all means for the preservation of the life of an enemy of his country.

The jury returned a verdict for the defendant; but, on the case being brought before the Court of King's Bench . . . in his lordship's opinion the fact of a contract was clearly established, and unless anything of an immoral or impolitic tendency could be proved, the agreement must be supported.

On the ground last mentioned, the rule was ultimately discharged and a new trial refused; the judges finding that such a wager was illegal, from its tendency to produce public mischief, as, on the one hand, an undue interest was created in the preservation of the life of a public enemy, and, on the other hand, a temptation might be induced to plot the assassination of Bonaparte.

SOURCE: *The Book of Days* (edit. R. Chambers), 1864, Vol. II p. 635.

WALCHEREN EXPEDITION, THE (1809). When the war between France and Austria was renewed, Britain planned to assist the latter by creating a diversion and causing France to withdraw some of her forces from the Danube valley. Objectives were the destruction of the French fleet in the Scheldt, the capture of the great arsenal and the taking of Antwerp. The expedition was led by John Pitt, second Earl of Chatham (brother of William Pitt) and Admiral Sir Richard Strachan (pronounced 'Strawn'). It was a dismal failure.

Great Chatham and Sir Richard Strachan

> *Great Chatham with his sabre drawn*
> *Stood waiting for Sir Richard Strachan;*
> *Sir Richard, longing to beat 'em,*
> *Stood waiting for the Earl of Chatham.*

Captain Gronow, in his *Reminiscences and Recollections*, 1862–1866, gives a slightly different version:

> *Sir Richard, longing to at 'em,*
> *Was waiting for the Earl of Chatham,*
> *The Earl of Chatham, all forlorn,*
> *Was waiting for Sir Richard Strachan.*

SOURCE: contemporary, but anonymous.

WALPOLE, SIR ROBERT, first **EARL OF ORFORD** (1676–1745). A corrupt politician, but a man of immense ability and grasp of affairs who is usually called Britain's first Prime Minister, though the title was not used. He worked for peace when the country most needed it and, in the words of Burke, 'preserved the crown to this royal family, and with it their laws and liberty to this country'.

i. *They will soon wring their hands*

They now ring the bells, but they will soon wring their hands.

(Sometimes rendered, more dramatically but less accurately, as

'Ay, you can ring your bells now. You'll be wringing your hands soon.')

SOURCE: a remark made on the Declaration of War with Spain in 1739; William Coxe, *Memoirs of Sir Robert Walpole*, 1798, Vol. i, p. 618.

ii. *Bolingbroke chokes at Walpole's table*

Viscount Bolingbroke (1678–1751) occupied a number of high offices but became deeply involved with the Jacobites, was dismissed, impeached and his name erased from the roll of peers. He fled into exile, worked for the return of the Stuarts, but, through the good offices of Sir Robert Walpole, was allowed to return to England in 1723.

Bolingbroke, at his return, could not avoid waiting on Sir Robert to thank him, and was invited to dine with him at Chelsea; but whether tortured at witnessing Walpole's serene frankness and felicity, or suffocated with indignation and confusion at being forced to be obliged to one whom he hated and envied, the first morsel he put into his mouth was near choking him, and he was reduced to rise from the table and leave the room for some minutes. I never heard of their meeting more.

SOURCE: Horace Walpole, *Reminiscences*.

WALSINGHAM, SIR FRANCIS (1530?–1590), statesman; Secretary of State under Elizabeth and maintained a secret service, largely at his own expense; father-in-law of Sir Philip Sidney.

Walsingham's 'lions'

I question not but my country customers will be surprised to hear me complain that this town is, of late years, very much infested with lions; and will, perhaps, look upon it as a strange piece of news, when I assure them, that there are many of these beasts of prey who walk our streets in broad day-light, beating about from coffee-house to coffee-house, and seeking whom they may devour.

To unriddle this paradox, I must acquaint my rural reader, that we polite men of the town give the name of a lion to any one that is a great man's spy. . . .

It has cost me a great deal of time to discover the reason of this appellation, but after many disquisitions and conjectures on so obscure a subject, I find that there are two accounts of it more satisfactory than the rest. In the republic of Venice, which has been always the mother of politics, there are, near the Doge's palace, several large figures of lions, curiously wrought in marble, with mouths gaping in a most enormous manner. Those who have a mind to give the state any private intelligence of what passes in the city, put their hands into the mouth of one of these lions, and convey into it a paper of such private informations as any way regard the interest or safety of the commonwealth. By this means all the secrets of state come out of the lion's mouth. The informer is concealed, it is the lion that tells everything. In short, there is not a mismanagement in office, or a murmur in conversation, which the lion does not acquaint the government with. For this reason, say the learned, a spy is very properly distinguished by the name of lion.

I must confess, this etymology is plausible enough, and I did for some time, acquiesce in it, till, about a year or two ago, I met with a little manuscript, which sets this whole matter in a clear light. In the reign of Queen Elizabeth, says my author, the renowned Walsingham had many spies in his service, from whom the government received great advantage. The most eminent among them was the statesman's barber, whose surname was Lion. This fellow had an admirable knack of fishing out the secrets of his customers, as they were under his hands. He would rub and lather a man's head, until he had got everything out of it that was in it. He had a certain snap in his fingers, and volubility in his tongue, that would engage a man to talk with him, whether he would or no. By this means, he became an inexhaustible fund of private intelligence, and so signalized himself in the capacity of a spy, that from his time a master-spy goes under the name of a lion.

SOURCE: Joseph Addison, *The Guardian*, No. 71, June 2, 1713.

WASHINGTON, GEORGE (1732–1799), general and first President of the United States of America.

i. *The cherry tree*

The following anecdote is ... too valuable to be lost, and too true to be doubted; for it was communicated to me by the same excellent lady. ...

'When George,' said she, 'was about six years old, he was made a wealthy master of a hatchet! of which, like most little boys, he was immoderately fond, and was constantly going about chopping everything that came in his way. One day, in the garden, where he often amused himself hacking his mother's pea-sticks, he unluckily tried the edge of his hatchet on the body of a beautiful young English cherry-tree, which he barked so terribly, that I don't believe the tree ever got the better of it. The next morning the old gentleman, finding out what had befallen his tree, which, by the by, was a great favourite, came into the house; and with much warmth asked for the mischievous author, declaring at the same time, that he would not have taken five guineas for his tree. Nobody could tell him anything about it. Presently George and his hatchet made their appearance.

'George,' said his father, 'do you know who killed that beautiful little cherry tree yonder in the garden?'

This was a tough question; and George staggered under it for a moment; but quickly recovered himself: and looking at his father, with the sweet face of youth brightened with the inexpressible charm of all-conquering truth, he bravely cried out:

'I can't tell a lie, Pa; you know I can't tell a lie. I did cut it with my hatchet.'

'Run to my arms, you dearest boy,' cried his father in transports, 'run to my arms. Glad am I, George, that you killed my tree; for you have paid me for it a thousand fold. Such an act of heroism in my son is worth more than a thousand trees, though blossomed with silver, and their fruits of purest gold.'

SOURCE: M. L. Weems, *Life of George Washington*, 1860 edition, p. 12.

ii. *George settles all disputes*

A very aged gentleman, formerly a school mate of his, has often assured me . . . that nothing was more common, when the boys were in high dispute about a question of fact, than for some little shaver among the mimic heroes, to call out:

'Well boys! George Washington was there; George Washington was there. He knows all about it: and if he don't say it was so, then we will give it up.'

'Done,' said the adverse party. Then away they would trot to hunt for George. Soon as his verdict was heard, the party favoured would begin to crow, and then all hands would return to play again.

SOURCE: M. L. Weems, *Life of George Washington*, 1860 edition, p. 23.

iii. *The dollar across the Potomac*

Mr. Evarts [William Maxwell Evarts, formerly Secretary of State], showed an English friend the place where Washington was said to have thrown a dollar across the Potomac.* The

* An American librarian has written to the editor: 'None of the reputable biographies have any reference to the silver dollar story, and having seen the Potomac at Mount Vernon, I am prepared to assert that it is apocryphal—the river is about half a mile wide at that point.'

English friend expressed surprise; 'but,' said Mr. Evarts, 'you must remember that a dollar went further in those days'.

A Senator met Mr. Evarts next day, and said he had been amused by his jest.

'But,' said Mr. Evarts, 'I met a mere journalist just afterwards who said, "Oh, Mr. Evarts, you should have said that it was a small matter to throw a dollar across the Potomac for a man who had chucked a sovereign across the Atlantic".'

SOURCE: George W. E. Russell, *Collections and Recollections*, Smith, Elder & Co., 1903, Ch. XIX.

iv. *Washington's two horses*

General Washington had two favourite horses; one a large elegant parade horse of a chestnut colour, high-spirited, and of a gallant carriage; this horse had belonged to the British army: the other was smaller, and his colour sorrel. This he used always to ride in time of action; so that whenever the general mounted him, the word ran through the ranks:

'We have business on hand.'

SOURCE: Thomas Byerley and Joseph Clinton Robertson, *The Percy Anecdotes*, 1820–1823.

v. *Washington's lucky escape*

Major Ferguson, who commanded a rifle corps . . . during some skirmishing a day or two previous to the battle of Brandywine, was the hero of a very singular accident, which he thus relates in a letter to a friend. . . .

'We had not lain long when a rebel officer, remarkable by a hussar dress, pressed towards our army, within a hundred yards of my right flank, not perceiving us. He was followed by another, dressed in dark green and blue, mounted on a bay horse, with a remarkable high cocked hat. I ordered three good shots to steal near to them; but, the idea disgusting me, I recalled the order.

The hussar, in returning, made a circuit, but the other passed within a hundred yards of us, upon which I advanced from the woods towards him. Upon my calling, he stopped; but, after looking at me, proceeded. I again drew his attention, and made signs to him to stop, levelling my piece at him; but he slowly cantered away. As I was within that distance at which, in the quickest firing, I could have lodged half a dozen balls in or about him, before he was out of my reach, I had only to determine; but it was not pleasant to fire at the back of an unoffending individual, who was acquitting himself very coolly of his duty; so I let him alone.

The day after, I had been telling this story to some wounded soldiers who lay in the same room with me, when one of the surgeons, who had been dressing the wounded rebel officers, came in, and told us that General Washington was all the morning with the light troops, and only attended by a French officer in a hussar dress, he himself dressed and mounted in every point as above described.

I was not sorry that I did not know at the time who it was.'

SOURCE: Thomas Byerley and Joseph Clinton Robertson, *The Percy Anecdotes*, 1820–1823.

vi. *'Away with it!' quoth Washington*

Reminiscence of an earlier Washington.

When the civil war broke out, the Washingtons took the side of the King. . . .

You all know the name of Sir Henry Washington, who led the storming party at Bristol, and defended Worcester. We have it, on the contemporary authority of Lloyd, that this Colonel Washington was so well known for his bravery, that it became a proverb in the army when a difficulty arose:

'"Away with it!" quoth Washington.'

SOURCE: Rev. J. N. Simpkinson, speech to a meeting of American citizens in London, 1862.

WATERLOO, BATTLE OF (June 18, 1815): one of the great decisive battles of history, which practically annihilated the French army and finally broke the power of Napoleon in Europe. Inevitably, many stories were circulated about the battle, many of them dismissed by Wellington himself as 'novels . . . which curious travellers have picked up from peasants, soldiers, individual officers, etc., and have published to the world as truth'. An example is the famous 'Up Guards and at 'em!' Wellington said his words were probably 'Stand up, Guards!' and that he followed with the order to charge. Captain Gronow said his precise words were 'Guards get up and charge'.

Pressed for stories about the battle, the Duke would declare that they were all already in print. But one evening he is said to have relented and told one which had not so far appeared.

i. *The button manufacturer on the battle-field*

In the middle of the battle he saw a man in plain clothes, riding about on a cob in the thickest fire. During a temporary lull, the Duke beckoned him and he rode over. He asked who he was, and what business he had there. He replied, he was an Englishman accidentally at Brussels, that he had never seen a fight, and wanted to see one. The Duke told him he was in instant danger of his life; he said, 'Not more than your Grace,' and they parted. But every now and then the Duke saw the cob-man riding about in the smoke, and at last, having nobody to send to a regiment, he again beckoned to this little fellow, and told him to go up to that regiment, and order them to charge—giving him some mark of authority the colonel would recognise. Away he galloped, and in a few minutes the Duke saw his order obeyed. The Duke asked him for his card and found, in the evening, when the card fell out of his sash, that he lived in Birmingham and was a button manufacturer! When at Birmingham, the Duke inquired of the firm, and found he was their traveller, then in Ireland. When he returned, at the Duke's request he called on him in London. His Grace was happy to see him, and said he had a vacancy in the Mint. . . . The little cob-man said it would be exactly the thing, and the Duke installed him.

SOURCE: John Timbs, *A Century of Anecdote* (Chandos Classics), Frederick Warne & Co., pp. 267–268.

ii. *A lady has her fill of French Generals*

In the confusion of retreat, following Waterloo, a French officer, Colonel Lemonnier Delafosse, was escorting his General, Foy, who had been wounded in the shoulder by a musket-ball.

On entering Beaumont we chose a house of superior appearance, and demanded of the mistress of it refreshments for the General.

'Alas!' said the lady, 'this is the tenth General who has been to this house since this morning. I have nothing left. Search if you please, and see.'

SOURCE: Colonel Lemonnier Delafosse, *Memoirs*.

iii. *Wellington sums up*

'My heart is broken by the terrible loss I have sustained in my old friends and companions, and my poor soldiers. Believe me, nothing except a battle lost can be half so melancholy as a battle won.'

SOURCE: letter written almost immediately after his return from the battle-field; quoted Sir Edward Creasy, *The Fifteen Decisive Battles of the World* (32nd edition, 1886), p. 607.

iv. *The apple-trees after Waterloo*

Early on the morning after the battle of Waterloo, I visited Hougoumont, in order to witness with my own eyes the traces of one of the most hotly-contested spots of the field of battle. . . . The apple trees presented a singular appearance; shattered branches were seen hanging about their mother trunks in such profusion that one might almost suppose the stiff-growing and stunted tree had been converted into the willow: every tree was riddled and smashed in a manner which told that the showers of shot had been incessant.

SOURCE: *The Reminiscences and Recollections of Captain Gronow*, 1892; abridged edition by John Raymond, Bodley Head, 1964, p. 72.

v. *Two opinions of the British cavalry:*

(a) *The Duke of Wellington.*

He had just been informed that the Prince Regent had made himself Captain-General of the Life Guards and Blues [the Horse Guards] because of their brilliant conduct at Waterloo.

'Ah! his Royal Highness is our sovereign, and can do what he pleases but this I will say, the cavalry of other European armies have won victories for their generals, but mine have invariably got me into scrapes. It is true that they have aways fought . . . gallantly and bravely, and have generally got themselves out of their difficulties by sheer pluck.'

(b) *Marshal Excelmann.* 'Your horses are the finest in the world, and your men ride better than any continental soldiers. . . . The great deficiency is in your officers, who have nothing to recommend them but their dash and sitting well in their saddles. . . . The British cavalry officer seems to be impressed with the conviction that he can dash and ride over everything; as if the art of war were precisely the same as that of fox-hunting.'

SOURCE: *The Reminiscences and Recollections of Captain Gronow,* 1892; abridged edition by John Raymond, Bodley Head, 1964.

vi. *Colonel Ponsonby hears of the French retreat in unusual circumstances*

Colonel Ponsonby, of the 12th Light Dragoons, was severely wounded and had a miraculous escape after being disabled in both arms, dragged along by his horse, receiving a further sabre cut which knocked him to the ground, taking a lance-thrust through the back, being robbed by a plundering soldier and ridden over by two squadrons of Prussian cavalry. At one stage a young French rifleman knelt down and fired over his body.

He knelt down and fired over me, loading and firing many times, and conversing with me all the while. . . . At last he ran off, exclaiming:

'You will not be sorry to hear that we are going to retreat. Good day, my friend.'

SOURCE: Ponsonby's own account, quoted Sir Edward Creasy, *The Fifteen Decisive Battles of the World* (32nd edition, 1886), p. 612.

vii. *The soldier who forgot the name of Waterloo*

About the time I joined the Coldstream in 1878, Colonel Fremantle was in the chair at a dinner of . . . the Regimental dining club in London. He proposed the health of the oldest Coldstreamer in the room, and a tall, slim, aristocratic-looking old gentleman, with white hair and a white moustache, rose to reply. He was then Lord Stradbroke. . . . Lord Stradbroke thanked everybody for so kindly drinking his health, and went on to say that he was very proud of having served in the Cold-stream Guards as a young man.

'I am also,' he continued, 'very proud to have been present with the Regiment at the famous battle of Quatre Bras [June 16, 1815]; but unfortunately I was wounded, and so was unable to be present at the much more famous battle which was fought on the following day—I mean the battle at which the great Duke of Wellington commanded the Allied Army, when it defeated the French under the Emperor Napoleon; but,' said Lord Stradbroke, 'you must excuse a temporary lapse of memory by an old man, for I cannot remember its name.'

Some-one said:

'Waterloo.'

'Waterloo—of course, Waterloo! How foolish of me not to remember.'

SOURCE: The Duke of Portland, *Men, Women and Things*, Faber and Faber, 1937, pp. 27–28. Waterloo was, in fact, fought two days after Quatre Bras.

WATSON, CHARLES (1714–1757), Admiral. Commander-in-chief in the East Indies, 1754–1757, working with Clive in the recovery of Calcutta, etc.; an officer of high principle and devotion to duty.

i. *The man who turned his back on the treasure-fleet*

. . . the man who [as captain of the *Dragon* in 1743], when detached by Admiral Matthews from off Toulon, as a special favour to a smart officer, to cruise off Cadiz just when the treasure galleons from the Spanish Main were expected to arrive, with additional instructions to go on afterwards to Lisbon and carry the merchants' treasure thence to England— the most lucrative employment a naval man could possibly look for—deliberately, on hearing at Gibraltar that a battle was likely to take place off Toulon, turned his back on a sum of prize-money that would have made him wealthy for life, saying 'He thought his ship would be wanted with the fleet.'

SOURCE: Edward Fraser, *Champions of the Fleet*, John Lane, 1908, p. 84.

ii. *The sailor who captured a fort*

On their way up the Hooghly to the relief of Calcutta, Watson's ships were held up by the fort at Baj-Baj, called by the English Budge-Budge, which held out despite a bombardment from the ships and a land assault by Clive's sepoys. A storming party was planned for the next morning, but that evening a sailor named Strahan, enlivened by his ration of grog, wandered up to the walls of the fort and climbed them where one of the guns had made a breach. He took on a party of the enemy with cutlass and pistol, gave three cheers and cried 'The place is mine!' Hearing the shouting, two or three other sailors turned up to give support, and the whole garrison fled, leaving eighteen guns behind.

. . . Strahan was brought before the Admiral by the master-at-arms to explain matters. Admiral Watson, we are told, thought it necessary to show himself displeased with a measure in which the want of discipline so notoriously appeared. He therefore angrily accosted this brave fellow with:

'Strahan, what is this you have been doing?'

The untutored hero, after having made his bow, scratched his head and, with one hand twirling his hat, replied:

'Why, to be sure, sir, it was I who took the fort, but I hope there was no harm in it.'

The Admiral with difficulty suppressed a smile excited by the simplicity of the answer, and the language and the manner which he used in recounting the several particulars of his mad exploit. Admiral Watson then expatiated on the fatal consequences that might have attended his irregular conduct, and with a severe rebuke dismissed him, but not without dropping some hints that at a proper opportunity he would certainly be punished for his temerity. Strahan, amazed to find himself blamed for an action that he thought deserved praise and for which he expected to have received applause, in passing from the Admiral's cabin muttered:

'If I'm flogged for this here action, I'll never take another fort by myself as long as I live!'

SOURCE: ibid., p. 94. Fraser uses the account given by Dr. Ives, surgeon on the *Kent*. Ives says that Admiral Watson, so that he could have a good excuse for pardoning Strahan, prompted several officers to come to him to plead for clemency in the matter.

WATT, JAMES (1736–1819), engineer.

The little extra

His father was a builder and contractor—also a merchant—a man of superior sagacity, if not ability, prudent and benevolent. . . . When boatswains of ships came to the father's shop for stores, he was in the habit of throwing in an extra quantity of sail-needles and twine, with the remark:

'See, take that too; I once lost a ship for want of such articles on board.'

SOURCE: *A Book of Days*, 1864; Williamson's *Memorials of James Watt*, 1856.

WEATHER, THE ENGLISH. The weather is traditionally the Englishman's staple topic of conversation. One suspects that it has always been so. Here is a small sample of the things they talked about over a period of a thousand years, from A.D. 800–1800.

i. *800*. On the ninth day before the calends of January, the day before the Nativity of our Lord, a mighty wind, blowing either from the south or south-west, by its indescribable force destroyed many cities, houses, and towns in various places; innumerable trees were also torn up from the roots. In the same year an inundation took place, the sea flowing beyond its ordinary limits. An extensive murrain also prevailed among the cattle in various places.

Roger de Hovenden.

On Christmas Even chanced a marvellous tempest of wind,
which overthrew whole cities and towns and trees in great
numbers, besides other harm by death of cattle, etc.

Holinshed.

ii. *874*. All the lochs, rivers, and all manner of other waters were
frozen in Scotland, from the beginning of November till the
latter end of April; and when the frost brake and the snows
melted there was such a flood flowing over all the plains as the
like had not been seen. Moreover, there was a mighty comet
seen, with fiery rays issuing forth from the same, during the
month of April, to the great horror of all who beheld it.

Holinshed.

iii. *970*. About this time, for the space of six months together,
there appeared no sun by day nor moon by night in any part
of the realm; but still was the sky covered with continual
clouds, and sometimes such outrageous winds arose, with
lightnings and tempests, that the people were in fear of present
destruction.

Holinshed.

iv. *1000*. The moon appeared of a bloody colour, to the great
terror of them that beheld it. In the summer next following,
corn failed and cattle died so generally that if there had not
been more plenty of fish got than was accustomed to be, the
people had been famished in many places. It rained stones.

Holinshed.

v. *1009*. Such wind came as no man before remembered, and
beat all the ships to pieces and cast them upon the land.

Anglo-Saxon Chronicle.

vi. *1040*. On Christmas day there was an earthquake. In the
summer the sea rose higher and flowed further into the land
than ever it had been seen at any other time. On Midsummer
day there was such a vehement frost that the corn and other

fruits of the earth were blasted and killed, so that thereupon followed a great dearth in all the country.

Holinshed.

vii. *1047*. There fell a marvellous great snow, covering the ground from the beginning of January until the seventeenth day of March. Besides this, there happened the same year such tempests and lightnings, that the corn upon the earth was burnt up and blasted, by reason whereof there followed a great dearth in England, and also death of men and cattle.

Holinshed.

viii. *1091*. A marvellous sore tempest fell in sundry parts of England, especially in the town of Winchcomb, where (by force of thunder and lightning) a part of the steeple of the church was thrown down. 17th of the same month much harm was done in London with an outrageous wind, the violence whereof overturned and rent in pieces about five hundred houses. Moreover, at Salisbury much hurt was done with the like wind and thunder, for the top of the steeple and many buildings besides were sore shaken and cast down.

Holinshed.

ix. *1114*. October 15. The sea so decreased and shrank from the old accustomed marks and coasts of the land here in this realm that a man might have passed on foot over the sands and washes for the space of a whole day together. The river Thames was so low for the space of a day and a night that horses, men, and children, passed over betwixt London Bridge and the Tower, and also under the Bridge, the water not reaching above their knees. Moreover, in the month of December the air appeared red as though it had burned. In like manner the winter was very extreme cold with frosts, by reason whereof at the thawing and breaking of the ice the most part of all the bridges in England were broken and borne down.

Holinshed.

x. *1135.* August 2. The day darkened over all lands, and the sun became as it were a three-night-old moon, and the stars about it, at mid-day. Men were greatly wonder-stricken and affrighted, and said that a great thing should come thereafter. So it did, for that year the king died.

Anglo-Saxon Chronicle. (*Note:* Henry I died in 1135.)

A mighty great tempest of thunder horrible to hear, and lightning dreadful to behold, the day Stephen arrived in England. Now because this happened in winter time it seemed against nature, and therefore was the more noted as a fore-showing of some trouble.

Holinshed.

xi. *1200.* About the month of December there were seen in the province of York five moons, one in the east, the second in the west, the third in the north, the fourth in the south, and the fifth as it were set in the midst of the others, having many stars about it, and went five or six times encompassing the other, as it were the space of one hour, and shortly after vanished away.

The winter after was extremely cold, and in the spring came a great glutting and continual rain, causing the rivers to rise with higher floods than they had been accustomed.

Holinshed.

xii. *1236.* Great tempests of rain which filled the earth full of water and caused monstrous floods, for this rain continued all the months of January, February, and part of March, and for eight days it rained in manner without ceasing; and upon the tenth of February, immediately after the change of the moon, the Thames rose with such a high tide that boats might have been rowed up and down in Westminster Hall.

Holinshed.

xiii. *1252.* Then began a sore drought, continuing a long time, the which, together with morning frosts and northerly winds, destroyed the fruits and other growing things, which were

blasted in such wise that, although at first it was a very forward
year and great plenty towards of corn and fruit, yet, by the
means aforesaid, the same was greatly hindered, and specially
in the summer season, when the sun's heat increased and the
drought still continued. The residue of such fruits as then remained withered away, so that scarce a tenth part was left. . . .
The grass was so burned up in pastures and meadows that if a
man took up some of it in his hands and rubbed the same never
so little, it straight fell to powder, and cattle were ready to
starve for lack of meat, and because of the exceeding hot nights
there was such abundance of fleas, flies, and gnats, that people
were vexed and brought in case to be weary of their lives. And
herewith chanced many diseases, as sweats, agues, and other. . . .
After so great a drought, which had continued by all the space
of the months of April, May, June, and July, there followed
good plenty of rain, the earth began to yield her increase most
plenteously, and so the cattle, which before were hunger
starved, fed now so greedily of this new grass that they died.
Apple trees and pear trees began again to blossom after the
time of yielding ripe fruit.

Holinshed.

xiv. *1309*. A sudden thaw after a great frost caused the waters
so fast to rise that Salisbury Cathedral was flooded, and the
king was enforced to leave the church as the executor did his
mass, lest they should all have been drowned, and this rage
endured for the space of two days, whereupon no mass could
be said in the said minster.

Holinshed. (*Note:* The king was Edward II.)

xv. *1347*. Having been fifteen months abroad, the King at last
landed at Sandwich on October 12 after a stormy crossing.

'Holy Mary,' he cried, 'why is it that when I go abroad the
weather ever smiles on me and frowns when I return?'

Philip Lindsay, *Kings of Merry England*.

xvi. *1348*. (The year of the Black Death.) From Midsummer to
Christmas, for the more part it continually rained, so that there

was not one day and night dry together; by reason whereof great floods ensued, as great sickness and other, neither sea nor land yielding such plenty of things as before. Whereupon victuals and corn became scant and hard to come by. About August the death began in divers places of England, continuing so for the space of twelve months following.

Holinshed.

xvii. *1395*. A certain thing appeared in the likeness of fire in many parts of England, now of one fashion, now of another, as it were every night, but yet in divers places all November and December. This fiery apparition oftentimes when anybody went alone it would go with him, and would stand still when he stood still. To some it appeared in the likeness of a wheel burning; to other some round in the likeness of a barrel, flashing out flames of fire at the head; to other some in the likeness of a long burning lance; and so to divers folks, at divers times and seasons, it showed itself in divers forms and fashions a great part of winter, specially in Leicestershire and Northamptonshire; and when many went together it approached not near them, but appeared to them as it were afar off.

Holinshed.

xviii. *1438*. Great dearth of corn. . . . Wherefore Stephen Brown, the Lord Mayor, sent into Prussia and brought to London certain ships laden with rye, which eased and did much good to the people, for corn was so scarce in some places that poor people made bread of fern roots.

> William Caxton. (*Note:* This was the year in which Caxton, aged about 17, came up to London from Kent to be apprenticed to Robert Large, a prominent mercer. The famine was the worst for about 120 years and was felt on the Continent as well as in England.)

xix. *1555*. September 30. By occasion of great wind and rain that had fallen was such great floods that that morning the king's palace at Westminster and Westminster Hall was overflown with water unto the stair foot. And that morning a wherriman rowed with his boat over Westminster Bridge.

Holinshed.

xx. *1586.* On Saturday, October 8, there arose the greatest storm that happened since the wind which some people do call Dover wind, which was in the reign of Queen Mary . . . where-withal fell such sharp showers of rain that the drops thereof beating against the faces of travellers made them so smart as with twigs of birch. Besides great harms which happened that night upon the seas, there were upon the land in every quarter overthrown thereby houses, cottages, barns, haystacks, tiles, chimneys, pales, and gates innumerable, and many trees, both great and small, were not only torn and rent asunder, but grubbed up by the roots, in so much as upon the Monday next in many places men could not pass on horseback in the high-ways by reason of the trees that lay blown and broken down cross overthwart the streets.

Holinshed.

xxi *1643.* March 10. I must not forget what amazed us in the night before, viz., a shining cloud in the air, in shape resembling a sword, the point reaching to the North; it was bright as the moon, the rest of the sky being very serene. It began about 11 at night, and vanished not till about one, being seen by all the South of England.

John Evelyn.

xxii. *1683–1684.* January 24th. The frost continuing more and more severe, the Thames before London was still planted with booths in formal streets, all sorts of trades and shops furnish'd and full of commodities, even to a printing press, where the people and ladies took a fancy to have their names printed, and the day and year set down when printed on the Thames; this humour took so universally that 'twas estimated the printer gained £5 a day for printing a line only, at sixpence a name, besides what he got by ballads, etc. Coaches plied from West-minster to the Temple, and from several other stairs to and fro, as in the streets, sleds, sliding with skeets [skates], a bull-baiting, horse and coach-races, puppet-plays and interludes, cooks, tippling and other lewd places, so that it seem'd to be a bacchanalian triumph, or carnival on the water, whilst it was a severe judgment on the land, the trees not only splitting as if lightning struck, but men and cattle perishing in divers places, and the very seas so lock'd up with ice, that no vessels could stir out or come in. . . . Nor was this severe weather much less intense in most parts of Europe, even as far as Spain and the southern tracts. London, by reason of the excessive coldness of the air hindering the ascent of the smoke, was so filled with the fulginous steam of the sea-coal, that hardly could one see cross the streets, and this filling the lungs with its gross particles, exceedingly obstructed the breast, so as one could scarcely breathe.

John Evelyn.

xxiii. *1703*. One continued storm from Wednesday, November 24, till Wednesday following, about one o'clock in the afternoon. It had blown hard about fourteen days past, and that so hard that we thought it terrible weather. Friday 26. It did not blow so hard till twelve o'clock at night, but that most families went to bed. But about one or, at least, by two o'clock, few people that were capable of any sense of danger were so hardy as to lie in bed. From two o'clock the storm increased till five, and from five till half-past six it blew with the greatest violence. . . . It kept blowing all Sunday and Monday, and Tuesday afternoon it increased again, and all Tuesday night it blew with such fury that many families were afraid to go to bed.

Daniel Defoe. (*Note:* This was perhaps the worst storm in English history. It sank twelve warships with their crews, killed something like 8,000 people, including the Bishop of Bath and Wells, who was killed in bed by a stack of chimneys falling on him; and destroyed hundreds of buildings, among them the Eddystone Lighthouse.)

xxiv. *1758*. 'When two Englishmen meet, their first talk is of the weather.'

Doctor Samuel Johnson, *The Idler*.

xxv. *1783*. The summer of the year 1783 was an amazing and portentous one, and full of horrible phenomena; for, besides the alarming meteors and tremendous thunder-storms that affrighted and distressed the different counties of this kingdom, the peculiar haze or smoky fog that prevailed for many weeks in this island, and in every part of Europe, and even beyond its limits, was a most extraordinary appearance, unlike anything known within the memory of man. By my journal I find that I had noticed this strange occurrence from June 23 to July 20 inclusive, during which period the wind varied to every quarter without making any alteration in the air. The sun, at noon, looked as blank as a clouded moon, and shed a rust-coloured ferruginous light on the ground, and floors of rooms. . . . The country people began to look with a superstitious awe, at the red, louring aspect of the sun; and indeed there was reason for the most enlightened person to be apprehensive.

Gilbert White, *Natural History and Antiquities of Selborne*, Letter LXV.

xxvi. *1800*. August 19. Pieces of ice as large as a hen's egg fell at Heyford, in Oxfordshire, the same storm doing great mischief in Bedfordshire, where hailstones fell eleven inches in circumference.

(Many of the above entries are to be found in T. H. Baker, *Records of the Seasons, Prices of Agricultural Produce and Phenomena Observed in the British Isles, c.* 1884).

WEBSTER, DANIEL (1782–1852), American statesman and orator; Secretary of State.

i. *Webster's picture of the power of England*

. . . a power, to which, for the purposes of foreign conquest and subjugation, Rome, in the height of her glory, is not to be compared; a power which has dotted over the surface of the whole globe with her possessions and military posts, whose morning drum-beat, following the sun, and keeping company with the hours, circles the earth with one continuous and unbroken strain of the martial airs of England.

SOURCE: Speech in the Senate, May 7, 1834.

ii. *The steam-engine in trousers*

Daniel Webster struck me much like a steam-engine in trousers.

SOURCE: Rev. Sydney Smith. Lady Holland, *Memoir*, 1855.

iii. *A great speech*

In 1830, Daniel Webster delivered 'one of the greatest speeches ever delivered in Congress' against Robert Haynes, of South Carolina, who had expounded an extreme version of states' rights.

There are many anecdotes about what took place between Mr. Hayne and Mr. Webster, and among them a great many absurdities. I had read a large number of these stories; and I asked Mr. Webster about the truth of them. Mr. Webster replied:

'Not one of them is true.'

He said, however, that it was true that, when he had finished his speech, some Southern member, whose name he did not mention, approached him cordially and said:

'Mr. Webster, I think you had better die now, and rest your fame on that speech.'

SOURCE: Peter Harvey, *Reminiscences and Anecdotes of Daniel Webster*, Boston, 1877.

WELLESLEY, ARTHUR, first DUKE OF WELLINGTON
(1769–1852), Field Marshal and Prime Minister.

i. *The Duke nominates a General*

The Government was contemplating the despatch of an expedition to Burma, with a view to taking Rangoon, and a question arose as to who would be the fittest general to be sent in command of the expedition. The Cabinet sent for the Duke of Wellington and asked his advice. He instantly replied:

'Send Lord Combermere.'

'But we have always understood that your Grace thought Lord Combermere a fool.'

'So he is a fool, and a damned fool; but he can take Rangoon.'

SOURCE: G. W. E. Russell, *Collections and Recollections*, Smith, Elder & Co., 1963, Ch. II.

ii. *The Duke tends a toad*

Nor has the repellent appearance of the toad hindered it from being much loved. The following anecdote shows both this ugly reptile and the stern Duke of Wellington in an unusually attractive light. One day the elderly soldier chanced on a small boy weeping bitterly and on asking the cause the child began to explain that he was going away to school next day . . . not waiting to hear more the Duke read him a severe lecture on his attitude, which was cowardly, unworthy of a gentleman and not at all the way to behave, etc. At last the little boy managed to explain he was not crying because he was going to school, but he was worried about his pet toad, as no one else seemed to care for it and he wouldn't know how it was. The Duke, a just man, apologized to the child for having wronged him, and being human as well as just, took down the particulars and promised to report himself about this pet. In due course the little boy at school received a letter saying 'Field-Marshal the Duke of Wellington presents his compliments to Master —— and has the pleasure to inform him that his toad is well.'

SOURCE: ibid.

iii. *The Duke—universal referee*

When the Queen came to the throne her first public act was to go in state to St. James's Palace to be proclaimed. She naturally wished to be accompanied in her State coach only by the Duchess of Kent and one of the Ladies of the Household; but Lord Albemarle, who was Master of the Horse, insisted that he had a right to travel with her Majesty in the coach, as he had done with William IV. The point was submitted to the Duke of Wellington, as a kind of universal referee

in matters of precedence and usage. His judgment was delight-
fully unflattering to the outraged magnate—
    'The Queen can make you go inside the coach, or outside
the coach, or run behind like a tinker's dog.'

SOURCE: W. E. Russell, *Collections and Recollections*, Smith, Elder &
    Co., 1963, Ch. II.

iv. *Wellington and Peel*

'I,' said the Duke of Wellington on a memorable occasion,
'have no small talk, and Peel has no manners.'

SOURCE: ibid., Ch. XIV.

WELLESLEY, ARTHUR RICHARD, second **DUKE OF
WELLINGTON** (1807–1884), son of 'The Iron Duke'.

The judge of donkeys

In dress the Duke was eccentric to a degree. . . . Being much
interested in animals, he once insisted on driving me down to
the Crystal Palace, where a donkey show was being held. On
our arrival there nothing would prevent him from walking on
the especial piece of ground marked out 'For Judges Only.' . . .
He continued to stroll . . . when presently an official approached
him and said:
    'Sir, may I ask, are you a judge?'
    'A judge of what?' thundered the Duke.
    'Of donkeys,' came the reply.
    'Certainly I am, and' (looking hard at the man) ' a very good
one too; leave me alone.'

SOURCE: *Reminiscences of Lady Dorothy Nevill*, (edit. Ralph Nevill),
    Thomas Nelson & Sons, 1906.

WENTWORTH, THOMAS, first **EARL OF STRAFFORD**
(1593–1641). Known as 'Black Tom Tyrant', from the harshness
and ruthlessness of his methods, particularly in the north of
England and in Ireland, where he ruled as Lord Deputy. With
William Laud, Archbishop of Canterbury, developed the con-

ception of government called 'Thorough', based on loyalty to the Crown and the annihilation of opponents. Strafford was a complex character, capable of nobility, but moody, arrogant and ambitious, without the saving grace of affability. There have been few men in English history who commanded such general fear and hostility. A Bill of Attainder was passed against him in 1641, and he was executed on Tower Hill, betrayed by Charles I, who had promised his protection, and who signed the act for fear of mob violence.

i. *The word of a King*

. . . I cannot satisfy myself in honour or conscience without assuring you (now in the midst of your troubles) that, upon the word of a King, you shall not suffer in life, honour, or fortune.

SOURCE: letter from Charles I to the Earl of Strafford, from Whitehall, April 23, 1641, less than three weeks before his execution.

ii. *'Put not your trust in princes'*

When Secretary Carleton waited on him with the intelligence, and stated his own consent as the circumstance which had chiefly moved the king, the astonished prisoner inquired if his majesty had indeed sanctioned the bill? And when assured of the fatal truth, he raised his eyes to heaven and, laying his hand on his heart, exclaimed:

'Put not your trust in princes, nor in the sons of men: for in them there is no salvation.'

SOURCE: Bulstrode Whitelocke, *Memorials of English Affairs*, 1682; John Macdiarmid, *Lives of British Statesmen*, 1820, p. 273. Strafford was, of course, quoting the 146th Psalm.

WESLEY, JOHN (1703–1791), evangelist and Methodist leader. Wesley is said to have preached 40,000 sermons and travelled 250,000 miles, chiefly on horseback.

i. *Wesley sleeps rough*

On a tour in Cornwall, Wesley and his companion John Nelson were listened to readily enough, but found the people slow to offer any hospitality. They were delayed at St. Ives for several weeks because of the illness of one of their company.

All that time, Mr. Wesley and I lay on the floor: he had my great-coat for his pillow, and I had Burkitt's *Notes on the New Testament* for mine. After being here near three weeks, one morning, about three o'clock, Mr. Wesley turned over and, finding me awake, clapped me on the side, saying:

'Brother Nelson, let us be of good cheer! I have one whole side yet, for the skin is off but one side.'

SOURCE: John Nelson's Journal; inc. in John Timbs, *A Century of Anecdote* (Chandos Classics), Frederick Warne & Co., pp. 448–449.

ii. *The world his parish*
I look upon the whole world as my parish.

SOURCE: John Wesley, *Journal*, June 11, 1739.

iii. *End of a marriage*
Non eam reliqui, non dimisi, non revocabo.
I did not forsake her, I did not dismiss her, I will not recall her.

SOURCE: John Wesley in his diary, after his nagging wife Mary had left him after twenty years, taking away many of his personal papers.

iv. *Wesley keeps an appointment*
One day when I was ostler at the London Inn, Helston, Mr. Wesley came and obtained my master's leave for me to drive him to St. Ives. On arriving at Hayle, we found the sands between that place and St. Ives, overflown by the rising tide. Mr. Wesley was resolved to go on; for he said he had to reach St. Ives at a certain hour and must be there. Looking out of the carriage window, he called:

'Take the sea, take the sea.'

In a moment I dashed into the waves and was quickly involved in a world of water. The horses were swimming, and the wheels of the carriage not infrequently sank into the deep hollows in the sand. I expected every moment to be drowned, but heard Mr. Wesley's voice and saw his long white hair dripping with salt water.

'What is your name, driver?' he calmly asked.

I answered, 'Peter'.

'Peter,' said he, 'Peter, fear not, thou shalt not sink.'

With vigorous whipping I again urged on the flagging horses and at last got safely over. Mr. Wesley's first care was to see me comfortably lodged at the tavern; and then, totally unmindful of himself, and drenched as he was with the dashing waves, he proceeded to the chapel and preached according to his appointment.

SOURCE: Peter Martin of Helston; quoted Garth Lean, *John Wesley, Anglican*, Blandford Press, 1964, pp. 44–45.

v. *A text for Billingsgate*

Wesley's preaching was always searching: but seldom terrible or severe, except when addressed to rich and complacent audiences.

'Sir,' said a friend to him after he had preached to a genteel congregation from the words 'Ye serpents, ye generation of vipers, how can ye escape the damnation of hell?' . . . 'such a sermon would have been highly suitable to Billingsgate; but it was highly improper here.'

'If I had been in Billingsgate,' replied Wesley, 'my text should have been, 'Behold the Lamb of God which taketh away the sin of the world.'

SOURCE: ibid., p. 46.

WHIG AND TORY.

i. '*These silly terms of reproach*'

These silly terms of reproach, whig and tory, are still preserved among us, as if the palladium of British liberty was guarded by these exotic names, for they are not English, which the parties so invidiously bestow on each other. They are ludicrous enough

478 ANECDOTES FROM HISTORY

in their origin. The friends of the court and the advocates of lineal succession were, by the republican party, branded with the title of *tories*, which was the name of certain Irish robbers; while the court party in return could find no other revenge than by appropriating to the covenanters and republicans of that class the name of the Scotch beverage of sour milk, whose virtue they considered so expressive of their dispositions, and which is called *whigg*. So ridiculous in their origin were these pernicious nicknames, which long excited feuds and quarrels in domestic life, and may still be said to divide into two great parties this land of political freedom.

SOURCE: Isaac D'Israeli, *Curiosities of Literature*, 1791. The terms seem to have been first used 1650–1660.

ii. *Coke of Norfolk and the Tories*

The vigour, heartiness, and sincerity of this political hatred put to shame the more tepid convictions of our degenerate days. The first Earl of Leicester, better known as 'Coke of Norfolk', told my father that when he was a child his grandfather took him on his knee and said:

'Now, remember, Tom, as long as you live, never trust a Tory'; and he used to say, 'I never have, and, by George, I never will'.

SOURCE: George W. E. Russell, *Collections and Recollections*, Smith, Elder & Co., 1903, Ch. X. But, despite Coke's statement, Tories were as welcome as Whigs at 'Coke's Clippings', the meetings held for over forty years on Coke's estate to discuss agricultural problems; and not till political matters were allowed into the discussions, in 1821, did the meetings come to an end. See WOOLLEN INDUSTRY (vi).

iii. *Are Tories born wicked?*

A little girl of Whig descent, accustomed from her cradle to hear language of this sort, asked her mother:

'Mamma, are Tories born wicked, or do they grow wicked afterwards?' and her mother judiciously replied:

'They are born wicked, and grow worse.'

SOURCE: ibid.

iv. *Principles of cab selection*

I well remember in my youth an eccentric maiden lady—Miss Harriet Fanny Cuyler—who had spent a long and interesting life in the innermost circles of aristocratic Whiggery; and she always refused to enter a four-wheel cab until she had extorted from the driver his personal assurance that he never had cases of infectious disease in his cab, that he was not a Puseyite,* and was a Whig.

SOURCE: ibid.

v. *Doctor Johnson on Whiggism*

(a) Whiggism is a negation of all principle.

SOURCE: Boswell's *Life*.

(b) I have always said, the first Whig was the Devil.

SOURCE: ibid.

(c) Where you see a Whig you see a rascal.

SOURCE: *Anecdotes by the Rev. W. Cole.*

(d) Johnson signified his displeasure at Mr. Mason's conduct very strongly; but added, by way of shewing that he was not surprised at it:
 'Mason's a Whig.'
 Mrs. Knowles (not hearing distinctly):
 'What! a Prig, Sir?'
 Johnson: 'Worse, Madam; a Whig! But he is both!'

SOURCE: James Boswell, *The Life of Samuel Johnson.*

vi. *The ladies show their colours*

As I was standing in the hinder part of the box at the opera, I took notice of a little cluster of women sitting together in the prettiest coloured hoods that I ever saw. One of them was blue, another yellow, and another philamot [a light brownish-

---

* A follower of Dr. Pusey and his Tractarian teachings, a High Churchman.

yellow]. I looked with as much pleasure upon this little party-coloured assembly, as upon a bed of tulips, and did not know at first whether it might not be an embassy of Indian queens; but upon my going about into the pit, and taking them in front, I was immediately undeceived, and saw so much beauty in every face, that I found them all to be English. . . . I am informed that this fashion spreads daily, insomuch that the Whig and Tory ladies begin already to hang out different colours, and to show their principles in their head-dress.

SOURCE: Joseph Addison, *The Spectator*, No. 265, January 3.

vii. *Mrs. Carnegy does not rise*

A notion of the stiff manner in which these old ladies could vindicate their principles or their personal dignity is afforded by the various stories told of Mrs. Helen Carnegy, of Craigo. On one occasion, as she sat in an easy chair, having assumed the habits and privileges of age, Mr. Mollison, the minister of the established kirk, called on her to solicit for some charity. She did not like being asked for money, and, from her Jacobite principles, she certainly did not respect the Presbyterian kirk. When he came in she made only an inclination of the head, and when he said, deprecatingly, 'Don't get up, madam,' she at once replied:

'Get up? I wadna rise out of my chair for King George himsel', let abee a Whig Minister.'

SOURCE: John Timbs, *A Century of Anecdote, 1760–1860.*

viii. *The Whig Bible*

It is more than 300 years since the Genevan printer in 1562 sent out into the world the famous *Whig Bible*, so called because Matthew v, verse 9 is made to read 'Blessed are the place-makers' [instead of 'peace-makers'].

SOURCE: *Book-Lore*, August, 1886. The christening of the edition as the 'Whig Bible' is, of course, a Tory quip, place-men being supporters put into Government jobs—what modern terminology calls 'jobs for the boys'.

WHITEFIELD, GEORGE (1714–1770), Methodist leader and preacher.

i. *'By God! He's over!'*

He [John Wesley] was not dramatically eloquent like George Whitefield, whose description of a blind man tottering towards the crumbling edge of the precipice of sin could bring the urbane Lord Chesterfield to his feet crying, 'By God! He's over!' Nor had his voice the melody which made Garrick say he'd give a thousand guineas to be able to say the single word 'Oh!' like Mr. Whitefield.

SOURCE: Garth Lean, *John Wesley, Anglican*, Blandford Press, 1964, p. 45.

ii. *The ships that failed to get built*

Every Sunday that I go to my parish church I can build a ship from stem to stern under the sermon; but to save my soul, under Mr. Whitefield, I can't lay a single plank.

SOURCE: a shipbuilder; quoted ibid.

iii. *The white gutters in the coal grime*

... finding the churches denied to him [at Bristol] he preached on a hill at Kingswood to the colliers; and after he had done this three or four times, his congregation is said to have amounted to twenty thousand persons. That any human voice could be heard by such a number, is improbable; but that he effected a great moral reform among these colliers, by his preaching, cannot be denied.

'The first discovery,' he tells us, 'of their being affected, was the white gutters made by their tears, which plentifully fell down their black cheeks, as they came out of their coal pits.'

SOURCE: quoted *The Percy Anecdotes*, 1820–1823.

WILBERFORCE, SAMUEL (1805–1873), Bishop, successively, of Oxford and Winchester.

The only road to heaven

Samuel Wilberforce, the well-known Bishop of Oxford, lived not very far from us, and we used to see a great deal of this excellent and witty ecclesiastic. . . . He was an admirable talker, and very quick at repartee. There is a well-known story of some young men having endeavoured to drag him into controversy at a time when a series of tracts entitled 'The Road to Heaven' was creating a considerable sensation. The Bishop, however, proved too much for them, merely saying:

'The best and only road to heaven I know is to turn to the right and go straight on.'

SOURCE: *Reminiscences of Lady Dorothy Nevill* (edit. Ralph Nevill), Thomas Nelson & Sons, 1906.

WILBERFORCE, WILLIAM (1759–1863), philanthropist; parliamentary leader of the slavery abolition movement.

The watches of Mr. Wilberforce

. . . Mr. Wilberforce had a peculiar mannerism which was well-known to all with whom he was acquainted. He kept two watches, one in each side pocket, and he had a trick of taking these out and comparing the time indicated by each. If he found them exactly the same, he would, as though bored by this discovery, push on the hands of one a little, then replace both in his pockets, next take out the first one again, and finding it now, of course, a little slower than its fellow, he would push on its hands to correspond with the other. This curious trick he would continue absently repeating at intervals.

SOURCE: A. M. W. Stirling, *The Richmond Papers*, Heinemann, 1923.

WILLIAM I (1027–1087), King of England; called the Conqueror.

i. *Philip I jeers at William's corpulence*

The Conqueror was of 'extraordinary corpulence' according to William of Malmesbury and, though he was majestic, 'the protuberance of his belly deformed the royal person'. Philip I (1060–1108) pretended to think William was expecting a child.

When will this fat man be delivered?' . . .
To which the Conqueror replied that he would be churched *
at Paris with ten thousand lances by way of tapers.

SOURCE: Victor Duruy, *A Short History of France*, 1873; Everyman's Library edition, J. M. Dent & Sons, 1917, Vol. I, p. 188. William ravaged the countryside up to the walls of Paris, but died before the grim promise could be fulfilled.

ii. *The making of Domesday Book, 1086*

So very narrowly did he cause the survey to be made, that there was not a single hide nor a rood of land, nor—it is shameful to relate that which he thought no shame to do—was there an ox, or a cow, or a pig passed by, and that was not set down on the accounts, and then all of these writings were brought to him.

SOURCE: *Anglo-Saxon Chronicle*, trans., J. A. Giles, 1881.

WILLIAM II (1057?–1100), King of England. Called 'the Red' but, contrary to popular tradition, not because of his red hair. William of Malmesbury describes him as having fair hair and a florid complexion. The true story of his death from an arrow in the New Forest will probably never be known. The only man with any direct knowledge, Walter Tyrrel or Tirel, denied any complicity, though he crossed the Channel almost immediately. But there seems fair substance behind the story of the charcoal-burner who jolted the fallen King of England on his cart to Winchester.

The lineage of the charcoal-burner

About sun-down, one Purkiss, a charcoal-burner, driving homewards with his cart, discovered a gentleman lying

---

* Churching is the church ceremony of thanksgiving for a woman after child-birth.

weltering in blood, with an arrow driven deep into his breast. The peasant knew him not, but conjecturing him to be one of the royal train, he lifted the body into his vehicle, and proceeded towards Winchester. . . .

There is a tradition that, for this service, he had some rods of land, to the amount of an acre or two, given to him; and it is very remarkable that a lineal descendant of this charcoal-burner, bearing the same name, does now live in the hut, and in possession of the land, and is himself a charcoal-burner; that all the family, from the first, have been of the same calling, and never richer or poorer, the one than the other; always possessed of a horse and cart, but never of a team; the little patrimony of land given to their celebrated ancestor having descended undiminished from father to son. This family, therefore, is rightly esteemed the most ancient in the county of Hants.

SOURCE: *The Book of Days* (edit. R. Chambers), 1864, Vol. II, pp. 160–161.

WILLIAM (WILHELM) II (1859–1941), Emperor of Germany; usually called in England 'The Kaiser' or, less politely, 'Kaiser Bill'.

The withered arm

I . . . had an audience of the Kaiser at Potsdam. William II was then, I suppose, at the summit of his strange and ill-starred career [in 1900]. To me he was gracious and cordial. I had been warned that he was acutely sensitive about his physical deformity and disliked his withered left arm being looked at. But members of his court and others who knew him said that the curiosity of human beings is such that everybody, meeting the Kaiser for the first time, found his gaze drawn automatically and irresistibly to the left side of his uniform. While I awaited my audience I said to myself over and over again:

'You won't look at his arm, you *won't* look at his arm.'

He strode into the room; my eyes became a law unto themselves, and there I was staring at his left arm. Fortunately for me, I suppose, he must have been so accustomed to this happening that he did not let it diminish the warmth and courtesy of his greeting.

He held out his right hand and shook hands with me. This was literally a crushing experience. As a compensation for his deformity the Kaiser had, from childhood, determined that his right hand and arm should be so strong that they would do the work of two. He took constant, vigorous exercise; every day he had at least twenty minutes' fencing; he played lawn-tennis often for two hours at a time; and undertook all manner of other remedial exercises. The result was an immense development of strength in his right hand and arm; one of its effects was this appallingly powerful handshake. I am told that mine was no unusual experience. The Duchess of Teck (later the Marchioness of Cambridge) told me that she—like most other women with whom His Imperial Majesty shook hands—had the greatest difficulty in not letting out a cry of pain as he took her hand in his.

SOURCE: *The Memoirs of Aga Khan*, Cassell & Co., 1954, p. 66.

WILLIAM III (1650–1702), King of England.

i. *A famous non-juror*

Non-jurors were those—mainly, but not entirely clergymen—who refused to take the oath of allegiance to William III and Mary at the Revolution of 1688. Among the well-known non-jurors was Francis Cherry (1665?–1713), of Shottesbrooke, Berkshire.

A stout Nonjuror, Cherry would not acknowledge William and Mary, and when he found that William was following him pretty closely in stag-hunting, he suddenly leaped his horse down a steep and dangerous bank into the Thames, hoping that 'the usurper' would follow him and break his neck; but the King turned away.

SOURCE: C. R. L. Fletcher, *Historical Portraits*, 1700–1850, Clarendon Press, 1919, Part I, p. 20.

ii. *To be included in the next edition*

Lord Molesworth, who had been Ambassador at the Court of Copenhagen, published, at the end of the last century, an esteemed work, entitled, *Account of Denmark*. This writer spoke of the arbitrary government of that kingdom, with the freedom which the liberty of England inspires. The King of Denmark, then reigning, was offended at some reflections of the author, and ordered his Minister to complain of them to William III, King of England.

'What would you have me do?' said William.

'Sire,' replied the Danish minister, "if you had complained to the King, my master, of such an offence, he would have sent you the head of the author.'

'That is what I neither will, nor can do,' replied the King; 'but if you desire it, the author shall put what you have told me in the second edition of his work.'

SOURCE: Mr. Addison (pseud.), Interesting *Anecdotes, Memoirs, Allegories, Essays* . . . etc., 1794.

iii. *William III is put to the torture*

Mr. Carstairs [William Carstairs or Carstares, 1649–1715], afterwards principal of the university of Edinburgh, was deeply concerned in those unfortunate transactions, which brought Argyle to the scaffold in Scotland, and Russell and Sidney in England. He was seized in England, and being sent to Scotland, was, on the 5th of September, 1684, tortured with the thumb-iken before the secret committee of the privy council, in order to force him to reveal the names of his associates. . . .

After the revolution [of 1688], the privy council of Scotland presented Mr. Carstairs with the identical thumbiken with which he had been tortured in 1684. . . .

There is an anecdote handed down among the descendants of Mr. Carstairs, in regard to this instrument, which is narrated in the fifth volume of *The Statistical account of Scotland*.

'I have heard, principal,' said King William to him, when he waited on his majesty after the revolution, 'that you were tortured with something they call the thumbiken; pray what sort of instrument of torture is that?'

'I will shew it you,' replied Carstairs, 'the next time I have the honour to wait on your majesty.'

The principal was as good as his word.

'I must try it,' said the king. 'I must put in my thumbs here—now, principal, turn the screw. O, not so gently—another turn—another. Stop! Stop! No more. Another turn, I'm afraid, would make me confess anything.'

SOURCE: *The Waverley Anecdotes.*

See also BOYNE, BATTLE OF THE.

WILLIAM IV (1765–1837), king of Great Britain and Ireland. Succeeded to the throne at the age of 64, having served as a naval officer and, from 1827, as Lord High Admiral.

i. *The Lord High Admiral approves of disobeying Admiralty orders*

Nor was he likely to endear himself to officials at the Admiralty by shouting out, at a public dinner, to an officer who had obeyed his orders in preference to written orders from the Admiralty:

'You did quite right, sir, and I would not give a damn for any officer who did not know when the good of the Service required his disobeying written orders.'

SOURCE: Roger Fulford, *Royal Dukes*, Gerald Duckworth & Co., 1933, p. 118.

ii. *The new King swears in his Privy Council, 1830*

Suddenly the doors were flung open and a short, red-faced figure bustled in and, without acknowledging anyone, walked up to the table and, seizing a pen, signed with a bold splutter 'William R.' The whole room heard him say:

'This is a damned bad pen you have given me.'

SOURCE: ibid., p. 124.

iii. *The King publicly castigates the Duchess of Kent*

William IV and his sister-in-law the Duchess of Kent, mother of the future Queen Victoria, were often at daggers drawn. The climax came when, in defiance of the king's decision, she took over seventeen rooms in Kensington Palace, though, in William's opinion, she already had adequate accommodation there. At a dinner to celebrate the King's birthday, attended by over a hundred guests, including the Duchess of Kent, William, in replying to the toast of his health, expressed the wish that he might live another nine months, since by then Victoria would be of age to reign, and would not need a Regent, in the shape of her mother. He referred to:

'. . . a person now near me, who is surrounded by evil advisers and who is herself incompetent to act with propriety in the station in which she would be placed.'

SOURCE: quoted ibid., p. 146.

iv. *The King with the head like a pineapple*

'What can you expect' (as I forget who said) 'from a man with a head like a pineapple?' His head is just of that shape.

SOURCE: *Greville Memoirs.*

See also BROUGHAM, LORD (ii).

WILLIAM OF ORANGE (1533–1584), Prince of Orange and Nassau, called 'William the Silent'; founder of the Dutch Republic; assassinated by a Burgundian fanatic.

i. '*The most beautiful epitaph known to history*'

As long as he lived, he was a guiding-star of a whole brave nation, and when he died the little children cried in the streets.

SOURCE: John Lothrop Motley, *The Rise of the Dutch Republic*, 1856. Motley took the words from a state document of 1584.

ii. *The confederacy of 'The Beggars'*

In 1566 the leading noblemen and gentlemen of Holland formed a league to resist the oppression of Spain and the atrocities of the

Inquisition. When they approached the governor, Margaret of Austria, to remove the Inquisition, her adviser, the Count de Berlaymont, contemptuously referred to the deputation as 'only a set of beggars' (*ce ne sont que des gueux*).

There was an earnest discussion as to an appropriate name to be given to their confederacy. Should they call themselves the 'Society of Concord', the restorers of lost liberty, or by what other attractive title should the league be baptized? Brederode was, however, already prepared to settle the question. He knew the value of a popular and original name; he possessed the instinct by which adroit partisans in every age have been accustomed to convert the reproachful epithets of their opponents into watchwords of honour, and he had already made his preparations for a startling theatrical effect.

Suddenly, amid the din of voices, he arose, with all his rhetorical powers at command. He recounted to the company the observations which the Seigneur de Berlaymont was reported to have made to the Duchess upon the presentation of the request, and the name which he had thought fit to apply to them collectively. Most of the gentlemen then heard the memorable sarcasm for the first time. Great was the indignation of all, that the state-councillor should have dared to stigmatise as beggars a band of gentlemen with the best blood of the land in their veins. Brederode, on the contrary, smoothing their anger, assured them with good humour that nothing could be more fortunate.

'They call us beggars!' said he, 'let us accept the name. We will contend with the Inquisition, but remain loyal to the King, even till compelled to wear the beggar's sack.'

He then beckoned to one of his pages, who brought him a leathern wallet such as that worn at that day by professional mendicants, together with a large wooden bowl, which also formed part of their regular appurtenances. Brederode immediately hung the wallet around his neck, filled the bowl with wine, lifted it with both hands, and drained it at a draught.

'Long live the beggars!' he cried, as he wiped his beard and set the bowl down. '*Vivent les gueux!*'

Then for the first time, from the lips of those reckless nobles rose the famous cry which was so often to ring over land and sea, amid blazing cities, on blood-stained decks, through the smoke and carnage of many a stricken field.

SOURCE: John Lothrop Motley, *The Rise of the Dutch Republic*, 1856. Another group, who placed themselves under the leadership of Count Horn to resist the Spaniards in the Zuyder Zee, took the name of 'The Sea Beggars'.

WILLOUGHBY, SIR JOSIAH NESBIT (1777–1849), Admiral. One of the most curious cases in English history of the entire neglect of a great hero, whose exploits far exceeded many of his better-known contemporaries.

The consummate gallantry, indeed, the utter disregard of self, and the exalted devotion to his country's interests which have emblazoned the acts of this hero's career, in every rank and under every circumstance . . . we confess to have never seen surpassed in any of the myriad soul-stirring deeds which have necessarily passed in review before us.

SOURCE: William R. O'Byrne, *A Naval Biographical Dictionary, comprising the Life and Services of Every Living Officer in Her Majesty's Navy . . .*' 1849.

O'Byrne reckoned that Willoughby earned the C.B. on ten different occasions. Among the many exploits he chronicles are:

i. (1804) During the operations against Curacoa, where for 25 days he was exposed to three and four diurnal attacks from the enemy, he again distinguished himself by a display of marked firmness and daring. Landing on that island on 31 Jan., he first of all commanded a party at the storming of Fort Piscadero. . . . He had the good fortune, on the morning of 5 Feb., to defeat, with not more than 85 seamen and marines, as many as 500 of the Dutch and French, after a hard fight and a loss of 23 men killed and wounded. . . . During his occupation of the advanced battery, he frequently, for the purpose of inspiriting the depressed portion of his men, took his meals in an awfully exposed situation, under a full shower of the enemy's missiles. 'The earth,' says Mr. James,* 'was ploughed up all around, and one man, we believe, was killed close to the spot; but still the table and chair, and the daring young officer who sat there, remained untouched'. . . . On March 14, we find Mr. Willoughby capturing, in command of the *Hercule*'s boats, *La Félicité*, French privateer. . . . When the same ship, on 6 of the following Sept. was caught in a fearful hurricane off the Silver Keys, during which 300 vessels are supposed to have been lost, this meritorious officer, although at the time on the doctor's list, was the first person—even the oldest seamen being appalled—who summoned courage to mount into the foretop and clear away the wreck of the foretopmast, which had been blown over the side, thus saving the lower mast, which already was in a tottering state.

ii. (1807) During a land attack. . . . he was struck by two pistol-balls, one of which entered his head just above the right jaw, and, from the upward position of his head at the moment, took a slanting direction towards the region of the brain, where it has ever since remained. The other shot cut his left cheek in two, and he lay for six or seven minutes apparently lifeless on the ground; but at the very moment that his companions began to retreat, one of his arms was observed to move, and he was carried off to the ship as one of whom no hopes were entertained. In short, so desperate was his case that the surgeon of the *Royal George* also considered him to be mortally wounded, and officially reported him as such for three days afterwards.

iii. (1810) . . . while on shore at Ile Platte, a small island near the northern extremity of the Mauritius, and in the act of exercising his men at small arms, a musket in the hands of a marine burst, inflicting upon Captain Willoughby a dreadful

* William James, *The Naval History of Great Britain*, first published 1822.

wound, supposed at the time to be mortal. His lower jaw on the right side was badly fractured, and his neck so lacerated that the wind-pipe lay bare. For three weeks he could not speak.

iv. (1811) The *Nereide* was taken . . . after she had been reduced to a mere wreck, and had incurred—during a glorious resistance unparalleled even in the brilliant annals of the British navy—a loss, out of 281 persons, of about 230 killed and wounded. Among the latter was the chivalrous Willoughby himself, who, to his former wounds, had now to add, besides a splintered cheek, the loss of one eye . . . and the most serious injury to the other.

(1812) We next . . . find him volunteering into the service of Russia, where he fought against the French, until taken prisoner by the latter after their defeat of General Steingell—a misfortune which was occasioned by an act of generosity in giving up his own horse, and that of his attendant Cossack, to the use of two Russian soldiers who were attempting with bleeding and mangled limbs to withdraw from the scene of slaughter. He then for a time became involved in all the horrors of the retreat from Moscow.

SOURCE: All from O'Byrne's *Naval Biographical Dictionary*, 1849 (see above). It may be added that Willoughby was court-martialled three times, and dismissed the service on one occasion. He lived in retirement at Brighton and, when William IV was promenading on the sea-front during a visit, he saw the battered old warrior limping along, halted, and hailed him as a hero before all the company. As a final contribution to the navy, he wrote *Extracts from Holy Writ and Various Authors, intended as Helps to Meditation and Prayer, principally for Soldiers and Seamen*, 1839, for free distribution in the services.

WOLFE, GENERAL JAMES (1727–1759).

i. *The madness of Wolfe*

Reply of George II to someone* who expressed the opinion that Wolfe was mad:

* Apparently the Duke of Newcastle, when the King proposed giving the command of the Quebec expedition to Wolfe.

'Oh! he is mad, is he? Then I wish he would bite some other of my generals.'

SOURCE: Francis Thackeray, *History of William Pitt, Earl of Chatham*, 1827, Vol. i, Ch. 15.

ii. *General Wolfe recites on the eve of the Battle of Quebec*

The General ... repeated nearly the whole of Gray's Elegy ... adding, as he concluded, that he would prefer being the author of that poem to the glory of beating the French tomorrow.

SOURCE: J. Playfair, *Biographical Account of J. Robinson* in Transactions of the Royal Society, Edinburgh, 1814, vii, 499.

iii. '*See how they run*'

After our late worthy General, of renowned memory, was carried off wounded to the rear of the front line, he desired those who were about him to lay him down; being asked if he would have a surgeon, he replied:
'It is needless; it is all over with me.'
One of them cried out:
'They run, see how they run.'
'Who runs?' demanded our hero with great earnestness, like a person aroused from sleep. The Officer answered:
'The Enemy, Sir; Egad, they give way everywhere.'
Thereupon the General rejoined:
'Go one of you, my lads, to Colonel Burton; tell him to march Webb's regiment with all speed down to Charles's river, to cut off the retreat of the fugitives from the bridge.' Then, turning on his side, he added:
'Now, God be praised, I will die in peace.'

SOURCE: Captain John Knox, *Historical Journal*, 1769, p. 79.

iv. *The 'best written epitaph'?*

On the death of general Wolfe, a premium was offered for the best written epitaph on that brave officer. A number of poets of all descriptions started as candidates; and among the rest was a poem sent to the editor of the *Public Ledger*, of which the following was one of the stanzas:

> *He march'd without dread or fears*
> *At the head of his bold grenadiers;*
> *And what was more remarkable—nay, very particular,*
> *He climbed up rocks that were perpendicular.*

SOURCE: Stephen Collet, *Relics of Literature*, 1823, p. 248.

WOLSEY, CARDINAL THOMAS (1475?–1530). Cardinal-Archbishop of York and Lord Chancellor. Lost favour, and in 1529 arraigned on a list of forty-four charges but, through the generosity of Henry VIII, received a general pardon. Shortly afterwards, while journeying north, charged with high treason and died at Leicester on his return journey to London.

'If I had served God . . .'

Master Kyngston bade him good morrow, for it was about 7 of the clock in the morning, and asked him how he did.

'Sir,' quoth he, 'I tarry but the will and pleasure of God, to render unto him my simple soul into his divine hands.'

'Not yet so, sir,' quoth Master Kyngston, 'with the grace of God, you shall live and do very well, if ye will be of good cheer.'

'Master Kyngston, my disease is such that I cannot live; for I have had some experience in my disease, and thus it is. . . .'

'Nay, sir, in good faith,' quoth Master Kyngston, 'ye be in such dolour and pensiveness, doubting that thing that indeed ye need not to fear, which maketh you much worse than ye should be.'

'Well, well, Master Kyngston,' quoth he, 'I see the matter against me, how it is framed; but if I had served God as diligently as I have done the king, he would not have given me over in my gray hairs.'

SOURCE: George Cavendish, *Negotiations of Thomas Woolsey*, 1641. Cavendish wrote his life of Wolsey in about 1557, and Shakespeare must have seen one of the MSS. in order to have followed the scene so exactly in Henry VIII, Act III, Scene ii:

> Had I but serv'd my God with half the zeal
> I serv'd my king, he would not in mine age
> Have left me naked to mine enemies.

Did Colbert (see separate entry) also know Cavendish, or read Shakespeare?

WOOLLEN INDUSTRY, THE. The raising of sheep, both for home use and for exports, and woollen manufactures, early assumed great importance in England. Large numbers of sheep were sent to Spain as early as 1273 and again in 1394, this time as part of the dowry of Catherine Plantagenet, daughter of John of Gaunt, when she married Henry III of Spain. Holinshed records that 'on the occasion of a treaty of alliance between Edward IV of England and Henry IV of Castile, license was given for certain Cotswold sheep to be transported into the country of Spain, which have there so multiplied and increased, that it hath turned the commodity of England much to the profit of Spain'. In 1354, in the reign of Edward III, 31,651 sacks of wool and 3,036 cwt. of fells were exported, according to exchequer records.

The continued growth of the industry had pronounced social and political repercussions. Great areas of land were turned from arable into pasture; rents and prices increased; towns and villages grew because of it; and a new class of wealthy merchants appeared on the scene, building great houses, endowing fine churches, etc. The new race is in a sense exemplified by John Winchcomb, known as Jack of Newbury, who is said to have run a hundred looms in his own house in Berkshire, and who sent, at his own expense, a hundred armed men to fight for the King against the Scots at Flodden Field.

It is not surprising that English literature and history abound with stories of shepherds, who are usually presented in a very favourable light. Their habits and customs were handed down through long centuries and their craft was often preserved in the same families through many generations. In 1911, a family on a farm near Lewes had been shepherds since the time of Cromwell.

i. 'The Shepherd Lord'—Henry de Clifford, 14th Baron Clifford (1455?-1523)

The life of Henry Clifford, commonly called the Shepherd Lord, is a striking illustration of the casualties which attended the long and disastrous contest between the Houses of York and Lancaster. The De Cliffords were zealous and powerful adherents of the Lancastrian interest. In this cause Henry's father had fallen at the battle of Towton. . . . But scarcely had the Yorkists gained this victory, which placed their leader on the throne as Edward IV, than search was made for the sons of the fallen Lord Clifford. These were the two boys, of whom Henry, the eldest, was only seven years old . . . but their mother's anxiety had been too prompt for the eagerness of revenge. They could nowhere be found. Their mother was closely and peremptorily examined about them. She said she had given direction to convey them beyond the sea, to be bred up there; and that being thither sent she was ignorant whether they were living or not. . . . Certain it is that Richard, her younger son, was taken to the Netherlands, where he shortly afterwards died.

But Henry, the elder, the heir to his father's titles and estates, was either never taken out of England, or, if he were, he speedily returned, and was placed by his mother at Londesborough, in Yorkshire, with a trustworthy shepherd. . . . Here in the lowly hut of this humble shepherd was the heir of the lordly Cliffords doomed to dwell—to be clothed, fed, and employed as the shepherd's own son.

In this condition he lived month after month, and year after year, in such perfect disguise that it was not till he had attained the fifteenth year of his age that a rumour reached the Court of his still being alive in England. Happily the Lady Clifford had a friend at Court, who forewarned her that the king had received an intimation of her son's place of concealment. With the assistance of her then husband, Sir Lancelot Threlkeld, she instantly removed 'the honest shepherd with his wife and family into Cumberland', where he took a farm near the Scottish borders. Here, though his mother occasionally held private communication with him, the young Lord Clifford passed fifteen years more, disguised and occupied as a common shepherd; and had the mortification of seeing his castle and barony of Shipton in the hands of his adversary, Sir William Stanley, and his barony of Westmorland possessed by the Duke of Gloucester, the king's brother.

On the restoration of the Lancastrian line by the accession of Henry VII, Henry Clifford, now thirty-one years old, was summoned to the House of Lords and restored to his father's titles and estates. But such had been his humble training that he could neither read nor write. . . . Having regained his property and position, he immediately began to repair his castles and improve his education. He quickly learnt to read and wrote his own name; and, to facilitate his studies, built Barden Tower, near Bolton Priory, that he might place himself under the tuition of some learned monks there, and apply himself to astronomy, and other favourite sciences of the period. . . .

His training as a warrior had been equally defective. Instead of being practised from boyhood to the use of arms and feats of chivalry . . . he had been trained to handle the shepherd's crook, and tend and fold and shear his sheep; yet scarcely had he emerged from his obscurity and quiet pastoral life when we find him become a brave and skilful soldier—and an able and victorious commander. At the battle of Flodden he was one of the principal leaders and brought to the field a numerous retinue.

SOURCE: *The Book of Days*, edit. Robert Chambers, 1869.

ii. *A 1542 method of counting sheep*

It was used in Cornwall and described by Andrew Borde or Boorde (1490?–1549), physician and traveller.

1. Ouyn	5. Pimp
2. Dow	6. Whe
3. Tray	7. Syth
4. Peswar	8. Eth

9. Naw	15. Pymp-deec
10. Dec	16. Whe-deec
11. Unec (one-	17. Syth-deec
ten)	18. Eth-deec
12. Dowec	19. Naw-deec
13. Tredeec	20. Igous
14. Peswar-deec	21. Ouyn-war-igous, etc.

Andrew Borde said: 'No Cornish man doth number above thirty . . . and when they have told thirty they do begin again, one, two, three, and so forth, and when they have counted to 100, they say "kans", and if they number to 1000 they say "myle".'

Such forms of scoring were common in all parts of the country, with local variations, and probably survived for a thousand years from the ancient Britons, with inevitable corruptions and interpolations. For comparison, here is a Lincolnshire 'score' still in use by old shepherds in about 1910:

1. Yan	11. Yan-a-dik
2. Tan	12. Tan-a-dik
3. Tethera	13. Tethera-dik
4. Pethera	14. Pethera-dik
5. Pimp	15. Bumpit
6. Sethera	16. Yan-a-bumpit
7. Lethera	17. Tan-a-bumpit
8. Hovera	18. Tethera-bumpit
9. Covera	19. Pethera-bumpit
10. Dick	20. Figgit (or Jiggit)

SOURCE: article by Walter Skeat, *The Sheep-Counting Score*, 1910, in Adelaide Gosset, *Shepherds of Britain*, Constable, 1911.

iii. *The Isle of Sheep*

It would seem by the dedication of the name that this island [Isle of Sheppey, Kent] was long since greatly esteemed either for the number of the sheep, or for the fineness of the fleece, although ancient foreign writers ascribe not much to any part of all England (and much less to his place) either for the one respect or for the other: but whether the sheep of this realm were in price before the coming of the Saxons or no, they be now (God be thanked therefore) worthy of great an estimation both for the exceeding fineness of the fleece (which passeth all other in Europe at this day, and is to be compared with the ancient delicate wool of Tarentum, or the Golden Fleece of Colchos itself) and for the abundant store of flocks so increasing everywhere, that not only this little isle which we now have in hand, but the whole realm also might rightly be called Sheppey.

SOURCE: William Lambarde, 1576 edition, *Perambulation of Kent.*

iv. *Queen Elizabeth is addressed by a shepherd*

'This lock of wool, Cotswold's best fruits and my poor gift, I offer to your Highness: in which nothing is to be esteemed but the whiteness, Virginity's colour: not to be expected but duty, shepherd's religion.'

SOURCE: address by a shepherd to Queen Elizabeth, on a visit to Sudely Castle.

v. *A 17th Century church notice*

The Clerke shal give notice on Trinitie Sondaye after divine service is ended publickly in the Chuche that one score and three straye sheepe hav bin vounde in David Pugsley his bartone* with a clippette† in ye lefte eare.

SOURCE: notice found in 1864 in the parish chest at Luccombe, Somerset; William Andrews, *Curious Church Customs*, 1896; quoted Adelaide Gosset, *Shepherds of Britain*, Constable, 1911.

vi. *'Coke's Clippings'*

One of the greatest influences on sheep-breeding in the late 18th and early 19th Centuries was Thomas William Coke of Holkham, Norfolk (1752–1842), created Earl of Leicester in 1837.

Not until 1778, two years after Coke had first collected the farmers together to discuss matters agricultural, did this local gathering at Holkham in Norfolk assume a definite character. ... First, the farmers brought with them their relations and friends. These in turn brought others from a yet greater

* Barton = farm-yard.   † Clippette = owner's brand-mark.

distance. Next, agriculturalists from more remote parts of the kingdom wrote to ask if they might attend. Swiftly and steadily grew the fame of 'Coke's Clippings', as they were called locally; till scientists of note turned their attention to them, and men of celebrity from other countries came to England in order to be present at them; till, year by year, they assumed greater proportions, so that they became representative of every nationality, British and foreign; of every phase of intellect, scientific and simple; of every rank from crowned heads to petty farmers.

It was Lafayette's greatest regret that he had never witnessed a Holkham sheep-shearing. In 1818 the Emperor of Russia sent a special message to say how he wished he could be present. Among the most famous names on the page of contemporary American history are men who journeyed from the other hemisphere expressly to take part in so unique a gathering.

And meanwhile the rule which had characterised the meetings in their early simplicity was never departed from; all united thus in a common interest, met on common ground; the suggestions of the simplest farmers were treated with the same respect as the conclusions of the most noted scientists; ... the same courtesy and hospitality were experienced by the most, as the least distinguished guest. . . .

Never until 1821 were politics tolerated at a Holkham sheep-shearing; and then it was subsequently recognised to have been an evil omen, for that sheep-shearing proved to be the final one. Thus, the 'Clippings', which were always dated from 1778, extended over a period of forty-three years, until that ominous year of 1821; and during that time, it is said not a single year passed without some discovery being made . . . and some practical benefit accruing to the human race. . . .

In 1812, Dr. Parr was present, and relates how, previous to the public gathering, he watched Coke personally working amongst his shepherds, and inspiring the men with his own remarkable energy. This confirms the account given some years before by Arthur Young, who stated how 'Mr. Coke readily assists, not only his own tenants, but other neighbouring farmers. . . . He puts on his shepherd's smock and superintends the pens, to the sure improvement of the flock, for his judgment is superior and admitted. I have seen him and the late Duke of Bedford, thus accoutred, work all day, and not quit the business till the darkness forced them home to dinner.'

SOURCE: A. M. Stirling, *Coke of Norfolk*, John Lane, 1908.

vii. *A famous wager*

In June, 1811 a wager was made for 1000 guineas that a coat could not be made from freshly shorn wool between sunrise and sunset in a single day. The attempt was made on Tuesday, June 25, 1811.

On the day above stated at 5 o'clock in the morning Sir John Throckmorton, a Berkshire baronet, presented 2 Southdown sheep to Mr. Coxeter of Greenham Mills, near Newbury, Berkshire. The sheep were immediately shorn, the wool sorted and spun, the yarn spool'd, warp'd, loom'd, and wove. The cloth burr'd, mill'd, row'd, dy'd, dry'd, sheared and pressed. The cloth having thus been made in 11 hours was put into the hands of the tailors at 4 o'clock in the afternoon, who completed the coat at 20 minutes past six. Mr. Coxeter then presented the coat to Sir John Throckmorton, who appeared with it the same evening at the Pelican Inn, Speenhamland.

The cloth was a hunting kersey of the admired dark Wellington colour. . . . It was supposed that upwards of 5,000 people were assembled to witness this singular unprecedented performance which was completed in the space of 13 hours and 20 minutes. Sir John and about 40 gentlemen sat down to a dinner provided by Mr. Coxeter and spent the evening with the utmost satisfaction at the success of their undertaking.

SOURCE: contemporary account, included in Adelaide Gosset, *Shepherds of Britain*, Constable and Company, 1911, p. 242.

viii. *Sheep-dogs in church*

I have a vivid recollection of an anecdote which my father used to relate, nearly if not quite half a century ago, with regard to dogs being taken to public worship in Scotland. In a rural kirk where this was the practice, the shepherd's dogs were permitted to occupy the gallery over their master's heads, where they remained during service time, and, it is fair to suppose, conducted themselves in an inoffensive manner; but on one occasion, presumably that of a larger assembly than usual, a strange dog was introduced among them. This was a signal for a general commotion upstairs, which terminated by the sudden bolting of the intruder over the front of the gallery into the body of the church, and as speedily out of it by the door, pursued by the same route in his headlong exit by the whole dog congregation. . . .

In 1839 a relation of mine was fishing on the Whitadder when a small building attracted his attention, and he asked a shepherd:

'Pray, is that a kirk? It looks very small'; to which the shepherd answered:

'Aye, aye; but it's no sae sma'; there's aboon thirty collies there ilka Sabbath.'

SOURCE: Adelaide Gosset, op. cit., pp. 168–169.

ix. *A young drover*

Until comparatively recent times, it was common to see drovers moving immense numbers of sheep and cattle about the countryside to markets and fairs, and sometimes to pasture them in other counties when the home fields needed to recover. A fifty-mile walk was nothing, and the drover might have charge of five or six thousand sheep or three or four hundred head of cattle for ten days or a fortnight. The toll-gates, where large sums had to be paid, were a constant annoyance; and, where possible, the drovers sometimes took the old down-land tracks which, though more circuitous, avoided the toll-gates.

Having rambled to the junction of the two roads upon Chalk Hill on the sultry morning of July 24, 1797, I rested until a boy, trudging and singing at a great rate, came up to me.

'Come along the old road, sir,' said he; 'it is a mortal sight nearer, and I suppose you are thinking which to take.'

I found my companion a most famous little chatterer, not

much above three feet high, and fifteen years of age. He told me he had been to Smithfield with some sheep; that he went every week, and had thirty miles to walk before night. His frock [i.e. smock] was compactly bound up and tied across his shoulders. The straps of his shoes formed a studied cross below the buckles, which he took care to tell me had cost him nine-pence in London the Saturday before. Turnpike tickets were stuck in his hatband, noticing the number of sheep he had paid for; and the lash of his whip was twisted round the handle, which he converted into a walking stick.

I soon found, though so small a being, he was a character of no little consequence upon the road, and he told me any returning chaise or tax-cart would give him a lift for nothing. He was familiar with every one we passed. He wanted no hints to make him loquacious, and thus his busy mind unfolded itself:

'Now, sir, do you know, I have a very good master; and he promises if I behave well to make a man of me. When I went to live with him I was a poor, ragged, half-starved parish boy, without father or mother, or never had any as I know of. I have now two better coats than this' (which, by the by, was all one complete shred of darn and patch-work), 'and I have a spick-and-span new hat I never had on but Whit-Sunday last, and I am to learn, too, my master says, to write.'

. . . I asked him if he could read.

'Aye, in the Testament. I have almost finished the Gospel according to St. John; and I can repeat the Lord's Prayer and Belief too'—the latter of which he ran over as quick as possible, and asked me if he had missed a word. . . .

On parting, as I was turning a corner which took me out of sight, he shrilled out:

'God bless you!'

SOURCE: *The Gentleman's Magazine*, 1797.

x. *Three maxims*

From the conversation of James Gardner, of North Cobbinshaw, Midlothian (b. 1840), shepherd and dog-trainer.

No insult would wound me deeper than a look of distrust from one of my dogs.

The noblest lessons in truth, sacrifice, and duty I have got from my dogs.

When a dog bites a man, that man is sorely in need of chastisement.

SOURCE: Adelaide L. J. Gosset, *Shepherds of Britain*, Constable and Co., 1911, pp. 88–89. Much of the above material is extracted from this admirable compilation, now, unfortunately, rare.

WORLD WAR I (1914–1918).

i. *The 'scrap of paper'*

'Just for a word—"neutrality", a word which in war-time has so often been disregarded, just for a scrap of paper—Great Britain is going to make war.'

SOURCE: Von Bethmann Hollweg's words to Sir Edward Goschen, August 4, 1914; dispatch from Goschen to the Foreign Office.

'What is a treaty, says the German Chancellor, but a scrap of paper? Have you any £5 notes about you? Have you any of those neat little Treasury one-pound notes? If you have, burn them. They are only scraps of paper. What are they made of? Rags! What are they worth? The whole credit of the British Empire! Scraps of paper! I have been dealing with scraps of paper in the last few weeks. We have suddenly found the commerce of the world coming to a standstill. The machine had stopped. Why? The machinery of commerce was moved by bills of exchange. I have seen some of them; wretched, crinkled, scrawled over, blotted, frowzy; and yet those scraps of paper moved great ships, laden with thousands of tons of precious cargo, from one end of the world to the other.'

SOURCE: Rt. Hon. David Lloyd George in a speech at Queen's Hall, London, September 21, 1914; *British Historical and Political Orations*, Everyman's Library, J. M. Dent & Sons, pp. 342–343.

ii. *'The lamps are going out . . .'*

A friend came to see me on one of the evenings of the last week —he thinks it was on Monday, August 3. We were standing at a window of my room in the Foreign Office. It was getting dark, and the lamps were being lit in the space below on which we were looking. My friend recalls that I remarked on this with the words:

'The lamps are going out all over Europe; we shall not see them lit again in our lifetime.'

SOURCE: Edward, Viscount Grey of Falladon, *Twenty-five Years*, Hodder and Stoughton, 1925, Vol. II, p. 20.

iii. *'They shall not pass'*

Ils ne passeront pass.

SOURCE: Marshal Pétain, at Verdun, February 1916.

iv. *'Lafayette, we are here'*

In 1917, when America entered the war, Major General John Pershing was selected to command its troops. He arrived in June 1917 and was given a memorable reception. In Paris, he was taken to the Picpus Cemetery in the suburbs, where many of the heroes of France, including the Marquis de Lafayette who fought on the side of America against Britain in the War of Independence, lie buried.

General Pershing advanced to the tomb and placed upon the marble slab an enormous wreath of pink and white roses. Then he stepped back. He removed his cap and held it in both hands in front of him. The bright sunlight shone down on his silvery grey hair. Looking down at the grave, he spoke in a quiet, impressive tone four simple, all-meaning words:

'Lafayette, we are here.'

SOURCE: Floyd Gibbons, *'And They Thought We wouldn't Fight'*, New York, 1918.

WORLD WAR II (1939–1945).

i. *The fourteenth child*

By January 1936 the stage was set for the Second World War. Three more years passed before the shooting started, because certain rough edges remained to be ironed out. One of them was the remilitarization of the Rhineland. Hitler undertook this job on March 7, 1936. . . .

'This is the end of Hitler', said I and made haste to London, where the League of Nations Council had called an emergency session. . . .

The Council met at . . . St. James's Palace, in the Queen Anne's Room, a royal salon Frenchified with complicated window drapes and three-tiered candelabra. Ancestors in skirts and on horseback watched from the walls. . . .

Queen Anne had thirteen stillborn children, and after I had listened for a while to the speeches in Queen Anne's Room I remarked that we were witnessing the stillbirth of the fourteenth.

SOURCE: Emery Kelen, *Peace in Their Time*, Victor Gollancz, 1964, pp. 325 and 328.

ii. *'I'm glad we've been bombed'*

It became his [George VI's] habit to come up from Windsor each morning to work at Buckingham Palace or to inspect the damage done in recent air raids. And one morning the Palace was bombed while the King and Queen were in it.

'I'm glad we've been bombed,' the Queen said. 'It makes me feel I can look the East End in the face.'

SOURCE: Sir John Wheeler Bennett, *King George VI*; Christopher Hibbert, *The Court at Windsor*, Longmans, 1964, p. 282.

iii. *The Duke of Windsor challenges the enemy*

It was curious no word of it reached us earlier, but I had no radio, nor did any other member of the staff, so that it was not until the evening of Sunday, September 3, 1939, that I came to know what the rest of the world knew already, that we were once again at war with Germany. . . .

The moment the last guest had left and the front door was locked, the Duke turned to me and said:

'Oh, King, would you come up to my room.'

I at once headed for the staff lift, but he stopped me, calling; 'No, come up this way with me.'

I had no idea what he wanted and not until we reached his dressing-room did he speak again, then he said:

'King, you might put out my kilt, will you?'

His kilt? At near midnight? I was naturally puzzled. Even more so when, while doing as he asked, I saw him take his bagpipes from a cupboard in his room. After he had changed from his dinner-jacket and trousers he took the lift up to the flat roof of the villa, carrying his bagpipes with him, and after a few minutes I could hear him marching up and down letting fly with a mighty 'blaw' on the pipes. I don't know who else heard him. It must have been strange indeed to hear the weird, wild notes of the pipes carrying across the water in the silence of the warm Mediterranean night. An eerie, flaunting challenge to our enemies, I thought.

SOURCE: Ernest King, *The Green Baize Door*, William Kimber, 1963, pp. 70–71.

iv. *Something Hitler should have known.*

Devonshire told me a curious story tonight which illustrates vividly the attitude of the British public. On saying goodnight to his chauffeur he remarked:

'Well, Gibson, and what do you think about Hitler?'

'Well, your Grace,' the man answered, 'it seems to me that he should know by now that he is none too popular in this district.'

SOURCE: Harold Nicolson, *Diaries and Letters*, 1930–1939, Collins, 1966.

v. *An unpardonable error*

During the war the Cunard liner *Queen Elizabeth* was used for conveying troops, prisoners of war, etc. On one six-thousand mile journey from Rio to New York, Captain Fall gave advance notice that he would be passing the Ambrose Light at 4 o'clock on the afternoon of June 6th.

Moving at an average speed of twenty-nine knots, we chased up the coast, rounded Cape Sáo Roque, and plunged along on a north-easterly course, heading for New York. We saw no sign of the promised escort, so as wireless silence could not be broken, there was nothing for us to do but push on.

After a late lunch on June 6th, I was standing beside the Captain on the bridge. There was a heat haze about and our speed had dropped to ten knots. I was peering through the grey wreaths of mist, hoping to catch sight of the coastline, when I saw, a little to starboard and ahead, a red light-ship looming up with the word 'AMBROSE' painted on one side in large white capitals. I glanced at Captain Fall, who grinned and nodded his satisfaction.

Suddenly a nasal American voice bellowed from a loud hailer, 'Ahoy! What ship is that?'

An expression of utter disgust suffused Captain Fall's weather-beaten countenance. He snatched off his cap, hurled it to the deck and jumped on it. '. . . Did you hear that?' he rasped. 'Does he think we're the —— *Mayflower*?'

Choking back my laughter, I quickly looked at my watch.

'Captain Fall, wasn't our expected time of arrival sixteen hundred hours?' I asked quietly.

'Yes,' snapped the irate Captain. 'What about it?'

'Well, it's only fifteen fifty-eight. We're two minutes ahead of time!'

Captain Fall's grim expression relaxed. He seized me by the shoulders, gave me an affectionate shake and chuckled appreciatively.

'How right you are lad!' he exclaimed. 'We've zigzagged across six thousand miles of ocean, without an escort, and we're a couple of minutes too soon for our appointment with the

Ambrose Light. An unpardonable error. We must do better next time.'

SOURCE: Colonel Michael O'Brien-Twohig, *Diplomatic Courier*, Elek Books, 1960, pp. 15–16.

vi. *American nurses are insulted*

On one Atlantic crossing, the *Queen Elizabeth*, in addition to many British personnel, was carrying 150 members of the American Army Nursing Corps, who were the object of much attention from British officers. On the second day out the Chief Nurse approached Colonel O'Brien-Twohig, O.C. Troops on the ship, and objected to the deliberate insults they were receiving. He promised to investigate the complaint at once and asked for instances.

'Oh, we're not beefing about your officers' behaviour, Colonel. On the contrary, my girls surely appreciate their little attentions, like offering them chairs and opening doors. But no well-brought up girl likes to be called "Sister" all the time, that's all.'

Naturally, when I explained to the Chief Nurse how the misunderstanding had arisen, she was highly diverted. She wanted to rush off and pass the information on to the other nurses, but I suggested that a public announcement would help ease the embarrassment that had been caused. . . . Thus it was that at twenty-thirty hours exactly my voice, amplified considerably by the loud-speaker system, cut across the hum of conversation in the ship's immense first-class lounge. I began with a humorous reference to the various connotations of the word 'sister' and pointed out how that particular epithet had led to a regrettable deterioration in Anglo-American relationships since leaving New York.

'The ladies of the American Army Nursing Corps,' I continued on a more serious note, 'have been shocked and hurt by British officers using this apparently harmless little word as a mode of address. Anyone acquainted with our hospitals and their organization could tell them that far from being disrespectful, we are punctiliously observing normal hospital etiquette— at least according to British standards. When hospitals such as St. Bartholomew's were started in the Middle Ages, the nursing was done by nuns who were known as Sisters of Mercy. Later on, the nuns withdrew from medical work and secular nurses took over, but the title "Sister", together with the religious head-dresses, were retained. Under the present system a trainee or probationer is referred to as "Nurse" by staff and patients alike. After qualifying she becomes a "Staff Nurse", but it is not until she is promoted to assume full control over a ward that she attains the coveted rank of "Sister". For the information of the American nurses, I have asked my Adjutant —the Highland gentleman easily identifiable by his Scottish kilt—to stand near the door of the lounge. He has with him the British Army List, open at the pages concerning our nursing services, so that the ladies may satisfy themselves that "Sister" is a definite grading in our forces. In future they may rest assured that when a British officer addresses one of them as "Sister", he is employing the word in an honourable sense.'

SOURCE: Colonel Michael O'Brien-Twohig, *Diplomatic Courier*, Elek Books, 1960, pp. 17–19.

vi. *The fleet that retired towards the enemy*

Our ships have been salvaged and are retiring at high speed towards the Japanese fleet.

SOURCE: William Frederick Halsey, radio message, October 1944, following Japanese claims that the U.S.A. Third Fleet had been sunk or were retiring.

WORTHINGTON, THOMAS (1549–1622?), President of the English College at Douay; imprisoned in the Tower, 1584, and banished.

End of an argument

If not the same (which for his vivaciousness is improbable) there was a Father Worthington, certainly his kinsman and countryman, very busy to promote the catholic cause in England, about the beginning of King Charles. He dining, some thirty years since, with a person of honour in this land (at whose table I have often eaten) was very obstreperous in arguing the case for transubstantiation and the ubiquitariness of Christ's body.

'Suppose,' said he, 'Christ were here.' To whom the noble master of the house (who till then was silent) returned:

'If you were away, I believe he would be here.'

SOURCE: Thomas Fuller, *The English Worthies*, 1662; 1952 edition, George Allen & Unwin, p. 303.

WOTTON, SIR HENRY (1568–1639), diplomatist and poet; ambassador at the Court of Venice, etc.

An Ambassador's definition of an Ambassador

Peregre missus ad mentiendum Respublicae causa—An ambassador is an honest man sent to lie abroad for the good of his country.

SOURCE: Sir Henry Wotton; written in the album of Christopher Fleckmore, 1604; mentioned by Gasper Scioppius in a diatribe against James I, 1611.

WREN, SIR CHRISTOPHER (1632–1723), architect; rebuilder of London after the Great Fire; designer of St. Paul's Cathedral.

i. *Objection*

Ladies think nothing well without an edging.

SOURCE: comment when he objected (vainly) to a stone balustrade being put round St. Paul's, 1717.

ii. *Inscription*

Si monumentum requiris, circumspice.

If you seek his monument, look around you.

SOURCE: inscription, attributed to Wren's son. over the interior of the North Door, St. Paul's Cathedral.

ZISKA, JOHN (1360–1424), Bohemian general; called by Carlyle 'Rhinoceros Ziska'. A gifted leader and daring originator in the religious war following the burning of John Huss at the stake in 1415.

i. *One of nature's generals*

Ziska was one of nature's generals. Under the rigid discipline of this stern and disinterested commander an army was formed of a type hitherto unknown in Europe. The followers of Ziska were religious and racial enthusiasts. They condemned games and dancing, music and drunkenness. To their fierce and sombre temper the flute, the drum, and the trumpet were as obnoxious as a foul oath, a loose woman, a rich wardrobe, or a German burgess. As they marched into action, with their huge flails and roaring the Ziska psalm behind the sacred chalice, they struck terror into armies whose inner moral principle was weaker than their own.

SOURCE: H. A. L. Fisher, *A History of Europe*, 1936; one-volume edition, p. 357.

ii. *15th Century tanks*

Meanwhile in Bohemia a man of very great genius, John Ziska, was baffling some of the finest men-at-arms in Europe by meeting them with armoured wagons and a peasantry armed at first only with flails. Enforcing very strict discipline he trained his men to manoeuvre these wagons with great accuracy and skill so that at any moment they could be drawn into a ring, presenting an impregnable front on every side. It was a favourite manoeuvre of his to lure his enemy to the attack of apparently helpless wagons in front, and then, wheeling the outer wagons inwards, to enclose him and beat him to death with flails. The unit of organisation was the wagon, to each of which was allotted a driver, two men appointed for his special protection, and seventeen others armed with missile weapons. Every thousand of his force was made up of nine hundred foot, one hundred horse and fifty wagons.

[These wagons can fairly claim to be the origin of the modern armoured tank.]

SOURCE: Sir John William Fortescue, *Medieval Warfare*, in *Universal History of the World*, Amalgamated Press, Vol. 5, p. 2950.

CHRONOLOGICAL INDEX

513

SIXTEENTH CENTURY

SEVENTEENTH CENTURY

EIGHTEENTH CENTURY

NINETEENTH CENTURY